MASTERY

THE ART OF MASTERING LIFE

E. STANLEY JONES

ABINGDON PRESS
NASHVILLE

MASTERY: THE ART OF MASTERING LIFE

This book is printed on acid-free paper.

ISBN 978-1-5018-4963-3

17 18 19 20 21 22 23 24 25 26—10 9 8 7 6 5 4 3 2 1

MANUFACTURED IN THE UNITED STATES OF AMERICA

CONTENTS

PUBLISHER'S PREFACE

Abingdon Press is pleased to bring back into circulation E. Stanley Jones's *Mastery: The Art of Mastering Life*. Originally published in 1955, this page-a-day devotional has helped people all over the world explore the art of mastery—within and without—with the experience of Pentecost and the nascent Christian movement as the guiding example.

For this edition, the publisher has made some minor revisions but has also made every effort to retain E. Stanley Jones's voice for today's readers. The updates include spelling, punctuation, capitalization, and some language usage and references that would distract or confuse the reader. But there have been very few changes to content or style. Some references that were specific to the 1950s still have relevance for our time.

References to humanity, no longer expressed as men and mankind, have been updated.

Some references to God have been recast to avoid masculine pronouns. In the prayers, thee, thou, and thine have been changed to you, your, and yours.

It is a privilege for Abingdon Press, publisher of E. Stanley Jones's books since 1925, to introduce him to a new generation of persons seeking to grow in faith, one day at a time.

Introduction

The art of living is the least learned of all arts. Humankind has learned the art of existing, of getting by somehow with the demands of life, of escaping into half answers; but we know little about the art of living, about being able to walk up to life, with all its demands, humbly conscious that we have within us a mastery that is able to face this business of living with adequacy. That is life's central lack. All others are marginal lacks. The modern person knows everything about life except how to live it!

There are just two great human needs: *light on the mystery of life*, and *life for the mastery of life*.

We have made a great deal of progress in finding light on the mystery of life. Through the discoveries of science in the realm of the physical universe, the mental universe, and the spiritual universe, we know a lot about life. We see its mechanisms, its workings, as no other age has seen them. We are enlightened, but I question whether we are more enlivened. We are more nervous, more jumpy, more twitchy, more tense; but I question whether we are more enlivened. To be really enlivened is to be the possessor of an inner life adequate to meet outer life with joy and confidence. That is lacking. Our light has outrun our life. We thought that to analyze our problems was to solve them.

But to know is not necessarily to know how to live. We need life for the mastery of life. But even that is inadequate unless you put it this way: We need Life for the mastery of life.

If it is life trying to master life, then we will fail. In order to live, life must come in contact with Life or cease to be life; it becomes existence.

Mastery is not gained by trying to be masterful—by clenching your teeth and asserting your life against life. That results in the big I over against the little you—an unlovely personage. Mastery is gained by humbly relating your life to a Life that is masterful, effortlessly so. You take that effortless mastery and make it your own and live by it—effortlessly. You learn the art of receptivity, which is the art of life. To be able to receive is to be able to live, and to be able to receive abundantly is to be able to live abundantly. Life is gauged by its capacity of receptivity. I know there is the counter truth that life is gauged by its capacity to release. Receptivity and release are the alternate beats of the Christian heart. But it is first receptivity; without that there is nothing to release.

That leads me to the heart of this book: In a period of thirty years—one generation—120 people and their immediate spiritual descendants introduced more basic changes in human living, individual and collective, than have been introduced in any generation in any part of the world before or since. And those changes have embodied the ruling ideas of real civilization ever since. This period we call the "Acts of the Apostles." But just as rightly it could be called the "Acts of the Risen Christ." This Risen Christ through the Holy Spirit put into the inner life of a group of very ordinary people such extraordinary moral and spiritual mastery that within the space of thirty years they had effected a revolution so great that it has been at the basis of all great constructive revolutions ever since in every part of the world. And its force has not been expended. It is still working, vitally and masterfully. By all the rules of the book, this revolution should have expended itself long ago. Revolutions do. They come and go and have their day. But this one has not had its day; it is moving on to nothing less than that which can be described as the Day—the Day of its ultimate world triumph—the Day to which all creation moves—the Day!

When people looked on what was happening, they described with rare insight this revolution in these words: "These that have turned the world upside down are come hither also" (Acts 17:6 KJV). They called it a turning of the world upside down, and it was, but in a far deeper sense than they guessed. They thought it was a change of religious allegiance and customs. It was far deeper than that; it was a turning of the world upside down in its basic outlook, its personal and collective allegiance, and its economic, social, and political structure. It was a total revolution affecting the total life.

But never did a revolution come in so unobtrusively. It stole in under religious forms and terms so quietly and unobtrusively that people, for the most part, have missed the basic revolutionary character of the movement. They looked on it as the spread of a religion that could be superimposed on the framework of human society and could leave that society unchanged basically. It wasn't. It wasn't a religion at all—a religion that could be put alongside other religions—it was a kingdom demanding a total obedience in the total life. That was—and is—revolutionary!

And that leads me to my real point. Jesus said, "I assure you that some standing here won't die before they see God's kingdom arrive in power" (Mark 9:1). And again: "I assure you that some standing here won't die before they see the Human One coming in his kingdom" (Matt 16:28). Did that come true? If not, then Jesus was mistaken; and if he was mistaken in this, then why couldn't he be mistaken in other things? We can't rest our full weight down on him. That is the worm that has been eating at the heart of the faith of honest believers in all ages. Jesus said that there were some standing there who should not taste death—very specific!—until they saw the kingdom of God come with power—very specific! Did it happen? If not, then he was wrong—and wrong not on a marginal issue but on a central one; and wrong there he is not completely trustable. But suppose he was right, that the kingdom of God did come and did come with power during the lifetime of those present; then that makes us go with eagerness back to the account to see what really did happen. Did the kingdom of God come with power in the revolution that began with the descent of the Holy Spirit at Pentecost and ramified [spread] into the individual and collective life of society in the next thirty years? I believe it did! Not fully, of course. The full consummation of that kingdom will come only when Jesus returns in his second coming to consummate it. But the kingdom did come in miniature. The essence and nature of that kingdom was revealed in the revolution that took place with the coming of the Holy Spirit and the Spirit's impact upon the individual and society. The kingdom didn't come "at Pentecost," as some have suggested; but it began there and produced individuals and a society that became the kingdom in cameo. It was a preview of the final consummation, which will come when Jesus returns to consummate that kingdom. The coming of the kingdom and the coming of the Son of Man seem to be in two phases—the preview and the final consummation. But the point is that we have in the preview the outline and spirit of the kingdom that is to be and yet is. I am persuaded that we have in the first half of the Acts of the Apostles the kind of individual and the kind of society that will constitute the final kingdom. That final kingdom will be more than, but not different from, what we find revealed in Acts.

Is it possible that the kingdom stole in upon people almost incognito and was there ready to be revealed when they were able to receive it? Jesus said it would be so: "Being asked by the Pharisees when the kingdom of God was coming, he answered them, 'The kingdom of God is not coming with signs to be observed; nor will they say, "Lo, here it is!" or "There!" for behold, the kingdom of God is in the midst of you'" [in the margin, "within you"] (Luke 17:20-21 RSV). In these words Jesus provided for the coming of the kingdom, which would not be by signs to be observed; nor could men say, "Lo, it is here!" or "There!"; but it would be in your midst, yes, within you. And that happened in this movement that was inaugurated with the coming of the Holy Spirit—the kingdom was within them and in the midst of them—personal and corporate.

And this seems to be the method of God in revealing God's deepest secrets. In the incarnation, God stole in among us almost incognito.

A Babe appeared in a lowly manger, grew up in an obscure village, worked in a carpenter shop, and then after a public ministry of three years quietly asked his intimate companions, "Who do you think I am?" And it dawned upon them that they were looking into the face of the Eternal God. The incarnation is both the veiling and the unveiling of the hidden God. So it is with the kingdom. Jesus speaks of the "open secret of the Realm of God" (Mark 4:11 MNT); it is a secret—hidden in the nature of reality, but it is our open secret—open to those who have eyes to see and hearts to learn. And just as Jesus, the incarnation of the Eternal God, stole in, in lowly human guise, so the incarnation of the kingdom of God also stole in, in a very lowly movement—the movement that began in the hearts of 120 ordinary people. When Jesus said, "Don't be afraid, little flock, because your Father delights in giving you the kingdom" (Luke 12:32). it seemed laughable. The group of nobodies rule the ages? Absurd. But they have! They have literally ruled the development of the ages—they have held the kingdom. Any departure from their thoughts and principles and spirit has been visited by the silent judgment of God with decay and doom. And any rediscovery and re-embodiment of their thoughts and principles and spirit has been visited by the silent approval of God with revival, release, and open vistas—life has become living, and more—worth living.

These nobodies became the somebodies who have been the real rulers of the ages. Not the Caesars, the Alexanders, the Napoleons, the Hitlers, the Mussolinis, the Stalins, or the Croesuses have been the rulers of the ages—these nobodies have. To them, the little flock, has been given the kingdom. They rule even now. Not because of what they were, but because they presented in their own attitudes and proclaimed with their voices a new kingdom. They were identified with the final order, the kingdom; hence their word was final—and is final. Why have our eyes been "holden" (KJV) that we could not see this? Often truths are hidden until events force our attention upon them, and then they burst into meaning. It has been so with the kingdom of God. It has lain within the pages of the New Testament as a truth, inoperative as a working way; it was a far-off dream to be realized in heaven, or if on earth it has been reduced to the compass of the Church. The Church and the kingdom were identified, and the kingdom thereby reduced. But now with the rise of the human totalitarianisms—Fascism, Nazism, and Communism—

demanding a total obedience in the total life, we as Christians have been stung into the necessity of finding something to match against these totalitarianisms. And to our glad surprise we find that we do have a totalitarianism—God's totalitarianism—the kingdom of God. It demands a total obedience in the total life, individual and collective. The kingdom of God is the end of human destiny, and it is the way to the fulfillment of that destiny. Therefore it is the Way. "And he entered the synagogue...pleading about the kingdom of God; but when some were stubborn and disbelieved, speaking evil of the Way..., he withdrew" (Acts 19:8-9 RSV). Here the *kingdom of God* and the *Way* are used synonymously. The kingdom then is the Way. It is true that Jesus said, "I am the way," and we will take up later the relationship between Jesus and the kingdom, but suffice it to say now that the kingdom is the Way.

But how could we know what the kingdom as the Way is like unless we could see it in actual operation, at least in miniature? If the universal Christ, not incarnate, had been proclaimed as the Way, it would have been words. We had to see the Way in operation in the incarnate Jesus. The word of the Way had to become flesh in a Person. Then it lived! It is the same with the kingdom. Had the kingdom been proclaimed verbally as the Way, it would have left us with proclamation but no demonstration, words with no fact. Just as the Divine Person, the Son of God, had to become flesh in Jesus, so the Divine Order, the kingdom of God, had to become flesh in a group. It did. The new order of living that arose from the impact of the Holy Spirit upon the framework of human living became the Order, the kingdom of God. Imperfectly, of course, because made up of very imperfect people; but it was in a real and recognizable way the revelation of the nature of the kingdom of God. In this study of the Acts of the Apostles we turn then to inquire into the nature of that human living in both the individual and the collective, which became in a real way the kingdom of God. People standing there did not taste death until they had seen the "kingdom of God come with power"—with such power that the nature of human individuals and society underwent profound changes, and that those changes are ruling the development of the best life on this planet today.

The Acts of the Apostles is not merely a study in the history of early Christianity and its spread through that ancient world—it is that—and more! It is also an exploration into the nature of the Order that is and is to be—the nature of the kingdom of God. For here in small events great meanings are revealed. And those forces have not been expended. They are pressing at the basis of all wrong human living, individual and collective, and are pushing the foundations out from under all evil everywhere. Evils continue to exist, but they belong to the "dethroned." They are destined to the dust.

Perhaps as a missionary—an evangelist traveling through the world in East and West, and especially the East, for forty-five years—I have had more opportunity than most people to observe and feel these silent forces of conflict, of collapse, of conversion, of construction. And perhaps I've thus been able to see more clearly in this world context the meaning of the movement that began with the coming of the Holy Spirit.

Jesus said that the kingdom would not come "with observation," by outward sign and show—"the kingdom of God is within you," or "among you," as the margin puts it (Luke 17:20-21 KJV, NRSV). The only lasting revolution begins there—"within"—and goes there—"among." All other revolutions begin "among"—imposed from without.

They go to pieces upon the rock of unchanged human nature. There is not enough of the "within" to sustain the "among"—hence failure. Communism will fail because it is deliberately from the "among" to the "within"; change the order and you change the people. Upon the rock of that half-truth it will go to pieces. The whole truth is with the kingdom; therefore it will wear down all movements based upon half-truths or falsehoods. The mastery is from "within" to the "among." A group of people waited for ten days after the ascension to receive a Divine reinforcement within. God moved into them. And then they went out to move into human society to effect the greatest changes, and the most lasting, that have ever appeared in human history.

To the exploration of that Divine Impact and those consequent changes in the structure of human society we now turn. It will be an exciting adventure, for we shall be exploring the shape of things to come, the destiny of our race. For here in history the norm has been fixed, the pattern has been set. We see what the consummated kingdom will be like; it will be like this order universalized.

The thesis of this book will be: A group of ordinary people were mastered by the risen Christ moving into them in the Holy Spirit; and thus mastered, they moved out to master their circumstances and their relationships into a miniature kingdom of God. It is Mastery, within and without.

The book is arranged after the pattern of the rest of my devotional books—a page a day. This is for personal use. But it is also arranged in topics of a week each, so it can be used as a study book for group study. At the same time there is one developing theme, so it can be read straight through as an ordinary book. This may be the last of my devotional books, for my autobiography comes next; but of this I cannot be sure, for I have wondered if each one wasn't the last. In each one I seem to write myself empty and then comes the filling up again, apparently from Eternal Springs. But if this should be the last devotional, I would not be sorry that my last one pointed people to the possibility of mastery. It is our greatest need, for we are more weak than wicked.

E. Stanley Jones

THE MASTER

Philippians 2:9-11

To find the secret of mastery, you need a Master. You cannot say to yourself, "Come now, I will be masterful." You will not be masterful—you will be silly—or obnoxious. To be masterful, you must get in touch with the resources of a Master, one who is inherently masterful and who knows how and is willing and ready to impart, to those who accept his ways, his own mastery.

The Christian way is centered in such a Master. Jesus Christ was the most masterful Person this planet has ever seen. He walked into time and quietly divided it into before and after—BC and AD. He walked into the realm of thought and altered all our conceptions about God and life and destiny. He walked into our moral conceptions and codes, and now we are good or bad according to whether we embody his spirit or not. He walked into our sundered relations with God and healed them by his cross. He walked into the chaos of human relationships and projected a kingdom that is destined to gather all our chaos into cosmos, to be the goal and end of human history. He walked into our moral weakness and sin and imparted to the defeated and collapsed a moral and spiritual mastery that made them go out and impart to humanity such a stimulus that a movement was begun, which is destined to change the world. The Master mastered people into masterfulness.

That sounds like a strong-man stunt. It wasn't. It was all done quietly, unobtrusively, and effortlessly. People quietly got in touch with him, imbibed his secret, and found themselves doing things they couldn't do, thinking thoughts they couldn't think, and loving people they couldn't love. They were a surprise to themselves and others. It was no clenched-teeth type of mastery; it was as gentle and quiet as the dawn—and as effective—awakening the slumbering world to light and life. Mastery is primarily caught, not taught. Mastery is gained by contact with the Master. In contact with him we learn the same effortless striving, the same easy accomplishment, the same serene effectiveness.

O Lord, as we begin this quest for mastery, save our feet from bypaths and help us to walk the Way—Your Way. Amen.

AFFIRMATION FOR THE DAY: I will know mastery to the degree that I know the Master.

THE MASTER IMPARTS HIS MASTERY

Luke 24:45-49

We come now to study how ordinary people got in touch with extraordinary power and did extraordinary things beyond their power of accomplishment. This account of the divine reinforcement is found in the "Acts of the Apostles," or as it has been called, "The Acts of the Holy Spirit through the Apostles." And yet that too is scarcely accurate; for the movement, as we shall see, transcended the apostles, was given over into the hands of a lay group that went beyond the apostles and went on sometimes in spite of the apostles. The movement used whatever instruments were at hand and sensitive to the spirit and goal of this amazing redemption.

The Acts of the Apostles is the bridge between the Gospels and the Epistles. Without it there is a vacuum. How did the Christianity of Jesus become the Christianity of Paul? The Acts tells us. It is the transition from the Jesus of history to the Christ of experience, the transition from the localized Teacher to the universal Transformer. In the Acts the ideas of Jesus became flesh; they became incarnate in a group; they walked. And they not only walked, they ran; they danced along life's way; they sang; they shouted; they laid healing hands on the souls, the minds, the bodies, of people and made them whole, every whit whole. And in the process they quietly laid the mines of thought and idea that blew existing civilizations to pieces and turned the world upside down and laid the foundations of a New Order, the kingdom of God. This description comes in retrospect. At the time the movement seemed a local tempest in a teapot instead of a cleansing storm that would blow through the brains, the souls, the customs, the societies of people; cleansing away the miasma of superstition and cruel customs, and bringing a breath of fresh heavenly air to all life everywhere. And as in Ezekiel's vision, this breath of God breathed upon valleys of dry bones, upon dead or decadent civilizations, and they lived.

But that universal storm came out of a quiet—an upper room where people waited in silence to receive God.

O Lord, let this cleansing storm blow through my inmost being, cleansing away all that is not of you. Amen.

AFFIRMATION FOR THE DAY: I, too, am an ordinary person, but I can link with Extraordinary Power.

"JESUS BEGAN" ALMOST EVERYTHING!

Luke 4:16-21

Luke, the author of the Gospel of Luke and the author of Acts, opens the account with these words: "In the first book, O Theophilus, I have dealt with all that Jesus began to do and teach" (Acts 1:1 RSV). Note the word "began." The life and teaching and death and resurrection of Jesus were but a beginning, a prelude, the first chapter of a Book. This Book will never be finally written with *finis* at the end; it will eternally be in the writing, the Lamb's Book of Life.

The test of a person's life is this: Is the person dead when dead? Or does that person live on with greater power after death? Judged by that test, Jesus has really lived; for he was more powerful after his death than before. During his lifetime, through incessant teaching and preaching, he gathered at the highest estimate "five hundred brothers and sisters" (1 Cor 15:6); but after his death he drew, through people filled with himself, five thousand disciples in a single day.

When Jesus was about to die upon the cross, he cried, "It is finished" (John 19:30 KJV). Something was finished that day that will never have to be done again. We were reconciled to God by that offering of himself; once offered, our redemption was sealed. But while something was finished, something was left unfinished and will be forever unfinished until we awake in his likeness. Even then will it be finished? I question.

"Jesus began"—what?—everything that is now working in humanity for the uplift and renewal of the human race. Trace it back to its origin and you will come out at the foot of the cross. The high-school young people of Helsinki, Finland, go dressed in their school uniforms once a year to a national cemetery; and marching up to a knoll, they lay flowers at the foot of the cross in gratitude for the privilege of studying. If we had eyes to see, we would see that all our liberties, all our schools, all our hospitals, all our democracies, all our fellow feeling, all our increasing corporate sense—all these and much more "Jesus began." The Gospels are the first chapter of the greatest Book ever written.

O Jesus, I thank you that you are beginning in me something that can never, never end. It has the feel of the eternal upon it. Amen.

AFFIRMATION FOR THE DAY: The beginnings of the Never-Ending are beginning in me.

THE WORD BECOME FLESH

John 1:1-4

We have looked at the mastery of the Master. He has been the starting point and stimulus of everything that is working for the redemption of the human race. For since he is the "true light that shines on all people...coming into the world" (John 1:9), so he is the life of all that leads toward Life. People have been and are often unconscious of the source of that light and life within, urging them to better individual and collective living, but the source has been Jesus, for "through the Word was life, and the life was the light for all people" (John 1:4).

That leads us to inquire what lay behind the mastery of those who laid masterful hands on life around them and changed it profoundly. Did it just happen? Was it a historical departure from the ordinary, an aberration—what is called in biology a "sport," a kind of life that lives and dies within itself and will not be repeated? Or was this the working out of something that has divine purpose and plan behind it and is capable of being duplicated wherever conditions are met? What lay behind this amazing burst of spiritual mastery?

The answer is in the opening verses of the Acts. There Luke lays down the seven things upon which the Christian gospel rests. They are the pillars sunk deep in the purposes of God and going down to the very bedrock of the foundations of the universe.

The first pillar is Jesus: the Word become flesh of "everything Jesus did and taught from the beginning" (Acts 1:1). Our starting point is Jesus. But someone objects and says, "The gospel begins with God." No, for until Jesus came, there were views about God and there was news about God, but no good news. Apart from Jesus we know little about God, and what little we know is not good news. The conception of the character of God apart from Jesus is questionable. In Jesus our question marks about God turn into exclamation points. In the face of Jesus we know what God is like and what we must be like if we are to be good. If God is other than Jesus, God is not good; if like Jesus, God is good. That is an astounding thing to say; yet when I say it, I hear the ages give a resounding Amen. And it reverberates through all things.

O Lord, I see you in a Face. And that Face is the express image of your Face. I thank you. Amen.

AFFIRMATION FOR THE DAY: I am beginning not with an idea but with a Fact, so fact must come out of it.

THE GOSPEL IS GOD'S SEARCH FOR HUMANITY

John 1:9-13

We began yesterday with the first of the seven pillars upon which the Christian gospel rests: *Jesus—the Word become flesh.* The gospel doesn't begin with God; it begins with Jesus. You cannot say *God* until you have first said *Jesus.* For Jesus puts content into God. You cannot say *Christ* until you have first said *Jesus,* for Jesus puts content into Christ. You cannot say the *Holy Spirit* until you have first said *Jesus,* for Jesus puts content into the Holy Spirit. You cannot say the *kingdom of God* until you have first said *Jesus,* for Jesus puts content into the kingdom of God. You cannot say *Life* until you have first said *Jesus.* You can say life, but not Life. You cannot say *Truth* until you have first said *Jesus.* You can say truth, but not Truth. You cannot say the *Way* until you have first said *Jesus.* You can say the way, but not the Way.

You cannot begin unless you begin with Jesus. You can begin a series of bypaths, a lot of tangles, of complications and frustrations; but you can't begin to live. For you can't live life without Life, know truth without Truth, nor be on the way without the Way.

The gospel then begins with the incarnation. All religions are humanity's search for God; the gospel is God's search for humanity; therefore there are many religions, but one gospel. All religions are the Word become word; the gospel is the Word become flesh. Therefore all religions are philosophies; the gospel is a fact. Philosophies may be good views; the gospel is good news. The gospel is not primarily a philosophy—it is a Fact. The philosophy grows out of the Fact. The Fact of Jesus is our starting point and is our gospel.

It is the gospel of Jesus before it is the gospel of God or the gospel of the kingdom. The gospel lies in his person—he didn't come to bring the good news—he was the good news. This gospel is not spelled out, therefore verbal; it is lived out, therefore vital. Jesus didn't come to bring the forgiveness of God—he was the forgiveness of God. There is no other way to God, for Jesus is the Way from God. He is God coming to us. Therefore there can be no other way.

O God, in Jesus the lines of your face grow tender and beautiful. We thank you for what we see—in him. Amen.

AFFIRMATION FOR THE DAY: When I begin with Jesus, I have the key, the key to everything: God, life, mastery.

THE LIFE BECOMES LIGHT

John 1:14-18

We saw yesterday that we don't begin with God, and we don't begin with people; we begin with the God-Man. And from him we work up to God, and from him we work down to people. In his light we see life. Christians are people who believe in God and humanity and life through Jesus.

The second pillar on which the Christian gospel rests is the Word become revelation, "all that Jesus began to do and teach" (Acts 1:1 RSV).

The first step was the *Word become flesh*, and the next step is the *Word become revelation*. The one follows the other as the sunlight follows the sun. The gospel had to be real before it was revelation.

The life of Jesus became Light for the life of humanity.

But note the order: "To do and teach"—first the doing, then the teaching. The deed became the creed. Therefore it was realism. A great many people think that the Christian gospel is idealism, something imposed on life. But the gospel is not something imposed on life; it is something exposed out of Life. It is the revelation of the nature of Reality. Jesus was not a moralist imposing a moral code on humanity—a moral code for which humanity is badly made—he was not a moralist in that sense at all. He was a revealer of the nature of Reality: first, of God. He said, "If you want to know what God is like, look at me." And when we do, our hearts almost skip a beat as we say to ourselves: "Is God like that? Is God a Jesus-like God?" If so, I could ask nothing higher; I could be content with nothing less.

In Jesus we do not hear what God is like; we see what God is like. We are a kindergarten race and need the visual—seeing is believing.

All of Jesus' "teaching" was an interpretation of what he was and what he did. So it is out of Life to life. It was Deep speaking to deep. Hence his words were not words; they were facts clothed in words.

Therefore they strike you with authority, a strange new authority that is self-verifying. He did not argue; he disclosed. And all his preaching was not preaching; it was revelation. When he spoke, people saw.

O Jesus, we thank you that you let us see as no one lets us see, and what we see satisfies—absolutely. Amen.

AFFIRMATION FOR THE DAY: All I say and do today shall be revelation— revelation of Reality.

ETERNAL GREATNESS IN THE PASSAGE OF TEMPORAL FACT

Matthew 7:28-29

We saw yesterday that the second pillar was the *Word become revelation*—"all that Jesus began to do and teach." His teaching came out of his doing; it was his doing made vocal. And that made a difference. All other teachers have pointed beyond themselves to truth. Jesus pointed to himself and said: "I am the truth." And somehow or other we believe it; for if we could sit down and try to imagine a perfect illustration of abstract truth translated into life and action, we could not think for the life of us of a better illustration than Jesus of Nazareth, a man who lived two thousand years ago. And now when I think of truth, I do not add truth to truth to get Truth—I think of Jesus. When I say *Truth*, I think of Jesus. When I say *Goodness*, I think of Jesus. And when I say *God*, I think of Jesus. If I don't, I miss Truth, I miss Goodness, I miss God.

So our Christian faith is not a following of an impossible ideal; it is the following of the Ideal become Real. Whitehead says: "I hazard the prophecy that that religion will conquer which can render clear to popular understanding some eternal greatness incarnate in the passage of temporal fact."* That has happened in Jesus. The victory goes to him for "in any battle of ideas the victory goes to those ideas which are guaranteed by the facts."** In the Christian faith all the ideas are guaranteed by the fact of Jesus.

All the ideas of the Christian faith set forth not idealism but realism. For all the ideas look out at us from tender eyes and touch us with warm redemptive hands; therefore they shake us like a passion. Jesus never used words ending in "ity"—abstractions. He did not teach us to respect personality; he taught us to love persons. He did not glorify purity; he said the pure in heart see God. In Jesus we see realism so far ahead of us that we think it idealism. But it is Realism. It has all been worked and worked where you and I have to work it, namely, in the stream of ordinary human history. And the working has been so wonderful that we have never gotten over the spell of it. And never will.

O Lord, we have seen the authentic in Jesus. And seeing him, we see all. Our hearts can never rest this side of him. Amen.

AFFIRMATION FOR THE DAY: Since I have seen the Real, I must be real in thought, word, and deed.

* Alfred North Whitehead, *Adventure of Ideas* (New York: The Free Press, 1933), 33.
** No published source was found for this quotation.

MASTERY MUST BEGIN WITH MORAL MASTERY

Romans 3:22-26

We saw yesterday that the Word became revelation. And that revelation was Realism. But suppose it had stopped there. Is a revelation all that we need, even though that revelation be perfect and final? Hardly. For the revelation would leave us with light on the mystery of life, but would not give us Life for the mastery of life. It is not enough to see; we must be able to make operative within us what we see. But what is within us? Those who know themselves and others best know that within them is a dark, ugly thing called sin. And this dark, ugly thing is not an occasional, exceptional something here and there—in some people and not in others—it is universal. Something stands between us and God and between us and ourselves and between us and our fellow people and between us and living. It is a life block. And it is something for which we seem to be responsible. The thought of it brings a sense of guilt.

Obviously until that dark, ugly something is removed, we are incapacitated for mastery. For sin makes us feel not merely wicked but weak. It lays a paralyzing hand on all we think and do and are. This sin seems anti-life as well as anti-God—it is anti-us. It seems alien and makes us estranged from God, ourselves, our brothers and sisters, and from life.

Any revelation therefore that would pass from light on the mystery of life to Life for the mastery of life must deal with this tragic fact of sin. To skirt this fact and try to solve mastery would bring us not mastery but misery, not fruitfulness but frustration. All attempts at mastery without being saved from sin have ended, and will end, in disillusionment and despair. If we are not saved from sin, we are not saved from anything; we are not saved. Therefore the first word about Jesus was: "you will call him Jesus, because he will save his people from their sins" (Matt 1:21). The Savior was to save—from sin. But how? Would he fence us off from sin by a law? Would he force us to be good by compulsion? Or would he bear our sins in his own body on a cross?

O Lord, we have come to the very heart of the mystery of Love. Give us eyes to see, really see. Amen.

AFFIRMATION FOR THE DAY: If I am not saved from sin, I am just not saved.

LOVE BEARS AND SHARES

Romans 5:6-11

We come now to the third pillar upon which the Christian faith rests: the *Word become vicarious*—"he presented himself alive after his passion" (Acts 1:3 RSV). Note the word "passion"—it points to a cross. The cross is the place where God deals with this awful fact of sin. The cross is the price that God pays to get to us in spite of our sin. God being what God is and humanity being what it is, the cross became inevitable.

For wherever pure love meets sin in the loved one, at the junction of that love and that sin a cross of pain is set up. It is the nature of love to insinuate itself into the sorrows and sins of the loved one and make them its own. All love has the doom of bleeding upon it as long as there is sin in the loved one—inevitably so. If God is love, then when that love comes into contact with sin in the loved ones, a cross of pain will be set up at the junction of that love and that sin. But how would I know there is a cross upon the heart of God—God is a Spirit, and I am bounded by my flesh—how could I know there is the unseen cross on the heart of God? How would I know except God shows me—shows me by lifting up a cross in human history so that I can see through the outer cross the inner cross upon the heart of God? That has happened.

The cross lights up the nature of God as vicarious, suffering Love.

The outstretched arms of the cross are the arms of God stretched out to gather to God's heart all the sin and sorrow of the world to make it God's own.

A lifer, now transformed, wrote me from prison these lines:

"I love you big—this much," a child will say,
And thrust his arms out wide;
So baby Christ grew to love that way,
With outstretched arms he died—
"I love you—big—this much."

The cross is God saying just that: "I love you enough to bear your sins in my own body and make them my own." The cross is Love caring and sharing and bearing.

O Lord, through the cross I see you—the real you—and what I see sends me to my knees. Amen.

AFFIRMATION FOR THE DAY: If God's attitude toward me is suffering Love, my attitude toward others will be suffering love.

HE LIVES!

Romans 6:5-11

We have seen that the third pillar upon which the Christian faith rests is the *Word become vicarious*. That leads us to the fourth: the *Word become triumphant*— "presented himself alive" (Acts 1:3 RSV). The resurrection of Jesus is God's seal of acceptance on the offering Jesus made upon the cross. Without the resurrection we would have been forever in doubt as to whether goodness is power. Will goodness not forever writhe on the cross in the grip of a more powerful thing—evil? The answer of the resurrection is No! Not only is goodness good—it is all powerful and has the last word in human affairs.

Without the resurrection the song of life is pitched forever in a minor key, the sadness of ultimate defeat running through it. With the resurrection the note of sadness, which runs through lower nature and through human living, is transposed to a higher, triumphant key and ends with the burst of the "Hallelujah Chorus." The worst that humanity can do has been done—we have crucified the Son of God. Then the best that God can do has been done—God has raised that Son of God and made him alive forevermore. Our worst and God's best came into clash on that first Easter morning and the result was that the "guards...became like dead men" (Matt 28:4), and the One supposedly dead was alive and triumphant.

Without the resurrection the Christian faith would not have been the Christian faith. It would have been the Christian failure—a religion of unfulfilled promises, a vast might-have-been. It would have meant that Jesus tried to redeem humanity but couldn't make the grade. But the resurrection says that he made the grade—and more! I saw a church dedicated to the Virgin Mary and called "To Our Lady of Sorrows," and my inner comment was: "Hasn't she heard of her son's resurrection?" Without the resurrection our religion is a "Religion of Sorrows," but with it, it is a faith that sings an invincible song—Victory! The resurrection is God saying, "I still have charge of affairs and have the last word; whoever has the word of the first day or the second day, I have the word of the third day; and that last word is Victory!" He lives!

O God, our Lord, we thank you that your mastery is over death and the grave. We face everything without fear. Amen.

AFFIRMATION FOR THE DAY: If my Redeemer is alive, I, the redeemed, must live as though I were alive.

WHO HAS THE FINAL WORD?

Matthew 28:18-20

We have seen the fourth pillar upon which the Christian faith rests: the *Word become triumphant*. We now come to the fifth: the *Word become final*—"up to the day when he was taken up" (Acts 1:2). And Peter adds: "Being therefore exalted at the right hand of God" (2:33 RSV). So his being taken up meant that he was taken to the right hand of God; in other words, to the place of final and absolute authority.

And this had to be. It is not enough for Jesus to be triumphant in an event like the resurrection; what we want to know is whether he will be triumphant in all events, everywhere? Has he the final word? If not, then his resurrection fades into insignificance; for it was an isolated event and not a part of a triumphant whole. If the end doesn't spell out victory, then the resurrection must be spelled out as a victory and not as Victory! Unless it is a part of a larger Victory, the resurrection is not Victory! It is the winning of a battle but the losing of a war.

But just as the cross is guaranteed by the resurrection, so in turn the resurrection is guaranteed by the fact of Jesus being at the place of final authority—at the right hand of God. He is Alpha—the Jesus of initial victory, the resurrection—but he is also Omega—the Jesus of final victory. That makes us stand amid the flux of events with confidence that these events will not have final significance unless they fit into his mind and purpose. They will break themselves upon the fact of Jesus at the place of final authority. You cannot fight God without getting hurt. Saul of Tarsus tried it and found he was only hurting himself in kicking against the goads.

At the right hand of God means that Jesus is at the place from which the laws of the universe have their source and sanction. Therefore all the laws of the universe point to him as their source and end. They all work for him. They are the silent sentinels who stand guard over the universe on behalf of their Lord. And no one gets past these silent sentinels. If anyone or anything cannot give the password "Jesus is Lord," then these silent guards apprehend them as alien intruders into the universe—a danger to themselves and others. He is the Christ of the final word.

O Christ, we thank you that you are where you are. Goodness is on the throne, and we are safe. Amen.

AFFIRMATION FOR THE DAY: I will get away with nothing that is not truth and reality.

11

GOD'S TOTALITARIANISM AND HUMANITY'S

Colossians 3:16-17

We have seen that the fifth pillar upon which the Christian faith rests is the *Word become final*. That is assuring, but not fully assuring. For the question arises, can all this be projected back into life as a total way of life? Or must it all rest in Jesus but incapable of being transferred into us as our way of life now? The answer to these queries is given in the sixth pillar: the *Word become a total way of life—the kingdom of God*. "He appeared to them over a period of forty days, speaking to them about God's kingdom" (Acts 1:3).

Fortunately the account tells us what he talked about during the forty days he stayed with them after his resurrection. He talked about the thing that was most upon his heart in his preaching ministry and now was most upon his heart as he prepared to leave them: the kingdom of God. He seemed to be saying, "Get this straight, for if you go wrong here, all the ages will go wrong with you. Get this right, and all the coming ages will go right with you." The future of humanity was bound up with his being able to get them to see this. If this whole scheme, worked out by redemptive love, could not be projected back into life as a total way of life, then it failed at the place where it counted—namely, at the place of life itself. If it cannot function there, it cannot function.

So the kingdom was God's head-on and sweeping answer to humanity's total need, individual and collective. It was God's totalitarianism, offering and demanding a total obedience in the total life, but which, when totally obeyed, gives total freedom. Here is an essential difference between human totalitarianism and God's: When we totally obey human totalitarianism, we find total bondage; but when we totally obey God's totalitarianism, we find total freedom. Only God could have thought out the idea of giving total bondage and total freedom at one and the same time. It seems incredible, but the fact is that it works. If I seek first the kingdom of God, then I find my freedom— yea, my very self—being added to me. But if I seek something else first, then I find my freedom—yea, my very self—being subtracted from me. The laws of the kingdom are the very laws of my being, the thing for which I am made.

O Lord, I thank you that the kingdom and I are not alien but affinities to each other, the very homeland of my soul. Amen.

AFFIRMATION FOR THE DAY: Nothing above the kingdom, nothing outside the kingdom, everything within the kingdom.

NO COSMIC LOOM?

Colossians 1:16-18

We considered yesterday the sixth pillar upon which the gospel rests: the *Word become a total way of life—the kingdom of God.* Humanity needs something to obey totally, so that through that obedience all life is brought into coherence and total meaning. Without this life is at loose ends and lacks drive, for it has no total goal. In sonnet cxxxvii, Edna St. Vincent Millay notes the chaos of an interminable stream of "unquestioned" facts that is "daily spun; but there exists no loom / To weave it into fabric."

There is "no loom to weave it into fabric"—no cosmic loom on which these unrelated facts can be woven into the fabric of total meaning. Life lacks meaning. Hence our minds are uneasy. We haven't found the ultimate It! We turn to the totalitarianisms of the day—Fascism, Nazism, Communism—to find something we can totally obey and thus find total meaning. But these half answers let us down and disillusionment sets in. For we are really looking for the kingdom, God's answer to our total need. We are homesick for our native land—the kingdom of God—and don't know what's the matter with us. When we find the kingdom, we know instinctively that this is it! The quest is over. A businessman, who had spent a fortune on pagan psychiatrists but grew worse, when he heard the message of the kingdom, took it joyfully saying, "This is it! My quest is over." And he rose to magnificent spiritual heights in following the way of the kingdom.

It would be a strange thing for God, who has put order and law in the atom and the cell, in fact in everything God has made, to leave humankind without plan and meaning and goal where we need it most—in our total life. To leave us at loose ends there would be a cosmic blunder. But God hasn't left us at loose ends—God gave us the kingdom of God, God's head-on and total answer to our total need.

O Lord God, we thank you that love provided for our needs and for our greatest need—the need of the kingdom. Amen.

AFFIRMATION FOR THE DAY: The kingdom shall be the cosmic loom upon which I shall weave all the facts of my life this day.

* Edna St. Vincent Millay, sonnet cxxxvii, *Collected Poems* (Harper & Row). Copyright © 1939, 1967 by Edna St. Vincent Millay and Norma Millay Ellis.

THE APPLIED EDGE OF REDEMPTION

2 Corinthians 1:21-22

We come now to consider the last of the seven pillars upon which the gospel rests: the *Word become dynamic—the Holy Spirit.* "While they were eating together, he ordered them not to leave Jerusalem but to wait for what the Father had promised. He said, 'This is what you heard from me: John baptized with water, but in only a few days you will be baptized with the Holy Spirit' " (Acts 1:4-5).

Here in this last step all the other six come into contact with the immediate problem; the problem of so changing and reinforcing the moral and spiritual life of people that they will be willing and able to put into operation in actual life what God has provided. It is not enough for the Word to become flesh, for the Word to become revelation, for the Word to become vicarious, for the Word to become triumphant, for the Word to become final, for the Word to become total program for the total life—all these are good, but not good enough unless and until they can move on the inside of humanity as immediate dynamic and power to enable us to accept and appropriate and make use of all that God has provided in Jesus. For all these six things are on the outside of us; and nothing is ours until it moves on the inside and becomes a part of us. This happens in the last step—the promise of the gift of the Holy Spirit. For the Holy Spirit is the applied edge of redemption. The Spirit is redemption where it counts, namely, down amid the driving urges on the inside of us. If the Holy Spirit can move in and cleanse and control and consecrate these driving urges, then salvation has come and has come where it counts, namely, within.

Otherwise these first six basic facts are all outside of us in history. The historical must become the experimental. The Jesus of history must become the Christ of experience. For nothing is ours until it becomes us. If all the redemption that Jesus has wrought had remained in history and had stopped this side of experience, then it would have stopped short of redemption. For it is not redemption until it redeems us, and it does not redeem us unless it can get into the inside of us. In the Holy Spirit, God takes the final step in redemption—God steps within. And that is where God has always wanted to be.

O Holy Spirit, you are the Lord and the Son stepping within me to remake and refashion me into the divine image. Amen.

AFFIRMATION FOR THE DAY: The Holy Spirit is with me now; my lowered barriers invite God within.

14

FROM PREPARATION TO PROMISE TO PERFORMANCE

Ephesians 5:24-27

We have looked at the divine preparation as seen in the first five pillars on which the Christian faith rests and then at the divine promises as seen in the last two pillars. We must now look at the divine performance as seen in the rest of the Acts. This is the greatest drama ever enacted—the drama of redemption of humanity moved from preparation to promise to performance. The preparation was the Lord become flesh, the Word become revelation, the Word become vicarious, the Word become victorious, the Word become final. The promise was a new and total way to live—the kingdom of God—and the offer of a divine dynamic to make it all possible—the Holy Spirit.

But someone objects: Where is the church in all this; is it not one of the pillars upon which the Christian faith rests? The church is more a product than a pillar. It is something that emerged out of the impact of these divine facts upon human life. It was a product of the divine performance. It is the building that was reared on these divine pillars. Where you have these seven things in vital operation, you have the church as a result. Where they are vitally absent, then you do not have the church; you have an organization, not an organism. You have a building built on sand, and the gates of hell do prevail against it; it falls or slowly decays, and great are both the fall and the decay thereof.

So in the opening chapters of Acts the church is not mentioned either by Jesus or by the disciples, for it was not yet born. Even by the descent of the Holy Spirit at Pentecost the church was not born.

So when we say that Pentecost was the birthday of the church, this is only partly true. Forces were loosed that produced the church through producing the fellowship, the *koinonia*. The *koinonia* became the soul of the church. Out of it the church grew. It was the organism out of which grew the organization. And where there is no fellowship, no *koinonia*, there is no church. But we will return to this later.

We must now turn to the vital fact, and factor, which produced this amazing moral and spiritual mastery, namely, the Holy Spirit. The Holy Spirit was God in action—and how!

O God, we thank you for this amazing divine impact—the Holy Spirit. We let the Spirit impact us. Amen.

AFFIRMATION FOR THE DAY: The Holy Spirit and my spirit shall be in accord in every act this day.

NOTHING IS OURS UNTIL IT GETS WITHIN

Ephesians 3:14-19

We now turn to the Holy Spirit, who is the applied edge of redemption—redemption where it counts, namely, down in the midst of me—within me.

Our need is greatest in the inner dynamic. We believe in all these things—God, Jesus, the kingdom of God—but they all lie like an empty, inoperative dream, above actuality, with no feet on the ground and no power to walk. As a Christian movement we have stopped short of the one thing that would make all God's preparation and promises into performances in and through us. That one thing is the Holy Spirit. We have tied God's hands just when God was at the point of dumping everything into our laps. We have stopped short of receiving the Holy Spirit and therefore of everything. For it is in and through the Holy Spirit that God gives us everything now. Luke tells us that Jesus "had given commandment through the Holy Spirit to the apostles" (Acts 1:2 RSV). He was from that time on commanding and working *through the Holy Spirit*. If we don't receive the Spirit, we are cutting ourselves off from Christ and God. Their dealings are now from within. It was external; now it is internal—a religion of the Spirit. If you do not receive the Spirit, you automatically shut yourself off from all God promised and Jesus procured for us. That is one reason Jesus emphasized something that has seemed odd to some. He said all manner of sin and blasphemy shall be forgiven, but not blasphemy against the Holy Spirit. Why? Because the Holy Spirit is the "finger of God" casting out the evil spirits within us, and then filling us with presence and power. But if we reject God's outstretched hand by refusal to cooperate or by positive blasphemies as God offers us grace, then God can give us nothing. We have tied the process of redemption in knots, just where it would be operative.

The blasphemy against the Holy Spirit is seldom committed, and hence the danger from it is infinitesimal. But the silent neglect of the Holy Spirit within our churches is infinitely more devastating, for it leaves a devastating barrenness—forms without force, liturgy without life, maneuvers without mastery.

O Lord, forgive us that we have stopped the fountain just when it was about to flow. In Jesus' name. Amen.

AFFIRMATION FOR THE DAY: If sin is missing the mark, it is also stopping short of the mark. I shall not stop short.

IMPOTENT INSTEAD OF OMNIPOTENT

Ephesians 3:20-21

If what I have said about the comparative impotence of the churches in the face of world need seems severe, then note what a medical psychotherapist, J. A. Hadfield, says:

> Looking at the Church of today, one cannot but be struck with its powerlessness. It contains men of intellect; it produces a type of piety and devotion which one cannot but admire; it sacrifices itself in...beneficence, but even its best friends would not claim that it inspires in the world the sense of power. What strikes one is its sense of impotence and failure. This want of inspiration and power is associated with the fact that men no longer believe in the existence of the Spirit in any effective practical way. They believe in God the Father, and they are reverent; they believe in God the Son, and...humbly try to "follow in His steps"; but for all practical purposes they are like that little band at Ephesus who had "not so much as heard whether there be any Holy Ghost," and lacking the inspiration of such a belief, they are weak and wonder why.*

We repeat the creeds Sunday by Sunday, and say, "I believe in the Holy Spirit"; but for all practical purposes we are about as confused about its meaning as when a little boy, coming back from church, said to his mother, "I understand everything about the creed except one thing: What do they mean when they talk about the 'Holy Cats in the Church'?" It wasn't too bad a mistake, for nearly every church has some "holy cats" in it! But seriously, what are we to think of a movement that comes in sight of the ultimate reality for which it is set, then fails to cash in on it? We sell ourselves short by stopping short of the source of mastery and power—the Holy Spirit.

The car of Christianity is beautifully streamlined, the gas tank of potential power full, the road before us; but there is no spark of the Spirit to start it and send it powerfully on its way. It fails at the place of operation; so to all intents and purposes it fails. A Spiritless Christianity is a counsel of perfection, demanding something that cannot be done. It lays an impossible burden on the will, too heavy to bear. But with the Holy Spirit everything is possible. The same power that worked in Jesus works in us with the same quality of results. And it is done so effortlessly. We let the power that works in creation work in us, and we become creative too.

O Holy Spirit, work in me the works of creation, and may I lay a creative hand on everything I touch. Amen.

AFFIRMATION FOR THE DAY: Through the Spirit of creation I shall become the center of creation today.

* J. A. Hadfield, *The Spirit*, ed. B. H. Streeter (Macmillan Co., 1919), 109.

17

SYMPTOMS OF THE MINUS

Ephesians 5:1-3

We come now to consider some facts among the disciples, showing the Spirit had not yet been given. True, they had a measure of the Spirit, but the Spirit had not been given without measure. He was with them but not in them ("for he dwells *with* you, and will be *in* you" [John 14:17 RSV, italics added]). They possessed the Spirit, but the Spirit did not possess them. They were using God; but after the coming of the Spirit, God was using them. What were some signs that the transition had not been made?

First, the disciples were struggling for position, place, and power. A dispute arose among them as to which of them was the greatest. They were assertive instead of surrendered. They were seeking first their own personal kingdom, where they could rule others, instead of the kingdom of God, where God would rule them. They were self-seekers instead of God-seekers, at least at times. They were a moral blur.

Second, they showed resentments against those who did not receive them in a Samaritan village, and asked Jesus if they should call down fire upon them, even as Elijah did. They mingled religiosity with resentments—"from heaven" and "even as Elijah did" (see Luke 9:54), quoting religious precedent. But stripped of this religious cloakage, there was just plain ugly resentment down underneath.

Third, there was self-righteous pride. "Though they all fall away..., I will never fall away" (Matt 26:33 RSV) Peter was taking a "they"-"I" relation to the rest—superior and full of pride. The humbling holiness of the Holy Spirit had not taken possession of them.

Fourth, they were spiritually impotent before the task of getting evil spirits out of a boy. They could not cast it out. The boy had a better case of devil possession than they had of God possession. They didn't have enough within to match against outer demand—the without was greater than their within.

Fifth, they were behind closed doors for fear of the Jews, and this even after the Resurrection, which was great, but not great enough to get them from behind closed doors. Intellectually they were convinced, but emotionally they were held by fears—deep-down fears.

So unsurrendered self, resentments, self-righteous pride, spiritual impotence, and fear showed they were not filled with the Spirit.

O Lord, help me not to stop this side of my full freedom from these and other crippling sins. Amen.

AFFIRMATION FOR THE DAY: I'm walking out from behind closed doors of fear by the power of the Spirit.

THE SEVEN ROAD BLOCKS

Matthew 17:14-20

To the five things showing the disciples had not entered into their inheritance—the Holy Spirit—we must add two more.

They were still held by pre-Christian notions: "Lord, are you going to restore the kingdom to Israel now?" (Acts 1:6). They were spiritually dull. They kept trying to jam his universal kingdom into their own narrow, nationalistic molds. They were a spiritual disappointment to him; his kingdom was too great for their small hearts.

Then they were still guided by outer events instead of inner spiritual illumination. "Lord,...show us clearly which one you have chosen from among these two....When they cast lots" (Acts 1:24, 26). The seat of religion was still in the outward; it had not moved into them.

It was obvious from these seven things that these men who were to master the world were still mastered by the world. Things and circumstances and wrong attitudes were on top of them instead of their being on top. They were not yet spiritually fit to turn the world upside down, for a lot of things in them were wrong side up.

The first step in their mastery of the world around them and within them was that they should be mastered. But how? It must all be entirely voluntary. There must be no compulsion except love. They had given up a good deal to follow Jesus—fishing nets, boats, parents, home, occupation—everything except themselves. They had never really surrendered the center, the citadel. They gave the marginal things but not the center. The unsurrendered self was the central block keeping redemption from flooding them. Everything was ready except the receptacle, which was still in their hands, not God's. Their inmost selves had not been surrendered. So for ten days they waited in prayer in an upper room, asking God for something God was aching to give if only they would let the last barrier down. It took them ten days to get to the end of themselves. And at the end of themselves was the beginning of God. God took over when they turned over themselves. They offered their all, and that cleared the way for God's all. God can give marginal blessings, but God can't give the divine self—the Holy Spirit—until we give ourselves unconditionally and absolutely.

O Lord, help me not to stop this side of giving that last thing, myself; for I want and must have the Holy Spirit. Amen.

AFFIRMATION FOR THE DAY: The big road block is my unsurrendered self; that goes and goes today.

19

THE KEY LOG IN THE JAM

Acts 2:1-4

We saw yesterday that the central block in the way of the coming of the Holy Spirit was the unsurrendered selves of the disciples. Everything was ready—except them.

The day on which the Holy Spirit came—the day of Pentecost—was a day that set a favorable atmosphere for the self-offering. Pentecost was the day of the offering of the first fruits of the harvest as a symbol that the whole of the coming harvest belonged to God. Here in this group, men and women were being offered as the first fruits of the new humanity coming to harvest through the redemption of Jesus. They were the sign and symbol that all humanity—the coming harvest—was to belong to him. But would all of this amazing prospect be blocked by the refusal of the first fruits to offer themselves? That could have been, but it wasn't. For these first fruits did offer themselves wholly and utterly. When their "all" was lifted up to meet God's "All," then the All of God flooded their all with light and power, with Godself, the Holy Spirit. They were drenched with God. They were so drenched they looked as though they were drunk. They were—drunk with God.

The Holy Spirit came as though, pent up for ages, he was free to come freely. Why? For the first time in history a group had been schooled three years in only one thing—in self-surrender, receptivity. For three years Jesus was getting them ready for this hour when they would take down the last barrier—the unsurrendered self. When they said yes, God said yes. And what a yes! In the flood of that divine yes all their negativism, fear, guilt, and hesitation were swept away. They were rid of everything they didn't want and filled with everything they did want.

In a river log jam there is usually a key log that holds up the whole thing. When that log is pried loose or breaks loose, then everything breaks loose with it. The key log that holds us up spiritually and keeps life jammed up and getting nowhere is the log of the unsurrendered self. When that goes, everything goes with it. It took the disciples ten days to frame the word yes; it need take us only ten minutes or ten seconds to say it.

O Lord God, I've come to the very crux of the whole matter, and I do say yes with all my ransomed being. Amen.

AFFIRMATION FOR THE DAY: The key log has been pried loose; now let the glorious flow begin.

THE FIRST NEED: TO BELONG

Romans 1:1-6

Psychology says that the human personality has three basic needs: the need to belong, the need for significance, and the need for reasonable security.

Note the first need is "to belong." The rogue elephant put out of the herd by the younger males turns destructive, tearing up trees, houses, gardens, everything, because he doesn't belong. He is uneasy and unhappy. The modern person has that same feeling—he or she doesn't belong. Old sanctions of life are gone, and no new ones take their place; hence modern people are destructive to themselves and others. We need to belong.

The group in that upper room decided to belong, to make Jesus Lord, to bank their all upon him, to surrender to him. The consequence was that, when they surrendered to him, they didn't surrender to anything else—everything else surrendered to them! Low at his feet, they stood straight before everything else. Bound to him, they walked the earth free! Belonging to him, everything belonged to them. They were mastered, and as a result became masterful.

Moreover, they had significance. They had the significance of the thing to which they belonged. They found that the thing to which they belonged was Ultimate Reality. Therefore they went out with the sense that Ultimate Reality was behind them, backing them and approving of them. Hence they were afraid of nothing. As long as you belong only to yourself, you are uneasy, for you have no cosmic backing; nothing sustains you except yourself. And you know deep down that this isn't enough to sustain you. Hence your uneasiness.

And the third need of the disciples was met; they had reasonable security. When they let go their false securities of pride, of self-assertion, of possessiveness, and took God's security, the wavering went from their wills; they walked the earth conquerors.

Self-surrender was the key. Not world-surrender, as some think, but something deeper—self-surrender. It is possible to give up the world and not give up yourself. The Naga sadhus, "the sky-clothed," the naked sadhus of India,* renounce the world; but they are self-assertive and difficult to handle, for they haven't given up themselves.

O Christ, master me. I consent. Then I am in safe hands; then I can let my whole weight down. I belong. Amen.

AFFIRMATION FOR THE DAY: My first step in mastery is to be mastered at the place of the self.

* The Naga are an Indian people group. A *sadhu* is a religious ascetic or holy person.

21

FROM SECONDHAND TO FIRSTHAND

Acts 1:1-8

We come now after these preliminaries to look at the mastery that came into life with the coming of the Holy Spirit. For the Holy Spirit is redemption applied. In him the potentialities become the actualities. The word of redemption becomes flesh in us. All that Jesus accomplished for us in the way of redemption was accepted by the believers when they received the Holy Spirit—the accomplishment became an acceptance. Redemption was applied where it counts, namely, on the inside of us. Nothing is ours until it moves from the outside to the inside, becomes us.

That happened to the disciples—the secondhand became firsthand. "Are you a mystic?" a radiant friend of mine was asked. "No," he replied, "I'm not a mystic; I'm just a first-hander." The disciples were not mystics but first-handers. Before they had been catching what they could from Jesus; now, through the Spirit, they were the centers of contagion. Their realization of God was no longer in quotation marks but in direct statement—very direct indeed!

This is seen in the changed attitude of Jesus toward them. The disciples asked him, "Lord, are you going to restore the kingdom to Israel now?" And his reply, "Rather, you will receive power" (Acts 1:6, 8) Note "are you...? "Rather, you...." The emphasis was shifted from him to them. Hitherto they had been looking to him to do everything; now he was looking to them to do everything.

He was not only going to work miracles on the inside of them; they themselves were to work miracles, for they were miracles.

This shift of emphasis is seen where it says: "After he had given commandment through the Holy Spirit to the apostles whom he had chosen" (Acts 1:2 RSV). Hitherto his commandments were given from the outside; now they would be from the inside: "given commandment through the Holy Spirit." He would speak from within through the Holy Spirit. That changed their religion from a religion of authority to a religion of the Spirit. They were being commanded not from without but from within. And no authority is real authority until it becomes identified with us. Then it is real authority. These apostles became authoritative.

O Lord, my inmost being is the place of your throne; rule me from there, and then I shall be ruled. Amen.

AFFIRMATION FOR THE DAY: If he is to command me from within, then my within must be clear and attuned.

MASTERING OUR JERUSALEMS

1 Corinthians 16:8-9

We have seen that these disciples were mastered by Christ and mastered from within. His authority was within them by consent. They were no longer cringing vassals, governed from without; they were conquering victors, governed from within. Since the seat of authority was within them, they became authoritative. They took on the authority of that with which they were identified. And since they were identified with the risen Christ by complete surrender to him, they took on his authority. He had said: "All power is given unto me in heaven and in earth" (Matt 28:18 KJV). And since they were identified with him who had all power in heaven and on earth, they began to be manifestations of that "all power." Not that they tried to be; they just were. It was effortless power and effortless authority.

So mastered at the center, they became masterful at the circumference. Life around them felt the impact of a new moral and spiritual mastery. A new, strange imponderable had come into being. And all life had to come to terms with it.

Look at the masteries that were coming into being. First, there was the *mastery of the disciples' greatest problem—Jerusalem*. Jerusalem was the center of both political and religious hostility, so hostile that they combined and crucified their Lord. Before the storm of that awful hostility the disciples bent, and some broke, in betrayal and denial. And what breathtaking thing did Jesus tell them to do? Nothing less than "not to leave Jerusalem." And the account begins: "he *ordered* them" (Acts 1:4, italics added). The only time it is said that he "ordered" his disciples. Why this insistence and emphasis? Apparently this: Jerusalem was the place of their failure; there they all forsook him and fled. They caved in. Suppose they had gone off to Galilee to a quiet mountain to receive the Holy Spirit, what would have happened? Down underneath they would have the feeling that all this would work in the quietness of Galilee, but it wouldn't work in Jerusalem; that was too tough. But here was Jesus asking them to walk up to their most difficult problem—Jerusalem—face it and master it. And they did just that! Having mastered Jerusalem, they were ready for anything.

O living Christ, how relentless you are, not bending to our weakness but holding us to your highest. I thank you. Amen.

AFFIRMATION FOR THE DAY: I am determined to walk up to all my Jerusalems today and face them, not dodge them.

ON WALKING UP TO EVERYTHING!

Genesis 15:1; Deuteronomy 1:17

We have seen that the disciples were first called on to master Jerusalem—the center of their deepest problem. Jesus was going to make the place of their greatest failure the place of their greatest success.

What would that do to their mentality? Something fundamental and necessary: wipe out all escapism, running from problems, dodging unpleasant issues, failure of nerve. It would save religion from something that has plagued it in all countries and all ages, and earned it the opprobrium, "opium of the people." The disciples came near falling right into that morass. After the resurrection and before the Spirit came, the account says: "As he blessed them, he left them and was taken up to heaven. They worshipped him and returned to Jerusalem overwhelmed with joy. And they were continuously in the temple praising God" (Luke 24:51-53). "Praising God"—and dodging the issues! The temple authorities had crucified Jesus, and here were his followers in that same temple "praising God" and raising no questions, not confronting the hierarchy with their crime but retreating into their inner happiness—escapism. Had this been the outcome, we would never have heard of the gospel again. It would have died, wrapped in its mystical states, or drugged with devotion and emotion and incapable of shouldering its world task.

Jesus, seeing this possibility, "ordered" them to wait for the Spirit, knowing if the Creative Spirit came upon them, they would not compromise with this guilty religious system but confront it with a demand for repentance. This they did, and Jerusalem responded with tears and repentance, and multitudes were converted in a day. The worst had been met and mastered. Henceforth they were ready for anything. If they could face Jerusalem and master it in his name, they could face anything and master it in his name! Everything else was a play spell—they had met and conquered the real thing. Someone said, "Whenever you raise a question, raise it in its most acute form. Solve it there, and you solve it all down the line." Jerusalem was their problem in its most acute form. They solved it, and henceforth they could face everything and everybody unafraid. Religion wasn't opium—it was open possibility. It was victory!

O Gracious Spirit, wipe out of my mind and heart all attitudes that would try to escape and give me the power to confront. Amen.

AFFIRMATION FOR THE DAY: The Spirit within me is more than a match for anything outside me.

A CAUSE OF NEUROSIS: REFUSING RESPONSIBILITY

Daniel 6:10; Acts 4:31

We noted yesterday that a first mastery that came into being with the coming of the Spirit was the mastery of their supreme, immediate problem—Jerusalem. They weren't looking within at their own supreme happiness, thus not looking at Jerusalem; they weren't looking down at the dust, symbol of their downcast souls, afraid of Jerusalem; they weren't looking above Jerusalem to the New Jerusalem, thus escaping the unpleasantness of having to face the Jerusalem of the here and now; rather they were looking at Jerusalem level-eyed and unafraid, knowing they had something Jerusalem did not have and desperately needed. They gave it, and Jerusalem took it—by the thousands.

The mastery of their hardest problem right off is psychologically sound. There are two great schools of psychological thought—led by Freud, who found the basis of neuroses in childhood, and Jung, who said, "I no longer seek the cause of neurosis in the past, but in the present. I ask, 'What is the necessary task which the patient will not accomplish?'"* In other words, what is the patient running away from and refusing to face? Why is the patient dodging into subterfuges and unreality?

The Christian movement at this juncture could have retreated into Galilee, where people were more favorable, could have retreated into inner mystic states, could even have retreated into the temple "praising God" for such a wonderful fact as the resurrection. It would have ended in spiritual neurosis instead of spiritual nerve. It would have chased around in circles instead of walking straight into its world tasks.

A visitor to a mental hospital saw workmen hauling materials for a new building. Among them was a patient with a wheelbarrow, but turned upside down. When the visitor asked him why he had it upside down, he replied: "Do you think I'm crazy? If I had it turned up, they would fill it." Had the disciples not accepted the responsibility of facing Jerusalem, they would have been running around in circles instead of joyously and maturely undertaking the assigned task of making a new order on earth. They would have been, as many religious movements are now, spiritual mental asylums instead of a curative and curing movement.

Lord, save me from all halting before responsibility and tasks. Help me to walk up to everything in your name. Amen.

AFFIRMATION FOR THE DAY: My wheelbarrow is going to be turned up for God to put into it any responsibility he will.

* C. G. Jung, *The Essential Jung: Selected and Introduced by Anthony Storr* (Princeton University Press, 1983), 52.

RETREATING INTO UNCONSCIOUSNESS

Jonah 1:4-5

Let us pause to apply this principle of facing our most difficult problem and mastering it straight off, if we are going to know mastery. Don't deal with the problem of mastering marginal problems and leaving the central problem untouched. For that central, untouched problem will haunt the so-called solution of the lesser problems and taint them with the consciousness of the untouched central.

Many try to skirt the central problem by various methods. One is to retreat into sleep. It provides an escape; a temporary one, of course, but for the time being the problem is put off by oblivion. A very brilliant girl in Ceylon failed in her B.A. examination. It was a great blow to her pride. She began to develop various ailments. Above all she became drowsy, even falling asleep while teaching her classes. She would go to sleep on the slightest provocation. When the connection between her wounded pride and the sleep as a way out of the necessity of facing an unpleasant situation was pointed out, she surrendered herself and her wounded pride to God. The next day her face had changed, and the first thing she said was, "Don't you think I could take that examination over again and pass?" She had been insisting that her mind was so upset that she couldn't study. But now she was ready to face her central problem—the shame of having failed in an examination. She ceased her attempt at running away into insensibility through sleep. Life was tipped forward, not backward.

A colleague who didn't like to travel on planes, saying that he had a responsibility to his family and shouldn't risk things this way, was on a plane with me when we passed over the Sierras and dived into a dense fog bank on our way to Seattle. We had to go completely blind. I looked over at my friend; he was fast asleep, his chin on his chest. He was frightened and retreated into sleep when the going got tough. That is what Jonah did when his ship ran into a fierce storm, a storm that he knew his own running away from God had caused. He went below and fell fast asleep, retreated into unconsciousness out of his trouble.

To try to get away from our problem is self-defeating, for the running away puts the problem inside us; we become the problem.

O Lord, help me to run away to nothing except your arms. Help me to face all with your grace and strength. Amen.

AFFIRMATION FOR THE DAY: No checking out of responsibility, no excuses, no evasions, everything met unafraid.

THE REAL SHUT-INS ARE WALKING CASES

John 20:19, 26

There is another phase of the order of Jesus to the disciples not to leave Jerusalem until they were endued with power. The emphasis was upon the "power." For it was possible for them not to run away from Jerusalem but to stay as they were, "behind closed doors because they were afraid" (John 20:19). It is possible to stay in a situation but behind closed doors, shut in with fears. They could say to themselves: "We are not running away. We are still in our Jerusalem," and yet all the time not free, not confronting Jerusalem; they could be there but without power. The point was to get them not merely to stay there but to stay there with power, power to go out and meet Jerusalem positively and redemptively. Now they were meeting it fearfully and negatively. It is possible to stay in a situation and compliment yourself that you are not running away, but all the time the staying is behind closed doors in fear. You are staying, but behind barricades— behind closed doors. You are on the defensive against the situation; you are keeping it off by shutting your doors against life and against trouble. But that only shuts you in with your problem. You have not shut the problem out, you have shut it within; you become the problem, you are full of fears.

We speak of shut-ins, people who cannot get out of their homes, often not out of their beds. We have pity on them and often organize people to visit them. That is good. But the biggest class of shut-ins is not those physically unable to get out; it is the walking cases of shut-inism. They are outwardly out, but not inwardly out. They are free to walk out into their environment, but not free to walk out from behind their closed doors into usefulness and fellowship and outgoingness. They are tied-up souls. They are never relaxed, for they have to keep guard behind closed doors. Their energies are expended keeping guard against supposed or real enemies. They have little energy left to go out and positively achieve. They are so busy saying no to life and accomplishment.

Yet those disciples knew Jesus was risen from the dead; why then were they behind closed doors? Intellectually they knew he was alive, but emotionally they were held by the old fears. Only the Holy Spirit within could release them from those fears.

O Lord, I do not want to live behind anything. I want to live in the open—free— free to accomplish and attain. Amen.

AFFIRMATION FOR THE DAY: No behind closed doors for fear for me. I belong to the open road, adventuring with God.

INTELLECTUALLY MATURE, EMOTIONALLY IMMATURE

1 Corinthians 2:10-12

The church today is, in large measure, halfway between Easter and Pentecost and is behind closed doors in fear. The grandest good news that ever broke upon human ears had broken freshly upon them: Jesus was alive, yet that didn't free them; they were still locked behind closed doors.

One of the greatest fallacies of this age of intellectual progress is the fallacy that knowledge in itself is necessarily freeing. It may free you, it may not. Many intellectually mature people are emotionally immature. That accounts for the fact that many psychologists and psychiatrists are not integrated. They know, but they don't know freedom. Emotionally they are still bound by old fears and frustrations. That is the basic reason we need some powerful impulse within that will free us from our unreasoning fears and anxieties. That impulse within can be supplied only by the Holy Spirit. For the Spirit works within, down amid the driving urges.

A religion of rites, ceremonies, and outer observances may be good, but not good enough. For it does not touch within where fears and inhibitions hold the citadel. Only the Holy Spirit can touch those inner depths and free us there. All the knowledge about freedom and exhortation to freedom could not have got the disciples from behind those closed doors. They had to be emotionally freed. Only God within could unlock those doors and bid them walk out into freedom. And God within was the Holy Spirit. The Spirit is God in action, where it counts, down amid the driving urges where fears lurk.

Jesus said, "But if I throw out demons by the power of God's Spirit, then God's kingdom has already overtaken you" (Matt 12:28). The parallel passage of Luke is: "But if it is by the finger of God that I cast out demons" (Luke 11:20 RSV).

The Spirit is the finger of God, God touching us vitally within. The Spirit is redemption permanently settling within. He unlocks the doors from within and bids us be free. The Spirit is the "finger of God" that not only casts out demons but also keeps them out. His finger is on the doorknob, and no one gets in without his consent. The Spirit provides deliverance and security. Jerusalem is now in our hands as possibility for fruitfulness and not in our hearts as fear.

O Holy Spirit, come in and unlock the closed doors and give me freedom and glorious security. I consent now. Amen.

AFFIRMATION FOR THE DAY: I am intellectually and emotionally freed, for God is within me.

THE UNHEALED TRYING TO HEAL

Romans 2:19-23

We have been studying the fact that Jesus ordered the disciples not to leave Jerusalem. We have noted the word "ordered." It was the only time he ever ordered his disciples to do or not to do anything. It showed the importance he attached to facing up to your most difficult problem and solving it. For if you don't, everything else you do is canceled by your refusal to do this central thing.

For instance, a woman is out to set right the church and the world. She nags everybody she can about it, and then feels a martyr because there is no response. And there is none. For she is a frustrated woman trying to set everybody right. She is full of discord trying to produce concord. And the reason is seen at a glance; everybody senses it. The reason is she has never faced the need for personal self-surrender.

Her conflicting, festering, disrupted self sticks out, for the garment of defensive words has worn thin and is in shreds, and the untouched problem of an unsurrendered self protrudes. But if you try to get near that problem, she decoys you away from the nest of her personal problem by her flutter of wings of concern for the world's troubles. She wants attention—lots of it—and if you don't give as much as she demands, she is hurt, a martyr. But it all ends in frustration for everybody, for she is refusing to face her central problem—her Jerusalem. She is bypassing that and continually running into dead-end roads instead of walking the Way. She feels she has a mission, but the mission is used to hide omission. If she would face her need for self-surrender, she would find her life and work clicking; now they are only clacking. And the clacking gets on people's nerves. And that makes her feel that everybody is hard-hearted and unresponsive. No one comes to her with problems. People run away from her as a problem that refuses to acknowledge it is a problem—everybody else is the problem. So everybody's hands are tied. The problem is insoluble because unacknowledged.

But these Christians who had listened to the order of Jesus faced the multitudes; and the multitudes sensed they had faced their own central problem—their Jerusalem—and had solved it, so the people turned to them for solutions and got them.

O Lord, we know that unless we have found the Way for ourselves, we cannot point the way. Help us to find it. Amen.

AFFIRMATION FOR THE DAY: I shall begin to change the world by letting God begin in me.

THE MASTERY OF RELIGIOUS PARAPHERNALIA

Galatians 3:1-5

We saw yesterday that many try to go into all the world and solve all problems there instead of starting with their own Jerusalems. Many do this through an initial mental dishonesty, which through rationalization now seems mental honesty. Others shy away from their Jerusalems because they are confused as to the solutions offered or because of the feeling of sheer hopelessness of any solution.

That leads us to consider another mastery that came into being in the Acts. It was the *mastery of religious paraphernalia*. Since religion is humanity's search for God, it has manufactured ways of finding God. All sorts of things are intruded between us and God and proclaimed necessary if we are to find God. Paraphernalia is built up.

For instance, our Roman Catholic friends say that the Roman Catholic Church is necessary to find salvation, to find God. If you come to Christ, you must come through that church. A system is interposed between you and God. Without that system no salvation.

Others interpose a rite or ceremony between the soul and Christ. You cannot get to God without going through that rite or ceremony. For instance, baptism. If you do not take baptism from that particular group in that particular form, you are outside salvation.

Others would say that if you are outside a particular line of succession, the Holy Spirit is not mediated to you; you can find God only as specially prepared hands are laid on you. That special preparation is found within an unbroken line of succession from the apostles down to the present moment. Grace is mediated to those in "line."

Still others would say that you cannot get to God unless you come repeating a creed, a creed well defined with special accents. A creed is interposed between the soul and God.

Now all of these may contain something worthwhile. But according to the experience of the Acts, not one of them is required as absolutely necessary for receiving the Holy Spirit. When the Holy Spirit came upon this waiting body of believers, they were going through none of these things. They were undergoing no rite or ceremony, no hands were being laid on them, they were joining no church. There was nothing between.

O Lord, I thank you that the way is open to you and there are no hurdles. For you are coming to me, in Christ. Amen.

AFFIRMATION FOR THE DAY: Nothing will keep the living Christ out except my own wrong attitudes.

30

THE GREAT SIMPLIFICATION

Romans 10:6-13

We have seen that there was a mastery of religious paraphernalia in that, when these people received the Holy Spirit, God's highest gift, they were undergoing no rite, no ceremony, no laying on of hands on anyone, and they were not joining any religious body. There was nothing and no one between. There was one mediator—and only one mediator—between God and humanity, and that was Jesus. It was he who gave the Holy Spirit: "This Jesus, God raised up. We are all witnesses to that fact. He was exalted to God's right side and received from the Father the promised Holy Spirit. He poured out this Spirit, and you are seeing and hearing the results of his having done so" (Acts 2:32-33). That forever fixed the source from which we receive the Spirit; we receive the Spirit from Jesus and him alone, or we do not receive the Spirit. This gift comes from a nail-pierced hand or not at all.

To interpose a church, a rite, a ceremony, a worked-out creed, a line of specially qualified mediators of the Holy Spirit by the laying on of hands is to interpose people and things between the soul and God; and that is idolatry. For when a relative thing becomes an absolute thing, then that is idolatry. And there was no idolatry here.

Jesus was the Way. Humanity couldn't get to God, so God came to humanity— came in Jesus. This coming of the Holy Spirit was like a cleansing wind from heaven, cleansing the fetid atmosphere of religion from a thousand controversies and claims. Everything was simplified. The vast complications of law and ritual and rite and creed were all swept away before the vast simplification.

This group of one hundred twenty were doing what when the Holy Spirit came? Nothing but praying and surrendering to Jesus and through him to God. Nothing was needed except the open, surrendered, receptive heart. When that took place, then the Holy Spirit was given without measure. There was no special religious posture—they were not even kneeling—they were "sitting" (Acts 2:2).

This simple happening has rendered irrelevant and absurd all the controversies of the centuries as to what is essential or not essential. No "thing" is essential. But someone is—and only he. The air is cleared.

O Lord, your hand has brushed aside everything by this seed happening. We now see no man save Jesus only. Amen.

AFFIRMATION FOR THE DAY: I need nothing except to be in right attitudes to him—nothing.

I AM NOT RELIGIOUS: I'M HIS

1 Timothy 3:16

We pondered yesterday the mastery of religious paraphernalia. An added word is needed. Religious rites and ceremonies and creeds and laying-on of hands may be useful—in their place. But their place is not in the list of essentials. Aids? Yes, but not essentials. If these rites and ceremonies and practices point beyond themselves to Christ, and push you in that direction, then good. But if they stop you at themselves as essential, then not good—idolatry.

Religion, which is to help you to Christ, often stands between you and Christ; you can't see the person for the paraphernalia.

The fact is that Jesus never used the word *religion*, nor did the early disciples use it. *Religion* means literally "binding back"—a binding back to God. It is humanity's attempts to bind ourselves back to God by various expedients. But the gospel was not a series of expedients to bind us back to God; it was the good news of God's coming to us in incarnation, in redemption. Jesus didn't come to set one religion against other religions—a little better, a little bit more moral. He came to set the good news over against human need, whether that need be found in this religion, that religion, or no religion. Religion is our search upward; the gospel is God's reach downward. There are many religions; there is but one gospel.

What terms did Jesus use if he didn't use the term *religion*? He used the "kingdom of God" and the "Way," and both were embodied in himself: "I am the way." All these terms are inward pushes toward the person Jesus and through him to God.

In the book *Growing Spiritually*, I gave the beginnings of the story of "Mary," the simplest and the most spiritually profound person I've seen in East or West. Some psychiatrists, challenged and puzzled by her immediate insights and radiance, suggested that she ought to be psychoanalyzed. When I reported this to her, her reply was: "Why do they want to psychoanalyze me? I don't know anything to psychoanalyze. Do they think I'm 'off' on religion? I'm not religious; I'm his." Here she cut straight through paraphernalia to the person of Jesus. Life was simplified; she belonged to him.

O Lord, I thank you that I am now reduced to simplicity, I'm yours. That is central—all else marginal. Amen.

AFFIRMATION FOR THE DAY: I am emancipated from the many things to give myself to the One person of Christ.

NOT A VAGUE POWER, BUT A VITAL PERSON

John 14:25-26

We meditated yesterday on the mastery of religious paraphernalia. It was all so immediate. And the immediacy was not that of a vague impersonal power. They had immediate contact with a person. And that contact deepened into a communion—they communed in the heart with a Divine Person. The Holy Spirit is not an *it*. "He will guide you in all truth" (John 16:13); the Holy Spirit is a *he*. And not a vague depersonalized person; he is a person with a very definite personalized content. And the content is the content of Jesus.

The fact is that the terms "Holy Spirit" and "Spirit of Jesus" are used interchangeably: "...the Holy Spirit kept them from speaking the word in the province of Asia....They tried to enter the province of Bithynia, but the Spirit of Jesus wouldn't let them" (Acts 16:6-7). The consciousness of the Holy Spirit was the consciousness of Jesus. And it was the consciousness of the Lord: "but the Spirit of my Father is doing the talking through you" (Matt 10:20). So the Holy Spirit deepens the consciousness of the Lord. The fact is that I cannot tell where one ends and the other begins in my experience. It all seems to melt into one, yet there is an experience of all three—a social experience and yet a separate experience. How rich a fellowship!

One who had just entered into the experience of the Holy Spirit said: "I used to say I love Jesus more than the Father. But since I've experienced the Holy Spirit, it is like saying no longer, 'I love Mama more than Daddy,' but 'I love both.' Now I love the Father, and I love the Son, and I love the Holy Spirit." The Holy Spirit hadn't absorbed the love of the Father and the Son in his coming—he had intensified the love of each. The communion with the Spirit is an intensely personalized experience and an intensely social experience, the richest experience a human being is capable of experiencing. So the Trinity, instead of being an insoluble puzzle to be explained, is an intimate experience to be realized and enjoyed. You feel your inner life socialized while doing the most solitary thing one can do—communing with God. It can't be explained; it has to be experienced. And what an experience!

O Spirit, you make Father and Son inwardly real, and you make me real in the process. I thank you. Amen.

AFFIRMATION FOR THE DAY: I am taking hold of and am being taken hold of by the Redeeming Spirit within.

HOW DO WE RECEIVE THE HOLY SPIRIT?

1 Timothy 2:3-6

We have been thinking about how the Holy Spirit is given. The most important question in religion is just here, in the words of Paul, "Did you receive the Spirit by the works of the Law, or by hearing with faith?" (Gal 3:2 NASB). That penetrates to the very heart of our religious problem. Humanity's mediatorial religion says you get the Spirit by undergoing this rite, going through that ceremony, accepting this creed, undertaking that discipline, joining this group, believing that book, obeying this law, offering that sacrifice, worshiping this idol. All this is gently but decisively swept away in the coming of the Spirit upon that group of one hundred twenty believers. None of these things was present; hence none was necessary.

But every one of these things, now no longer necessary, came back again cleansed, related, and useful. They were redeemed. Since they were no longer looked on as redemptive, they themselves were redeemed. The rite of baptism, no longer a necessity, became beautifully useful in proclaiming outwardly an already inward fact (see Acts 10:47-48). Holy Communion, instead of mediating the Lord's death, proclaimed it: "for as often as you eat this bread and drink the cup, you proclaim the Lord's death" (1 Cor 11:26 RSV). The joining of a group, the fellowship, was the outward manifestation of an inner fact; they were one in Spirit and became outwardly one in the fellowship. They produced the books of the New Testament out of their experience of the Holy Spirit. That experience produced this expression. The Law of the Old Testament became an inner law, written not on tablets of stone but in the fleshly tablets of the heart. The sacrifices of animals and grain to propitiate and buy favor with God now became the sacrifice of God in Christ, offering himself upon the cross for our redemption. Jesus took the place of idols, since he was the express image of God's person. The idol misrepresented God; Jesus represented him.

Only God could wipe out all this paraphernalia of religion with one hand and then bring it all back with the other, now no longer necessary, but useful in pointing us to the reality in Jesus. Mediatorial religion was replaced by the one Mediator.

O Lord, I thank you that I have direct access to you through Jesus Christ my Lord. Amen.

AFFIRMATION FOR THE DAY: He takes away all my second bests to replace them with his best.

WHY NOT GO DIRECT TO GOD?

John 14:6-9

There is one thing we must consider before we leave this subject of the mastery of religious paraphernalia. All human mediatorial acts and rites and ceremonies are pushed out of the center as necessary and placed on the margin as helpful accessories; and one Mediator, Jesus Christ, takes the center as the only necessity between God and people.

But someone asks: Why Jesus? Why not go to God direct? Why a mediator at all? The answer is that no one goes to God direct. God has to be mediated to us. If you try to go to God direct, you go through the category of your conceptions of God. Those conceptions of God mediate God to you. But they are not God, they are your conceptions about God. They are more or less false and more or less true—false God.

Apart from Jesus we know little about God. Jesus is God disclosing the divine self to us in understandable terms, human terms. Jesus is not our view of God but God's view of Godself. God is the divine self-disclosure. Jesus is not therefore a third person, standing between us and God. He is God come to you; and when you take hold of Jesus, you take hold of the very self of God. So Jesus is a mediator only in the sense that he mediates God to you.

Just as the word mediates the thought of the speaker—so that when you take hold of his word, you take hold of his thought—so Jesus is the Word of the Eternal Mind. He is the Mind come to you in the Word. If you take hold of the Word, Jesus, you take hold of the thought, God.

That is not theory, it is fact—fact attested through the centuries. The more you deepen the Christ-consciousness, the more you deepen the God-consciousness. Jesus doesn't rival or push out God; he intensifies God. A man of Unitarian faith said to me, "I wish you would come to our convention and help us to get God back; we are becoming a humanism." Interesting that they who had focused on God were losing him, and I who focused on Jesus Christ had found God, or rather God had found me. Jesus mediates God to us—the one Mediator.

O Jesus, I thank you that in you I find God, and what a God! My heart bows in the utmost satisfaction. Amen.

AFFIRMATION FOR THE DAY: When I know God in terms of Jesus, then I know God, the authentic God.

THE ETERNAL QUEST AND THE ETERNAL FINDING

Luke 11:5-8

We come now to a mastery of real importance—*the mastery of the eternal quest by the eternal finding.*

A Jewish rabbi said to a friend of mine, "Our faith is an incomplete faith. We are always looking for a Messiah who has not come and for a kingdom that is not here. Ours is a religion of quest, of hopes unfulfilled." The vast majority of humankind, inside and outside the Christian church, belongs to the category of the unfulfilled faith. They belong to the eternal quest instead of the eternal finding.

But these followers of Jesus in the Acts belonged to the eternal finding. They weren't dealing with a future but with a fact. They could say, "This is what was spoken through the prophet Joel....This Jesus...was exalted to God's right side and received from the Father the promised Holy Spirit. He poured out this Spirit, and you are seeing and hearing the results of his having done so" (Acts 2:16, 32-33). They used the word "this" instead of "that"; it was present possession, present experience. The eternal quest had become the eternal finding. They had found God because God had found them, found them in Christ.

I have lived the larger part of my life in a continent of seeking, India. In India is to be seen the greatest God-hunger that we have ever found on this planet in any period of human history. It is a God-thirsty nation. But the impression one gets is that it is a quest rather than a finding. I have listened in at my Round Table Conferences, where the best representatives of India's religions were found, have listened for the note of finding. But I have listened in vain except where people, whether within or without the Christian church, were in contact with Christ. There the note of finding was heard. And it was heard to the degree of that contact with Christ. Where people were in contact with Christ, there the eternal quest had become the eternal finding. They weren't looking for something; they had it. And that made them witnesses—witnesses instead of mere worshipers. In Christ, God invades us, and that invasion becomes a pervasion. God comes within.

O Lord, we thank you that the dissatisfied quest is over, and the satisfied quest takes its place. We thank you. Amen.

AFFIRMATION FOR THE DAY: I am passing from the eternal seekers to the eternal finders through Jesus Christ my Lord.

DRUNK...WITH GOD

Luke 11:9-13

We mentioned yesterday our Round Table Conferences, where we invite people of all faiths and of no faith to tell what their way of life is doing for them in experience. We urge upon them that no one argue, no one talk abstractly, no one preach at the rest of us, but that we simply tell how our way of life is working—what do we find in experience? When we say that, the climate changes, arguments and abstractions and idealisms are out—only finding counts. Those intoxicated with the wine of their own wordiness become sober and serious. And the verb "is" becomes all-important. There the sincere Christian is at home. It is our native air. We are in contact with the Word become flesh, and in us, in turn, that Word again becomes flesh in experience. We have something.

Non-Christians often interpret this fact of finding on the part of Christians in a very interesting way. One Muslim man said to me as we walked away from a Round Table Conference, "We Hindus and Mohammedans must have been more sincere and honest than you Christians." When I asked him why he thought so, he replied, "Because we all said we had found nothing, but all you Christians said you had found something; therefore we must have been more honest and sincere than you were." I replied, "That's one interpretation. There is another possible one: Jesus is the Way. And when we come to him, we find." We do. And the degree of the coming is the degree of the finding. It works.

God can give himself in Christ, not arbitrarily but because Jesus represents, in his own person, the reality about God. God is like Jesus. Therefore, when we come through him, we come through that which God can approve about Godself. Hence God gives himself. We find. And when we give ourselves wholly, we find wholly. The disciples appeared "drunk" at Pentecost; they were—drunk with God. They gave all and got all. We give lightly and are affected lightly. When we are all out in our giving, then God is all out in giving to us. We are filled with God's Spirit. And the filling becomes an overflowing. The inflow becomes an outflow. We gush.

O Lord, I thank you that my seeking can become a finding and my finding becomes more finding. Amen.

AFFIRMATION FOR THE DAY: I will take from God with both hands today; it's all my heritage.

AT THE SIGHT OF THIS...I AM DOWN

1 Corinthians 1:20-24

We have been looking at the mastery of the eternal quest by the eternal finding. God cannot be found at the end of a syllogism—the way of logic and philosophy; nor at the end of a laborious and costly sacrifice—the way of priesthood; nor at the end of a long vigil of self-mutilation—the way of asceticism; nor at the end of a long and concentrated meditation—the way of the mystic; nor at the end of a long climb upward—the way of the seeker. God is found at the foot of the cross.

This is vividly put in the words of "T. V. K.," the greatest living Tamil scholar. He has written more than sixty books, some of which have gone into twenty editions. He has now written a book which the Tamil literary critics say is his best. In the introduction he says:

> Man somehow or other sins. He wants to get freedom from sin and suffering. The different religions of the world are attempts to wean men away from sin and give them freedom. But there is only one true way by which he can obtain his freedom from sin. That way is at the foot of the Cross where Christ is being nailed. Unless you are healed at that fountain there is no hope. I am not a Christian. No Christian padre ever taught me Christianity. Yet I tell you the truth. Go to the foot of the Cross or you perish.

Then he goes on and in the first lines of the book says:

> I took delight in learning various languages, studying various religions and philosophies and in debating with everybody. In logic, in argument my opponents feared me and I was successful everywhere. But today I see a humble man stretched on the Cross and his enemies nailing him. This victim is saying: "Father, forgive them." This was a new experience to me. At the sight of this gone is all my debate. I am down.... Various war lords drew their mighty swords and slew millions that they might live alone. They are all gone. Here is one who threw away the sword and was slain. He lives. Well, I have found the way to live. It lies at the feet of him who was slain and yet lives.*

So the eternal quest is not our search for God but God's search for us. God's quest and ours meet at the foot of the cross, where God finds us and we find God. The eternal quest ends, ends in finding and being found.

O Christ, we could not get to you so you came to us; come to us bearing our sins in your body. Amen.

AFFIRMATION FOR THE DAY: If God's quest for me and my quest for God meet at the cross, then for me the cross forever.

---

* No published source was found for these quotations.

THE ETERNAL FINDING

2 Corinthians 3:17-18

In our last day of considering the mastery of the eternal quest by the eternal finding, we note that while the finding is once and for all, yet it is an *eternal* finding.

In Acts, the people impress us as people without strained longings and dissatisfied yearnings but as people who had found what they were looking for. They were satisfied to the very roots of their being. They knew they knew and were sure they were sure. Their question marks had turned into exclamation points. Their religion was not an everlasting reaching out but a present realization within. God was the most real fact of their lives. If they should reach out to touch God, they would reach too far; God was within—gloriously so.

But while the eternal quest had been mastered by a finding, yet it was an eternal finding. They had found, but they knew that it was only the beginning of finding. They had found but knew there was more to be found. They had arrived only to start on an endless journey every moment of which was a new arriving. Every realization of God set them on fire to realize more—and then more. They were not dissatisfied but forever unsatisfied. Realization and reach were the alternate beats of their hearts.

And this will continue forever. I am persuaded that we begin the next life where we leave off this one, and there will be an eternal growth in the divine image, the finite forever approaching the infinite in character and life, but never becoming the infinite. In that growth in the divine image will be our eternal happiness. We are happy only as we fulfill the laws of our being, and those laws demand growth and creation for their fulfillment. To sit down forever and rest might fit the life of a man of a tropical country who said, "God is good. He made the nights to sleep in and the days to rest in." But it wouldn't be the heaven of an alive man. To be alive is to be alive to creation and development. God, the eternal Creator within us, would make us eternally creative.

We find, but we find that there is more to be found. Every experience becomes an exploration—for more.

O Lord, we thank you that we need not be afflicted forever with a spiritual itch that can't be alleviated. We find and are found in Jesus. Then comes the eternal "more." Amen.

AFFIRMATION FOR THE DAY: I have found, but the finding sets me on fire to find more, so more is my cry.

MASTERY OF THE TIMES-AND-SEASONS MENTALITY

Luke 17:20-21

We come now to note another mastery—*the mastery of the times and seasons totally, by the mentality of receiving power for the business of witnessing.* "Those who had gathered together asked Jesus, 'Lord, are you going to restore the kingdom to Israel now?' Jesus replied, 'It isnt for you to know the times or seasons that the Father has set by his own authority. Rather, you will receive power when the Holy Spirit has come upon you; and you will be my witnesses'" (Acts 1:6-8). Here the disciples were turned from studying doubtful traps of the future to receiving power to live effectively in the present.

This is important; for had this mastery not taken place, this redemptive movement would have dissipated in the sands of speculation about the future instead of being turned into channels of redemption to meet human need here and now. A little twist of interest toward times and seasons, and all Jesus had accomplished in his life, teaching, death, and resurrection would have been canceled or rendered inoperative. The Christian movement would have died. Paul checked this tendency:

> I asked you to stay behind...so that you could instruct certain individuals not to...pay attention to myths and endless genealogies. Their teaching only causes useless guessing games instead of faithfulness to God's way of doing things. The goal of instruction is love from a pure heart, a good conscience, and a sincere faith. Because they have missed this goal, some people have been distracted by talk that doesn't mean anything. (1 Tim 1:3-6)

Paul called them from religion as talk to religion as doing, from guessing games to love that issues from a pure heart.

When we see how much time is wasted and attention diverted by trying to understand times and seasons in religion, we see why Jesus turned them from maps of the future to roads into the present, from mysteries to masteries. They would have been prognosticators of events instead of preachers of the Event. The Christian movement would have been relegated to the growing pile of might-have-beens. But Jesus closed that door—"it isn't for you to know"—and opened the door to power through being his witnesses.

O Jesus, my Lord, save me from bypaths and help me walk the Way. When my mind is seduced from single devotion to you and your emphasis, save me. Amen.

AFFIRMATION FOR THE DAY: I shall not be curious about coming events but consecrated to that which has taken place, the cross.

DESTINY IN THE STARS?

Isaiah 8:19-20

I must pause and emphasize the need for mastery over times-and-seasons mentality in religion—times and seasons instead of power to witness effectively to the living, saving Christ.

Three distinct tendencies are pulling many devoted men and women from being effective witnesses to Christ into speculators on the future. One is the astonishing number of people trying to read their destiny in the stars—astrology addicts. I use the word *addicts* advisedly; for just as alcohol and drugs pull you away from the real world into a false world of fantasy and illusion, so gazing at the stars to find your destiny and your direction takes you out of the real world of guidance through your Christian faith into a false world of guidance through stars. As if lumps of matter floating in space could decide my destiny as a moral being. My destiny is decided by my moral choices. Under the guidance of my Christian faith I make those moral choices. All the stars in their courses cannot alter the slightest the moral choices themselves or the results of those moral choices. Yet five million people in America, I am told, decide their lives on the basis of the supposed effects of the stars. This is always a sign of moral decay; when people haven't nerve enough to make their own decisions, they weakly turn to the stars for direction, a moral abdication.

Then there are those who try to get in contact with the dead and get moral and spiritual direction from them. One can sympathize with this desire on the part of those who have lost loved ones. But the guidance and information supposedly coming from behind the veil are meager and innocuous. Apparently no worthwhile revelations and certainly no moral renovations or impulses have come from that quarter. This emphasis drains off our attention from getting the power of the Holy Spirit to witness effectively for Christ in the here and now. That is what the departed, if they are in touch with Christ there, would have us do here.

We must master the marginal interest and give ourselves to the central.

O Holy Spirit, check us when we are drawn from the simplicity of devotion to Christ to the devotion to curiosity, for in Christ is Life and Life eternal. Amen.

AFFIRMATION FOR THE DAY: The big enemy of the central is the clamoring marginal. I belong to the central.

WORKING EMPHASIS IS THE FIRST COMING, NOT THE SECOND

Acts 1:9-11

We note the third tendency toward times-and-seasons religion instead of power for witnessing. The New Testament teaches, I believe, the second coming of Christ. So I believe he will come again to reign. But of that coming I have no timetable, nor do I have any map of the future. He said I wouldn't know and added, "It isn't for you to know"; it isn't in his purpose for us to know. It is purposely veiled. Why? For the simple reason that if he had pulled aside that veil, we would have been so drawn by curiosity that we would have fixed our attention upon future events as Christ will unfold them instead of fixing our attention on events now as we can and should mold them. Religion would have been escape, escape into the future instead of making the present livable for ourselves and others. Instead of making a new age, we would speculate on the next age; this one would decay. That is exactly what has happened to many people. I know of a nurse devoted and able and effective until she got wrapped up in "signs of the times" and in his coming again. It completely unfitted her to carry on her nursing profession. She is a complete failure as a human being, living on relief and compensating for her ineffectiveness by getting more and more intensely interested in the things to be. In the meantime, the things that are, deteriorate—her health, her influence, her very person. She is a times-and-seasons Christian instead of a witnessing and winning Christian.

The working emphasis in the New Testament is on the coming of Jesus in incarnation; in his death and resurrection; on the coming of the Holy Spirit giving power to witness to the living, serving Christ now. Its gaze is upon that; its glance is toward the Second Coming. But if we gaze at the Second Coming and glance at the first, then we have lost the "single eye"; and the "whole body" of effectiveness is "full of darkness." The times and seasons will take care of themselves if we witness to him who controls them.

Lord, help me to live this day so that if, at nightfall or noonday, your Son should come, I would lift my eyes from my task and greet him with joy. Amen.

AFFIRMATION FOR THE DAY: My gaze is on Jesus; my glance is on the past and on the future.

LORD, WILL YOU? ... BUT YOU

Matthew 17:14-18

We come now to look at another mastery—*the mastery of looking to Jesus to do everything.*

"So when they had come together, they asked him, 'Lord, will you...?' He said to them,... 'But you....'" (Acts 1:6-8 RSV). The emphasis had now shifted; they had been looking to him to do everything—"Lord, will you?"—and now he was going to look to them—"But you."

That change from Jesus himself doing everything to his doing everything *through* them is of the utmost importance. For if their attitude had not changed, the movement of redemption would have resulted in a shabby group of pietists, folding their hands and rolling their eyes and saying, "Jesus will do it all." The movement would have died and ought to have died, for it would not have been worth surviving. It would have weakened the persons involved, taking away their initiative, their very personalities.

Up to this time they had watched him do everything: heal the sick, preach the good news, feed the multitudes, die, rise again, instruct them. He was taking the initiative. They were in the dependent stage—of childhood; then for forty days they were in the independent stage—of adolescence—for he came and went and left them on their own. Now they were passing into the interdependent stage—of maturity—where they were working things out together.

While he was looking to them to be the center of activity, he was more than with them, he was in them in the Holy Spirit. "Rather, you will receive power when the Holy Spirit has come upon you, and you will be my witnesses" (v. 8). There was interplay here. They were in the stage of maturity—of interdependence. Now they were grown-up human beings working with Christ within them and working out his purposes. He had brought them to the stage where he wanted them—of upstanding human beings who, now morally independent, choose to be morally interdependent and to work out things in cooperation with him—a cooperative endeavor. They would supply willingness, and he, power.

O Christ, you are so thoughtful, so considerate, guiding us but not overriding us, making us the center and yet yourself the center at the same time. We thank you. Amen.

AFFIRMATION FOR THE DAY: I am facing life not on the unit principle but on the cooperative plan.

HE CONCEALS AND REVEALS

John 14:18-21

We passed quickly yesterday over one of the three stages—dependence, independence, and interdependence—and we must now go back to it for a little further elucidation. It is the stage of independence, the stage between his resurrection and the coming of the Holy Spirit, a stage of forty days.

Many have been puzzled as to why he came and went after his resurrection. "It was still the first day of the week. That evening...Jesus came and stood among them. He said, 'Peace be with you.'" (John 20:19). "After eight days...Jesus entered and stood among them" (v. 26). "Later, Jesus himself appeared again to his disciples" (21:1). Why did he not stay with them continuously? Why did he come and go?

He was preparing them to pass from the stage of dependence to independence, and eventually for the stage of interdependence.

During his absences, they made some mistakes. Peter did at least two unguided things and took the others with him. "Simon Peter told them, 'I'm going fishing.' They said, 'We'll go with you.'" And that whole night "they caught nothing" (John 21:3). That was unguided fishing, so they caught nothing. But under the guidance of Jesus "there were so many fish that they couldn't haul in the net" (v. 6). He was there, leaving them on their own to make their own blunders but also ready to cover their blunders and help them out.

Then again Peter suggested an unguided move in selecting a successor for Judas. They presented two persons for God to select from, narrowing God's choice through the method of casting lots—a method never used again—and in the whole idea of selecting someone by their choice, for God had another in mind: Paul. "Am I not an apostle?" asked Paul. He was, for he was chosen by Christ. Here Christ again covered their mistakes. They blundered into blessedness. But in their blundering, they became independent persons, sufficiently independent to invite in the Holy Spirit to take them and make them over and to cooperate with him. They could not come to interdependence except through independence.

O Christ, you hide yourself in order to reveal yourself more fully. You let me stand on my own feet in order to be free—free to invite you in forever. Amen.

AFFIRMATION FOR THE DAY: My independence shall only make me more dependent on you.

I MUST HAVE FREEDOM TO SURRENDER

Acts 19:1-6

The fact must be emphasized further that we must pass through the stage of independence to get to that of interdependence.

Some have wondered why the Holy Spirit is a believer's gift, given subsequent to conversion. "Jesus said this concerning the Spirit. Those who believed in him would soon receive the Spirit" (John 7:39). Why a gift for believers? Why not when we come in repentance and faith seeking forgiveness? Well, no doubt there is a measure of the Spirit given in conversion: "no one can say 'Jesus is Lord' except [in] the Holy Spirit" (1 Cor 12:3). But the coming of the Holy Spirit into believers is not merely in the Holy Spirit. The Holy Spirit is in you—permanently—and shall abide with you forever!

Before Pentecost the Holy Spirit was with them, but after Pentecost the Spirit was in them: "The Spirit of truth…dwells with you, and will be in you" (John 14:17 RSV). Before Pentecost they possessed the Spirit, but after Pentecost the Spirit possessed them. They were using God—calling God in to help them out—but after Pentecost, God was using them.

How did this change happen? They became sufficiently independent to offer themselves sovereignly in surrender to God. When we come to conversion, we are in the stage of dependence; we are children, not sufficiently mature to make sovereign decisions. We can only take forgiveness; we are in the receiving stage. But when we come to the stage of adolescence, of independence, then we are met by an offer: If we will give our all, God will give his all. If we will give ourselves, God will give himself. This is a mature offer to persons sufficiently mature to accept it. Hence it has to be a post-conversion experience.

Full self-surrender can be made only when the self is sufficiently independent to surrender to Another. It is the free act of free persons. Penitent sinners are too bound to give themselves freely to Another. They can only ask for freedom and status.

The most sovereign act of an independent person is to give the one thing we own—ourselves. Then God gives the most precious thing God owns—himself. Then we are filled with the Holy Spirit.

O God, you have given me freedom; now I choose your bondage forever. I give you back the life I owe. And now I take within what I've always wanted—you. Amen.

AFFIRMATION FOR THE DAY: My freedom I use to do its freest act, to surrender to you, my Lord.

GOD INVITES US TO SHARE HIS THRONE

John 14:12-14

Let us pause one more day to note the significance of Acts 1:6-8—"Will you?"..."But you..."—the shift from the disciples looking to Jesus to his looking to them. Hereafter everything he does, he will do through them.

This simple fact is the most astonishing revelation of the nature and purpose of God I know of. If it means anything, it means that the divine is tying its hands to the human and limiting itself to what the human will do. Of all the delegations of authority that is the most astonishing.

After all the ages of preparation to redeem humanity, bearing with their sins and stubbornness and blindness, he then takes incarnation, dies upon the cross for their redemption, rises again, goes off to heaven, and. says to a handful of his followers: "From this point on I'm trusting my movement of redemption to you. From now on I'm working only through you. The movement survives or perishes through you. I'm trusting you." That is a breathtaking act of faith in people on the part of God. And it reveals God's purpose. God is not jealously sitting tight on the throne of the universe demanding that we grovel before him; God is determined to produce beings who will share God's authority, carry out God's plans voluntarily, and cooperate with God in the remaking of the world.

Jesus shows God moving over, as it were, and inviting us to share the throne. "As for those emerge victorious, I will allow them to sit with me on my throne, just as I emerged victorious and sat down with my Father on his throne" (Rev 3:21). God is producing not puppets but persons great enough to share God's authority. That reveals the nature of God and of God's purposes. It also reveals our destiny. We are to be the heart of Christ, loving others through us; the brains of Christ, thinking his thoughts; the hands of Christ, stretched out in helpfulness; the feet of Christ, seeking the lost; the lips of Christ, speaking his message. We are to be an extension of the incarnation.

This is the greatest entrustment ever entrusted to man. It puts back my shoulders, makes my blood run faster, and sets me on fire to be at it and to be true.

O Christ, your blessed faith in me sends me to my knees. I am humbled at your confidence in me. Now help me to be in some measure worthy of your faith. Amen.

AFFIRMATION FOR THE DAY: My brain, my hands, my feet, my lips, are sacred; for he has no other.

THE MASTERY OF SPECIAL PRIVILEGE AND STANDING

Colossians 3:10-11

This mastery we have just been considering—the mastery of looking to God to do everything instead of standing on our own two feet and playing our part—leads to another mastery, akin to it: *the mastery of special privilege before God and humanity.*

In this epoch-making event of the coming of the Holy Spirit, who were the recipients, a special group with special privilege and standing before God and hence before humanity? No, there were one hundred twenty in that group who received the "promise of the Lord." Suppose it had been the twelve only who received the Holy Spirit, as one Bible teacher maintained. It would have changed the very nature of the Christian faith. It would have introduced into the Christian faith a group with special privileges and special standing before God and hence before people. The Christian faith would have put its stamp of special approval on the various Brahmanisms through the structure of human society, and Christianity would have been just one more glorified caste system. On the contrary, when the 0 was added to the 12, making it the 120 instead of the 12, that was the most important addition in human history. It meant that before God no one person was higher or lower than any other person; the highest gift of God, the Holy Spirit, was open to a person as a person.

It showed that God wasn't dealing with apostles but with persons. The Holy Spirit was given, not to a priest, a prophet, or a pope, but to a person. There is no more important event in history than just that. It is a seed event—the future of humanity in the womb of that event. For if God treats with humanity as humanity, then people must treat with people as people. If there is no special privilege before God, then there must be no special privilege before people. That lays the foundation of democracy in a conception of God, and hence of humanity, and makes it rest, not on a written constitution made by people, but written into the very constitution of the universe. That gives democracy a foundation in the nature of things. Before God we are equal; therefore before people we must be equal.

O Lord, I thank you that I can stand before you, neither above nor below any other person. Help me to take that privilege and give it to every other person. Amen.

AFFIRMATION FOR THE DAY: Since I stand equal before God, then every person shall be treated equally by me.

HAVE ALIEN IDEAS INVADED US?

James 2:1-4

If what has been said is true, namely, that a person as a person can and does receive the Holy Spirit, and there is no special standing or pull in the reception of this gift, then what happens to all this hierarchy of privilege and standing built up in the Christian system? Is it an alien intrusion into the Christian faith from surrounding society built on special privilege and status? It is.

The president of Harvard University, speaking at a large church, announced in opening his address: "I have been looking for the title of my address this morning and did not see it till I saw it on the church door as I came in: 'Push!'" When the people turned around to see the sign, they saw "Pull!" Are there special inside "pulls" within the Christian churches? There are. Why do some churches have special seats in which no one can sit but a bishop? Why is there a special color for a bishop—purple? Why do bishops alone lay hands on candidates at confirmation? Can bishops alone give the Holy Spirit? Why do ministers alone give the Holy Communion? Why do they partake of it separately, either first or last? Why is the wine in the Communion given only to the clergy in some churches? Why is "His Holiness" attached to a man who occupies a certain position regardless of character and life? Why, when the World Council of Churches met, did *Time* magazine put the Archbishop of Canterbury on its cover page as symbolizing the council? Is that the focus of attention?

Is all this because we have been invaded by a pagan society based on special privilege and status, and forgotten the revolutionary idea of any person receiving God's highest gift, the Spirit?

This simple fact sweeps into oblivion all alien assumptions. It is the most cleansing idea ever dropped into the human mind. It puts back the shoulders of the common human being and makes him or her infinitely worthwhile before God, hence infinitely worthwhile before all human beings. This simple fact has put more meaning into democracy and religion than all the disquisitions of philosophers put together. This is the word of democracy, spiritual and social, become flesh in a group.

O Lord, I thank you that your highest gift is open to all on equal terms. That makes me walk the earth a free person, free before you, hence free before others. Amen.

AFFIRMATION FOR THE DAY: I ask no special privilege, for as a human being I have the highest privilege. I am equal.

UNDERLYING IDEAS BECOME OUTER FACT

James 2:5-9

We have been studying the effects of the simple fact that the one hundred twenty instead of the twelve received God's highest gift, the Holy Spirit. When we lose sight of the meaning of that fact, then alien ideas and practices invade the churches and make their influence for democracy weak and halting. For basic religious ideas sooner or later come out and show themselves in the structure of society.

Why has Latin America not achieved democracy, except where it has been skeptical or antagonistic toward religion? It has republics but not democracies. Elections are for the most part superseded by military revolutions, overthrowing the government by force. Why? Is it not because the dominant religion is based on special privilege and special status, in fact on an autocratic conception? Out of that underlying conception democracies do not grow. They cannot. If we are unequal before God, then we must be unequal before humanity. Democracy is impossible.

Why did Kurusu, the Japanese special envoy to Washington, say to us after World War II, "Japan will never become a democracy until Japan becomes Christian"?* Did he see that the underlying idea of the emperor being descended from the Sun Goddess—a Son of Heaven—had to be replaced by the idea that persons as persons are children of God? One idea will not sustain democracy; the other will. But Kurusu's statement has to be modified, for it depends on what kind of Christianity becomes the basis of Japan's life as to whether real democracy is produced.

Some types of Christianity do not produce democracy. They make society into their own image—autocracy. The barons of Briton said to their king: "We who are as good as you are say to you who are no better than we are that we will elect you as our sovereign liege and lord provided you protect our liberties and our laws; if not, then not."** That was good, as far as it went. But the people then had to have their say to the barons. For the people must rule. "I saw thrones, and people took their seats on them" (Rev 20:4). The "people" finally rule, and that fact comes out of the basic fact that a person as a person receives the Holy Spirit.

O Lord, I thank you that my faith and my form of government are not at war. Help us to Christianize it, and then it will be truly democratic. In Jesus' name. Amen.

AFFIRMATION FOR THE DAY: If I bend low before God, then I will stand straight before humanity.

*Quotation attributed to a personal conversation between Dr. E. Stanley Jones and Saburō Kurusu.
** For more information, see Magna Carta of 1225.

MASTERY OF THE INFERIOR STATUS OF WOMEN

Galatians 3:26-28

We come now to consider something related to what we have been studying, namely, *that women received the Holy Spirit on the same basis as men.* "All were united in their devotion to prayer, along with some women.... They were all filled with the Holy Spirit" (Acts 1:14; 2:4). The "all" included the women.

That unobtrusive little fact is one of the most important and explosive facts ever introduced into life. There is enough dynamite in it to blow our existing institutions and attitudes into bits. For this simple fact meant that a woman as a woman received God's highest and best gift—the gift of the Holy Spirit. If this highest gift was open to women, then what about the lesser gifts of life—are they open to women too? They haven't been.

Every day, the pious Jew thanked God that he was not born a woman, a leper, or a Gentile. The women might note their company! This intrudes itself into the pages of the New Testament and applied even to our Lord, "(It's written in the Law of the Lord, 'Every firstborn male will be dedicated to the Lord')" (Luke 2:23). Why "every male"? Why not every child, male or female? Because of the revolutionary fact that a woman as a woman had not received the Holy Spirit on the same basis as a man.

And this held among the Gentiles. A Roman father, writing from Alexandria to his wife, said, "I will send you some money as soon as my wages begin. If the coming child you're to have is a boy, keep him; if a girl throw it away."

The Aga Khan, head of an enlightened Muslim sect in India, who was once given his weight in platinum, said to his women disciples: "Nag your husbands until they allow you to take part in public prayers." He didn't mean that they were to lead the prayers or to pray audibly on their own, but just to be in the same congregation with the men and go through the same congregational prayers.

These statements give us the view of women in societies in which the Holy Spirit was not given to women as women. That simple fact changed their relationship to God and man and society.

O Lord, I thank you that your love is broader than man's mind, that you are oblivious of the things that divide us into inferior and superior. I thank you. Amen.

AFFIRMATION FOR THE DAY: I shall treat everyone as a child of God regardless of birth, color, class, or sex.

YOUR DAUGHTERS SHALL PROPHESY

Acts 21:8-9

The fact of women receiving the Holy Spirit on the same basis as men made Paul lay down this basic principle: "There is neither Jew nor Greek [race distinction]; there is neither slave nor free [social distinction]; nor is there male and female [sex distinction], for you are all one in Christ Jesus" (Gal 3:28)—"nor is there is male and female"—that is the new attitude.

Peter took this attitude immediately when he saw women had received the gift as the men:

> In the last days, God says,
> I will pour out my Spirit on all people.
>> Your sons and daughters will prophesy
>> Your young will see visions.
>> Your elders will dream dreams.
> Even upon my servants, men and women,
>> I will pour out my Spirit in those days,
>>> and they will prophesy. (Acts 2:17-18)

"All people" included women, and "daughters will prophesy." Here prophesying means not to foretell events but to forth-tell the good news. And this wasn't for particularly high-class women but women of all classes—the maidservant at the bottom of the social ladder included.

It is strange that Paul with this background would order that "women should be quiet during the meeting." He could do it only by adding: "just as the Law says" (1 Cor 14:34). He turned back to the Law for this unchristian position, for the gospel had a different one. In the new order the "daughters" were to prophesy.

In my last book, *Growing Spiritually*, I dealt with "Mary" as an amazing example of growing spiritually. In a crisis she saw she could possess and be possessed by the Holy Spirit. After a night of struggle she went to an early Communion and found herself like a glass jar being slowly filled. When the teacher of this important conference did not come, she was asked to take the Bible hour. She took it without batting an eye—effortlessly, powerfully. One of the other speakers said, "She took this group by storm." She did it without trying.

It was an example of a "daughter" prophesying. All question of male and female was gone. The Spirit was speaking through her, and we could but listen and respond.

O Lord, we thank you for wiping out all distinctions based upon the extraneous. We are distinct if we speak from you distinctly—no male and female. Amen.

AFFIRMATION FOR THE DAY: The Spirit is seeking instruments of his power, seeking regardless of sex.

51

THE INCOMPATIBLE PRINCIPLE

Amos 9:7; Acts 17:24, 26

A thinker has said:

> There is no greater method of reform than this: If alongside of a corrupt practice you lay an incompatible principle, then that incompatible principle will silently work against that corrupt practice and will overthrow it. Thus Christianity laid alongside the corrupt practice of slavery the incompatible principle of the equal worth of each individual before God and silently overthrew it.

Alongside the almost universal practice of the subordination of women to men, the Christians laid the incompatible principle that women can and do receive the highest gift of God, the Holy Spirit; and it has silently worked against that evil practice and is in the process of overthrowing it.

In India, at question time, a Muslim man sent up this question: "In Christianity women are in the lowest degradation; they have no rights of any kind. They are considered an object of scorn. While Mohammed said: 'To her is due what is due from her.' Is this no improvement on Christianity?" I could scarcely believe my eyes! I didn't argue that Mohammed permitted four wives and Jesus founded the home on the loyalty of one man and one woman; I simply pointed to a row of Christian women nurses and doctors on the front row, among them Ida Scudder, the most influential person in the city and a queen through service. I said, "I feel sorry for these poor degraded Christian women." The crowd roared. The opponents of early Christianity exclaimed, "Heavens, what women these Christians have!" They still have them! And behind their rise is the fact that the highest in God is open to them, and hence the highest in society must be open to them. That is the incompatible principle that is working against every disability laid on women everywhere. And it will win their complete emancipation—is winning their complete emancipation.

If women want to take a pilgrimage in thought to the shrine of their emancipation, let them go back to an upper room where women and men both received the Holy Spirit on the same terms. There woman's freedom began.

O Christ, we thank you that the silent coming of the Holy Spirit in our hearts is working a silent resolution everywhere. Then evermore give us this Spirit. Amen.

AFFIRMATION FOR THE DAY: My life today shall be the incompatible principle laid alongside all evil.

THE MASTERY OF PRIVILEGE BASED ON BLOOD

Genesis13:8; Matthew 23:8

We now pass on to another mastery that emerged with the coming of the Holy Spirit: *the mastery of privileges and standing based on blood relationships.*

Among those who waited in that upper room for the coming of the Holy Spirit was "Mary the mother of Jesus, and his brothers" (Acts 1:14). Into that innocent-looking statement is packed a world of new meaning and a world of emancipation from nepotism. For a great deal of our society is based on privileges based on blood relationships.

But note what happened: Mary, the mother of Jesus, did not sit out apart, superior, smiling patronage on this group who were waiting for the Holy Spirit. She took her place among them and sought and found the Holy Spirit on the same basis as the rest— on exactly the same basis. That simple happening canceled all rights and privileges based on mere blood relationship. Mary was equal to, but no higher than, any other human being. She needed the coming of the Holy Spirit within her just like the rest. The angel said to Mary, "The Holy Spirit will come over you and the power of the Most High will overshadow you. Therefore, the one who is to be born ... will be called God's Son" (Luke 1:35).

Note the "Holy Spirit will come over you," and the "power of the Most High will overshadow you"; "over" and "overshadow" but not "in" you. The Holy Spirit came over her for that particular work, but nowhere is it said that Mary was filled with the Holy Spirit as her own continuous personal possession. That came only at Pentecost and on the same conditions as the rest—surrender and faith. This was the divine plan. If people had planned it, they would have slipped into the prevalent pattern of special privileges based on blood; and the ages would have gone astray with them. This happened in Islam, where there are many modern blood descendants of the prophet Mohammed, all receiving special privileges and honors and standing.

We were saved all that by a simple seed happening; Mary was equal before God, but not more than equal.

O Lord, I thank you that you have no favorites, all on the same footing with you. Help me to grasp that and take it in its full meaning for myself and others. Amen.

AFFIRMATION FOR THE DAY: My blood relations through ancestry may be poor; my blood relations to the Son of God are wonderful.

AN ASSUMPTION!

Philippians 2:1-6

We saw yesterday that the last thing we see of the Virgin Mary in the pages of Scripture was that she was waiting with the rest to receive the Holy Spirit on the same basis. When the curtain went down on Mary's marvelous drama, she was not seated on a throne of privilege next to the Son of God, but seated on the floor with heart and possibly hands uplifted to receive God's best gift, the Holy Spirit. All else beyond that simple scene is tradition and mostly fiction. Ending there it is beautiful and right and befitting.

But human imagination and vested interests have turned her into a demigoddess, being prayed to, and through to Jesus, and through him to the Lord. So we have a hierarchy of mediators—saints, Mary, Jesus. The New Testament says there is "one mediator between God and humanity, the human Christ Jesus" (1 Tim 2:5). The Roman Church adds two more—saints and Mary—and thus pushes Jesus away from immediate contact with people. A sign in a library said: "Think of Mary, and Jesus will grow in your heart." My reaction was: "Think of Jesus; and you'll find God within you." To set up a human being as a mediator between God and people is idolatry pure and simple. And the nemesis of idolatry comes inevitably; God is pushed further away by the idol.

Someone asked me what I thought of the "Assumption of the Virgin," and I replied, "It is well named; it is an assumption." Everything is an assumption beyond the simple fact of the blessed Virgin receiving the Holy Spirit on the same basis as the rest. There is where the divine drama closes for her. It is a beautiful closing. Mary is in her place, and so are we. It is the place of equality for all. That is worthy of the drama of redemption. Had it ended with Mary on a throne, it wouldn't have been redemption; it would have been God putting divine imprimatur on the structure of society of that day with its deep injustices and special privileges based on blood. A caste system instead of a world community would have resulted. A little twist here would have twisted the shape of things to come into the old nepotisms instead of the new fellowship.

O Lord, I ask for no special privilege except the wonderful privilege of being a person, no heredity except being descended from you. Amen.

AFFIRMATION FOR THE DAY: My place will be with Mary and all other saints, praying for the Holy Spirit.

THE NEW COMMUNITY BASED ON DIVINE BLOOD

Philippians 2:6-11

We must look further into the application of the incompatible principle that a blood relationship does not confer special privileges beyond the fact that the family grows up together. After that the person stands in society on his or her own, no longer bolstered by special privileges conferred by family. This was true of the brothers of Jesus. They were there seeking for the Holy Spirit too.

That fact is important. In one place it is said, "For even his brothers did not believe in him" (John 7:5 RSV). But they had been won by the facts, especially the fact of the resurrection. The reticence of Scripture is seen in the fact that Scripture tells of their unbelief but did not report their belief. If people had written this, they would have put that out in big headlines: "Brothers of Jesus become his followers." But the Scripture brings it out only in an incidental way, saying that his brothers were there seeking the Spirit.

While being a blood relation to Jesus didn't give special privileges, neither did it bring special disabilities. The way was open for them, too, on their own merits. James, Jesus' brother, became head of the council in Jerusalem: "When Barnabas and Paul also fell silent, James responded: 'Fellow believers, listen to me'" (Acts 15:13). That sounds authoritarian and dictatorial, but only for the moment; for he says later, "The Holy Spirit has led us to the decision" (v. 28). That was the highest kind of collective guidance. James was under the guidance of the Spirit instead of their being under the guidance of James. They listened to him as he listened to the Spirit and no more. If James was emancipated from any thought of superiority based on blood, the rest of the disciples were emancipated from any inferiority based on a lack of blood relationship. There was a new heredity in their veins; they belonged to the One Blood. And that new heredity was open to all, James and his brothers included. They were all leveled up. Why think in terms of human heredity when a new divine heredity was open? They had had a blood transfusion from the Son of God. What else?

O Lord, I thank you that my bad blood can be canceled by your good blood. I can be directly descended from you. What else? Amen.

AFFIRMATION FOR THE DAY: I feel the blood of the new heredity coursing in my veins; I belong to a new line.

THE BACKWARD LOOK AND THE FORWARD!

1 Peter 1:14-19

The Gospels of Matthew and Luke begin with genealogies, a dying kick of an ancient custom. That was the backward look. It ceased with these two writers. For the Gospels are really interested not in origins but in destinations. Mark and John strike the new note. Mark 1:1: "The beginning of the good news about Jesus Christ, God's Son"; it looks not back but up—and then out. And John 1:1: "In the beginning was the Word, and the Word was with God, and the Word was God." That too looks up—and then out.

All life was based on the new heredity—the divine heredity and the new destination—"it hasn't yet appeared what we will be. We know that when he appears we will be like him" (1 John 3:2). The human blood heredity was irrelevant, a dead leaf that dropped off.

But it hasn't dropped off with us. We cling to these grave clothes, literally, dressing ourselves up in the clothes of our dead ancestors. The best part of some people is like potatoes—underground! And we base life upon it. Kings and queens comb the world to find royal blood for suitable marriages. Character and ability are secondary; blood is first. And some of the blood is very doubtful blood when the outcome in intelligence and ability is considered. We pass on huge fortunes to children without any thought of their character and ability to handle the fortunes for their own good and that of humanity. Heiresses flit from husband to husband, each getting a rake-off as he departs, and all this for no other reason than the heiress has certain ancestral blood in her veins.

These doubtful customs make us inwardly squirm with uneasiness, for we feel the pressure of the incompatible principle laid down by our faith, when all blood privileges were canceled and nullified by the fact that the mother of Jesus and his family did not ask for and did not get any special privileges or rights before God or people or society. The position of our faith holds the future; our customs are based on a dying order.

O Christ, we thank you for the glory of our faith. We feel our feet touch rock—the Eternal Rock. Our faith holds the Rock upon which we must build or go to pieces. Amen.

AFFIRMATION FOR THE DAY: I belong not to a dead past but to a living present and a more living future.

THE MASTERY OF SACRED PLACES

1 Peter 2:9-10

We now look at a new mastery which came into being with the coming of the Holy Spirit: *the mastery of sacred places.*

The Holy Spirit came upon the waiting group, not in the temple or in a synagogue, but in the upper room. And the upper room was a home: "they went up to the upstairs room, where they were staying....All were united in their devotion to prayer..." (Acts 1:13, 14). The Holy Spirit came upon them when they were in the most common place—a place where we all live—a home. Under that apparently insignificant fact lays a deep significance. It was an amazing emancipation for religion. For up to this time religion had been associated with sacred places, sacred vestments, and sacred persons. Now the center of gravity in religion shifted from places to persons, from vestments to vitality, from services to service. It was a most important shift. It saved religion from sterility and saved humanity to vitality. Religion was put where it belongs—in the human heart. Paul, brought up under the spell of temple holiness, announced this extraordinary shift: "Don't you know that you are God's temple and that God's Spirit lives in you?...God's temple is holy, which is what you are" (1 Cor 3:16-17). Here holiness had shifted from places to persons. And rightly so.

There is no such thing as a holy place. A place has no moral qualities since it has no moral choice. "There is nothing good but a good will, and there is nothing bad but a bad will," said Kant.* And we may add: there is nothing holy but a holy person; there is nothing unholy but an unholy person. Holy persons gathered together make a holy place, not the other way around.

This coming of the Holy Spirit on persons, rather than on places, was one of the most important happenings in history. It took religion out of the magical and put it in the moral, and in doing so universalized it. And further it saved the temple. For the temple was no longer the center; the persons in the temple were. As such the temple could be used.

O Lord, we stand in awe at your gentle but powerful revolutions. And now our hearts are your temple. That heightens our responsibility. Help us to be true. Amen.

AFFIRMATION FOR THE DAY: Since I am the temple of God, I shall keep that temple unprofaned this day.

*This direct quotation was not located, but see *Kant's Critique of Practical Reason and other Works on the Theory of Ethics*, trans. Thomas Kingsmill Abbot (London: Longmans, Green & Co., 1879).

THERE IS NOTHING HOLY
BUT A HOLY PERSON

Acts 7:46-50

We are meditating upon the fact that the Holy Spirit came upon the people not in a temple but in a home. Suppose the Holy Spirit had come upon them when they were in the temple, what would have happened? Then we would have associated the Holy Spirit with ornate ritual, sacred vestments, and awesome precincts. That would have been the native air of the Spirit. To get the Spirit, we would have to repair to the temple. The Spirit would be found there and only there. And if we didn't really find the Spirit there, we would try to bring him there by hocus-pocus—as is often done in East and West.

All that had to come down that real religion might live. It was no mere chance that Jesus predicted the temple would be destroyed and not one stone be left upon another. It had to be. The center was now the human heart; religion was moralized in that it was put down within the heart amid human choices. It was not something done to us by sacred places and sacred services; it was something done in us and through us. God now made every human heart that would let God in, the place of the Shekinah Glory.

Does that mean we should tear down or desert all our churches and cathedrals? No, we simply put them in their places. Their place is that they have no inherent holiness, only derivative holiness. The place in itself is not holy; it is holy only when holy people use it for holy purposes. The center of holiness is in the persons and their purposes. If the people come to the church or the cathedral in pride, in self-seeking, in narrow exclusiveness of race or class denomination, in an unconscious attempt to attain approval of their fellows, then the place is unholy, regardless of who dedicated it to a ritual holiness. It is intrinsically unholy.

The Holy Spirit makes holy persons, and where holy persons are, there the place is holy. Where the Holy Spirit is, there is the church; where the Holy Spirit is not, there is not the church. No holier spot on earth than the Upper Room.

O Holy Spirit, here is my heart. Make it your temple. I would offer the sacrifice of a continual flame of devotion to you, to the Son, and to the Lord. Amen.

AFFIRMATION FOR THE DAY: I shall be the center of holiness this day, for my choices will be God's choices.

58

THE SECULAR BECOMES SACRED

Luke 21:5-6

The coming of the Holy Spirit upon the group in the home instead of the temple put the center of religion in the streams of human life—the home. There it was to function as adequate living. It was to function, not merely as church attendance once a week, but as the very breath of life in all we do wherever we are.

When the Holy Spirit came upon the people in the home, God thereby put the stamp of approval on the ordinary. But the ordinary was not to remain the ordinary; it became the extraordinary. Everything was lifted up into the sacramental. Everything became an expression of something beyond itself. Everything took on meaning. They began to do the little things in a great way. The fact is that there were no little things, for the little things were great with meaning.

Just as the Eternal God became incarnate in a human body and made that body the center of meaning and destiny, so now every little act and attitude had meaning and destiny beyond itself. Life began to burst with value because it was bursting with meaning.

The power of the Holy Spirit was no longer to be associated merely with sacred places; it was available to people everywhere to do the so-called secular things in a sacred way. The housewife sweeping her home could draw on the power of the Spirit just as definitely and immediately as the priest preparing the Communion. The artisan could become the artist, for he would put the artistry of the Spirit in otherwise drudgery and make it into a dedication.

If the Holy Spirit is given in the house, then realization means relationships. The Holy Spirit makes all relationships a relationship with God. To do it to them is to do it to God. And to refuse to do it to them is to refuse to do it to God.

It means above all that the highest power is available for the lowest duty. God is naturalized in all life, and God's power can be laid hold of to do anything that ought to be done. Then we do the minute, the tiniest thing, magnificently.

O Lord, I thank you that the fire of the Spirit can burn in my heart as I do the little and the big. Help me to do all things for your love this day. Amen.

AFFIRMATION FOR THE DAY: I shall do every little thing today in a big way and make it big with destiny.

MASTERING RELATIONSHIPS BETWEEN YOUTH AND AGE

1 John 2:12-14

We come now to another mastery—*the mastery of the relationships between youth and old age*. Peter, interpreting what had happened with the coming of the Holy Spirit, said:

> *I will pour out my Spirit on all people...*
> *Your young will see visions,*
> *Your elders will dream dreams.* (Acts 2:17)

There has been a strain between youth and old age in all generations everywhere. Youth wants change, and old age wants the beloved old; one is radical, and the other is conservative. So the strain between the radical and the conservative comes to a head in the relationships between youth and old age. This happens everywhere in all ages. The oldest bit of writing in the world is a papyrus in an Istanbul museum, on which is said to be written, "Alas, times are not what they used to be. Children no longer obey their parents, and everyone wants to write a book." Sounds modern! It is and always will be. For the two great tendencies in human nature come to embodiment in youth and old age. The tendencies are radicalism and conservatism. One wants change, and the other wants to conserve values. Both have a function in life and are needed. We need to conserve the gains and values of the past, and we need to apply those values to larger and larger areas of life. If we were all conservative, we would dry up; if we were all radical, we would blow up! We need both tendencies and need them in a living blend; we need the radically conservative and the conservatively radical. We need youth and old age in a blend.

But they have not been in a blend. Old age has for the most part dominated the destiny of the world in East and West. Hence life has hardened into custom everywhere. I have often said that the real ruler of India has not been the Mogul, the Maratha, the British, or even the present Congress Government—the real ruler has been *dastur*, custom. Everywhere the living are ruled by the dead. The seat of government is the graveyard where the dead silently rule us. If you don't believe that, ask yourself the question: How many things do I do just because they have been done that way?

O Lord, you are stirring us to change. Your Spirit is the Spirit of Creation, and you are creating the eternally new. Help me to respond. Amen.

AFFIRMATION FOR THE DAY: I belong to the eternally new; therefore I challenge the *is* in the light of the *ought-to-be*.

YOUTH AND OLD AGE BOTH LEAN
TOWARD THE NEW

1 Timothy 4:12; Psalms 92:14

If there.is a conflict going on in every age between youth and old age, just how does the coming of the Holy Spirit resolve that conflict? It resolves it in a very simple way; it tips both youth and old age in the direction of change: "Your young will see visions. Your elders will dream dreams."

Both shall look in the direction of change, youth seeing visions of coming possibilities and old age dreaming dreams of a better order. That the dreaming of dreams on the part of the old is not dreaming of the past and sighing over its departed glories is to be seen in the fact that it is the Holy Spirit who makes them dream dreams, and the Holy Spirit is the Spirit of Creation—the Creative Spirit. It was the Spirit who brooded over chaos, and out of that chaos came cosmos. So when the Spirit comes upon us, we feel the stirrings of creation within us; we want to think things, feel things, do things, and be things. The hardened crusts of our thinking are broken up by the stirrings of new life within.

The Christian faith leans toward the radical, for it belongs to the Great Change—the kingdom of God on earth. It is the *ought-to-be* standing over against the *is*, demanding change. This is vividly seen in this passage: "Therefore every scribe who has been trained for the kingdom of heaven is like a householder who brings out of his treasure what is new and what is old" (Matt 13:52 RSV). Note "what is new and what is old"— the radical and the conservative. But note the new—the radical is first. Change is first in the Christian faith—conserving is secondary.

Note further it says that the "scribe who has been trained for the kingdom of heaven" brings forth the new. But the scribe was a copyist who created nothing; the scribe copied what had been created. But when the dry-as-dust copyist gets in touch with and is trained in the kingdom of heaven outlook and spirit, he brings forth the new. The noncreative becomes the creative. Old age dreams.

O Creative Spirit, create within me this day new life, new pulses, new concerns, new projects. For I am made for creation and am happy only as I create. Amen.

AFFIRMATION FOR THE DAY: I lean toward the new and gather up from the old all that fits the new.

61

THE KINGDOM PRIMARILY
A YOUTH MOVEMENT

Luke 9:59-62

We have been meditating on the mastery of the conflict between the younger and the older generation. It has been said that the conflict is resolved by making old age creative. The Holy Spirit brings into life an eternal youth—a rejuvenation—so youth and old age meet in a common life and a common outlook. They are both given to the same loyalty—the kingdom of God—and the kingdom is the most radical conception ever presented to the mind of humanity and the greatest challenge ever confronting our creative longings. When given to that, both youth and old age cannot help coming together in a common endeavor for change.

Note that youth seeing visions is mentioned before elders dreaming dreams. The emphasis is on youth. The Christian movement is a youth movement. Jesus was a young man when he lived and died for his cause.

But the moment I say that I know the reaction of youth; it disclaims the right of eminent domain in the kingdom. This was seen in one of our Ashrams when we asked the youth to bring a message to the older generation. The older had always advised "youth," now let youth speak to the older. They brought in a series of recommendations, and the first one was this, "We suggest that the older generation not lose confidence in itself by always saying, 'We've got to look to youth and turn the job over to them.' No, we've got to work it out together." When we asked youth to be radical, it turned conservative. When we suggested control, it suggested cooperation. That will almost invariably happen.

The angel speaking to Zechariah about the birth of John and seeing the meaning of the movement of change which the Baptist would inaugurate said, "He will turn the hearts of the fathers back to their children,...He will make ready a people prepared for the Lord" (Luke 1:17).

One would have thought that he would have said, "Turn the hearts of the children back to their fathers"—make the children conservative. No, it was to make the fathers radical—that was the remedy.

O Divine Lord, you entrusted to the Holy Spirit, the Spirit of Creation, the carrying on of your work; help us to trust the tasks of the kingdom to youth. Amen.

**AFFIRMATION FOR THE DAY: I align myself to that which is alive;
I shuffle off dead thoughts, dead customs.**

THE PARTNERSHIP MUST BE AN EQUAL ONE

Luke 5:4-7

Let us gather up the lessons we have been learning about the mastery of the conflict between youth and old age.

I am convinced, after seeing youth and old age living and working and playing and worshiping together in a close-knit fellowship in the Ashrams, that it is better to have them together rather than have youth conferences and old age conferences. Each needs the mental and spiritual cross-fertilization of the other. Each is poorer without the other, and each is richer with the other. But old age must not patronize or dominate youth; it must be an equal partnership.

I think Paul made a mistake here, a mistake that he rectified later. Why did John Mark leave Paul and Barnabas at Pamphylia and return home? Was he homesick? Weak-kneed? Or was it the position they gave him? This sentence would imply this reason: "John was with them as their assistant" (Acts 13:5). John was the "assistant minister" instead of the "associate minister," so in protest he silently went home. That was probable, for John was there "as their assistant"; they were the center with John at the edges assisting them. Barnabas took John and made him his associate (Acts 15:39). That he wasn't weak-kneed and afraid is seen by the fact that he and Barnabas sailed off straight to Cyprus, and he never turned again. He was an equal now. Paul later changed his attitude and asked for John Mark, but on a different basis: "Get Mark, and bring him with you. He has been a big help to me in the ministry" (2 Tim 4:11). Note "big help to me in the ministry." Before John Mark was profitable to minister to Paul; now he is profitable in the ministry—not "me" but the "ministry" the end. The years had changed Paul and taught him a needed lesson. He could get John to come only on a new basis.

Youth and old age must work together as partners, neither mastering the other. But both mastered by the kingdom, which could use both; for they were now one in being devoted to the great change.

Lord, we see that when we are both devoted to something beyond ourselves, we find ourselves and we find each other. You master us so gently. Amen.

AFFIRMATION FOR THE DAY: People shall not work for me but with me—a partnership in God.

THE MASTERY OF SOCIAL DISTINCTIONS

Matthew 20:25-28

We pass on now to study another mastery that came with the coming of the Holy Spirit—*the mastery of social distinctions.* Peter quoted the prophecy as having fulfillment in the coming of the Holy Spirit:

> *I will pour out my Spirit upon all people,...*
> *Even upon my servants, men and women,*
> *I will pour out my Spirit in those days,*
> *and they will prophesy.* (Acts 2:17–18)

Note the Holy Spirit was to come upon "servants, men and women," and they were to prophesy. These were not servants of God as we usually interpret them; but they were servants of people, in fact slaves. On the men slaves and women slaves the Spirit would be poured, and they would find a new occupation—they would prophesy, forthtell the good news.

Note the tender pronoun "my servants, men and women." When God speaks of the "accepted" classes, he uses "your sons and your daughters"; but when God speaks of the socially dispossessed, he uses "my servants, men and women." They were especially God's. And he introduces this section with special emphasis—"Even."

The mightiest movement for social freedom was being inaugurated, and it was done very unobtrusively and very effectively. The method was not to argue the equal rights of persons and to introduce social reforms from that basis. It was not a head-on attack; it was a flanking movement. The male and female servants were given God's highest gift, the Holy Spirit, on the same basis as the higher social classes, those who owned or employed these lower classes. If God's highest gift was open to them, then who could deny the lesser gifts of freedom and status? It was a deathblow to caste and class, and delivered so gently that many did not feel its impact till years later.

Not only was their status changed by receiving the same gift as their masters; their occupations too were changed—they prophesied; they forthtold the good news, the highest occupation given to humanity—preaching.

Dear Lord, O gently breaking our chains; but you are breaking them. We feel this new freedom coursing in our veins. We are free in you. Amen.

AFFIRMATION FOR THE DAY: As far as I am concerned, social distinctions are gone; I see a person for whom Christ died.

SLAVERY A DIVINE INSTITUTION

Ephesians 6:5-9

The movement for human social emancipation did not come until the Holy Spirit carne. Until then both Jews and Gentiles were in subjection to owners. And both believed slavery was a divine institution. Aristotle said some people are born as natural rulers and some as slaves, as a dog is naturally a dog and a cat a cat. Greek philosophers had time and leisure to philosophize about life, for beneath their glittering civilization was the toil of slaves, who outnumbered the free.

Forced labor built the Hebrew temple. "King Solomon raised a levy of forced labor out of all Israel; and the levy numbered thirty thousand men" (1 Kgs 5:13 RSV). Since he could use slave labor for the house of God, he would also use it to build his house, which took thirteen years. The temple was built in seven, simply because Solomon's house was large and more costly than the temple! That was the picture in Greece and Palestine when John announced that

> *Every valley will be filled* [depressed humanity raised],
> > *and every mountain and hill will be leveled* [exalted positions brought
> > down]. (Luke 3:5)

There was to be a leveling up and leveling down when Jesus inaugurated his movement. Mary, the mother of Jesus, took this up and broke into inspired song:

> He has scattered those with arrogant thoughts and proud inclinations [general
> revolution],
> He has pulled the powerful down from their thrones [literal revolution]
> > and lifted up the lowly [social revolution].
> He has filled the hungry with good things
> > and sent the rich away empty-handed [economic revolution]. (Luke 1:51-53)

Jesus took up the same theme,

> *The Spirit of the Lord is upon me....*
> *He has sent me....*
> > *to proclaim release to the prisoners...,*
> > *to liberate the oppressed.* (Luke 4:18)

The coming of the Spirit fulfilled all these prophecies.

O Lord, how can we thank you enough for your grace that frees the slaves so graciously and so effectively? Freed within they are freed without. Amen.

AFFIRMATION FOR THE DAY: The social revolution is on; I shall be a part of it, lifting everybody.

MORE THAN A SLAVE

Colossians 4:1; Luke 4:25-28

We saw yesterday that the method of emancipation of the depressed classes of society was by giving them the Holy Spirit on the same basis as the rest. That emancipated them at the center. The sense of inferiority was broken at the center—within. Emancipated there they began to be emancipated at the margin in social relations. Unless that inner emancipation takes place, the outer emancipation is ineffective. You can't get people out of the slums unless you get the slums out of people, for they will soon make their new environment into slums again.

We have found in India that you really can't raise the outcastes' standing before people until you raise their standing before God. When they realize they are children of God and as such equal before God and therefore equal before people, then they are really emancipated. Until that happens, the inner sense of inferiority pulls them down to an inferior position outwardly.

This is seen in the exquisitely beautiful letter of Paul to Philemon in regard to his converted slave Onesimus. Paul says, "Maybe this is the reason that Onesimus was separated from you for a while so that you might have him back forever—no longer as a slave but more than a slave—that is, as a dearly loved brother" (vv. 15-16). The whole method of Christian emancipation is summed up in that sentence—a slave silently walks out of slavery into brotherhood, and a "dearly loved" brotherhood.

When the master and the slave both knelt side by side and received the bread and wine in Communion, they arose knowing that the master-slave relationship was gone, killed at the heart. They heard the words, "Neither be called masters, for you have one master, the Christ" (Matt 23:10 RSV). And the chains fell off both master and slave. The master, too, was shackled by the shackles with which he had shackled the slave. He was in inner conflict over the system and needed emancipation—and got it.

Alongside the corrupt system of slavery was placed the incompatible principle that slaves received the Holy Spirit on the same basis as the rest. That killed the system.

O Lord, your silent forces working in our hearts are breaking our chains and making us free. We are free in every person's freedom and bound in every person's bondage. Amen.

AFFIRMATION FOR THE DAY: It is impossible to enslave a Bible-reading people.

A PERSON FOR WHOM CHRIST DIED

Revelation 14:6; 22:2

This equalizing of people before God and hence before humanity is seen in two marble tablets in a church in Agra, India. They are of the same size. One is to Sir Henry Havelock, the famous commander of the British forces in India: "He was every inch a soldier, and he was every inch a Christian." The other alongside is "To the memory of Pte. Robert Jones: he was a faithful soldier and a sincere Christian, a noble example to his comrades of Christian life in the barrack room. His last words were: 'The blood of Jesus Christ cleanses us of all sin. Now I have no doubts. Safe in the arms of Jesus. Blessed Jesus.'"

The private had more said about him than the general! They were both sons of God and therefore brothers.

This within-without method of producing a classless society is more thoroughgoing and more lasting. Without that within emancipation the without will come back again and take over. Russia is striving to have a classless society by the without-within method. But the without comes back where there is no within—comes back often hidden. I asked a waiter in a hotel in Moscow why the dining room was so empty; were there no guests in the hotel? He replied, "The hotel is full of government officials, military and civilian; but they dine in their rooms with their vodka and their girls, so they will not be seen." Special privilege had not been wiped out within.

Lest self-righteousness creep in and take over, let us be reminded that we have class in our society, largely based on money. It is just as insidious as that based on blood and family. Jesus said, "One's life isn't determined by one's possessions, even when someone is very wealthy" (Luke 12:15). If one's "life," then one's position in life, standing before society, should not consist in the abundance or meagerness of one's possessions. A person is a person—for whom Christ died.

The kingdom of God is a classless society; there is only one class, the class of the children of God. That simple fact dooms all distinctions set up to segregate person from person.

O Lord, your fatherly heart is breaking down our unbrotherliness, for you are intending a brotherhood and sisterhood, a family of God. Help us to cooperate. Amen.

AFFIRMATION FOR THE DAY: I will look on every person not for what he or she is but for what he or she can be in God.

THE MASTERY OF RACE DISTINCTIONS

Matthew 23:8-10; Luke 2:28-32

We have seen how the valleys are being filled and the mountains made low as people feel the impact of God's kingdom. Special privilege is more and more seen as intolerable. Someone has facetiously defined the "upper crust" as the "crumbs of society held together by their dough." Well, that crust is crumbling before the rise of humanity as a child of God. The incompatible principle is working.

There is another mastery of very great importance akin to this but going deeper—*the mastery of distinctions based on race*. The coming of the Holy Spirit dissolved the distinctions based on race. The new society that emerged was color-blind and race-blind—a new race made up of all races.

Race cleavages have gone deep. The Jews of Jesus' day prayed: "Lord...you have said you created the oldest age for our sake...that the other nations...are like spit" (2 Esdras 6:55-56). The Judeans despised the Galileans, who were supposedly of less pure blood. One charge against Jesus was, "he agitates the people...starting from Galilee all the way here" (Luke 23:5). The sting was in "starting from Galilee"— beginning with that racial group instead of with them!

The Samaritans were more bitterly despised, for they were mixed: "You are a Samaritan and have a demon" (John 8:48). To be a Samaritan was to have a demon! They were one.

The Jews despised Galileans, Samaritans, and Gentiles in an ascending order of contempt. The disciples were still tainted with this contempt even when following Jesus. They wanted to call down fire on a Samaritan village because it wouldn't receive them. And consider the disciples asking Jesus to send away the Syrophoenician woman calling after them and his reply that "it is not good to take the children's bread and toss it to dogs" (Matt 15:26). This can be fully understood only if the disciples had used the usual word "Gentile dog" in describing the woman. So Jesus picks it out of their mouths and uses it to shock them by repeating it. His look of correction must have carried his meaning, for he treated her not as a dog but as a child of God and healed her daughter.

O Lord God, forgive us; our contempt and pride that seem so silly are worse— wicked in the light of your love for all, and equally for all. Amen.

AFFIRMATION FOR THE DAY: I belong to a new race—children of the kingdom.

No, Lord; for I Have Never...

Acts 10:17-20

We have seen the racial background of the disciples before the coming of the Holy Spirit. Then something happened. The Holy Spirit actually came upon the Gentiles at the house of Cornelius, a Roman! That simple fact knocked into a cocked hat all their lingering race prejudices.

But it was not accomplished without a struggle. God let down the sheet with clean and so-called unclean animals in it and bade Peter kill and eat. And Peter protested, "Absolutely not Lord! I have never eaten anything impure or unclean." And the reply: "Never consider unclean what God has made pure" (Acts 10:14, 15). This was repeated three times as a gentle reminder of Peter's three-time denial of Jesus, thus hitting a blow at his self-righteous pride.

Peter reluctantly went to the house of Cornelius, and began patronizingly, "You all realize that it is forbidden for a Jew to associate or to visit with outsiders" (v. 28)—and I hope you appreciate what I am doing! But he began to preach his gospel and was carried away by it, and used a word beyond his own attitudes: "everyone" (v. 43). The account says, "While Peter was still speaking, the Holy Spirit fell on everyone who heard the word" (v. 44).

While Peter was still saying this—"everyone"—the Holy Spirit fell. The moment he took the attitude of "everyone" instead of "some," the Spirit fell. God could approve of the attitude expressed in that word, and gave the Holy Spirit as a seal of that approval. The account adds, "The circumcised believers... were astonished that the gift of the Holy Spirit had been poured out even on the Gentiles" (v. 45). At Jerusalem, when Peter was called to task, he repeated, "'If God gave them the same gift he gave us..., then who am I? Could I stand in God's way?' Once the apostles and other believers heard this, they calmed down. They praised God and concluded, 'So then God has enabled the Gentiles to change their hearts and lives so that they might have new life'" (11:17-18).

Their race prejudices were knocked in the head by a simple fact; God gave his highest gift to the Gentiles on the same basis as the Jews. The wall of partition had fallen before their astonished eyes. Humankind was one.

O Divine Redeemer, you are redeeming us from our narrowness and our prejudice; and in redeeming us from them, you are redeeming us. We thank you. Amen.

AFFIRMATION FOR THE DAY: When I look at Jesus and then at a person, I see that person differently.

I BELIEVE THE BIBLE, ALL EXCEPT...

Luke 13:28-30

God didn't argue the equal worth of all races before him. God did something more profound and gave to all races the same gift, the gift of the Holy Spirit. That simple fact did more to abolish race prejudices and distinctions than all the exhortations of moralists and the disquisitions of philosophers put together. It was a fact that couldn't be argued. It had to be accepted—or rejected, saying God was wrong. Some do. A friend from India was speaking in America and quoted the passage "[God] hath made of one blood all nations" (Acts 17:26 KJV). A man arose and said: "I believe the Bible—all except that verse."

Some accept the fact of the gift of the Holy Spirit to all races equally where they seek the gift, but dull the edge of the fact by saying in effect, "Yes, God does give the same gift of the Holy Spirit to all regardless, but it is a spiritual fact and has no social consequences." But this spiritual fact did, and does, have social consequences. One social consequence is that we enjoy the benefits of a Christian civilization instead of following pagan gods and sitting in pagan darkness; for the coming of the Spirit on Gentiles opened the door for the preaching of the gospel to us Gentiles and pushed the disciples through that open door!

An African American pastor said after one of my addresses: "He has time for the whitest and the blackest, and there is no difference. He says the same thing to white audiences he says to us." Why not? God was saying the same thing to both; why shouldn't I?

The facts, not arguments, are driving us into new attitudes. And the facts tell us that the brain and soul of humanity are one; that given the same stimulus and the same incentive, the brain and soul of every race will come out about the same; that therefore there are no permanently inferior races and no permanently superior races, only developed races and undeveloped races.

God knew what he was doing in giving the Holy Spirit equally to all, for down underneath is one basic humanity modified slightly by environment.

O God, my Lord, when I think of all this, hope springs up within my breast. When we are dreaming of a world community, it is not an idle dream; it is a possibility. Amen.

AFFIRMATION FOR THE DAY: If humanity is one down underneath, I will help to make it openly one.

THREE WAYS TO DEAL WITH RACE

Genesis 4:9-10; Malachi 2:10

Before we leave the mastery of race distinctions and prejudices, we must note three ways to deal with this problem, and these three ways are illustrated by the way three nations have dealt with it—Tasmania, Australia, and New Zealand.

Tasmania, south of Australia, is a beautiful land with lovely people; but a skeleton is in that national closet. A command was given by the governor to round up all natives on the island and transport them to another island, so the white man could have Tasmania to himself. The island was combed, and the aboriginals gathered into ships and taken away. On the new islands the natives died of homesickness. They would stand on a promontory, look toward their native land with tears streaming down their cheeks, crying, "My land, my land!" They died off as a race, died of broken hearts. That is one way to deal with the people of another race—genocide.

The second way is the way of Australia. The Australians didn't transport the aboriginals; they simply pushed them into more barren places as the white man took over the arable land. There isn't a sufficient economic basis to allow them to survive. So they are slowly dying off.

The third way is the way of New Zealand. A Christian governor and a bishop put through legislation in the early days that put an economic basis under the Maori. Standing in economic security, he has become the equal partner of the white man. There is little or no race intermingling by marriage. Yet there are mutual respect and equality of social and economic opportunity—each proud of the other. A Maori was prime minister of New Zealand at one time. Race relationships between the white man and the Maori are the best of the world. And the civilization produced is one of the highest of the world—both advancing, together.

Extinction, suppression, community—these three, and the greatest of these is community. The Christian way is the Way. "The wisdom of the just" (Luke 1:17 RSV)—it is not only good, it is wise to be just.

O God, our Lord, you are pushing us into community. We learn reluctantly and expensively. We take the hard way instead of your Way. And we get burnt. Forgive us. Amen.

AFFIRMATION FOR THE DAY: There is only one way to treat a person, and that is as a brother or sister—it shall be my way.

THE AMERICAN WAY OF DEALING WITH RACE

Matthew 5:21-24

A fourth way to deal with the people of another race must be mentioned—the way we are taking in America.

It is the way of giving equal rights but grudgingly and piecemeal. Slowly but surely the African American is coming into equal rights, privileges, and opportunity in our civilization. But it isn't being done graciously and grandly—we are doing it grumpily. We did it graciously and grandly on a legal level in the Supreme Court decision to desegregate the school system. But we dull the grandeur of that act by talk of evasion, postponement, downright rejection. We are not doing a big thing in a big way. We haggle and offer to compromise, and in the end give way. By that time the taste is gone. There are ashes in our mouths instead of a taste of sweetness. The African American is going to have equal rights and opportunities; it is destiny. Our democracy and Christianity both decree it. It will come, but it should come graciously instead of grudgingly.

The African Americans aren't a problem; they are a possibility, one of the biggest possibilities for development we have. If they go up, we go with them. And if they stay down, we stay down with them. Booker T. Washington once said, "One man cannot hold another man down in the ditch without remaining down in the ditch with him."* America's prestige in the world will be decided by the African American's prestige in America. They will be equal.

The church must lead the way. Now it is leading verbally but not vitally. For the greatest hour of segregation in American life is eleven o'clock Sunday morning. Churches are the greatest illustration of segregation in American life. We come together in conferences and conventions, but in the basic life of individual churches segregation is in operation—with few exceptions. For years I have been pleading that every white church should have at least one African American member and every African American church at least one white member. That wouldn't solve the problem, but it would be a symbol that we believe in and live in a kingdom that is class-blind and color-blind, seeing only persons—persons for whom Christ died.

O Christ, we thank you that our eyes are being opened, opened to see the possibility in every person, apart from everything extraneous. Help us to see and to heed. Amen.

AFFIRMATION FOR THE DAY: The American way isn't working in regard to race; it shall as far as I am concerned.

*Booker T. Washington, in an address on Abraham Lincoln before the Republican Club of New York City, February 12, 1909. (https://en.wikiquote.org/wiki/Booker_T._Washington, accessed March 8, 2017).

THE NEW TESTAMENT WAY OF DEALING WITH RACE

Matthew 8:5-13

If we should break up the segregation in the churches, it would not be a strange innovation; it would be a coming back to our original position, the place where we started.

Consider this illuminating passage, "The church at Antioch included prophets and teachers: Barnabas, Simeon (nicknamed Niger), Lucius from Cyrene, Manaen (a childhood friend of Herod the ruler), and Saul" (Acts 13:1). Two things may be noted: one, that Manaen, a member of the court of Herod, was a big fish and by our standards should have been Exhibit Number One; instead he is stuck into the list of prophets and teachers, not in the prominent first place or the prominent last place but in the middle. This society was class-blind. Two, that Simeon, called Niger, literally the Black, was a prophet or teacher in that church. Simeon was a member of the church and not on the edges; he was a prophet or a teacher. Moreover, he, among others, laid his hands on Paul and Barnabas and ordained them and sent them forth to preach the gospel in Asia and white Europe. We got our gospel from men who were ordained by a Black man.

If therefore every church would become an interracial church, it would only be going back to where we began. For our gospel came out of Antioch, and the Antioch church was interracial. If we did this, we would be richer for it. For instance, a woman came to one of our Ashrams, about as frustrated a piece of humanity as you could find; her nerves were tangled and, with them, her life situation. She left a week later one of the most radiant persons imaginable. Her husband came to take her home, and said: "I never saw such a change in a person in all my life." And *he* found Christ before he left! The woman told me that when she saw she was to live in the same room with an African American, she backed out and went to another room. "And to think," she added, "that woman was one of three women who took me aside and prayed and loved me into victory. My prejudices came near making me miss this!" Prejudices produce poverty.

O Jesus, help us to be enriched by the riches of all races. For as we give to them, we get from them. May we see beyond the extraneous to the interior. Amen.

AFFIRMATION FOR THE DAY: If I segregate another, I segregate myself and segregate myself into poverty.

THE MASTERY OF THE MATERIAL

Matthew 4:4; 6:24

We proceed now to another, very important mastery that began with the coming of the Holy Spirit—*the mastery of the material.*

To relate the spiritual life to the material life is one of the crucial problems of human living. Unless this adjustment is made, and made rightly, the spiritual life is one series of frustrations after another. There are three possible ways to relate oneself to the material. First, transfer the seat of one's life and live in the material as if it were the be-all and end-all of human existence. Second, try to run away from the material, reduce one's contacts with it to a minimum, and endeavor to live one's life in the spiritual entirely. Third, accept the material as God-given; dedicate it to God; and use as much of it as will make us more physically, mentally, and spiritually fit for the purposes of the kingdom of God. This third way is the Christian Way. The other two ways are unworkable save as they work disaster.

Take the first. Jesus said a very illuminating thing, "A man's life does not consist in the abundance of his possessions" (Luke 12:15 RSV). In all ages, our chief endeavor has been to disprove that, and there has been one result—and only one result—frustration and unhappiness. It works that way with as much precision as two plus two makes four. If the seat of one's life is in the material, then the seat of one's life is in unhappiness—invariably. We are inherently too big to be satisfied with a material existence.

The second alternative is almost as unworkable. You cannot run away from the material and try to act as though it weren't here. It is here, very much so. You must come to terms with it—right terms—or there is disaster. "Tell me, Sir, how to get rid of my body, it is my enemy; it drags down my soul," said an obviously unhappy *sadhu*, or holy man, of India. "Please don't talk to me, for you distract me and bring me into contact with the world," said one Indian ex-High Court judge, clothed in ashes and sitting in meditation.

O Lord, teach us how to relate ourselves to this world in which we live and move but in which we must not have our being. Teach us to live. Amen.

AFFIRMATION FOR THE DAY: My life shall not be directed by the material, nor shall I desert it; I shall dedicate it.

THE CHRISTIAN ACCEPTS THE MATERIAL

Genesis 1:4, 12, 18, 25, 31

We ended yesterday on the attempt to run away from the material. To the degree it has been tried in India, it has left that portion of its life in material and spiritual ruins. We are not made to be disembodied spirits trying to live disembodied in a material world. The attempt to be either immersed in the material or to become immune to the material ends in frustration.

There is only one workable way, and that is the Christian way of accepting the material as God-made and God-given, and to use as much of it as will make us more physically, mentally, and spiritually fit for the purposes of the kingdom of God. In the Acts of the Apostles, the Christians took the third way.

They accepted the material. The material was God-created and God-approved. God looked on it after creation and "saw that it was good"—good, not perfect—good for the purposes involved, namely, to provide an environment for the making and development of character. Moreover, the center of their faith was the incarnation, where the Divine Word became flesh—mind you, flesh. The Docetists, feeling an aversion to the material, said that Jesus, the Divine Word, became spirit. But John, protesting, said, "Every spirit that confesses that Jesus Christ has come as a human is from God, and every spirit that doesn't confess Jesus is not from God" (1 John 4:2-3). The Christian faith was planted firmly in material relations by the incarnation.

The followers of Jesus therefore made the material an agent of the coming of the kingdom of God and a part of its demonstration. Take the simple fact that the account says, "While they were eating together, he ordered them not to leave Jerusalem, but to wait for what the Father had promised" (Acts 1:4). "While they were eating together"— the most material thing we can do—"wait for what the Father had promised"—the most spiritual thing we can do. They were not incompatibles but com-possibles. When the Holy Spirit came, the breaking of bread, as distinct from the Communion, was made into a sacred ritual: "And they devoted themselves...to the breaking of bread and the prayers" (Acts 2:42 RSV).

Dear Lord, show us how to make every meal a sacrament and every relationship a revelation and every deed a devotion. May we make all life live. Amen.

AFFIRMATION FOR THE DAY: All my material relations will be demonstration points of the kingdom.

THE BREAKING OF THE BREAD BECOMES A LOVE FEAST

Luke 15:22-24

We ended yesterday with the statement that the breaking of bread was lifted up into a ritual—the Love Feast. It wasn't the ordinary meal as is seen by the passage, "On the first day of the week, when we were gathered together to break bread." This is followed by, "And when Paul had gone up and had broken bread and eaten" (Acts 20:7, 11 RSV). "Had broken bread" was different from "had eaten."

Ordinary breaking of bread had become sacramental; extraordinary breaking of bread—a Love Feast.

But ordinary eating apart from this Love Feast was a part of the manifestation of the kingdom: "And day by day, attending the temple together and breaking bread in their homes, they partook of food with glad and generous hearts" (Acts 2:46 RSV). The Love Feast in the extraordinary had become the feast of love in the ordinary. The ordinary was interfused with the divine extraordinary. Life was unified. The material and the spiritual were "according well" and "beating out music" faster than before.

This gathering up of the material and making it a part of the new order is seen in the very holiest moment of all—in the very coming of the Holy Spirit, which was accompanied by two material manifestations: the sound of the rushing mighty wind and the cloven tongues like as of fire (Acts 2:2-3 KJV). Why was the material thus associated with the spiritual? Both pointed to something beyond them. The sound of the rushing mighty wind helped their faith to take hold, for the words *wind* and *spirit* are the same in Hebrew—*ruach*. So when they heard the "wind," they said to themselves: the wind—the Spirit—is coming. Their faith stepped easily from one to the other. The "wind" blew them into "Spirit." The material helped the spiritual.

And the cloven tongues like as of fire sitting upon the head of each of them confirmed the fact by outer sign that God was giving to each one, as an individual, the Holy Spirit. The individual was important, and God was dealing not with a mass but with a person. The individual stood out.

O God, our heavenly Lord, we thank you that you are singling out each of us as important before you, therefore before others. It humbles us and lifts us. Amen.

AFFIRMATION FOR THE DAY: All my breaking of bread shall be a Love Feast this day.

INDIVIDUALISM AND COLLECTIVISM IN A LIVING BLEND

2 Corinthians 8:12-15

We saw yesterday that the cloven tongues as of fire sitting on the head of each of them pointed to the fact that the individual, as an individual, was receiving the Holy Spirit. This is important, for there are those who insist that the coming of the Holy Spirit is a group experience and not an individual experience, and they point to the fact that the Holy Spirit came upon groups in the Acts in all cases except one—Paul.

Now this insistence upon the Holy Spirit as a group experience is a good correction, for the emphasis has hitherto been too individualistic. The individual experience has not been corrected and enriched by the group experience. Hence it has resulted in the individual going off on a tangent into all sorts of marginal or odd emphases. Group mysticism, says Quaker theologian D. Elton Trueblood, is almost always a safer and more constructive type of mysticism than individual mysticism. But while we have needed this group emphasis, we need it only as a corrective. There is truth in the fact that the individual, as an individual, can and does and should receive the Holy Spirit.

When the one hundred twenty looked up and saw that every person had a tongue of fire resting on his or her head, then they knew that God was dealing with individuals, and each was precious before God. Thus individualism and collectivism were put together in a simple act, the group and the individual both receiving the Holy Spirit. The world struggle is over these two emphases—individualism and collectivism. Which will determine the future? The coming of the Holy Spirit meant that neither one was the full truth; each needs the other. Individualism forgets that life is social, and collectivism forgets that life is individual and personal. Here they were put into a living blend. And the society that emerged illustrated this emphasis on both. They took the hint, and embodied it.

These two physical accompaniments of the coming of the Holy Spirit were scaffolding, which was taken down when the new temple was reared. They had accomplished their purpose.

O Lord, we thank you that you are teaching us, using the material as a pointing rod to the spiritual. Help us to see where they point and follow. Help us to insights through eyesight. Amen.

AFFIRMATION FOR THE DAY: The material and the spiritual shall be blended today as the words and music of a song.

WHAT DOES THIS "OTHER TONGUES" MEAN?

1 Corinthians 12:27-31

We must look again at a physical phenomenon at the coming of the Holy Spirit—a phenomenon that pointed beyond itself to the spiritual. The statement has puzzled many, "And they were all filled with the Holy Spirit and began to speak in other tongues, as the Spirit gave them utterance" (Acts 2:4 RSV). What is this "other tongues," and what is its purpose?

I believe that a very important purpose was behind the speaking in tongues. If the disciples had spoken only in Hebrew to the throngs who had gathered from all of that ancient world—Africa, Asia, and Europe—on the day of Pentecost, the impression would have been that this was just one more religious movement within Judaism. It had no world significance. But when the people from all lands heard the message in their own language, they must have immediately pricked up their ears. This new redemptive movement was no mere Jewish movement; it had stepped straight off into a universal appeal and pattern. That simple fact broke the Jewish mold and universalized the gospel.

And while it spoke to the foreigners a message, it also spoke to the Jews. Their language was no longer sacred; God was speaking to all people everywhere in their own languages. That struck a tremendous blow for the freedom of the new movement. There was no longer one chosen people, with a chosen language and culture. Humanity as humanity was chosen. Peter expresses this in speaking of the new humanity in Christ, "But you are a chosen race, a royal priesthood, a holy nation, a people who are God's own possession....Once you weren't a people, but now you are God's people" (1 Pet 2:9-10). God was going to use all languages and all cultures as vehicles of the Divine. That was a startling innovation. Walls of exclusion went down, like Jericho's walls, not by the sound of a ram's horn but by the sound of a universal message, understood by all people in their very own languages.

When that purpose was accomplished, this scaffolding of speaking in tongues was taken down. This was a special miracle for a special purpose, and it fulfilled its purpose.

Lord, we thank you that you love all and you are speaking to all, each through our own language and culture, for you are intending to redeem a race. Amen.

AFFIRMATION FOR THE DAY: As God is breaking down walls of exclusion, so will I—I am for humanity.

GIFTS AND THE GIFT

1 Corinthians 14:1-3

We must spend another day on clarifying the meaning of speaking in tongues, for many have shied away from the Holy Spirit since some try to bind up his coming with speaking in tongues—no tongues, no Holy Spirit. That spoils it for many people, and rightly so. For that puts the gift of the Holy Spirit in the category of the weird instead of the wonderful.

Three times, the coming of the Spirit in Acts was accompanied by speaking in tongues: at Jerusalem, Caesarea, and Ephesus. All three point to our interpretation, for in all three this emancipation was necessary—at Jerusalem, as we have seen, there were Jews among foreigners; at Caesarea there were Romans among Jews (Acts 10); at Ephesus there were Asiatics with some Jews (Acts 19). This universalizing was needed in those three strategic places—the seat of Jewish nationalism, Jerusalem; the seat of Roman authority, Caesarea; and the seat of Asiatic paganism, Ephesus—and it took place. But once the lesson was learned, this temporary phenomenon disappeared.

What about the appearance in Corinth? At Corinth there appeared a different type of tongues—unknown tongues—needing an interpreter. At Pentecost no interpreter was needed, for everyone heard in their own languages the wonderful works of God. At Corinth the type of tongues that appeared was a gift of the Spirit.

> To each is given the manifestation of the Spirit for the common good. To one is given...gifts of healing..., to another various kinds of tongues, to another the interpretation of tongues. All these are inspired by one and the same Spirit, who apportions to each individually as he wills....Do all possess gifts of healing? Do all speak with tongues? Do all interpret? (1 Cor 12:7-11, 30 RSV)

The gifts of the Spirit are not to be confounded with the gift of the Spirit. The gift of the Spirit is for all, but the gifts of the Spirit God "apportions to each one individually as he wills." Paul urges seeking the two highest gifts of the Spirit—love and prophecy, power to love and power to forthtell the good news. These are necessary today and a permanent part of the coming of the Spirit.

O Holy Spirit, give me the power to love and the power to witness effectively for Jesus. For everyone needs love, and there are many who have never heard the good news. Amen.

AFFIRMATION FOR THE DAY: The gift of love and the gift to forthtell the good news—my quest for the day.

79

ON DIVIDING WHAT GOD HAS JOINED

Acts 6:1-6

One more comment on speaking in tongues. My conviction is the Pentecost type of tongues—the power to speak effectively in other languages without an interpreter—has disappeared; but the Corinth type of tongues—needing an interpreter—appears here and there. They are not the same. Many come to India hoping to reproduce the miracle at Pentecost and speak in the languages of India without an interpreter or learning the language. It hasn't happened. The wreckage of those hopes is strewn across India. You learn the language or use an interpreter, or you don't get your message across.

This special miracle at Pentecost, for this special purpose, served that purpose and disappeared. God performs miracles, but just enough, not too many. Too many would make us lazy. Too few would make us hazy. The miracle in the material pointed to the miracle in the spiritual and then passed away. The spiritual abides.

There is another incident in the Acts that offers a lesson regarding the relationship between the material and the spiritual. The apostles tried to separate the material and the spiritual, and God canceled the attempt and kept them together. The apostles called together the main body of believers and said,

> "It isn't right for us to set aside proclamation of God's word in order to serve tables. Brothers and sisters, carefully choose seven well-respected men from among you. They must be well-respected and endowed by the Spirit with exceptional wisdom. We will put them in charge of this concern. As for us, we will devote ourselves to prayer and to the service of proclaiming the word." (Acts 6:2-4)

This was done—the twelve appointed the seven. It seemed a highly wise and spiritual act. But sometimes a dangerous and disastrous thing can come in under the cover of spirituality. It did here. The apostles drove a dangerous wedge between the material and the spiritual. They would give themselves to the severely spiritual, and the seven would give themselves to the severely material. They separated what God had joined. In the incarnation, the material and spiritual were one—the Word became flesh. Here the Word became word. The material and the spiritual were separated.

O Jesus, in you all life is a living whole. In you we can't tell where one ends and the other begins. For all life lives in you and is resplendent there. Amen.

AFFIRMATION FOR THE DAY: Serving tables and serving the Lord will be the same today, for it is all unto him.

PUTTING GOD INTO THE TOTAL LIFE

Acts 6:8-10

We are considering the division the apostles made between the spiritual and the material by separating themselves for prayer and the ministry of the word and turning over to the seven the administration of food. By doing so they turned life into two compartments—the sacred and the secular. That division is not found in the Gospels or in the Acts up to this point. It was foreign to the Christian faith. Jesus taught, healed, and fed people, all as a part of the coming of the kingdom of God. Life was a unified whole.

But the apostles here separated what God had joined. They became more "spiritual" than their own Master, who fed people as a manifestation of the love of God and the fulfillment of human need. In separating the two, the apostles impoverished both. The spiritual was supposed to be on a higher plane but lifted out of material relations. It did not take shoes and walk; it took words and talked. It made for unreality. And it impoverished the secular; it was supposed to be on a lower plan, to be carried out by people with a lower calling, in a lower spirit and motive.

That division between the sacred and the secular has been the most disastrous move religion has ever taken. Its effects are more and more manifest every day in Christendom. It is news instead of the normal when a man puts God into his business. And it is news not normal if a minister works alongside the workers in a factory or on a project. And this division has made possible the Communists' move to allow religion to function as inner mystical experience or as worship in collective experience while they control the other parts of life—the economic, social, and political. Religion is pushed into the innocuous. The apostles in this move laid the foundations of that. And this is at the basis of the frantic attempt to get God back into life—the total life.

We will not get God back into the total life until we abolish, and abolish completely, the distinction between the secular and the sacred. All legitimate life has to become sacred again, and all legitimate occupations a manifestation of the kingdom.

O Lord, we your foolish children err from your ways like lost sheep. Help us to listen to your voice and to take your ways, and then life will click into total meaning. Amen.

AFFIRMATION FOR THE DAY: Everything that I touch today will be sacred, and I shall touch everything.

THE SPIRIT GIVES US SPECIAL SKILLS

Romans 12:6-8

Just why did the apostles make this move of separating the sacred from the secular? For two reasons, I think. First, they unconsciously, in the name of spirituality, adopted a pagan attitude toward the material—an import from Greek philosophy. Plotinus said he was ashamed that he had a body. This division between the secular and the sacred was not native to Judaic thought. The Spirit of God made Joseph a good food comptroller (Gen 41:38). The same Spirit made Bezalel a good artist and artisan (Exod 31:1-5). The Spirit of God came on Gideon, and he blew a trumpet and aroused and judged Israel (Jdg 6:34). The Spirit came on Azariah and made him a teacher (2 Chr 15:1-3). The Spirit of God was heightening and adding a plus to the powers of human beings and making them more skillful in their ordinary occupations. That turned the power of religion into the remaking of life in all its phases now. This move of the apostles turned the power of religion away from that into the so-called sacred. They adopted a foreign import.

Second, the apostles carried out a tendency that was manifesting more and more—to set themselves apart into a special class with special functions, honors, and privileges. They were too big to do this kind of work. They didn't say that—they put a spiritual interpretation on it—but nevertheless that apparently was part of the underlying reason. That same reason, dressed in spiritual garments, is with us today. A minister of a fashionable church came to an Ashram, and when the "work period" came, in which we all work with our hands, he remarked: "I've come here to develop my spiritual life, not to work with my hands." So he stayed out for a day. But the next day he took a broom and began sweeping out a hall. He came back radiant. He said jubilantly: "I didn't know a broom could do that for you. I'm going to go back to my church and preach the gospel of the Broom." Why was he jubilant? Well, life, which had been compartmentalized, came back into unity. The long-estranged twins, the secular and the sacred, were reconciled within him. Life was centrally unified, hence happy.

O Lord, give us the experience of making all life into a unity around your will. For your will comprehends and embraces all. May I walk in that will today. Amen.

AFFIRMATION FOR THE DAY: All my work will be worship today, hence sacred.

THE CENTER OF SPIRITUAL POWER SHIFTS

Acts 8:4-8

What happened as a result of this disastrous division between the sacred and the secular on the part of the apostles? One of the most important things in the history of religion happened. It was this: the center of spiritual influence and power shifted from the apostles to this group of the "seven." From that moment on the center of revival and the center of missionary advance were in this so-called lay group. It was Stephen, the leader of the seven, who precipitated the revival in Jerusalem. And also, by his straightforward boldness, precipitated his martyrdom and a persecution of the church.

If Stephen became the center of revival in Jerusalem, it was Philip, another member of the seven, who precipitated a revival in Samaria (Acts 8:4-8). They were scattered abroad by the persecution that arose over Stephen and "traveled as far as Phoenicia, Cyprus, and Antioch. They proclaimed the word only to Jews. Among them were some people from Cyprus and Cyrene. They entered Antioch and began to proclaim the good news about the Lord Jesus also to Gentiles. The Lord's power was with them, and a large number came to believe and turned to the Lord" (Acts 11:19-21). They founded the church in Antioch. And Antioch, not Jerusalem, then became the center of Christian influence and missionary activity. It was out of Antioch that Paul and Barnabas went on their missionary journeys and laid the foundations of Christianity in Asia and Europe, hence in America. We received our gospel from Antioch, not Jerusalem.

What did all this mean? It meant that God had tipped the weight of approval and hence influence and power toward this lay movement headed by the seven. They kept life a unified whole, and hence God put the stamp of approval on them. They were entrusted with God's movement of redemption and became the channels of God's power. And the apostles? They could apparently only try to regularize what they could not produce. They sent John and Peter to Samaria to lay hands on the products of Philip's revival and sent Barnabas to Antioch to encourage the new converts of the lay group.

Lord, we thank you that you are behind those who are behind your purposes. Help me to align myself with those purposes today; then I can expect your power. Amen.

AFFIRMATION FOR THE DAY: If I keep in line with God's purpose, I will keep in line with God's power.

THE APOSTLES DROP OUT OF THE ACTS OF THE APOSTLES

Galatians 2:7-13

We saw yesterday that the center of revival and the center of persecution shifted from the apostles to the lay group headed by Stephen, and later by Philip. The apostles escaped both revival and persecution. "At that time, the church in Jerusalem began to be subjected to vicious harassment. Everyone except the apostles was scattered throughout the regions of Judea and Samaria" (Acts 8:1). Why "except the apostles"? Were they braver than the rest? I used to think so, but I changed my mind. I think the edge of the persecution turned toward not them but this lay group for two reasons: (1) the apostles fitted into the Jewish system better than the lay group. They were conservatives; the lay group were radicals. (2) The Jewish leaders saw instinctively that when the apostles confined themselves to the severely spiritual; they were no longer dangerous. It was the lay group who held life together and demanded that it come under control of the kingdom; these were the dangerous ones.

When this interpretation dawned on me, I went to the commentaries to see how wrong I was. In the Speaker's Bible, edited by James Hastings, I found this:

> For a time, even though the Book in which the story lies be called "the Acts of the Apostles," the apostles disappear, and the whole crisis of which Stephen is the chief factor and which culminates in the conversion of Saul, and the opening of the world to the church, and her mission to the Gentiles, is achieved without one of them being present. Stephen stands alone to our view.*

It was Stephen who was in back of the conversion of Paul; and it was Paul, a product of the lay group, who took over from the apostles the lead in the movement. He shaped the thinking of the churches through his epistles. It was said of him, "Because they practiced the same trade, he stayed and worked with them. They all worked in leather" (Acts 18:3). And it was Paul who said, "Whatever you do, you should do it all for God's glory" (1 Cor 10:31). He held the secular and the sacred together in himself and helped the churches to do the same. The estrangement between the worker and the church would not have taken place if we had followed Paul's emphasis.

O Jesus, you who worked at a carpenter's bench and thereby did glorify all toil, help me to do everything I do in a sacred way. In your name. Amen.

AFFIRMATION FOR THE DAY: If I do all to the glory of God, then all I do will be glorified.

* James Hastings, *Speaker's Bible: The Acts of the Apostles* (Aberdeen, Scotland: The Speaker's Bible Office, 1927–1928), page number not available.

I FEEL GOD EVERYWHERE

Romans 12:1-2

Before we leave this mastery of the material by the spiritual, by making them both serve the same ends, we must apply this lesson to ourselves.

Someone has said our greatest need is to have the "spiritual mind in the man of the world." A Christian judge in India used to spend an hour in devotion from four to five, then still kneeling would write the court case judgments of the day. He tried to translate divine justice into terms of courtroom justice. When a Brahmin lawyer got out of hand one day, and the judge said, "I'm sorry, but I'll have to fine you for contempt," the lawyer replied, "Sir, if you fine me, I'll take it as the very judgment of God; for when you speak, God speaks." This same judge told me how the Spirit guided him to correct decisions. In one case the evidence was conflicting. He started to write in favor of the plaintiff when the Spirit whispered: "Why don't you look at the similarity of that handwriting?" He did and found a forgery, and wrote the verdict for the defendant. And he found he was right. Don't tell me that is a secular job; it's sacred when done in this sacred way. The renowned British preacher, John Henry Jowett (1863–1923), told of a man who before conversion was a burglar, and when Jowett asked him what happened when he received the power of the Spirit, he replied: "I feel God everywhere." That's it. There is no more secular when one is possessed of the Holy Spirit. Everything is sacred, for we see and feel God in everything.

Stephen and his group of seven were not supposed to do evangelistic work, but to serve tables. They lifted the secular into the sacred and became more effective as evangelists than the apostles who were supposed only to preach the Word. "They couldn't resist the wisdom the Spirit gave [Stephen] as he spoke" (Acts 6:10). His spirit and the Spirit had become one in a so-called secular job.

And the interesting thing is that the only person in the New Testament called an evangelist was Philip (Acts 21:8). He was not supposed to do evangelistic work!

O Lord, I thank you that you can help me to lift everything I do today with a new spirit—your Spirit—and then I shall make all things new. In Jesus' name. Amen.

AFFIRMATION FOR THE DAY: I shall take the eternal and show it in every passing event of time.

The Mastery of Inner Conflict and Decision

James 4:1-3

We have been studying the mastery of the various aspects of outer life, and we finished with the mastery of the material. One phase of this mastery of the material, namely, the basis on which the material goods are to be distributed, must await further consideration later. It is not being bypassed. We will run straight into it—later. We must now turn to some of the more personal masteries that lay behind these outer masteries.

We saw some of the things that were temporary accompaniments of the coming of the Holy Spirit; we must now look at three things that were permanent. One of them was *the mastery of inner conflict and division*. This *purity* seemed to be permanent. Peter described what happened in these words: "And God who knows the heart bore witness to them, giving them the Holy Spirit just as he did to us; and he made no distinction between us and them, but cleansed their hearts by faith" (Acts 15:8-9 RSV). Here Peter, describing what happened when the Holy Spirit came upon the Gentiles at the house of Cornelius, said that the Jews and the Gentiles both received the Holy Spirit and both without distinction were purified through faith. Here was a permanent element, passing from the Jews' Pentecost to the Gentiles' Pentecost; they were cleansed by the coming of the Holy Spirit. The cleansing was a cleansing from contradictory things within them.

They were obviously already converted when the Holy Spirit came upon them in that upper room. Jesus had said that they were not of the world even as he was not of the world (John 17:16). Note "of the world" (RSV); the sources of their life were not in the world but in Jesus. They were following him—not the world. Yet while they were not in the world, a good deal of the world was still in them. They were irritable—wanting to call down fire. They were self-seeking—a dispute arose over who should be greatest, and two wanted to outsmart the rest and get special seats at the right hand and the left. They still needed cleansing.

O Divine Spirit, reveal to me my deepest needs, and when you do, help me not to wince and whine and explain. Help me to face things boldly and honestly. Amen.

AFFIRMATION FOR THE DAY: If I am an inner contradiction, I shall be an outer blur. I will be neither.

PARTIALLY ON, LEAKY AND NOISY

James 4:7-8

We are studying the mastery of inner division and conflict. The disciples followed Jesus before the coming of the Holy Spirit but with certain areas reserved—unsurrendered. They were like the people described in Joshua: "'You are witnesses against yourselves that you have chosen to serve the LORD, to serve him.' And they said, 'We are witnesses.'" He said to them, "'Then put away the foreign gods. . . .' The people said to Joshua, 'The LORD our God we will serve, and his voice we will obey'" (Josh 24:22-24 RSV). They said they would serve and obey the Lord, not that they would put away foreign gods. They tried to live with divided loyalty.

In a hotel in San Jose, California, a sign over the radiator in each room reads: "Please turn the radiators all the way on and off. If turned partially on, they will leak and be noisy." That is absolutely true of the spiritual life; a halfway-on spiritual life is leaky, and it is noisy. It sets up inner friction. A great many people have just enough religion to set up a conflict within them. If it possessed them wholly, it would be a concord, but halfway it is a conflict.

Bonnie Brown Heady lived on the lower floor of her house as a respectable, cultured woman. On the upper floor she lived in a brothel. In 1953, she ended in an electric chair in Missouri for abducting and killing a child. That is dramatic, but many electrocute their very souls by divided loyalties and double-dealing—and do it silently without drama. It is just as tragic.

Now how did the disciples get rid of this divided loyalty within? Did Jesus set one side of their natures fighting the other? That is what people everywhere try. Seneca did that: "I am still toiling with all my might at my old task of eradicating my faults."* Another, a modern, says: "I intend to wring the last drop of self out of me." But the self, concentrated on the self, is hardly the way to get free from self. That ends in self-preoccupation and, it may be added, in frustration. It just doesn't work. There is a better way and more effective. The disciples found it—effortlessly.

O Lord, we would be free, free from the tyranny of a divided inner self. Free me there, and I shall be free indeed. Bound there, I am bound everywhere. Amen.

AFFIRMATION FOR THE DAY: I shall not fight with myself but surrender myself and let God control me.

*No published source was found for this quotation.

THE CLEANSING OF THE SUBCONSCIOUS

James 3:9-12

We are meditating on the "cleansing" that came to the disciples through the coming of the Holy Spirit. They had been cleansed of a great deal before this fuller and deeper cleansing. Jesus had said to them, "You are already made clean by the word which I have spoken to you" (John 15:3 RSV). The word he had spoken had cleansed them of wrong directions—they were converted and turned around; cleansed them from wrong relations with God—they were forgiven of sins committed; from wrong relationships with others—they had entered a fellowship; from wrong attitudes toward life—they were allied to life, not alien to it; from the kingdom of self to the kingdom of God—they had been "transferred" to the kingdom of God's beloved Son. They were in the family of God. They had been cleansed from much, but not from all. While they were in the family, the family spirit was not often in them. There were the outcroppings of the old through the soil of the new.

The cellar of their lives, the subconscious, needed to be cleansed. The ground floor—the conscious—had been cleansed and life's furniture set in order; but the cellar still had a lot of junk in it, left over from the old. Psychologists tell us that down in the subconscious—or the unconscious, as they prefer to call it—the primitive driving urges, or instincts, reside. These driving urges have been classified into more than a dozen by William McDougall (1871–1938), but have been reduced by many into three main urges or drives: self, sex, and the herd. These urges have come down through a long racial history, and through that contact with an erring race, have bent toward perverseness, toward evil. Stated thus, this uncovering of the subconscious squints toward what the theologians call original sin: sin born in us. Paul calls it the "flesh": "For I know that nothing good dwells within me, that is, in my flesh" (Rom 7:18 RSV). By the flesh he is speaking, not of his physical body (*soma*), but of the body of inner evil (*sarx*). By whatever name, everyone who knows himself or herself knows that it is there; and it is the center of our spiritual problems.

O Lord, I am now close, very close, to the sore spot. Help me not to wince or evade but to walk up to this problem and find the answer. In Jesus' name. Amen.

AFFIRMATION FOR THE DAY: I am persuaded God can save to the uttermost, and the uttermost includes the subconscious.

THE LEISURED HEART

Philippians 2:1-4

We saw yesterday that the disciples had been cleansed of much before the coming of the Holy Spirit—of much but not of all. The conscious mind had been changed and redeemed but not the subconscious.

With the coming of the Holy Spirit, the subconscious was cleansed and redeemed. They had gained *mastery of the self urge*, the first of the three main urges. How do we know? Only by inference. But the inferences are clear. A person with an unredeemed subconscious is constantly struggling with the self, preoccupied with sitting on a lid. The spiritual life is precarious, for it is always in danger of being upset from below. There is consequently a state of tension.

After the coming of the Holy Spirit, these disciples were not preoccupied with themselves and their own inner spiritual problems. They were set free to witness, to serve, to push a moral and spiritual offensive. In the Acts of the Apostles the consciousness of personal, inner problems is almost entirely absent. The problems shifted from the inner to the outer, from themselves to their environment. The fact is that we look in vain through the whole of the Acts to find raised one single inner, personal spiritual problem. All their problems were concerned with the reactions of the people to their witnessing. Here is the most healthy-minded group of people that has ever existed on the earth before or since. A people freed from their own problems, freed to turn their energies and interests into one channel, the channel of witnessing to others of what they had found. They certainly had learned how to live—and to live with hearts "at leisure to soothe and sympathize."* If psychologists want to study healthy mindedness, let them pour over the Acts and learn what it is to live. The word *problem* isn't mentioned once! They were not a problem-centered group but a power-centered group. Their problems were in their hands, not in their hearts. No wonder they turned the world upside down, for they had been turned inside out. Their civil war was over; there was peace and nothing but peace within, and now they could turn all their redeemed energies to the prosecution of an outside war, a foreign war.

O Christ, I thank you for what you have done for this group of followers. Help me to see, to seek, and to obtain my blessed freedom in you and obtain it now. Amen.

AFFIRMATION FOR THE DAY: I no longer belong to the problem-centered but the power-centered, for I am wholly his.

*"The Sympathy and Grace of Jesus, *Things New and Old*, vol. 4: (London: G. Morrish, 1861): 7.

WANTED TO TAKE A BATH

Jude 19-21

We have looked at the astonishing fact of a group of people who were buried deep in the problems of human living, yet seemingly had no inner problems of their own or none not being handled successfully or on the way to solution. Contrast this atmosphere of the Acts with that of modern church life. In our Ashrams, places of spiritual retreat, we ask the group the first day: "Why have you come? What do you want? What do you really need?" And we spend three to five hours in telling simply and honestly our needs.

One reaction was this, "Well, when I heard all these people telling their needs, I wondered if I hadn't landed in the center of all cracked souls, if not crackpots, of the country." No, he hadn't. He had looked into the souls of a cross section of modern church life—lay and clerical—and it spelled out one word: *problems.*

Is psychology with all its knowledge able to show anything better? Better? Worse. One woman who heard a lecture on psychology said she felt as though she "wanted to take a bath." What then is the difference between the modern atmosphere and that of the Acts? Do we just know more? Or is our knowledge just knowledge of problems and not knowledge of the way to solutions? Just what is the difference? The difference is that in the ordinary church today, and in modern psychology, little or nothing is known of the Spirit. This is an important lack, for the area of the Spirit's work is largely, if not entirely, in the subconscious. God who made the subconscious an integral part of us also provided for cleansing, controlling, and coordinating the subconscious. That provision is the Holy Spirit. Without the Spirit religion deals with the conscious, introducing new loyalties and moralities there, but not with deep-down, driving motives and urges. Hence it ends in frustration and disappointment; for it leaves the house of humanity divided against itself—conscious mind converted, subconscious mind left unconverted. Jesus said a house divided against itself cannot stand, and modern living is giving way under the pressures of modern living.

O Lord, I thank you that you have not left us without remedy where we need it most—in the depths of us. How can we thank you enough for the Holy Spirit? Amen.

AFFIRMATION FOR THE DAY: As I breathe the air into the depths of my lungs to cleanse them, so I breathe the Holy Spirit into the depths of my subconscious.

CALLED IN NOW AND THEN

2 Corinthians 3:16-18

We have seen that the difference between modern church life and the Acts is in the place the Holy Spirit occupies. In Acts, the Spirit was in control of life, and in modern church life the attempt is made to control the Holy Spirit in the interests of success. the Spirit is called in only to help out. We are at the center, and the Spirit is to help us. So he silently stays away—on those terms. We frustrate the grace of God and remain frustrated. Then we question whether Christianity will work. The truth is we are not working it.

The position of the church in regard to the Holy Spirit is like that of a man who courts a girl, admires her, enjoys her fellowship, but stops there and doesn't invite her to be his wife, to come into his home and take charge of it, to live life out with him. All else is preliminary to this; if it doesn't happen, there is a halfwayness, a frustration. The church has companionship with the Holy Spirit, seeks the Spirit's counsel, adores the Spirit—does everything but ask God's Spirit in to take over the within, including the subconscious.

The disciples in their simplicity had turned over to God their total beings, conscious and subconscious; and when they did so, the Holy Spirit moved in and took them over and made them over. They were released at the center of their beings. Now they were free and joyous and natural—and effective. God was pulling out all the stops and playing them all over. The conscious and the subconscious minds were not striking different and contradictory notes; they were under one control—the Holy Spirit—and now both conscious and subconscious were blended into an amazing harmony. Life harmonized; and the world, astonished at such heavenly music from such earthly instruments, crowded to listen and long and accept.

Just how did this happen? Did the disciples set their jaws, clench their fists, knit their brows, and throw all the adrenalin they had into the bloodstream to make them fight a little harder than the rest of humanity? No, it was all done effortlessly. They were not trying but trusting, not striving but surrendering; and the Holy Spirit did the rest.

O Holy Spirit, teach us how to accept your resources, to stop our futile struggling, and let you do in us and through us what we will not and cannot do. Amen.

AFFIRMATION FOR THE DAY: I am learning the art not of offering resistances but of accepting resources.

FIRST BIND THE STRONG MAN

2 Corinthians 2:14-16

We saw last week that the disciples had attained the unattainable: inward unity and coordination and outer power and effectiveness. I say "unattainable," for this cannot be attained, it must be obtained. It is the gift of God.

Just what happened? How did God work this miracle of amazingly effective living? Jesus gives a hint as to the method in these words: "How can one enter a strong man's house and plunder his goods, unless he first binds the strong man? Then indeed he may plunder his house" (Matt 12:29 RSV). He says there is no use trying to get something away from the strong man unless the strong man himself is bound. Bind him, and the rest is easy. In other words, don't try to conquer temper, pride, covetousness, irritability, sex desires—they are symptoms of something deeper—an unsurrendered self. The self is the strong man keeping these things going. Go straight to the center and bind the strong man—the self.

And how? The first step is our consent and cooperation. Christ cannot do it by our just asking him. In the asking there must be consent and cooperation. Consent that the strong man be bound and cooperate in surrendering him into the hands of God. In other words, self-surrender. You'll probably hesitate to surrender the one thing you own—the self—for you're afraid that this will make you a nonentity, a puppet in the hands of another. Actually the opposite happens. The strong man, the self, is bound that he may be free. Now he is free to create confusion and conflict and destruction. Then he will be bound to create peace and concord and construction.

How does the Holy Spirit bind the strong man? By stout ropes of increased inner resolution? No, by the silken cords of love. When we surrender the self to God, the Holy Spirit gently unfastens the cords of love, which the self had entwined around itself, and fastens them upon Jesus. The Holy Spirit makes us love Jesus. And loving him the self is freed from self-preoccupation. Really free to love, to serve, to create, and to fulfill its destiny.

O Lord, you have provided our freedom through a deeper bondage; I accept that bondage, which is freedom indeed. Make me a captive, Lord, and then I shall be free. Amen.

AFFIRMATION FOR THE DAY: To the degree I am bound to Christ, to that degree I am free in the world.

TWO METHODS OF BINDING
THE STRONG MAN

Colossians 3:12-15

When we allow the Holy Spirit to bind the strong man by the cords of love to Jesus, then his goods may be taken easily. Then temper, pride, covetousness, irritability, and rampant sex desires drop away as irrelevant. A consuming love for Christ takes possession of us, and by the "expulsive power of a new affection"* these lesser loves are cast out. We love something, Someone, better. Two illustrations of methods for binding the strong man illustrate what I mean:

> A man possessed by an evil spirit came out of the tombs, and no one was ever strong enough to restrain him, even with a chain. He had been secured many times with leg irons and chains, but he broke the chains and smashed the leg irons. No one was tough enough to control him. Night and day in the tombs and the hills, he would howl and cut himself with stones. (Mark 5:2-5)

That was one method—a failure. Then came the commanding word from Jesus, and this picture ensues: "They came to Jesus and saw the man who used to be demon-possessed...sitting there fully dressed and complete sane" (v. 15).

That is an illustration of the two methods of binding the strong man: one from without, a failure; and the other from within, a success. Is the self thus bound by cords of love and loyalty to the new center, Christ, reduced to a nonentity or canceled? No, the self, surrendered to God, is given back to itself. This man who was a torment to himself and others was told by Jesus, "'Go home to your own people...and tell them what the Lord has done for you.'...The man went away and began to proclaim in the Ten Cities all that Jesus had done for him, and everyone was amazed" (vv. 19-20). Here was a man who had been a problem to himself and others, who was now a proclaimer of good news about Jesus and himself. Only to the degree that we surrender ourselves to God does our self come back to us, released and happy and constructive. The deepest law of the universe is this: "Those who find their lives will lose them, and those who lose their lives because of me will find them" (Matt 10:39)—a self we can now live with and love, love because we love something more than ourselves. Love Christ supremely, and you can love yourself subordinately.

O Christ, you are teaching me how to find self-release. I find it at the foot of the cross, where I lay down my life, lay it down to find it again. Amen.

AFFIRMATION FOR THE DAY: I love Christ supremely; now my lesser loves fall into their places.

*Thomas Chalmers, *The Expulsive Power of a New Affection* (1857).

YOU ARE AKIN TO THE DIVINE BUT NOT DIVINE

John 14:16-17

We have been studying how effortlessly the disciples found release from themselves and then found themselves amazingly. They consented to be nothing and became everything.

A question was asked of a religious leader: "I can understand the body and the mind, but what is the spirit?" He replied: "The spirit is the Spirit." He identified the human spirit with the Divine Spirit.

But the New Testament is clear on that point: "The Spirit himself bearing witness with our spirit" (Rom 8:16 RSV). There they are not the same; the Spirit bears witness with our spirit. They are separate entities but deeply akin. If the Holy Spirit and our spirits are the same, then the attitude is self-realization, self-discovery, self-cultivation, self-knowing. But there is no place for self-surrender. There is nothing to surrender to—you are It! If we are not divine, however, but made in the image of the divine and therefore closely akin to it, then, being created, we find our life in self-surrender to the Creator, God. Having freely given the one thing we own, God gives it back to us. The self is realized, realized through renunciation. Try to realize yourself without renouncing yourself. It gives you an initial shot in the arm and makes you feel lifted for the moment, intoxicated by the wine of your own wordy assertion of divinity; but it ends in a letdown and disillusionment. So people wander from one cult to another looking for a new shot and a new boost to their essential egoism. It just doesn't work. But self-surrender, leading to self-realization, does work; and it works to the degree it is tried.

The people of the Acts were free from perplexing personal problems because they had solved the central problem—the problem of what to do with themselves. They solved it by self-surrender. When they consented and cooperated, the Holy Spirit took over their selves, cleansed these selves from selfishness, and then gave them back their selves—adjusted, free, and happy. Someone has said: "Modern man is a problem to himself." These men were not problems to themselves; they were only possibilities.

O Lord, your way is our way. When we take your way, we find our own. When we are most yours, we are most ourselves; bound to you, we are free. Amen.

AFFIRMATION FOR THE DAY: I am made a little less than God; today I shall be a little more like God.

I Do Not Account My Life of Any Value, If only . . .

John 16:32-33

We ended yesterday on the note that these men and women in the Acts were no longer problems to themselves; they were possibilities. They got this way, not by reducing their selves to a vegetable and then calling it victory, but by surrendering themselves to Someone beyond themselves. The moment they did so, they became self-aggressive. It was not an egoistic aggression ending in disruption but an aggression of love ending in a higher harmony. They were not going around apologizing for themselves or despising themselves or suppressing themselves. They accepted themselves—in God, loved themselves—in God, projected themselves—in God, found themselves—in God.

This passage sums up the mastery of self in an acute life situation:

> I am going to Jerusalem bound in the Spirit, not knowing what shall befall me there; except that the Holy Spirit testifies to me in every city that imprisonment and afflictions await me. But I do not account my life of any value nor as precious to myself, if only I may accomplish my course and the ministry which I received from the Lord Jesus, to testify to the gospel of the grace of God. (Acts 20:22-24 RSV)

Note this illuminating portion: "I do not account my life of any value nor as precious to myself, if only I may accomplish my course and the ministry." Paul's self was neither of value nor precious to him except in relation to the cause with which he had identified himself. There you find the secret of self-mastery. He was surrendered to and hence loyal to a cause beyond himself; hence his self dropped into the place for which it was made and became happy and adjusted and free and amazingly useful.

There is no other way to self-mastery. Everything else is an illusion and a snare and ends in a road with a dead end, whether it be religious, psychological, or plainly secular. The Holy Spirit cleansed their selves from selfishness, not merely by abiding within them in order to keep their selves in check, but by dedicating those very selves to the love of Christ and the purposes of the kingdom.

O Christ, I thank you that the way is open—upward. I offer all myself and all the powers of that self to you. Take it, make it, and break it to the multitudes. Amen.

AFFIRMATION FOR THE DAY: I do not account my life of any value, if only I can make it witness to God today.

THAT WHICH HAS BEEN MADE WAS LIFE IN HIM

1 John 5:11-12

Before we leave this subject of the cleansing of the self, we must note a very illuminating passage: "That which has been made was life in him" (John 1:4 RSV margin). Note "that which has been made"; every created thing brought into existence was made "life in him." Mere existence became life when it was in him by surrender to him.

Everything outside of him has mere existence and as such is bound to pass out of existence except as it is placed in him by surrender and consecration. Then it turns into life. Outside of him everything has existence; inside of him everything has life.

Self outside of Christ has existence, which I believe will come to an end; but the moment self is placed in Christ, it becomes life. And to such a quality of being that it must be spelled "Life"—and more, "Eternal Life." Outside of him is nothing but death; inside of him is nothing but Life. Yourself, your money, your talents, your work, your thinking, your loving—when placed in him by surrender become Life. If they stay outside of him, they have the touch of death. No wonder the Epistle to the Ephesians uses "in Christ," or its equivalent, so many times. For Paul saw that in Christ everything turned to life, danced with joy, scintillated with praise, grew amazingly, and was altogether effective.

There is no more beautiful and compelling picture in history—none in the Gospels— than Paul standing before Festus the governor and King Agrippa with Bernice his sister, and all the military tribunes and the prominent men of the city, and exclaiming to the king: "I pray to God that not only you but also all who are listening to me this day will become like me, except for these chains" (Acts 26:29).

This is a prisoner telling the cream of that economic, social, political, and military world, "I could wish nothing higher for you than for you to become like me." Then he adds graciously, "except for these chains." Here was a man bound and yet free, a prisoner gently passing sentence of condemnation upon the court. And the point is that they felt it was true. He had lost himself and had found himself with an amazing authority and self-realization.

O Christ, my Lord, I see that I must make you Lord if I am to find any authority over myself and others. There I shall desire no authority but will have it. Amen.

AFFIRMATION FOR THE DAY: All that I have shall pass from existence to life, for I shall place it in Christ.

CONSECRATED BY THE HOLY SPIRIT

John 17:16-19

We are studying the cleansing of the subconscious when the Holy Spirit moves in. The driving urges—self, sex, the herd—are mastered not by compulsion but by impulsion. A higher loyalty to Jesus as Lord breaks the tyranny of the lower loyalty. This gives us impulses toward the higher loyalty that swallow up the lower loyalties. But they swallow them up in order to assimilate them to higher purposes. The self becomes integrated when it is integrated into something higher than itself; it is cleansed when it is consecrated.

This consecration is made by the Spirit with our consent. We are "consecrated by the holy Spirit" (Rom 15:16 MNT). Jesus also was consecrated by the Spirit: "[Christ] offered himself to God through the eternal Spirit" (Heb 9:14). We often speak of consecrating ourselves to God. And when we do, we find we don't keep consecrated. We do the consecrating and have to stand before the altar, watchfully trying to keep self on the altar. We have to have periodic and continual "consecration meetings" to try to put the recalcitrant self back on the altar. It is a frustrating business. When we once and for all turn self over to the Holy Spirit by consent, then the Spirit, dwelling within, keeps the self and its powers consecrated. That relaxes the inner life. We don't nervously have to keep self on the altar. The Holy Spirit keeps it there by attaching its loyalties and love to Jesus; then out of loyalty and love to Jesus we will go anywhere, do anything, be anything. There is no altar where a helpless, bleeding sacrifice lays. There is nothing but love and glory and thanksgiving for the privilege of giving ourselves. We feel no sacrifice. Sacrifice? What sacrifice have I ever made? I laid at God's feet a self of which I was ashamed, couldn't control, and couldn't live with; to my glad astonishment the Spirit took that self, remade it, consecrated it to kingdom purposes, gave it back to me. Now it is a self I can live with gladly and joyously and comfortably. I've been hugging that self ever since that I had sense enough to give it up to God—the most sensible thing I ever did. For the moment I did, it became life in Christ.

O Gracious Spirit, how grateful I am for this inner relaxed confidence that you are keeping the self in your gracious keeping by keeping it in love with Jesus. Amen.

AFFIRMATION FOR THE DAY: I shall not struggle to keep self on the altar; I shall consent for the Spirit to keep it there.

ON MULLING OVER YOURSELF

John 21:15-17

Before we leave this question of the cleansing of the subconscious in relation to the self, let us look at it once more.

It is good that the instinct of self resides in the subconscious. That is where it should be. That is where it should stay. That produces un–self-consciousness. The Holy Spirit dwelling in the subconscious, cleansing the self from selfishness and consecrating it to purposes of the kingdom of God, is a perfect way to deal with the self.

But take the modern way of thinking about yourself, talking about yourself, picking yourself to pieces, analyzing your motives, trying to reorganize yourself, and mulling over yourself in general. That produces about as many problems as it solves. For it leaves you preoccupied. And that is disruptive. Center yourself on yourself, and yourself will go to pieces. The people who are always trying to regulate their health, paying attention to this, to that, and to the other, have little health to regulate. They upset the rhythm of the body by their very fussy attention. They get "attention pains." Obey the laws of health, get interests outside yourself, and the body will look after itself. It is made that way!

So is the soul. When Dr. David Livingstone came back from Africa, someone asked him about his soul. He replied, "My soul, my soul, I almost forgot I had a soul." He was so interested in the souls of his beloved Africans he almost forgot his own. That was healthy. And the secret was found in his statement, "All I am and all I have, I hold in relation to the kingdom of God."* That released his self from self-interest and turned it toward kingdom-interest.

The self is sufficiently in the conscious mind for us to decide consciously to turn it over to the Holy Spirit in the subconscious. Then hidden in the subconscious, it reveals itself unconsciously in the conscious as a self of blessing and power and influence for the kingdom. It is refreshing to see in the Acts people who were personally problem-less, helping people right and left to solve their problems.

O Holy Spirit, thank you for controlling where we can't control, cleansing where we can't cleanse; and all we have to do is to say yes. Blessed be. Amen.

AFFIRMATION FOR THE DAY: I have no problems, for in Christ all my problems are possibilities.

*No published source was located for these quotations.

THE MASTERY OF SEX

2 Timothy 2:20-22

We have been looking at the cleansing by the Holy Spirit of the first driving urge in the subconscious—the self urge. We must now look at *the mastery of the second—the sex urge.*

We are astonished to find in the Acts not one reference to sex. Women are there, naturally and normally; but there is no emphasis on their sex relationships. Acts is the least sex-conscious book dealing with men and women ever written. Women are there receiving the Holy Spirit, prophesying like the men, being raised from the dead, holding prayer meetings in their homes as with Mary, receiving Paul and his company as guests as with Lydia, becoming converts as with the prominent women in Thessalonica; but not one sex question is raised. Paul takes up the question of sex in the local churches such as Corinth in his epistles, but in the Acts there is a strange silence. This is the more strange since Paul spent a great deal of time at Corinth, which in an age notoriously loose in sex was especially loose, for the saying of the time, "he lives like a Corinthian" revealed the condition. Then why didn't sex creep into the Acts?

The fact is Jesus said little about sex. Only four references to it are in the four Gospels: "Every man who looks at a woman lustfully has already committed adultery in his heart" (Matt 5:28). "Whoever divorces his wife except for sexual unfaithfulness forces her to commit adultery. And whoever marries a divorced woman commits adultery" (Matt 5:32). "It's from the inside, from the human heart, that evil thoughts come: sexual sins,...adultery,...unrestrained immorality" (Mark 7:21-22). And the woman taken in adultery (John 8:1-11). The Acts omits it altogether. Why? Was sex taboo? No, for Paul deals with it plainly in his epistles. Was it suppressed? Apparently not, for the relationships between men and women were natural and normal.

Apparently this had happened: the men and women in the Acts had become so preoccupied with the Holy Spirit and the Spirit's work within them and around them that sex was relegated to the margin.

They were released from sex tensions by Spirit attention.

O Spirit Divine, become so real in me and around me that you occupy the center of attention. Then all else will fall into its place, subordinate, and I shall be free. Amen.

AFFIRMATION FOR THE DAY: I shall master sex attention by Spirit attention.

99

SEX MASTERY BY KINGDOM MASTERY

1 Corinthians 6:9-11

We saw yesterday that the Acts of the Apostles hasn't a single sex reference in it, yet men and women mingled freely. And we saw that the probable reason was that in an age obsessed with sex they had found a new obsession. They became obsessed with the Holy Spirit and the Spirit's work in human lives. The higher obsession absorbed the lower obsession into itself.

That is an eminently sane solution. The attempt to get rid of the dominance of sex desire by repression ends only in the desire coming back stronger. A hermit of India told me he had not looked on the face of a woman for forty years. It was the first thing he told me! Evidently it was uppermost in his mind. For forty years he had been running away from sex and turned round, and the first thing he thought of was sex. I saw a group of *sadhus* trying to murder sex desire by mutilating their sex organs, and you could see they were obsessed with sex. The attempt to get rid of all desire, as in Buddhism, results only in another desire, namely, the desire to get rid of desire. It was said of Immanuel Kant, the philosopher, that when he dismissed his coachman, Henry, and was troubled about the dismissal, he put up two signs at the place where he walked up and down in philosophic meditation: "Don't think of Henry." The attempt to do so only brought Henry back into mind!

The modern solution is to think of sex frankly and openly. But that too is just as great a failure as suppression. For as I've had to say again and again, whatever gets your attention gets you. Sex gets the attention of the modern man and woman, and it gets them. They become sex-obsessed, and therefore get the least out of sex, except disillusionment. The lust turns to disgust. This isn't chance; it's law, inherent law. The people who pay most attention to sex get the least out of it.

Sex must find its place if it is to find itself. And its place is not first place. God is God—not sex. Sex trying to be God ends in frustration instead of in fruitfulness. God intended it to be fruitful. How?

O Lord, you have written your laws within us. We thank you for them. For your laws are your preventive grace, preventing us from hurting ourselves and others. Amen.

AFFIRMATION FOR THE DAY: Sex will not master me, for Christ already has the mastery of me.

100

THE FOUR USES OF SEX

1 Corinthians 7:32-35

Just how did it happen that the book most filled with the Spirit of God is the book least filled with the problems of self and sex? Is it cause and effect? Yes.

What is the remedy for the dominance of sex urges within us? We cannot act as though they are not there. They are in every normal person, and they are an integral part of us and intended to be. We cannot ignore them; they come back stronger or disguised as various neuroses or illnesses. You cannot suppress them by sheer willpower and strength. Like a suppressed spring the reaction is stronger than ever.

These people got rid of sex dominance not by tense striving but effortlessly They did with sex what they did with self: they surrendered it to God. Then God took it over, not by sitting on a throne and ordering sex to be subservient, but by coming into the subconscious and taking over sex at its source. The Holy Spirit is God working within and in the deepest within—the subconscious. There the Spirit doesn't deal with the manifestations of sex, but with sex itself. God takes it over, cleanses sex from sexuality. Sexuality is perversion, perversion of the natural to the unnatural. The Spirit cleanses from perversion and brings sex back to its intended uses—intended by the Creator. These uses are four: (1) Sex was intended to help us to love; (2) through that love to set up a home. That home is intended primarily for fellowship. Sex when used properly augments that fellowship. (3) Procreation, which in turn produces the love of parents for a child; (4) for creative activity within the home or apart from it. The sex urge is the creative urge. It can physically create, or it can spiritually create, or both.

Suppose one has no home with a life partner, is he frustrated? Hardly. The two men who left the greatest creative impact on human living in any age, anywhere, were Jesus and Paul. They were both without homes, both unmarried. They weren't querulous, crotchety, frustrated; they were adjusted and creative, amazingly so. So the sex urge can be creative apart from and beyond physical manifestation.

O Lord, I thank you that you have provided for continuous creation through us, making us creative clear up to the end of life, and beyond. I thank you. Amen.

AFFIRMATION FOR THE DAY: My creative urges will become more creative because surrendered to the Creator.

THIS SEEMED MORE IMPORTANT

Acts 19:18-20

What had happened to lift this whole account in the Acts above sex preoccupation? Evidently it was the Holy Spirit. The Holy Spirit brought such a deep emotional satisfaction that the emotions of sex were pushed to the margin. A stronger and more satisfying emotion occupied the center.

"Mary," of whom I have written in *Growing Spiritually*, illustrates this; for she went through the experience of being filled with the Spirit. She was aglow with it. The doctor had said that there must be an operation to remove a cyst. She wrote me after seeing the doctor, at which meeting it was to be finally decided whether there was to be an operation. But she didn't mention the matter. When I wrote asking about it, she replied: "Oh, I forgot to tell you the doctor said: 'No operation.' I forgot to tell you, for I seemed so preoccupied with this glorious coming of the Holy Spirit that this seemed more important." That is exactly what happened in the Acts: "this"—the coming of the Holy Spirit—seemed more important.

But the sex urge was not eliminated or suppressed; it was expressed on another level. The sex urge, or the creative urge, was expressed in creating faith, hope, new spiritually born souls, new movements, new life in general. The Holy Spirit, who is the Creative Spirit, was now creating on the highest level, the level of remaking human personality. God, who in the beginning of creation had brooded over chaos and brought cosmos out of it, was now doing the same on another level. The Spirit was brooding over the chaos and darkness of human personality and producing the cosmos of changed, coordinated, harmonious human living. But this time the Spirit was creating through created beings—a cooperative endeavor. And God was doing it through the sex urge, which had been converted to creation on a higher level. This was more than sublimation, as psychology uses it, it was creation. Sublimation is "to divert the primitive urges." This was to convert these urges into the higher creation. The human personality was never more fulfilled than in this creation.

O Spirit of God, you have brought us to our own fulfillment when you take the lower urges and turn them into the highest uses. I glow to your purposes. Amen.

AFFIRMATION FOR THE DAY: My primitive urges will be not diverted but directed to higher creative ends.

EROS PASSES INTO *AGAPE*

John 15:12-13, 17

Humanity comes to its highest fulfillment through the sex urges, the creative urges, when those urges are turned by the Holy Spirit within into creation on the moral and spiritual level. This means that the urges—which when given the reins and used in the purposes of selfish impulses can make human beings lower than the beasts—can now under the direction and impulses of the Spirit make human beings higher than the angels, can make us share the very creative activity of God. We rise highest through the lowest.

And it does something else. It allows the Holy Spirit to fulfill his purpose in creation. The Spirit was able to create matter into higher forms, but not able to create spirit into higher forms except here and there through an occasional opening. But now the Holy Spirit found an instrument of higher creation: a group of one hundred twenty surrendered, responsive spirits. And God created through them an epitome of the new order—the kingdom of God amid human society.

We do not know the mysteries of the divine nature, for instance, whether God can come to a deeper self-fulfillment; but certainly the Holy Spirit, who is God in action, came to a deeper fulfillment in purpose in creating this higher humanity and, through them, a new order: the kingdom of God. The Spirit, who created the creative urge, the sex urge, saw that urge come to its highest fulfillment in creating new spiritual persons, new purposes, new hopes, a new order.

Sex, which was *eros*, or sex love, until the Spirit took over, now became *agape*, or divine creative love. Love was cleansed of sexuality. It began to function through sex into higher creation. It is said in Heb 9:19, "Moses took the blood...and sprinkled both the Law scroll itself and all the people." The Law was cleansed, signifying that it needed to be cleansed and made into Love. That happened in Christ. Law was no longer mere law; it was Love. So sex was sprinkled by the atonement of Jesus and cleansed and made into the most creative force ever let loose upon our planet. It functioned as creative love. And there is nothing, absolutely nothing, more potent and creative than creative love.

O Holy Spirit, thank you for taking hold of our lowest and making it into the highest, our basest and making it into the best, our clay and making it into a temple. Amen.

AFFIRMATION FOR THE DAY: My lowest can become your highest by surrender to your highest.

FOUR POSSIBLE ATTITUDES
TOWARD THE HERD

1 John 2:15-17

We now pass to another of the primitive urges which were taken over and cleansed and made into construction. We have looked at the mastery of self urge and the sex urge, and now we must look at *the third—the herd urge, or the social urge.*

When we turn to the Acts to see what happened to the herd urge, we are struck with the fact that only in the people not in the Christian movement did the herd urge seem to be the dominating motive and influence. Within the movement itself the power of the herd urge was broken, or better still, was fastened upon a higher society, the kingdom of God. Note the places where the herd was dominant: "Herod...had James, John's brother, killed with a sword. When he saw that this pleased the Jews, he arrested Peter as well" (Acts 12:1-3). The herd instinct decided his conduct. And "Since Felix wanted to grant a favor to the Jews, he left Paul in prison" (24:27). The conduct of these high officials was determined by desire to please the herd.

When we look around and within, we see how many things are done because others do them. A woman was losing her husband, their marriage was drifting on the rocks, and over a small matter—red fingernails. Someone remonstrated with the woman and suggested that if the husband didn't like red fingernails, why not give them up? The wife's reply was, "How can I? Everybody does it." That settled it; husband or no husband she would have to do what society silently decreed. "Everybody does it" is perhaps the most powerful incentive for conduct now operative in human affairs.

We can take these possible attitudes toward the herd: (1) We can try to run away from it. But that makes the unsocial type. (2) We can stay within it and fight it. But that makes the pugnacious, cantankerous type, *agin'* everything. (3) We can stay within the herd and surrender to it. But that makes the echo, the nonentity, the zero. (4) We can do with the herd urge what we do with the self urge and the sex urge: we can surrender it to God. That makes for inner freedom yet sends us back into the herd constructively. The disciples did just that.

O Lord God, I bow my knee to nothing but you. I want to be free—free to love only you supremely. Free there, I shall be free to love everyone freely. In Jesus' name. Amen.

AFFIRMATION FOR THE DAY: Emancipated from the herd, I shall go more deeply into it and love it.

SO DIFFERENT THAT THEY MADE A DIFFERENCE

Matthew 5:13-16

We have been thinking about how many things we do on account of the herd instinct. I write this on September 13, a week after Labor Day; and that is the day when all straw hats are supposed to disappear and be replaced by felt hats. I still have mine on as I sit in this railway station. For the life of me I can't help feeling "different," out of step. I laugh at it as silly, but nevertheless it is there. Many succumb to this herd pressure, not only in such trivial matters as wearing straw hats, but in the matter of morals and behavior and life directions. They succumb to a gray, average conformity. They conform, hence do not create.

But the disciples were different, so different that they made a difference. They began to be so creative that they ushered in the mightiest revolution in human affairs this planet has ever seen. They broke with the lower order because they gave themselves to a higher order, the kingdom of God. They surrendered the herd to God. They were no longer supremely loyal to it. They fastened the herd instinct upon the highest order, the kingdom of God. That broke the power of the lower loyalty—the expulsive power of a new affection. This difference of loyalty made such a difference that when people saw the resultant radiance and happiness, some sneered: "They're full of new wine" (Acts 2:13). They dismissed it as a lower manifestation of living. Others thought it dangerous, because different, and tried to suppress it by threats and force: "They threatened them further, then released them. Because of public support for Peter and John, they couldn't find a way to punish them" (Acts 4:21). Note "because of public support." Those under the dominance of the herd didn't know what to do with those under the dominance of Christ and his kingdom. The disciples' reply to the command not to speak in this name was simple, "It's up to you to determine whether it's right before God to obey you rather than God. As for us, we can't stop speaking about what we have seen and heard" (Acts 4:19-20). They had slipped out from under the dominance of the herd and were baffling to those still under its dominance. You cannot escape, struggle with, or succumb to the herd—you must surrender it to God.

O Lord, to get free from the herd we must be bound to you in a supreme loyalty. Obeying you we can bend the knee to nothing else. Then we stand straight. Amen.

AFFIRMATION FOR THE DAY: I will love people with the emancipating love of Christ.

SOCIAL AND YET SOLITARY

Ephesians 2:1-5

As has been pointed out, we cannot escape the herd by running away from it physically or by retreating inwardly in spiritual isolation; nor can we stay in it and fight it by being always on the defensive, taking a negative attitude toward everything it stands for or proposes; nor can we succumb to it, for if we do, we become a herd-centered person with all personality and morality flattened out of us. The only Christian attitude we can take is to surrender the herd to God.

Does that mean that we live in God apart from the herd? No, it means that we go more deeply into the herd, but now we go in emancipated. Our inmost souls are cleansed from herd dominance. It has been replaced by God dominance. God is Lord, not the herd. Now emancipated, we can love the herd, because we love something more than the herd. It falls into its right place. This keeps us social and yet keeps us solitary. We have a solitary supreme loyalty, and yet we have a secondary social loyalty to the herd.

This relationship is seen in the commission of Paul, "I will rescue you from your own people and from the Gentiles. I am sending you to open their eyes" (Acts 26:17-18a). He was sent to people, therefore social; but he was delivered from people, therefore inwardly solitary. You cannot serve people unless you are delivered from people. For instance, if you are a pastor under the dominance of the herd, afraid of what they will say about you or think of you, you are tied up and unable to contribute to them. Only as you walk out of your solitude, where you have bent the knee to God supremely, are you able to stand straight and unafraid and relaxed before people. Now you can see straight horizontally, because you have first seen straight vertically. Now you can pour out your emancipated love to people, for you have a hidden shrine within where you bend the knee only to the Lord. Only free one can make others free.

The Christians in the Acts were inwardly free—free from the herd—therefore able to change and give to the herd. And how!

O Lord, I thank you that only as I become intensely solitary, can I be intensely social. Cleansed of a thousand conflicting loyalties, I can now give and give freely. Amen.

AFFIRMATION FOR THE DAY: "They say...; what will they say? Just let them say."

MANIFESTATIONS OF A CLEANSED SUBCONSCIOUS

2 Corinthians 4:2-6

We have seen that the disciples were cleansed at the place of the subconscious by the Holy Spirit. How do we know that? Well, of course, only by implication. We see that the driving urges—self, sex, and the herd—that reside in the subconscious mind were now functioning constructively and redemptively and freely. We therefore imply that some power is working in the subconscious. That power is obviously the Holy Spirit. Jesus said, "you will know them by their fruit" (Matt 7:20). And by their fruit we know these men and women. They were not tense, anxious, strained, holding down something within. They were free, joyous, and natural. They were "letting nature caper."

Take this passage as revealing the amazing steadiness of the inner life of these Christians: "They had them beaten. They ordered them not to speak in the name of Jesus, then let them go. The apostles left the council rejoicing because they had been regarded as worthy to suffer disgrace for the sake of the name. Every day they continued to teach and proclaim the good news that Jesus is the Christ, both in the temple and in houses" (Acts 5:40-42). Note the victory at the place of self: "they had them beaten. . . . The apostles left . . . rejoicing." Not resentful or full of self-pity, they left "rejoicing because they had been regarded as worthy to suffer disgrace for the sake of the name." The self was under divine control. Take the sex, or creative, instinct: "They continued to teach and proclaim the good news that Jesus is the Christ." Pressure and threats could not suppress the creative urge. Take the herd urge: they "ordered them not to speak. . . . Every day they continued . . . both in the temple and in houses." They were entirely emancipated from the herd pressure represented in the council.

How could these men be so free in the outer manifestations if they were not free in the inner? The manifestations were cleansed, so we must take it for granted that the men were cleansed. So we are driven to the conclusion that the Holy Spirit had cleansed, coordinated, and consecrated the subconscious.

O Holy Spirit, you cleanser of the depths, we offer to you now our depths for you to cleanse. Brood over our depths and bring order and harmony out of them. Amen.

AFFIRMATION FOR THE DAY: Out of my good store—my cleansed subconscious—I shall bring forth good.

MASTERY OF THE ART OF WITNESSING FOR CHRIST

1 Thessalonians 1:2-8

We have seen one thing as permanent in the coming of the Holy Spirit: the cleansing of the heart. And the "heart" included the subconscious. We come now to the second permanent thing: *power to witness for Christ.*

Jesus said, "Rather, you will receive power when the Holy Spirit has come upon you, and you will be my witnesses in Jerusalem, in all Judea and Samaria, and to the end of the earth" (Acts 1:8). Here was something permanent that would persist from Jerusalem to the end of the earth, namely, the power to be his witnesses. The first permanent thing was purity; the second was power. Purity for myself, power for others; these two constitute my real needs for successful spiritual living.

But note the power offered here is not "power"—full stop. It is power of a particular kind—the power to be witnesses for Christ. As long as we witness to him, the power is operative. But if we begin to witness to ourselves, our denominations, our groups, then the power is turned off. Many of us want power so we can become prominent and important through that power. So the power never comes. It eludes us. For God withholds it. Only when we begin to witness to Jesus, does the power begin to flow. Then channels are open. God can give all out when we are holding up Jesus. For that is what God witnesses to, "This is my Son, my chosen one. Listen to him!" (Luke 9:35). When we and God witness to the same thing, then the power of God is available for us. It was said of Stephen: "They couldn't resist the wisdom the Spirit gave him as he spoke" (Acts 6:10). The translators just could not translate the "Spirit" with a small *s*, for it wasn't Stephen's spirit; it was the Holy Spirit speaking through Stephen's spirit. And his hearers were nonplussed at this Plus.

"What did you learn at the Ashram?" someone asked of "Mary," and she replied: "I learned that people argue with the 'Mary' spirit, but they don't argue with the Jesus Spirit." This is power. Apart from this we represent powerlessness.

O Lord, make my eye single that I will see Jesus only, my heart cleansed that I love him supremely, my tongue bold to speak of him only. Amen.

AFFIRMATION FOR THE DAY: Only as I am linked with God's purposes, can I expect God's power.

THE TWO GROUPS OF TWELVE

Acts 19:1-7

We are studying the second permanent thing in the coming of the Holy Spirit. The first was purity, and the second was power—power to witness effectively for Christ. Some speak dead truth with no kindling, converting power.

The difference between a group with power and a group without power is seen in the two groups of twelve—the twelve apostles and the group of twelve at Ephesus (see Acts 19:7). The twelve apostles were part of a movement turning the world upside down. The Ephesian group of twelve were turning nothing upside down. They were noncontagious, huddling together for protective purposes. Paul sensed a lack in them, and asked them point blank, "Did you receive the Holy Spirit when you came to believe?" (Acts 19:2). They replied in words that many modern Christians could use, "We've not even heard that there is a Holy Spirit" (v. 2). A Holy Spiritless Christianity is Christianity without witness and without power. It lacks the vital spark. Nothing happens.

Then the Holy Spirit came upon these twelve at Ephesus, and things did begin to happen. "Many of those who had come to believe came, confessing their past practices. This included a number of people who practiced sorcery." Suppose believers today would come confessing and divulging their practices! A revival would be on! "They collected their sorcery texts and burned them publicly. The value of those materials was calculated at more than someone might make if they worked for one hundred sixty-five years." (Acts 19:18, 19). When the real thing came, they couldn't tolerate the spurious. When people are out of touch with God, they will turn to half-gods, any superstition that will get them in touch with anything beyond themselves. For people want God.

This summed up what had happened, "In this way the Lord's word grew abundantly and strengthened powerfully" (v. 20). Here was the power of contagion, the power to change men and situations. Here was mastery. The difference came when the Holy Spirit came. The spiritual desert began to blossom as a rose. Life was bursting into meaning and power—power to win.

O Holy Spirit, touch the barrenness of our hearts into life and bud and flower and fruit. Make us fruitful through you. Then will be fulfilled your purposes and our persons. Amen.

AFFIRMATION FOR THE DAY: I will belong to the Ephesus "twelve" after the coming of the Spirit—adequate.

THE MASTERY OF DISUNITY

1 Corinthians 3:1-4

We have come to see that there were two permanent factors in the coming of the Holy Spirit—purity and power. We come now to a third, in five parts; first—*an amazing unity with God.*

Wherever life is self-centered, there centrifugal forces are at work, and life tends to fly apart. Where there is egoistic aggression, there division takes place automatically. But where there is the aggressiveness of love, there life tends to come together. Love unifies, and egoism divides. These disciples had surrendered their egoism to God, and the result was that an amazing unity came into being—a unity that extended from the inner life clear out into racial and material relations. They found what Paul calls the "unity of the Spirit" (Eph 4:3). That unity of the Spirit wasn't just a sense of oneness in a small group, as we sometimes think; it was a unifying principle and power that tended to bring all life into a living unity and coherence.

We will now note the mastery of the centrifugal forces in favor of the centripetal. The first unity was a unity with God. "They were all filled with the Holy Spirit" (Acts 2:4). The Holy Spirit is God, intimate and within. They and God were no longer at cross-purposes. Every area of their lives had been brought under the will of God by self-surrender. God had them. And what God has, God fills and empowers. When they thought of God, they did not think of conflict but of concord. There were no leftover issues between them and God. The relationship was comfortable, with a sense of at-homeness. They had settled down in God. God could count on them, and they could count on God; the mutuality was complete.

But it was a mutuality; they were not submerged in God, nor did God override them. God was God, and they were they; but Person flowed into person, Will into will, Mind into mind, and they could scarcely tell where they ended and God began. God was closer than the blood in their veins and nearer than their own heartbeats. If they should reach out to touch God, they would reach too far.

O Indwelling Spirit, I thank you that we can think the same thoughts, feel the same feelings, will the same purposes, and become the same being. Amen.

AFFIRMATION FOR THE DAY: Today I shall be God-infused and therefore God-enthused.

UNITY WITHIN THE PERSONAL SELF

Ephesians 4:11-13

We have looked at the first unity that came into being with the coming of the Holy Spirit—unity with God. The second unity was *unity within the personal self.* "And they were all filled with the holy Spirit...[and] began...to express themselves" (Acts 2:4 MNT). Now they could "express themselves," for they had selves they could express. They were unified within. And unified within, they could express themselves without. Why were they unified within? Because they belonged to Another and not to themselves. Belonging to Another, they now began to belong to themselves. That is the inflexible paradox. They could live with themselves because they could live with God. If you won't live with God, you can't live with yourself. But if you do live with God without conflict, you can live with yourself without conflict.

You are no longer fighting with yourself. All self-hate and self-rejection are gone. You can love yourself now because you love something more than yourself. Self-hate is as bad as other-hate. Christianity delivers us from both. It makes you love yourself as you love your neighbor, Not less and not more but "as."

The cults of self-expression try to make you express yourself while still centered in the self. That makes for artificiality and artfulness. A young man who had tried self-expression, trying to put on an ingratiating smile, found the real thing through self-surrender. Then a real smile came. He laughingly said, "I felt the corners of my mouth twitching nervously after I ceased putting on an artificial smile." It was twitching from habit even after the artificial attempt to smile had been taken away. Now he could smile from the inside out; before he was attempting to smile from the outside in. Unnatural expression! When the Holy Spirit took over the group on the day of Pentecost, they could express themselves naturally because they expressed themselves supernaturally. In God they were themselves. Now they expressed themselves artlessly. They had natural joy, natural self-expression, because they were naturalized in God. They had selves they could express—beautiful selves.

O Lord, I thank you that I can be at home with you and with myself. My life's music is now no longer off key; it is on key, and it plays divine music through a human instrument. Amen.

AFFIRMATION FOR THE DAY: All self-hate, self-rejection, are gone. I gladly accept myself—in God.

UNITY AMID THE INTIMATE BODY OF DISCIPLES

John 17:20-23

We have seen the second unity that came with the coming of the Holy Spirit—unity within the person. That leads us to the third unity—*a unity amid the body of immediate disciples—the twelve.*

They had not always been unified. They found themselves at cross-purposes again and again. They disputed over who should be first, and two of them tried to pull an inside deal by which they would get seats on the right and left of Jesus in his kingdom. "Jesus knew the dispute that occupied their minds" (Luke 9:47 MNT). What a lovely thing to occupy the minds of disciples on the way to Jerusalem and to the cross! Their outer lives were united around a common loyalty to Jesus, but their inner lives were far apart, divided by self-interests and jealousies. Then came the Holy Spirit, and their inner lives were fused into a "unity of the Spirit."

This unity is seen in this statement: "Peter stood with the other eleven apostles" (Acts 2:14). Before he had stood against the eleven; now he stood "with" them. The difference was so real that Luke noted it and used not "among," as he did before the coming of the Holy Spirit (Acts 1:15) but the more intimate "with."

The critical attitude gave way to the cooperative attitude. Not only were they one in purpose, they were one in person. Their very inner lives had a common basis, the Holy Spirit.

It is not easy to have unity with those who are in the same field with us. Ministers tend to be critical of ministers, professors of professors, politicians of politicians. It is easier to be unified with those who are not competing with us. It is mastery when we are. This mastery came through two things: they were mastered by a common loyalty to the kingdom of God and by a common life within—the Holy Spirit. So the outer loyalty to the kingdom and the inner life of the Spirit brought unity among a difficult group to unify. Without those two things—outer loyalty and inner life—life remains apart, divided.

O Holy Spirit, quicken our common loyalty to the kingdom and quicken our life in the Spirit that we may have an unbreakable unity with those who compete in the same field. Amen.

AFFIRMATION FOR THE DAY: Loyalty to the kingdom, life of the Spirit, these two things shall unify me with others.

THE UNITY OF ALL BELIEVERS

John 17:7-11

We have seen the unity amid immediate disciples through the coming of the Holy Spirit. We come now to the fourth, a larger unity, *the unity of all believers*. "All the believers were united and shared everything" (Acts 2:44).

All the believers kept together. Today all the believers keep separate. I am writing this in a town of two thousand people, Pembroke, North Carolina; and there are ten churches within the town and seventeen pastors living within its precincts. All are Christians with a common loyalty to Christ and working for the same purpose, the kingdom of God. But nothing binds them together. They are more or less competing with one another, dividing the community at the place of its deepest loyalty, its spiritual loyalty. Moreover, they are canceling one another out. Each has to magnify its minute points of difference to justify its separate existence. There is no sense of solidarity among the Christians. They are not primarily Christians; they are primarily Baptist, Methodist, Presbyterian, Pentecostal, and whatnot. The emphasis is upon the marginal differences instead of upon the central fact, Christ. They have no sense of solidarity as Christians.

And this in the face of world corporate evils, such as Communism. When Eisenhower was about to invade Europe, he turned to his aides and said, "It's one team, or we lose." Again for us "it is one team, or we lose." For a divided church is no match for a united Communism. The next great step is for the churches to get together outwardly. Inwardly, Christians are one. We share a common life. We don't have to seek for unity; we have it—have it in the deepest thing in life, namely, in life itself. We share the life of Christ in common. The church then is at once the most united body on earth and the most divided. We are united at the center and divided at the margin, united in Christ and divided in the expression of Christ. But we have unity; all we have to do is to express it. These early Christians had unity, and they expressed it. Therefore they hit that ancient world with power.

O Christ, we know that those who belong to you belong to one another automatically and inescapably. Help us to recognize, rejoice in, and act on that unity. Amen.

AFFIRMATION FOR THE DAY: I am united with every Christian by unities deeper than the differences that divide.

UNITY BETWEEN FORMER ENEMIES

Romans 12:17-21

We are studying the unities that come into being with the coming of the Holy Spirit. We come now to the fifth unity—*the unity with enemies.*

When Peter and these Spirit-filled followers of Christ faced the multitudes in front of them on that great day of the coming of the Spirit, they faced people whose hands were red with the blood of their Master. Were they filled with a desire for revenge and retaliation? Did their resentments boil? Or did they bridge that gulf of hate and bitterness? They bridged it, and apparently they did it effortlessly. It is done so gently that we scarcely see anything happening. But something did happen and something very important. They mastered evil with good, mastered hate by love, mastered the world by a cross. And they did it so graciously.

Note: "Brothers and sisters, I can speak confidently. . . . I know you acted in ignorance. So did your rulers" (Acts 2:29; 3:17). Calling the murderers of Jesus "brothers and sisters"! That was magnanimous. And in saying to them, "I know you acted in ignorance," they echoed the prayer of their Master on the cross: "Father, forgive them; for they know not what they do" (Luke 23:34 RSV). They had caught the spirit of their Master and were applying it in a very acute situation. Gone was the spirit of wanting to call down fire from heaven on those who wouldn't receive them; gone was the drawing of the sword to cut off right ears. They were actually doing what he told them to do: "Love your enemies." And the result? Good will begat good will. The conscience-stricken multitudes responded in kind, "When the crowd heard this, they were deeply troubled. They said to Peter and the other the apostles, 'Brothers, what should we do?'" (Acts 2:37). When Peter called them "brothers and sisters," these former enemies responded and said "brothers." Like produced like. Hate produces hate; love produces love. When they turned their enemies into friends and then into brothers, there was produced the greatest close-knit fellowship the world has ever seen—the *koinonia*—the fellowship. And this fellowship was made out of former enemies.

O Lord, we thank you for this miracle of love. Help us to show the power of that miracle day by day in all our relationships, beginning with the next person. Amen.

AFFIRMATION FOR THE DAY: Today I shall have no enemies, for I shall have no enmity. It is simple.

THE MASTERY OF THE ECONOMIC

Matthew 20:9-16

We come now to discuss the sixth unity, which is so breathtaking that it is embarrassing—*the unity in the economic.*

This unity is described in these words:

> All the believers were united and shared everything. They would sell pieces of property and possessions and distribute the proceeds to everyone who needed them.....
>
> The community of believers was one in heart and mind. None of them would say, "This is mine!" about any of their possessions, but held everything in common....There were no needy persons among them....[Proceeds from the sales of properties] was distributed to anyone who was in need. (Acts 2:44-45; 4:32-35)

When we come to this description of the earliest Christian society, we take a mental vault and skip it, or we explain it away as an interim ethic. Jesus was returning soon, so why keep possessions? They were given away in the light of the near coming of Jesus to set up his kingdom. This is the usual explanation. But that explanation overlooks two facts: one, that the return of Christ is not mentioned in connection with the distribution of goods; the other, that this unity in the economic was the direct outcome of the coming of the Holy Spirit. It is set in the framework of the coming of the Holy Spirit and not in the framework of the coming again of Jesus. It was based on a spiritual experience. They were one in spirit, why not one in the material? Life was held together as a whole. They refused to compartmentalize it. Were they wrong? If so, then it casts doubt on the whole spiritual experience in back of it.

It is possible, however, for them to be fundamentally right and yet wrong in the interpretation and application of that experience. I believe that happened. They were right in seeing that distribution should be according to need. They were wrong in thinking that having all things in common was the method of providing distribution according to need. They were fundamentally right and marginally wrong.

O Lord, help us to see your truth amid irrelevancies. Help us to face your truth, for only your truth can make us free. We need to be free. Amen.

AFFIRMATION FOR THE DAY: I will sift fundamental truth from marginal error, for I would be fundamentally right.

WHY HAS COMMUNISM FAILED?

Galatians 6:1-5

We have seen that the unity in material goods was founded on a truth and a wrong application of that truth. I am persuaded they were fundamentally right in seeing that distribution should be according to need, but wrong in thinking that the method of achieving that distribution was the method of having all things in common.

This method of having all things in common has been tried here and there through the ages. It has invariably failed after being sincerely tried. The Christian church tried it for three centuries. One of the church fathers in the third century could say, "We have everything in common except our wives."* Then it faded out. But it has come back again in many places in all ages. In India we tried it for a time in the Ashram at Sat Tal and Lucknow. It produced a wonderful fellowship, but as an experiment in communal living it failed. In the present day it is seen in the Amish and the Bruederhoef Mennonite settlements. Why have they failed to make any significant contribution to human living? And why have the Communists of Russia and China and elsewhere hesitated to apply the pure form of Communism? They say they are in the stage of state socialism but only on the way to Communism. And to make their state socialism work, they have to appeal to personal incentives by offering extra income for extra effort. Why do Communistic communities or states begin with a big spurt and then ultimately break down or slow down and become sterile, without driving force? Is it because Communism is appealing to one urge—the social urge—and fails to awaken and appeal to the personal urge? People apparently cannot live by the social urge alone. Bees can. But we are not bees. So human society cannot be a hive where only the social urge is at work. Nor can we live in a society where the drive is, "every man for himself and the devil take the hindmost!" Not only does the devil take the hindmost, but all. We are feeling after something beyond an anthill and a prize ring.

O Lord, guide our steps toward your order, your plan for humanity. We know you have a plan, and that plan will be good and good for us. Help us to find it. Amen.

AFFIRMATION FOR THE DAY: My life shall be a blend, an equal blend, of the personal and social urges.

*Attributed to Tertullian.

BEYOND INDIVIDUALISM AND COMMUNISM: THE KINGDOM

2 Corinthians 9:6-10

We saw yesterday that purely Communistic societies fail or slow down and become stagnant. Why? Because there are two urges in human nature: the egoistic (personal) and the altruistic (social). Both of them have to be held in a living blend and, further, in a living balance. The Christian faith puts them in a living balance—"You shall love your neighbor [altruistic] as yourself [egoistic]" (Matt 19:19 RSV). Note the "as"—exactly balanced.

Communism is a half-truth; it forgets that life is individual and personal. Individualism is also a half-truth; it forgets that life is social. There is something beyond each—the Christian order—where you love your neighbor as you love yourself. The meaning of the world crisis is apparently this: Something beyond Communism and beyond individualism is struggling to be born, God's order, the kingdom of God. We swing from one to the other, oscillating between Communism and individualism. We will probably come to equilibrium at the kingdom of God.

Let us note that the communism of the Acts was quite different from modern Marxist Communism. The early Christian type was voluntary and spiritual. Peter said to Ananias, who had kept back a part of the price of land sold, "Wasn't that property yours to keep? After you sold it, wasn't the money yours to do with whatever you wanted?" (Acts 5:4). This showed that sharing of goods was voluntary. There was no compulsion or expulsion, if goods were shared. This is quite different from the compulsory Communism of the present day.

Also, while it was set off as a distinct type, it failed for two obvious reasons: first, it was only partially applied, namely, to distribution and not to production. They gave away what they had, so they were soon poor, and collections had to be taken for the "poor among the saints" at Jerusalem. Second, even if it had been applied to production as well as to distribution, it would have failed ultimately, for it appealed to only one urge—the social urge. Life built on that half-truth was based on an insufficient foundation, and hence it broke down. Yet it had a very great truth wrapped up in it; that truth is alive today.

Dear Lord, give us insight to see your mind and your purpose. For you are intent on redeeming people and nations. When we see light, may we walk in it. Amen.

AFFIRMATION FOR THE DAY: I will have insight to see God's pointings, and I will follow those pointings.

DISTRIBUTION ACCORDING TO NEED

Luke 19:28-34

We saw yesterday that communisms, secular and religious, apparently break down after a certain length of trial. God apparently does not intend that they should succeed, so they break down, frustrated.

But what is the truth—the very great truth—at the heart of this Christian experiment in the first century? I believe it to be this: distribution according to need (Acts 2:45; 4:34-35). Is that the basis on which economic goods should be distributed? I believe it is. We need what we need, not more than we need or less than we need. Need is written across our bodies. If we eat less than we need, we are unhealthy. But if we eat more than we need, again we are unhealthy.

Someone has said that we live off half we eat, and the doctor lives off the other half. But need is not merely written across our personal bodies; it is written across the body of society. Two of my friends are in charge of the problem children of certain cities, one in Canada and one in America. They give exactly the same conclusions. In both cities there are three economic classes: 25 percent below the privilege line, 25 percent above the privilege line, and 50 percent in the middle class. Invariably the problem children come from classes below the privilege line and from classes above the privilege line. Apparently too little produces problem children, and too much also produces problem children. I picked up my morning paper one day, and the headlines told of the arrest of the heir to millions, arrested for possession of narcotics. His accompanying picture was pathetic, the face of a man on skid row. If I have tears—bitter tears—for the underprivileged, I just as bitter tears for the overprivileged. All incentive to struggle and achieve is taken away, and they have nothing to do but spend unearned millions, become playboys and playgirls, play with fire and get burned.

The normal and adjusted children come out of the middle classes, where they do not have too little or too much. Is God speaking to us here at the place of the economic, and is God's voice unmistakable?

O God, our Lord, you are speaking and speaking plainly. Help us to listen and to heed. For if we cross your mind, we get hurt, invariably and inexorably. Amen.

AFFIRMATION FOR THE DAY: The right to receive according to need was apparently basic then and is now.

THE TREND IN AMERICA TO DISTRIBUTION ACCORDING TO NEED

Luke 21:1-4

We noted yesterday that God apparently does not approve of too little or too much. God seems to be bearing down on the necessity of distribution according to need.

Interestingly enough, that seems to be the tendency in world development. Socialists and Communists frankly say they want distribution of economic goods according to need. And they intend to get it by collective action—the socialists by the ballot and the Communists by the bullet, if necessary—but by force in any case.

But there is a third development taking place—partly by compulsion and partly by impulsion. That third development is seen in America. We are slowly but surely coming to distribution according to need.

When the Ford Company announced the principle that if you don't raise the wages of the workers, they will not be able to buy back your products, it was important. To lift the other is to lift yourself. If you don't meet the other's needs, you don't meet your own. A generation or so ago, those who had wealth put up huge mansions, far beyond their needs. In large measure they served for show. Result? Those huge mansions have become white elephants; they are being cut up into apartment houses or being given away to charitable organizations for the public benefit. Why? They didn't meet a need, and hence they ended in futility and frustration. Houses are now being cut down to need—perforce!

Take another important development. Why did the richest nation on earth begin at the close of the war to distribute its wealth throughout the world, not by millions but by billions? We did it partly through fear of Communism and partly through Christian impulse. We saw that if we didn't meet the needs of the depressed and despairing portions of humanity, they would turn to Communism. So the fear of Communism became the beginning of social wisdom. But we also gave these millions because our Christian conscience felt that these depressed millions were in need and we must do something to meet that need.

O Christ, you are knocking at the door of our hearts, knocking through these clamoring needs of others. Help us to hear and to respond and do it quickly. Amen.

AFFIRMATION FOR THE DAY: I shall watch the movements of God and follow them, for God wills the best for us.

BY COMPULSION OR IMPULSION?

James 2:5-7

We were studying last week the fact that the principle of distribution of material goods according to need was sound and was slowly but surely being adopted as the basis for human living. There are two approaches to that distribution: one the method of force and compulsion, the way of Communism; and the other the way of impulsion, the way of freedom, the way of democracy and Christianity. The social revolution is on. The depressed portions of humankind are on the march. They are through with exploitation and are knocking at the gates of privilege with no uncertain knock. There are just two patterns that social revolution can take: one the pattern of Communism and the other the pattern of the Christian faith, best expressed in democracy and freedom. I am convinced that the Communists have betrayed the social revolution, guiding it into channels of compulsion and tyranny. The cure is as bad as the disease. We must guide the social revolution into channels of Christian freedom and democracy. But if we do, then the basis of distribution must be according to need. Not according to greed, but according to need. We can't have a world half-stuffed and half-starved.

Just how did early Christians fasten upon need as the basis of distribution? After two thousand years we cannot find a better basis. This basis has survived scrutiny and struggle of the sifting centuries. And it is being adopted by both opposing camps— Communism and free enterprise. One says the distribution according to need will come by force and compulsion; the other says it will come by consent and freedom. The point is that they are both aiming in varying degrees at the same thing in this particular. That is the most interesting and important fact in the collective life of the world today. And the important thing is that the Christians discovered this basis and put it into operation from the beginning. How did they discover it? They knew nothing economics or sociology. They must have found that basis through inspiration. It must be God's will and plan to distribute the goods of the world according to need.

O Lord, if you are teaching us the lessons of life the hard way because we wouldn't take them by the way of grace, forgive us and give us sense. Amen.

AFFIRMATION FOR THE DAY: I shall take life from the hand of grace instead of from the hand of judgment.

INTERIM ETHIC OR SPIRITUAL BASIS?

James 5:1-5

Yesterday we saw that the early Christians fastened on need as the basis of distribution. They must have done it through divine inspiration. This inspired insight has lain dormant for centuries. But the pressure of a false method of distribution according to need, as seen in Communism, has forced us to rethink our position. To our glad surprise we find that we have, as an inherent part of our gospel, the fact and method of distribution according to need. The method is through insight into the law written into our personal and social lives and the Christian impulse of love.

God had distributed spiritual gifts according to each one's needs; why not material gifts on the same basis? Life was one. So this distribution was not out of an interim ethic; it was out of an inspired ethic. They were working out the will of God in material relations.

An underlying question comes to the surface: If distribution is according to need, will not people sit down and do nothing since their needs are met? What will keep people from becoming dependent and without initiative? The Christians provided for that possibility by announcing another principle: "If anyone doesn't want to work, they shouldn't eat" (2 Thess 3:10). If a person will not work according to his or her ability, then he or she should not get according to need. That appeals directly to our hearts and consciences as sane and wise and basically sound. How did Paul arrive at that conclusion? I am persuaded that it came directly through the inspiration of God.

Two principles, then, emerge out of New Testament Christianity: to each according to need and from each according to ability. Someone objects and says that is socialism, but you can't scare me with a word. Long before socialism or Communism was ever thought of the Christians arrived at these two conclusions. God led them to them. Shall we now throw them overboard out of fear, because socialism and Communism have adopted them? Not if we are wise and Christian.

O God, our Lord, we thank you for stirring our minds and consciences to think your thoughts in regard to material relations. Help us to follow. Amen.

AFFIRMATION FOR THE DAY: Economic relations will work in God's way and only in God's way.

YOU SHALL LOVE YOURSELF, OR YOUR NEIGHBOR AS YOURSELF?

James 2:14-17

We are pondering two principles in the pages of the New Testament: to each according to need and from each according to ability. It is interesting that the most bitterly anti-Christian movement in the world today has adopted from Christianity these two basic principles, which are the most worthwhile things in their movement. These two things are making the movement float. Take them out, and the movement will sink.

It is interesting that the Communists in Russia have put into their constitution, in quotation marks, this statement of the New Testament: "If anyone will not work, let him not eat." Perhaps they think it was from Lenin! Don't tell them it was from Paul; they would probably take it out, if possible!

But the further question arises: Can these two principles fit into a free-enterprise economy? Not if free enterprise is based on "loving yourself"—a pagan principle. But it can fit into it if free enterprise is based on "love your neighbor as you love yourself"—a Christian principle.

It is an interesting and important fact that industry is putting those two principles into operation. Profit-sharing and labor-capital management are more and more being applied. And when they are applied, relations between management and labor are better and production goes up. On the basis of trial and error these principles are proving to be better operating principles. They put oil in the industrial machine—oil where there was sand before. In other words, life is rendering a Christian verdict. Life says, "Work life in a Christian way, or life won't work at all."

Take the principle "If anyone doesn't want to work, they shouldn't eat"—is life approving that? Yes. For if you don't work, you aren't healthy. We used to say, "That man is well off; he doesn't have to work." Result? The man who doesn't work gets nervous and upset, gets into the hands of a psychiatrist, who sends him to a sanitarium, where he is put to work at occupational therapy to regain his health!

O God, you are driving home certain lessons, and those lessons are inescapable. Help us to learn them not the hard way but your way as seen in the kingdom. Amen.

AFFIRMATION FOR THE DAY: I must be creative if I serve the creative God; if not, I decay inevitably.

How Can We Deal with Parasites?

2 Thessalonians 3:7-12

We saw yesterday that life approves of the principle that if a person will not work, neither shall they eat; approves of it by producing mental and emotional illness when we refuse to obey the principle. There is another important consideration: those who inherit money and live only to spend it soon have nothing to spend. "From shirtsleeves to shirtsleeves is three generations," goes the saying, meaning that those who earn by shirtsleeves pass it on, and in three generations they have run through with it and are back at work in shirtsleeves. Who decrees that? Life! And who decrees that life shall work in this way? God! People who were inspired of God discovered these two principles two thousand years before modern people; experimenting with this business of living they came out at the same place.

So these two principles supplement and correct each other. If we take one principle— to each according to need—and do not require the second—from each according to ability—we have a parasitic group without incentive to work. If we take the other principle—from each according to ability—and do not give according to need, we have slave labor, disgruntled and inefficient.

These two principles are the alternate beats of the heart of economic living; if either beat is absent, the heart stops, and the body of economic relationships breaks down and dies.

Why should Christians look askance at and shy away from two principles deeply embedded in their faith? And why should they turn them over to alien ways of life for them to try to put them in operation? The principles cannot grow in the climate of Communism with its compulsions and hates. They can grow only in the climate of the Christian faith with its liberty and its love. Then let the Christians boldly and gladly accept them and make them operative. Then free enterprise will be free—free from ruthlessness that pushes the weaker to the wall and free to reconstruct through love and good will. Then industry will not be a war; it will be a worship.

O Divine Redeemer, redeem our relationships from wrong attitudes and wrong methods and help us to cooperate with you in making a new world for everybody. Amen.

AFFIRMATION FOR THE DAY: We must create an economic climate in which Christianity can freely operate.

THE UNITY OF THE SPIRIT

Ephesians 3:1-6

We have seen the six unities that came into being with the coming of the Holy Spirit. They are an amazing list: unity with God, with themselves as persons, among the inner circle—the twelve—unity of all believers, with enemies, and in material relationships. To these must be added some unities we have seen previously: unity of the secular and the sacred, of all classes, all races, all ages—old and young—both sexes in spiritual equality, the ministry and the laity. Everybody and everything was brought into a living unity, called the "unity of the Spirit."

This was the profoundest unity ever seen in any age in any place.

It was not a unity of picked people. It was a unity that included people who a few weeks before had crucified Jesus, their Lord and Savior. The one hundred twenty had been with Jesus more or less for three years; but the unity that was now manifested included murderers, the dishonest, the sexually loose, the morally depraved in general. And more astonishingly it included proud Pharisees, the separatists who claimed moral superiority. All these were welded into a living unity in a matter of days, if not of hours. It was a miracle in human relationships.

"Don't use the word *fellowship* here," said a professor in a Christian college in India, "for the word has a bad odor. We have tried to have fellowship, but it is all very unreal and hollow." Here was a picked group of Christian people, college professors, who tried to have fellowship and failed. Why? Because it was from the outside in. Fellowship in the Acts was from the inside out. They didn't *try* to have fellowship; they just had it, had it in the Spirit. A common bond held them together. It was not the bond of race or economic class or common social origin; it was the bond of the Spirit. They shared a common Life, and hence they shared a common life. The Spirit that had brooded over the chaos of matter in the beginning of creation had now brooded over the chaos of human relationships and had brought out of it a cosmos—a fellowship, a unity of the Spirit.

O Divine Spirit, brood over the chaos of conflicting and diverse human hearts and make out of us a fellowship so deep within that it will be undisturbed without. Amen.

AFFIRMATION FOR THE DAY: I will let the unity of the Spirit lead me into unity with everyone who is unite-able.

THE *KOINONIA*

Ephesians 4:1-6

The unity that came into being with the coming of the Holy Spirit was so comprehensive, so thoroughgoing, so deep, that it was an utterly new thing. It was so new that a new word had to be coined to describe it—*koinonia*. It was a new word with a new content. For all the old words broke down under the weight of new meaning. Writers such as C. A. Anderson Scott think that the emergence of the *koinonia* was the central and fundamental thing that happened at Pentecost.

Many think it was the church that was born at Pentecost. There is no evidence from the Scriptures that this was so. The writer of the Acts seems to be at a loss to say just what it was the converts were coming into, "The Lord added daily to the community those who were being saved" (Acts 2:47). "Many who heard the word became believers, and their number grew to about five thousand" (4:4). "And more than ever believers were added to the Lord" (5:14 RSV). The word *church* is not used in the Acts until the eighth chapter: "And on that day a great persecution arose against the church in Jerusalem" (v. 1 RSV). This *koinonia*, or fellowship, was antecedent to the church and formed the soul of the church. The description of the fellowship is found in Acts 2:42: "The believers devoted themselves to the apostles' teaching, to the community [*koinonia*], to their shared meals, and to their prayers." But Scott says:

> The introduction...of the article [the] before the word *koinonia* justifies, if indeed it does not require, the recognition of the phrase into an independent one. *It is not the teaching and fellowship of the Apostles to which the community adhered, but the teaching of the Apostles and the Fellowship.* It was a new name for a new thing, community of spirit issuing in community of life: that was the primary result of the coming of the Spirit.*

The intense reality of the oneness of the fellowship is indicated in these words: "The community of believers was one in heart and mind" (Acts 4:32). "It was something approximating to a corporate personality that had come into being."**

O Spirit Divine, come upon us and melt us into such a living unity that all our barriers will go down before it. Make us into a living koinonia of the Spirit. Amen.

AFFIRMATION FOR THE DAY: My unity with others shall be not the unity of compulsion but the unity of the Spirit.

*C. A. Anderson Scott, *The Spirit*, ed. B. H. Streeter (Macmillan Co., 1919), 133; italics original.
** Ibid.

125

THE RELATION OF THE *KOINONIA* TO THE CHURCH

Ephesians 5:25-27

The fellowship, or *koinonia*, was antecedent to and formed the soul of the church. Out of it the church grew. The soul secreted its skeleton. The fellowship was the organism that produced the organization, the church. The first act of that organism into organization was the choosing of the "seven."

This brings an important truth to light: Where there is the fellowship, the *koinonia*, there is the church. But where the fellowship is absent, there we have an organization but no organism. We have a body but no soul—we have a corpse.

Where the Holy Spirit is, there is the fellowship—the fellowship of the Spirit—and where there is the fellowship, there is the church. In other words, where the Holy Spirit is, there is the church; and conversely, where the Holy Spirit is not, there is not the church. The symbol of this unity was the loaf—"the breaking of the loaf." This is not the Eucharist, or the Lord's Supper, as some have thought. The "Fellowship of the Loaf" meant that just as the grains from scattered hills and valleys had been brought into one loaf, so these diverse and scattered peoples had been brought into the one loaf, the one bread, the one body.

This Fellowship of the Loaf had another significance; it signified their unity in not only spiritual things but material things as well. They ate one bread. Hitherto they had been eating many breads; each one was on his or her own economically. Now the fellowship included the responsibility for the bread of each. It fulfilled the prayer of Jesus: "Give us this day our daily bread"—not "give me" but "give us."

This Fellowship of the Loaf, the Love Feast, dropped out; and the Lord's Supper became the sole rite connected with the breaking of one bread. Was that symptomatic of what had happened? Did they find it easier and less demanding to eat the Lord's bread—what he did for us—than to eat the bread of the Love Feast—what we should do for one another? It seems so.

O Lord, we thank you for this fellowship that came into being; help us to recapture it and reincarnate it, for our togetherness has been broken. In Jesus' name. Amen.

AFFIRMATION FOR THE DAY: I belong to the Fellowship of the Loaf, scattered humanity gathered into one.

126

THE KINGDOM IN MINIATURE

Ephesians 3:14-19

We have been studying the emergence of the fellowship, the *koinonia*, as the most wonderful human society ever seen on our planet. In it the word of the kingdom had become flesh. The following describes it:

> And day by day, attending the temple together and breaking bread in their homes, they partook of food with glad and generous hearts, praising God and having favor with all the people. And the Lord added to their number day by day those who were being saved....
>
> Now the company of those who believed were of one heart and soul, ... and great grace was upon them all. (Acts 2:46-47; 4:32-33 RSV)

Note the fivefold relationship: (1) corporate worship—"attending the temple together," (2) home relationships—"breaking bread in their homes," (3) personal—"partook of food with glad and generous hearts," (4) Godward—"praising God," (5) societyward—"having favor with all the people." It was no lopsided spirituality, developing in one direction and letting the other sides of life atrophy. It was all round and hence sound. It was spiritually functioning as life, total life. Life was no longer at loose ends; it was under a single control and directed toward a single end. Life was whole. This fellowship was the kingdom of God in miniature. Universalize that and you have the answer. This is the fulfillment of the word of Jesus, "I assure you that some standing here won't die before they see God's kingdom arrive in power" (Mark 9:1). Here was the kingdom in preview. When the final order is set up with the return of Jesus, it will not be different from, it will only be more than, this order realized. We now know the shape of things to come. We are sure of where we must head if we are to get to the goal of the kingdom. And we see the very nature of that kingdom. It is a society ruled by love in all the relationships of life, including the social and the economic, and including them especially. The phrase "and great grace was upon them all" gives the source of this fellowship. It was no worked-up, trying-to-be-nice, kind of fellowship; it was rooted in grace, and grace is God's love in action, and that love in action produced the kingdom in cameo.

O Lord, we thank you for what we have seen. We have seen your order, and our hearts are aflame to see it everywhere in everyone. Help me to begin now. Amen.

AFFIRMATION FOR THE DAY: Grace will make me gracious to all I meet this day.

THE RELATIONSHIP OF THE KINGDOM AND THE CHURCH

Ephesians 2:17-22

The fellowship of which we have been thinking was antecedent to the church. C. A. Anderson Scott puts it this way: "And this *Koinonia*, called into being by the Holy Spirit, was prior to the organised Ecclesia: it was related to it as the life to the organization."* Out of this *koinonia*, the fellowship, came the *ecclesia*, the church.

But there was something beyond and above both the fellowship and the church, and that was the kingdom. The kingdom was best seen in the church as it, in turn, embodied the fellowship, but it was not to be identified with the kingdom. The kingdom is the absolute; the fellowship and the church are relatives. They are related to something higher than themselves—the kingdom. The kingdom is not related to something higher; it is the absolute order confronting all relatives with an offer of grace and demanding complete surrender and obedience. "Seek [first God's] kingdom, and these things shall be yours as well" (Luke 12:31 RSV). The kingdom is first; all else, including the fellowship and the church, is to be related to it. If they become first, they become idolatry; for where a relative order becomes an absolute order, there is idolatry. The fellowship and the church are not ends but means to the ends of the kingdom.

You cannot go out and say, "Repent, for the church is at hand." It would sound absurd. But it doesn't sound absurd when you say, "Repent, for the kingdom of heaven is at hand." For we feel that here we are confronted with the Absolute to which all life must be related or perish. The church contains the best life of the kingdom but cannot be identified with the kingdom. "Christ is head of the church, that is, the savior of the body" (Eph 5:23). Christ saves the church but not the kingdom. The kingdom is salvation; it offers salvation to all, including the church. The church must lose its life in the kingdom, and then it finds itself again. But if it saves its life—makes itself the end—then it loses itself. The fellowship within it dies; and when that dies, the church is dead. The kingdom is universal, for all worlds; the church is particular, for this world.

O blessed Spirit, you have brought into being the way to live corporately. Then help us to yield to you so that in us that fellowship may be realized again. Amen.

AFFIRMATION FOR THE DAY: The kingdom is my absolute; I hold all things in relationship to it.

*C. A. Anderson Scott, *The Spirit*, ed. B. H. Streeter (Macmillan Co., 1919), 138.

THE DISCIPLES WERE FIRST CALLED CHRISTIANS IN ANTIOCH

Acts 11:19-26

We have seen the relationship of the church to the kingdom and of the fellowship to the church. We must now look into the nature of the New Testament church and, seeing it, bathe our spirits in its spirit. For here the water is pure, gushing out of Reality.

In one church in the Acts of the Apostles this fellowship came to embodiment. The fellowship was born in Jerusalem but had to find a complete embodiment elsewhere. Christian faith did not come to its own in the Jerusalem church. For two reasons: it was in an exclusively Jewish setting, and it caught some of the surrounding racial pressures. Peter was an example; amazingly full of the Spirit, he nevertheless had his reservations about the Gentiles, "You all realize that it is forbidden for a Jew to associate or visit with outsiders" (Acts 10:28). This was characteristic of the Christianity at Jerusalem. Hence it never came to its own there. It was too bound up with racialism. It had to be transplanted to a totally different environment, free of these inhibitions, before it could come to full flower.

There was another reason Christianity couldn't come to its own in Jerusalem. The apostles were tending more and more to become the center of authority; things had to be referred to them for decision. The church was taking on the pattern of the society around them with its authoritarian heads. Jesus had said, "You know that the ones who are considered the rulers by the Gentiles show off their authority over them and their high-ranking officials order them around. But that's not the way it will be with you" (Mark 10:42-43). But it was becoming so with them, and the pattern had to be broken. A fresh beginning had to be made, and it was made in Antioch. There, in a pagan environment, and thus not inhibited by a religious tradition, Christianity came into its own. It was no mere chance that "It was in Antioch where the disciples were first labeled 'Christians'" (Acts 11:26). They gave names in those days to express characteristics, so they gave the name *Christians*, for they saw the marks of Christ upon this society.

O Lord, we thank you for the church, the best life of the kingdom. Help us to make our church fellowship as near the life of the kingdom as possible. Amen.

AFFIRMATION FOR THE DAY: When the people think of me, may they think of one thing: the Christian.

OUR SPIRITUAL ROOTS ARE IN ANTIOCH

Acts 13:1-3

We saw yesterday that Christianity came to its own not in Jerusalem but in Antioch, that names were given according to characteristics, that the Spirit of Christ had come to embodiment in a group and they were thus called Christians. The name was rightly given, for as we examine this society, we find the fellowship producing a church—a real Christian church.

This is important for us because the roots of our spiritual lives are in Antioch, not in Jerusalem. The missionary journeys Paul and Barnabas took were begun in and continued to be centered in Antioch. Those journeys took them into Europe and laid the foundation of the Christian faith there, and from there we got it. Antioch is the mother of our spirits. We can well be proud of our spiritual heritage, for the marks of Christ were truly on this church. We must see ourselves in the light of it. As someone has said, "It is the depravity of institutions and movements that, given in the beginning to express life, they often end in throttling that very life, so they need recurrent criticism, constant readjustment, and a perpetual bringing back to original purposes and spirit." This is particularly true of the Christian movement and more particularly of the Christian church. We must see what the pattern of the New Testament church really is before we can make our churches into its image.

Let us go back and look at the real thing. Someone has written a book titled *The Heresy of Antioch*, but it was not a heresy; it was Jerusalem with its racialisms and its authoritarianisms that had become a heresy. Antioch was the real thing. This was orthodoxy because it was orthopraxy. In Jerusalem, the word of the kingdom was tending to become words, but in Antioch it became flesh. Therefore it became power. The center of spiritual power and evangelism shifted from Jerusalem to Antioch. One scholar remarks on the "relative ineffectiveness" of the apostles after the first few years. They drop out of the story.

The story centers on Antioch, Paul, and Barnabas as the effective centers of power. That is important, for it shows what God approves. We must catch God's mind.

O Lord, you are putting your approval upon those movements that express the mind of your Son. Help us to study his approvals and thus catch his mind. Amen.

AFFIRMATION FOR THE DAY: Nothing shall hinder my effectiveness as an illustration of the Christian Way.

THE CENTER OF GRAVITY IN THE PEW

Acts 6:8-10

We come now to look at the church at Antioch as having within it the marks of the New Testament church.

We must note first of all what went into the making of that church. It was founded by the lay group that was scattered through the persecution that arose over the martyrdom of Stephen. "Now those who were scattered as a result of the trouble that occurred because of Stephen traveled as far as Phoenicia, Cyprus, and Antioch. They proclaimed the word....The Lord's power was with them, and a large number came to believe and turned to the Lord" (Acts 11:19-21). The founding of the church by a lay group is important. It put Christianity just where it ought to be—not in the profession but in the person. Adolf von Harnack, the historian, says, "All the early conquests of Christianity were carried out by informal missionaries."* No movement is strong unless it is a lay movement. If the church is organized around the minister, it is a weak church. The center of gravity must be not in the pulpit but in the pew. The minister must be the guide, the stimulator, the spiritualizer of an essentially lay movement. Every Christian, as a Christian, must be the bearer of the good news. A century ago the church in Norway was a minister's church; the laity were forbidden by law to teach the Bible lest they teach heresy. A farmer began to read and teach the Bible in his home. He was put in jail and spent seven years there. But this lay movement became the center of mission activity at home and abroad. The clergy are now cooperating with the laity in these missionary enterprises. But the laity are the driving force.

The movement of Christianity passed from the hands of the apostles to this lay group, which was centered in the seven. It was the seven, not the twelve, who became the center of revival and the center of missionary activity. So God set the stamp of approval on a church centered in the laity by making them the center of God's drive outward into the nations. The Antioch church was a lay church.

Lord, put the sense of your power and approval on what we do and say this day. May we have a sense of carrying out your program with your power. Amen.

AFFIRMATION FOR THE DAY: Whatever God approves, God uses. God's approval must be on all I do.

* No source was located for this exact quotation, but see Adolf Harnack, James Moffatt, *The Mission and Expansion of Christianity in the First Three Centuries* (New York: G. P. Putnam's Sons, 1908).

131

THE MARK OF THE CROSS UPON THE CHURCH

1 Corinthians 2:1-2

We continue our study of the founding of the first Christian church at Antioch. We saw that it was founded by a lay group.

The second thing that went into the founding of that church was the fact that it was founded by people who suffered for their faith: "Now those who were scattered as a result of the trouble..." (Acts 11:19). The persecution in Jerusalem had not shattered them; it only scattered them. Near the Ashram at Sat Tal in India, there is a tree with large pods, which when ripe explode with a crack like that of a pistol. A second later the falling of the seeds can be heard fifty feet away. The persecution explosion at Jerusalem landed the seeds of the kingdom at Antioch. The church at Antioch had the marks of the cross upon it—people who suffered for their faith founded it. If our faith is costing us nothing, it will be worth nothing. "As soon we cease to bleed we cease to bless."* Cities were founded in the old days with the blood of the firstborn in the mortar of the foundation. This church was cemented, not by the blood of the firstborn, but by the very blood of the founders themselves. So the blood of the martyrs became the seed of the church.

The third thing that went into founding this church was an in international mind. "Among them were some people from Cyprus and Cyrene. They entered Antioch and began to proclaim the good news about the Lord Jesus also to Gentiles. The Lord's power was with them" (Acts 11:20-21). Jews who came down from Jerusalem spoke the gospel to the Jews only, but the group from Cyprus and Cyrene also spoke to the Greeks. Their contacts with people in Cyprus and Cyrene made them realize these were people like themselves, with common needs.

This bringing of the international mind into the making of the church at Antioch was important; for when God wanted to get the church to send out Paul and Barnabas on their missions to the Gentiles, God found an international mind ready to be guided. God guides us within the framework of our conceptions. If they are narrow, God can give us only narrow guidance; if broad, then broad guidance. The outlook determines the outgo.

Our Lord, enlarge our hearts that we may have enlarged guidance and thus have enlarged spheres of living. For we want your best, your very all. In Jesus' name. Amen.

AFFIRMATION FOR THE DAY: My sympathies are as wide as humankind; therefore God can lead me to humanity.

* John Henry Jowett, *A Passion for Souls* (New York: Fleming H. Revell Co., 1905), 30.

BARNABAS, A GREAT MAN
BECAUSE A GOOD MAN

Acts 4:36-37

We note the fourth thing that went into the founding of the church at Antioch. It was Barnabas. "When the church in Jerusalem heard about this, they sent Barnabas to Antioch. When he arrived and saw evidence God's grace, he was overjoyed and encouraged everyone to remain fully committed to the Lord. Barnabas responded in this way because he was a good man, whom the Holy Spirit had endowed with exceptional faith" (Acts 11:22-24).

The church at Jerusalem did here what they did in Samaria, they sent down representatives to regularize what they could not produce. The lay group produced the spiritual movements, and the apostles attempted to regularize them. They were trying to keep up. Be that as it may, they could not have sent a better man than Barnabas, a man who was always taking hold of people whom no one else would take and making them over again. He took Paul when the disciples at Jerusalem were afraid of him, and introduced him. He took John Mark when Paul refused to have anything to do with him, and made him over again so that Paul was later glad to get him back.

When Barnabas "saw evidence of God's grace"—saw it incarnate in a group—he rejoiced. He was big enough to rejoice in the work of another. Some of us are not. And when he saw the type of Christianity produced here, he conceived the idea of exposing the young man Saul to this type of Christianity. "Barnabas went to Tarsus in search of Saul. When he found him, he brought him to Antioch" (Acts 11:25-26). This simple statement was one of the most important things in history. For exposing Paul to the type of Christianity in Antioch determined the type of Christianity we would get in the West through his missionary work in founding the faith among us. Since through Paul our roots are in Antioch, then our faith has the stamp of Antioch on it. And there was not a better type found anywhere. This Christianity was the closest approximation to the Christianity of Christ that had emerged. It was a stroke of spiritual genius on the part of Barnabas to expose Paul to Antioch. We must remain forever grateful to him.

O Lord, let us be this day the instrument of your purposes in the world. For what we do and say may touch the ages. Help us to do and say it then in you. Amen.

AFFIRMATION FOR THE DAY: "Full of the Holy Spirit and of faith"
(Acts 11:24 RSV)—my aim for this day.

THE STRONG CORPORATE SENSE
OF THE CHURCH

Romans 12:4-8

We have seen the things that went into the making of the church at Antioch. We must now turn to the authentic marks of Christ as seen in that church.

First, *the church had a strong corporate sense.* They were not a group of individuals coming together periodically to worship, then returning home. They were an organism, not merely an organization. The *koinonia*, the fellowship, was at the basis of this church. How do we know? Two things let us see into its heart. The account says of Paul and Barnabas, "For a whole year they [were guests of] the church" (Acts 11:26 RSV; "were guests of" is the margin note). They weren't the guests of a rich individual in the church, but the guests of the whole church.

The next thing that lets us see the corporate sense of the church was the fact that when they fasted and prayed, the Holy Spirit could speak to the whole church and say, "Appoint Barnabas and Saul to the work I have called them to undertake" (Acts 13:2). They listened and obeyed as a corporate entity. They were so attuned to one another and to God that they heard corporately and acted corporately.

That is important, for it became one secret of the spread of the faith in that ancient world. The faith spread partly by its message and partly by the fact that the ancient society was decaying; a feeling of spiritual insecurity was pervading it. This new society in the church was an un-decaying society in the midst of a decaying society. So people pressed into it for spiritual security. Here they found love across all race and class lines; here they found a people who cared—for everybody. People need deeply to belong to something significant. When they joined this society, they inwardly felt: This is it. I've found ultimate Reality in human relations. This is the homeland of my soul. Here I belong. I asked an African American maid in a hotel, "Do you go to church?" She replied with her face all lighted up, "Yes, I *really* go to church." "I really go to church"; you could see for her it was a homeland.

The church at Antioch had a strong corporate sense; the organism was working itself out as an organization.

Blessed Savior, make our hearts into your home, a place where you can dwell and feel at home. Then let us welcome everyone of all races and classes to our home. Amen.

**AFFIRMATION FOR THE DAY: I am resolved not to go to church
but** *really* **to go to church.**

THE MATERIAL AN EXPRESSION OF THE SPIRITUAL

1 Corinthians 15:46-49

We are taking up marks of the New Testament church as seen in the church at Antioch. We come now to the second mark: *this strong corporate sense was not confined to the spiritual; it included the material.* "Agabus stood up and, inspired by the Spirit, predicted that a severe famine would overtake the entire Roman world. (This occurred during Claudius' rule.) The disciples decided they would send support to the brothers and sisters in Judea, with everyone contributing to this ministry according to each person's abundance. They sent Barnabas and Saul to take this gift to the elders" (Acts 11:28-30). They felt responsible for one another's economic condition.

This was important. It shows that this lay group, rooted in the seven, kept life a unit. The apostles at Jerusalem separated the spiritual from the material, said they would give themselves to the spiritual and turn over the material to others—the seven. Here the spiritual colleagues of the seven turn around and take care of the material needs of the apostles and their spiritual colleagues. The material is part of life; and if you put it out the door, it will come back by the window. As here, the "spiritual" apostles were dependent on the "material" laity. So the church at Antioch was in line with Jesus, who taught, healed, and fed people as a part of the coming of the kingdom. This was Jesus succession instead of apostolic succession. The Word was word among the twelve, but the Word was flesh among the seven.

And they sent "everyone . . . according to each person's abundance." Note "according to each person's abundance"; a sound basis for giving, the only basis for real giving. And note "everyone"; they were all in with all they had. They *really* went to church!

The test of the reality of the spiritual is whether it functions in material terms. If it doesn't, it is unreal.

Another illuminating thing is that the account said: "The disciples decided. . . . They sent. . . ." Their determination and their doing were parts of one whole. The Holy Spirit had both their minds and their wills, and above all their emotions. And the emotions, driven by love, made the determination pass into the deed. They were whole persons holding all life in a living whole.

O Lord, help me to bring all life into a living whole centered on your will and purpose. May my creeds and my deeds be one. May oneness characterize me and all I do. Amen.

AFFIRMATION FOR THE DAY: All my material relationships shall be an outer expression of the inner spiritual.

A NEW RACE MADE UP OF ALL RACES

Colossians 3:10-11

We have been noting the characteristic marks of the New Testament church as seen in the church at Antioch. We now come to the next mark: *the church was without race and class—a raceless and classless society.* "The church at Antioch included prophets and teachers: Barnabas, Simeon (nicknamed Niger), Lucius from Cyrene, Manaen (a childhood friend of Herod the ruler), and Saul" (Acts 13:1). Note the composition of that group: (1) Barnabas, from the island of Cyprus; (2) Simeon—probably identical with Simon of Cyrene (Mark 15:21)—a native of Africa, called Niger, literally the Black; (3) Lucius of Cyrene, also from North Africa, probably an African; (4) Manaen, a foster brother of Herod, the ruler, probably a Roman; (5) Saul, a Jew from Tarsus in Cilicia. In the group there were two Jews, two Africans, and a Roman.

This church was a church beyond race. A new race was emerging, made up of all races. We can see how far we've come from that original church when I remind you that in Jaffna, Ceylon, in the early days, there was a mission church with two pulpits: a higher pulpit from which the white man preached and a lower pulpit from which the Ceylonese preached, and there was no interchange. A daughter of a missionary was married in that church, and a cord separated the races, the white people coming in one door and the Ceylonese another. A burgher (mixed blood) wanted to enter the ministry; but since he was not "white," he would have had to speak from the lower pulpit. He refused to accept this position, gave up the idea of the ministry, and became attorney general for all Ceylon.

Now there is one pulpit in that church from which I have spoken. But the picture of the two pulpits is a symbol of the divided gospel we have been preaching on race. In the early church there was no division on the line of race—a person was a person, one for whom Christ died. They had the kingdom of God, and we have the kingdom of Race.

A religion that is identified with the superiority or the supremacy of one race is a backward eddy in the stream of history where people of all races and all colors flow toward oneness in community.

O Lord, we thank you that you have made of one blood all nations. What you have made, help us not to try to unmake, lest we unmake ourselves in the process. Amen.

AFFIRMATION FOR THE DAY: I belong to the kingdom of God; therefore I renounce the kingdom of Race.

A CLASSLESS SOCIETY

*Revelation 20:4 (MNT)**

We have been looking at characteristic marks of the church in the New Testament. We are now meditating on the fact that the church at Antioch was raceless and classless. Unless we can produce a modern expression of that, we will be no match for the Communists, who boast of a raceless and classless society. A friend of mine, a minister, was arrested in the Communist zone of Berlin. When he was taken before the authorities, the first question he was asked was, "How many lynchings of African Americans did you have in America last year?" He could answer "none for three years," but the question was significant—very. Unless we can sound a clear, unmistakable note on a raceless society, we are simply out of the running for a new world. Other hands will take it over and shape it.

The same with class. In the church at Antioch, Manaen, a member of the court of Herod, was obviously of high social standing. But he is not mentioned in the prominent first place or last place—he is stuck in the middle or near the end without any special emphasis on the "big name" they had won to their group. A new measuring stick had been brought into being: It is not who you are but Whose you are. If you belong to Christ, you stand equal with every other who belongs to him. You become great as you greatly give yourself to him and to others. Greatness was now in greatly giving, and only in greatly giving. That opened the gates of greatness to all. It was a new standard and a new opportunity for all.

One reason Christianity spread in that ancient world, which was founded on race and class exclusiveness, was because it was raceless and classless. The depressed multitudes saw in it new hope and an open door. The same thing is happening today. The maharaja of India once had a palace near where we have an Ashram in India; connected with the palace were kennels for two hundred dogs, with doctors taking their temperature twice a day. Today the maharaja is dethroned, and his palace is being used as a public school. The masses are pushing out the maharajas; they are on the march.

O Lord, your children, aroused and marching, are looking for a spiritual home. Help us to make the church that home, where all classes and races are at home. Amen.

AFFIRMATION FOR THE DAY: I belong to the highest class on our planet—a child of God—let that suffice.

* "And I saw thrones with people sitting on them, who were allowed to judge—saw the souls of those who had been beheaded for the testimony of Jesus and God's word, those who would not worship the Beast or his statue, and who would not receive his mark on their forehead or hand; they came to life and reigned along with the Christ for a thousand years."

BLENDING THE CONSERVATIVE AND THE RADICAL

Matthew 5:17-20

We continue our study of the marks of Christ upon the church at Antioch. Another mark—*the church held together in a living blend the radical and the conservative.* The account says, "The church at Antioch included prophets and teachers" (Acts 13: I). Teachers are usually the ones who conserve the values of the past and pass them on to future generations—they are the conservatives. Prophets are the ones who demand that those values be applied to wider and wider situations in the present and future—they are the radicals.

Each has a function in human society. All progress is made between the tension of the two. If we were all conservative, we would dry up. If we were all radical, we would bust up. But between the pull back of the conservative and the pull ahead of the radical we make progress in a middle direction.

The church should hold both within its ample bosom and cherish and appreciate both. Its very life depends on keeping both in a living blend. The reason we have not been doing that is because we have felt that life could be interpreted in terms of one or the other. It can't. Life is bigger than conservatism and bigger than radicalism, but it includes both and goes beyond each.

The tragedy in American church life is that we have allowed a split to run straight through the denominations on this issue. We are fast dividing up into two camps: the conservative and the liberal. We are becoming two camps instead of one fellowship of the Spirit. Each needs the other. Each must spiritually cross-fertilize the other. For each is weak without the other. The conservative is weak, and the radical is weak. The strong person is the conservative-radical and the radical-conservative.

But the Christian faith leans toward the radical; the prophet was named before the teacher. Jesus said the disciple of the kingdom of God "brings out of his treasure what is new and what is old"—the new was first (Matt 13:52 RSV). The Christian faith leans toward the radical, for it is the *ought-to-be* standing over against the *is*, and demanding change. It is the Great Change.

O Lord God, help us to tip our lives in the direction of change, for we believe your heart is tipped in that direction. Help us to keep step with you. Amen.

AFFIRMATION FOR THE DAY: I shall conserve all values, but I shall apply all values to all situations.

HOLDING TOGETHER STRONG PEOPLE WHO DIFFER

1 Corinthians 3:3-9

We continue to look at the incarnation of the kingdom of God as seen in the church at Antioch. The next thing we note about that church is it *held together strong people who differed on principles and persons—Paul and Barnabas.*

An issue arose over taking Mark with them on the second missionary journey. He had turned back from Pamphylia. Why? Was he weak-kneed, homesick—the usual explanations? There is another: "John was with them as their assistant" (Acts 13:5). Or as the King James Version puts it: "to their minister," to minister to or serve them. Mark might have been, not an equal partner, but a glorified servant—at best an assistant instead of associate minister. They put him in a subordinate place; then Paul complains he left them. The relationship was basically wrong in the new society, a remnant of the old. John pulled out and came back the equal associate of Barnabas.

We often complain of people being unhappy and unadjusted in situations we have made for them, unjust situations. The fault is not in the persons but in the basic injustice of the situation we have created.

Paul argued they should keep the movement clean; they had to purge John, who turned back. Barnabas argued they should keep the movement redemptive; they didn't break a man because he made one blunder. Both ideas were good: one that the movement must be pure, the other that the movement must be redemptive. They parted over these principles—"in irritation," says Moffatt (15:39)—Paul taking Silas and Barnabas taking John Mark. But in the midst of that unhappy situation is this bright spot, "being commended by the brethren to the grace of the Lord" (Acts 15:40 RSV). The punctuation would imply both groups were commended to the grace of the Lord, as if to say, "You both need the grace of the Lord!" the church held both groups within its loving bosom. When they returned, they both returned to Antioch—the home of their souls. The church held together in its love and interest strong men who differed widely; it was the reconciling place of the strong. The church should do that today!

O loving Lord, help us to love across the chasms of difference and in spite of disagreements. Help us to love, and maybe our love will dissolve disagreements. In Jesus' name. Amen.

AFFIRMATION FOR THE DAY: I shall not break people who make a break; my attitude shall be redemptive.

A FELLOWSHIP OF THE SPIRITUALLY CONTAGIOUS

2 Timothy 4:1, 5

We now come to another mark of Christ upon the church at Antioch—*it was redemptive*. A spiritual contagion was inherent in its very Christianity. "The Lord's power was with them, and a large number came to believe and turned to the Lord....A considerable number of people were added to the Lord....teaching large numbers of people" (Acts 11:21, 24, 26). Evangelism was something, not imposed on the situation, but exposed out of the very heart of the situation. It was endemic.

The evangelism was so potent that it evangelized the evangelists, including Paul. Up until Antioch his name was Saul; after Antioch it was changed to Paul. And Paul, or Paulus, is the Roman form of the Hebrew Saul, a symbol of what took place in the soul of Saul. In the burning love of this fellowship the Hebrew bonds of Saul were dissolved, and a universal Christian emerged. If the Christian fellowship of Antioch had not burned up these Hebrew bonds, he would probably never have been the missionary and evangelist to all races. He was born a Jew but reborn a brother of all.

I love to feel, though it is not said, that Antioch had a living part in the remaking of Mark as well. It did indirectly through Barnabas, who was influenced by the Antioch church. Certainly Mark emerged a new man, so much so that Paul, after years apart, wrote, "Take Mark, and bring him with thee: for he is profitable to me for the ministry" (2 Tim 4:11 KJV). I like to think this version is correct; he was profitable "for the ministry." He started out ministering *to* Paul and Barnabas—they used him—but here he is profitable *for* the ministry of Christ. The angle and the attitude had changed, and Mark gladly came to Paul.

The church at Antioch redeemed everything it touched. For at its heart was the Spirit of Jesus, and he is redemption. The church today must be just that: a society of the being redeemed and a society of the redeeming. It should be the fulfillment of the question of the Korean woman, who knocked on the church door and asked, "Is this the place where they mend broken hearts?" It should mend broken hearts, broken homes, broken people.

O Jesus, you mender of broken lives, help me this day to be a mender of broken lives too. Help me to touch healingly everything I touch. And in the process I shall be healed. Amen.

AFFIRMATION FOR THE DAY: I shall be the person of the healing hands, healing situations through love.

THE CREATIVE SPIRIT

Ephesians 3:7-9

Before we leave the church at Antioch as the church that embodied the *koinonia*, let us look at one more mark of Christ upon that church—*the church was creative*. "As they were worshipping the Lord and fasting, the Holy Spirit said, 'Appoint Barnabas and Saul to the work I have called them to undertake.' After they fasted and prayed, they laid their hands on these two and sent them off. After the Holy Spirit sent them on their way..." and so on (Acts 13:2-4).

This church was "worshipping the Lord." The Lord here is Jesus. "Jesus is Lord." Where a group is worshiping Jesus as Lord, there the Holy Spirit begins to speak. For it is on the right center—Jesus—and when we are there contagion begins; creation sets in.

This was one of the most creative moments in human history. All Western civilization was bound up in this hour. Out of it went two men who went ultimately to Europe and laid there—and consequently in America—the foundation of Christian civilization. Had they not listened, we would not have lived—not as we are. We might still be groping in pagan darkness.

The most absolutely creative thing one can do is to listen to God. Out of that silence motives and movements are born. When a group listens, tuned to one another and to God, then bigger things may be born through bigger receptivity.

Wherever the Holy Spirit is, there is creation; for the Holy Spirit is the Spirit of Creation. Wherever the Holy Spirit is not, there are stagnation and death. It is a simple test, but a decisive one. If the church is reaching out in evangelism at home and in missions abroad, there the Holy Spirit is at work in some measure. When the church ceases to lay its hands on its members to send them forth, then the hand of the Lord is not laid on the church in blessing and grace.

Note "the Holy Spirit said, 'Appoint'" and "After the Holy Spirit sent them on their way"; they belonged primarily to the Spirit, secondarily to the church. Their primary responsibility was to the Spirit not the church. They were agents not ends. They went from Antioch to preach the glory not of the church at Antioch but of Antioch's Lord.

O Holy Spirit, speak to me today and send me forth on a big errand or little. May I be so attuned that I can hear, and hearing may I obey with alacrity and joy. Amen.

AFFIRMATION FOR THE DAY: I am made for creation; I am happy only as I create; then I shall create.

CONCORD OR CANTANKEROUSNESS?

Psalm 133

We have been exploring the vast and penetrating unity that came into being with the coming of the Holy Spirit. I say "vast and penetrating" for it included every area of life: all ages, classes, races, and both sexes. This outcome from the impact of the Spirit is strangely different from the phenomena we see in movements today that stress the Spirit. Here we find diversion over minute points of doctrine, emphases, and names. The spiritual climate is quite different. Here we find criticism and cantankerousness; there we find all-embracing concern and concord. Of modern movements stressing the Holy Spirit—with some exceptions—it can be said as was said of the church at Ephesus: "I know your works, your labor, and your endurance. I also know that you don't put up with those who are evil....But I have this against you: you have let go of the love you had at first" (Rev 2:2-4). The Spirit was not manifest as the Spirit of love—as in the Acts, "at first"—therefore modern movements dissipate their energies showing their inability to bear with those who differ from them in the slightest, hence are not producing the first fruit of the Spirit, which is love. They are whirling eddies instead of a mighty stream of redemption following through the total life of the church and surrounding society.

We have seen the fellowship of the Spirit, the *koinonia*, manifested in Jerusalem; and then we have seen that same *koinonia* transplanted to an environment, Antioch, where it became incarnate in a church. Out of that *koinonia* as the soul, the body—the church—was formed. That body became the body of Christ, so much so that a name was given to this group—Christians—for the Spirit of Christ had taken flesh and blood and was incarnated in a society.

We use glibly the statement that the church is the body of Christ. It is if at the center of that church is the *koinonia*, the fellowship of the Spirit. If that is absent, then the church is a religious organization, not a Christian organism. It has a form of life, but in fact it is dead.

O Lord, help us to know and realize and incarnate the Holy Spirit in our churches. May love from within be organized into all we do in the without. Amen.

AFFIRMATION FOR THE DAY: Love shall be the organizing principle of my life today, love for everything and everybody.

THE MASTERY OF MISTAKES AND BLUNDERS

Galatians 6:1-2

I don't mean to imply that the fellowships at Antioch or Jerusalem were perfect societies. They were not. In Jerusalem, against the background of complete sharing of soul and substance, Ananias and Sapphira kept back part of the price and the subsequent lying and tragedy that followed. In Antioch "Their argument became so intense that they went their separate ways. Barnabas took Mark and sailed to Cyprus. Paul chose Silas and left" (Acts 15:39-40). Insincerity and contention put up their serpent heads in these Edens of amazing sincerity and love.

However, two things are important: First, that in writing about both societies the writer did not hesitate to bring these blotches out into the open for the world to see. This shows how realistic was the approach and gives confidence that the description of the good was simple fact. And second, it shows the amazing vitality of the society, a vitality that could absorb its own mistakes and sins and go on its triumphant way. That is one of the tests of a person or a movement; can it go on with power to close in upon its own mistakes and sins and absorb them and even profit by them?

In both cases these groups rescued something constructive out of what would otherwise be pure calamities. In the case of Ananias and Sapphira it showed the moral climate of that fellowship. The moral tensions were so acute that if a man lied in that situation, he died of shock due to heart failure. God didn't strike him dead—he died of inner shock caused by moral tension. That fact shows the contrast with the moral climate of our church life today. One could lie and be dishonest in it, and nothing would happen. Not a ripple would be caused on the surface of events, and it would take a lie detector to register any increase in heartbeat. There are exceptions, of course, but this is the climate.

In the second case the contention between Paul and Barnabas resulted not in a paralysis of evangelism but in simply increasing it; there were two teams going out now instead of one. The contention became extension.

O Holy Spirit, give me power to profit even by mistakes and sins. Help me to have such inward vitality that I can absorb and profit by my blunders. In Jesus' name. Amen.

AFFIRMATION FOR THE DAY: I don't have to be perfect. I have to be sincere. If so, I can use even my blunders and mistakes.

THE POWER OF QUICK RECOVERY

Hebrews 12:12-15

We pause another day to meditate on *the mastery in a movement that makes it profit by its mistakes and sins*. That really is a test of mastery. If that power of quick recovery is absent, the movement is vulnerable and lacks stability and power of continuance.

I say "quick recovery" for, if the recovery is slow, it shows a lack of healthy rebound. The recoveries in the Acts were immediate. After the downfall of Ananias and Sapphira: "Trepidation and dread seized the whole church and all who heard what had happened....No one from outside the church dared to join them, even though the people spoke highly of them. Indeed more and more believers in the Lord, large numbers of both men and women, were added to the church" (Acts 5:11-14). A strange passage: "No one from outside the church dared to join them....more and more believers...were added to the church." A contradiction? No, the people had a double shock: the shock of unfaithfulness in a faithful society and fear at what happened through that unfaithfulness—the death of the unfaithful. So for a moment they didn't dare join them. But only for a moment, for they soon saw that this society could and did recover from that unfaithfulness, it was essentially sound. And it was essentially loving, for the people recognized that Ananias and Sapphira weren't killed by a stroke of divine wrath, but died of their own inner moral shock. So the people, seeing this power of amazing recovery, pressed into the society more than ever.

And the "quick recovery" was seen in the other incident of imperfection—the "intense" argument between Paul and Barnabas over John Mark. The account says, "Their argument became so intense that they went their separate ways. Barnabas took Mark and sailed to Cyprus. Paul chose Silas and left....He traveled through Syria and Cilicia, strengthening the churches" (Acts 15:39-41). Barnabas went on with his extended missionary work, and Paul went on with the business of "strengthening the churches." A weakened person can't strengthen others. Both of them recovered quickly and began anew the work of recovery. The movement was sound, essentially and fundamentally, in spite of missteps.

O Lord, give me this power to rebound into health and victory when I receive wounds from either my own mistakes or the mistakes of others. In Jesus' name. Amen.

AFFIRMATION FOR THE DAY: My soundness will be gauged by the quickness of my power of recovery. It should be instant.

THE MASTERY OF UNMERITED SUFFERING

Hebrews 12:6-11

This power of mastery over their inner moral lapses and mistakes leads us to consider *the mastery that this movement had over the sufferings and trials that came through the sins and injustices from others.* If they could recover from their own inner moral hurts, they could also recover from outer hurts inflicted on them by their environment.

First of all, we note that their faith did not save them from trouble and sorrow and suffering. Many modern interpretations teach that God will save followers from the sickness and calamities that fall on others. It is a sign of divine favor.

Of course it is true that the righteous are saved from many self-inflicted pains and illnesses and troubles that befall the unrighteous. The righteous know better how to live; they are not always barking their shins on the system of things. They know their way around better among the moral laws of the universe. But while this is true, nevertheless the righteous are not exempt from the ordinary sicknesses and accidents incident to human living in a mortal world. They get their share. And rightly so. Otherwise God would be bribing us into goodness, which would not be goodness. The sound position is the answer of the three Hebrew young men to the threat by Nebuchadnezzar that they would be thrown into a furnace of flaming fire if they didn't bow to the image. "If our God—the one we serve—is able to rescue us from the furnace of flaming fire and from your power, Your Majesty, then let him rescue us. But if he doesn't, know this for certain, Your Majesty: we will never serve your gods or worship the gold statue you've set up" (Dan 3:17-18). Note "Our God... is able to rescue us.... But if he doesn't... we will never... worship the gold statue." That was morality independent of any deliverance from its results. Right was right regardless of consequences.

How could a faith that has a cross at its center promise to exempt us from suffering when the center of that faith—Jesus—was not exempt? God let him die upon the cross; he never interfered to take him down. Why?

O Lord, we thank you that you do not exempt us from suffering and pain, but you do something better; you give us power to use it. Amen.

AFFIRMATION FOR THE DAY: I do not ask for exemption but adequacy and power to use anything that may come.

A THING OF BEAUTY WRAPPED AROUND TROUBLE

2 Corinthians 6:4-10

We ended yesterday with the question as to how a faith with a cross at its heart could offer exemption from suffering when the purest heart that ever beat was not exempt. But Jesus, while not exempt, was not passive in suffering. He took hold of this injustice and made something of it—turned it into redemption. When one can take hold of the worst thing that can happen to one—the cross—and turn it into the best thing that can happen to the world—its redemption—that is mastery of the very highest type ever exhibited upon our planet.

This mastery of unjust suffering was not a lone and unique thing—a lone star in the firmament—Jesus passed this power of mastery over to his disciples and their spiritual children. It became a characteristic of the Christian movement and of the individual Christian. They seemed to have the strange power to transform everything—good, bad, and indifferent—into something else, something better.

This power to transform the worst into the best is seen in a Philippian jail where Paul and Silas were in an inner prison with bleeding backs, and their hands and feet in stocks. What for? They had done nothing to deserve it; it was injustice from beginning to end. Did they whine and complain that God wasn't good, that God didn't take care of God's own? No, at midnight they prayed and sang hymns. One can understand the praying, for they were in a tight spot; but the singing of hymns—well, that showed a victorious mastery that was breathtaking. And they struck such high soprano notes that God had to bring in the earthquake for a bass! The jailer was converted before morning, and the foundations of a church were laid. Then Paul, writing to that church in later years, gives us one of the most beautiful epistles in our Bible, the Epistle to the Philippians. And that epistle specializes in joy. This was no cheap joy—joy in gifts and circumstances—it was a joy born out of the heart of pain and sorrow. It was like a pearl, "a thing of wonderful beauty wrapped around trouble."*

O Lord, I thank you for the power to face everything and to make something beautiful out of everything ugly, to make something sweet out of everything sour. Amen.

AFFIRMATION FOR THE DAY: Opposition shall be my opportunity—my opportunity to reveal the love of Christ.

*Attributed to Presbyterian minister and Chaplain of the United States Senate, Dr. Peter Marshall, in Richard H. Brooks, *Inherit the Wealth: Reflections on Living Well* (Bloomington, IN: 1st Book Library, 2003), 127.

A VACANCY INTO A VOCATION

1 Peter 2:19-23

We are considering the mastery of calamity and pain and making it contribute to the purposes for which we live.

The Meaning of Prayer is considered the best thing Harry Emerson Fosdick has written. But it came after a breakdown in the early days of his ministry. The breakdown threw him back on prayer; and out of that prayer experience a prayer expression—the book—was born.

A pastor's wife said to me as we were driving to an airport, "I've found a new vocation. I've learned I can write." She had never written a thing for publication until, on the verge of a breakdown, she was put in a hospital. While compelled to be quiet she began to write children's stories for her own amusement. She soon found that a publisher was eager to publish them. They have gone into school systems, over the radio, and on television. She, who was denied children of her own, has brightened and enlightened the lives of thousands of children by taking what she did have—an illness and a cat—and making something out of them. That cat became the mouthpiece of her insights, and that illness opened possibilities she had not dreamed were there. She used what came to her and transformed what could have been a vacancy into a vocation.

A girl failed in her music examination and was refused admission into a music school. It awakened and stimulated her into endeavor with the result that she became so proficient she stood out as the top student in the whole of the state. That failure could have sent her into a tailspin of inferiority and perhaps self-pity. On the contrary, she headed into the wind of this failure and rose to the very top. She made her failure make her. Everything furthers those who know how to use everything. Even our falls can further us. I let my coat fall in a dark room; and when I picked it up, I found that the fall had turned on my pocket flashlight. The light let me see where the coat was! There is nothing that cannot be turned into something better if you know how to use it.

O Lord, I am safe, for I can use everything. I can master calamities because calamities open doors for me. Everything is opportunity when I am in you. Amen.

AFFIRMATION FOR THE DAY: I shall turn everything into a testimony this day—good, bad, indifferent.

TAKING YOUR CAPTOR CAPTIVE

2 Corinthians 2:14-17

We have been looking at the mastery of pain and unjust suffering. The Christians mastered these by harnessing them and making them serve them. When they were kicked, they saw to it that they were kicked forward. Paul could say, "I take every project prisoner to make it obey Christ" (2 Cor 10:5 MNT). Everything served.

I saw a vivid and almost ridiculous possibility of making calamity into opportunity. We landed, a little late, at an airport in a southern city. Two pastors drove us back to the city, and because we were late, they drove too fast. A police car ran alongside and motioned us to the curb. The pastor who was driving said: "Oh, Officer, you are just the man I want. I've got to get this man into the city for a six o'clock meeting. We've got five minutes. Can you give us a police escort?" "Escort?" snapped the policeman, "I'm giving you a ticket." "All right," said the quick-thinking pastor, "Give me a ticket, but also give us an escort, please." The officer looked at him for a moment, incredulous, but said, "All right, fall in behind and follow me." We went through the traffic of the city with sirens going. Everything stood still for us. We ran all the red lights and came through in glorious triumph exactly on time. The officer looked at the pastor's license, smiled, and waved him on. We had taken our captor captive and made him lead us in triumph.

These early Christians knew that secret. They turned troubles into triumphs, sorrows into song. They made everything contribute.

This power of comeback and recovery is seen in the sign that a real-estate agent put up on a shack after the great Chicago fire had wiped out everything he had, "All gone except wife, children, and energy." That spirit of comeback could not be wiped out. It built a new Chicago out of the ashes of the old—and a better Chicago. When disease ruined all the coffee trees of Ceylon, the planters made opportunity out of it by turning their plantations into tea—and did better.

Everything serves those who serve God.

Dear Christ, I thank you that I can master all, if only I am mastered by you. Help me to make everything grist in my mill, even injustices. In your name. Amen.

AFFIRMATION FOR THE DAY: I am harnessing everything to the chariot of God's purposes. Everything serves.

ATTACK BUT NO HARM

Luke 21:12-15

We are meditating on the mastery of unjust suffering and pain. The Christian faith explains little and transforms everything. It takes hold of life as it is—good, bad, and indifferent—and makes the bad and indifferent into good, the good into better, the better into best, and the best into God's best.

This is illustrated in this passage:

> When they opposed and slandered him, he shook the dust from his clothes in protest and said to them, "You are responsible for your own fates! I'm innocent! From now on I'll go to the Gentiles!" He left the synagogue and went next door to the home of Titius Justus, a Gentile God-worshipper. Crispus, the synagogue leader, and his entire household came to believe in the Lord. Many Corinthians believed and were baptized after listening to Paul....
>
> So he stayed there for eighteen months, teaching God's word among them. (Acts 18:6-8, 11)

Put out of the synagogue, Paul moved next door and won the ruler of the synagogue to the faith. He went beyond the Jews to the Gentiles; in doing so he got the leading Jew. And he got many Corinthians. So opposition became just opportunity.

In the midst of it all, "One night the Lord said to Paul in a vision, 'Don't be afraid. Continue speaking. Don't be silent. I'm with you and no one who attacks you will harm you, for I have many people in this city'" (Acts 18:9-10). Note "I'm with you, and no one who attacks you will harm you." The Lord didn't say, "No one will attack you"; Paul was not to be exempt from attack. But the last phrase is the important one, "will harm you." We are not exempt from attack, but we are exempt from harm through those attacks. No attack can harm us unless we allow it to do so. It is not what happens to you but what you do with it after it does happen that determines the result. The kicking of Paul out of the synagogue kicked him into greater usefulness; he got Gentiles as well as Jews. The attacks didn't harm him; they helped him. That happened everywhere. Dammed up here, the Christians broke out there. They had found the secret of victorious vitality. Trouble pushed them further into new territories and further into the souls of people.

O Lord, give me this secret of victorious vitality, that I shall make all attacks upon me into an opportunity to exhibit the spirit of Jesus. In Christ's name. Amen.

AFFIRMATION FOR THE DAY: In Christ I am invulnerable, for everything serves those who serve Christ.

THE GAME OF THE HOUR

1 Peter 1:6-7

We have been noting the mastery of opposition and unmerited trouble and suffering. These people had the spiritual equivalent of the modern puncture-proof tire, which heals as quickly as it is punctured. They closed in immediately on wounds and healed them by the grace that was within them. And they did it quickly.

In over thirty years I've had many shocks and disappointments and sorrows, but I've found by God's grace that I could recover within the hour. Within the hour the equilibrium could be attained, and peace and joy were back again. It is a good game to play, the Game of the Hour. The hour is par. See if you can recover poise and victory within the hour. You can master many smaller shocks and reverses in a matter of seconds or minutes. But take the big ones and make them yield to victory within the hour. They, of course, may not be solved within the hour, but our attitudes toward them can be solved within the hour. By surrender of the problem into the hands of Christ and trusting him for guidance in the solution, you can regain your poise and inner confidence and be in a position to meet the problem constructively by God's grace and power.

A nationally known woman—creator of sixty-five charm schools across the country—had a nationwide radio hour and dealt with millions. She was converted under strange circumstances. While it seemed she was on top of her world of charm, she was inwardly miserable and unhappy and spiritually hungry. She took a book into her room, thinking it was a book on the history of New England, but it was *Pilgrim's Progress*. She was converted then and there. She walked out of her millions and misery into mastery. She had many difficult adjustments to make, for her former world of charm felt she had let them down, and the Christian world was not sure her conversion was real. She tells me that the Game of the Hour is working. She is enabled to adjust herself to every hard problem and hard bump within the hour.

O Lord, give me that resilience of spirit that can come back from any sorrow and shock and come back quickly. Help me to foreshorten my period of shocks. Amen.

AFFIRMATION FOR THE DAY: Today all my periods of recovery shall be below par, for I shall draw heavily on grace.

FROM INVALID TO WORLD CHAMPION

2 Peter 1:5-8

This power of comeback and quick recovery is seen in this amazing passage: "They stoned Paul and dragged him out of the city, supposing he was dead. When the disciples surrounded him, he got up and entered the city again. The following day he left with Barnabas to Derbe....Then they returned to Lystra...where they strengthened the disciples" (Acts 14:19-22). Note "supposing he was dead. He got up and entered the city again"—apparently under his own steam and not on a stretcher or in an ambulance, as with us. The vitality of the man! And more, "The following day he left with Barnabas to Derbe"—again under his own steam, though he must have been terribly bruised and battered from the stoning and the dragging. And note again "they returned to Lystra... where they strengthened the disciples." Paul didn't get the disciples to strengthen him; he strengthened them! From a victim of storm to a victor of strengthening—well, that is victory.

And it can happen today. I sat at lunch with a man who had won five world records and was once called the fastest human, Glenn Cunningham. Yet at five years of age he was so severely burned that for a year he was attended by a doctor in his own home. He overheard people talking in the next room: "Too bad Glenn is going to be an invalid for life." He determined he wouldn't be; he saw a medal and determined he would have it. After exercising muscles that had apparently gone, he ran his first race in blue jeans and tennis shoes—and won—but left for home half-frightened before he got the medal! That was the beginning. The boy who was to be an invalid won five world records and, at forty-five, told me he felt that with training he could equal those world records. But he was so busy going to high schools and colleges giving lectures on fitness—speaking especially against liquor and tobacco, that he didn't have time to train. He was training youth effectively, out of experience.

Whatever happens to us, justice or injustice, pleasure or pain, can be mastered and made to contribute to the ends for which we live. Everything is possibility.

O Christ, I see in you everything unfolding into possibility. You are Possibility. Help me to face everything today with the expectation of possibility everywhere. Amen.

AFFIRMATION FOR THE DAY: "In him who strengthens me, I am able for anything" (Phil 4:13 MNT).

THE MASTERY OF FEAR

2 Timothy 1:6-7

This mastery of unmerited suffering and making something out of it leads us to consider another mastery—*the mastery of fear.*

In the Gospel accounts Jesus is always saying, "Fear not." He said more about fear than he did about sin, for he saw a brooding sense of fear over the hearts of people. It was the basic plague in most lives. From the first statement of the angel to Joseph, "Joseph, son of David, do not fear" (Matt 1:20 RSV), to the statement of Jesus to his disciples after his resurrection: "Do not be afraid; go and tell my brethren to go to Galilee, and there they will see me" (28:10 RSV); he was lifting the plague of fear from the minds and hearts of humanity.

He was lifting this fear, not by slogans or tricks played on the mind or by a back-slapping attitude of "Buck up; don't be afraid"—no, not that—but by making men and women adequate to face anything that happened to them and thus making something out of it. That is the only real way of dealing with fear; everything else is dealing with symptoms. This is dealing with the disease. For the real disease is the feeling of inadequacy to face the problems of human living. That produces the fear. When the problem of inward inadequacy is solved, then fear drops away like a dead leaf. When we are inadequate, we don't know what to do with life, so we retreat into fear and anxiety. But when we do know what to do with life, then there is no room for fear and anxiety. Confidence and faith push out fear and anxiety.

And the remedy was seen at work. If the Gospels exhorted people not to be afraid, the Acts exhibit a people who were not afraid. Between that exhortation and exhibition an adequacy had been introduced into the hearts of people. They were healed at the heart, so they could say to life, "Come on!" Here in the Acts is the least fear-ridden society that ever appeared upon this planet at any time in any place. But it was not a society that had gained peace and confidence by retreating from life. On the contrary, they walked into life and raised every issue that could be raised about life—and they did it unafraid.

O Master of fear, help me to master fear. Help me to look life in the face level-eyed and not be afraid. I can do this only as your adequacy takes possession of me. Amen.

AFFIRMATION FOR THE DAY: I am drawing on the divine adequacy; therefore fears are pushed to the margin and beyond.

TASTING CHAOS AND TASTING COSMOS

1 John 4:17-18

We said yesterday that the society in the Acts was the most completely free from fear of any society before or since. The word of boldness had become flesh in a group. Not because there was nothing to fear, but because they were now unafraid of fear. In the light of the vast adequacy that had taken possession of them there was nothing to fear, for they could make something out of everything that came upon them. Threats? They turned threats into testimonies. The more they were threatened, the more they testified. Beatings? They turned beatings into blessings; after the beating they left the council rejoicing (see Acts 5:41). The beatings only beat the glory out. Prisons? Prisons only freed their spirits for opportunity to write immortal epistles to the churches. Death? Death became unbelievably impossible, for deathlessness reigned in their bosoms. Poverty? They had chosen to be poor for Jesus' sake because they were infinitely rich in him. Lies and false witness? Lies, when they fell upon them, turned into light, as in the case of Stephen; for the more they lied about him, the more his face shone. The future? They knew that Jesus is Lord, and that he held the future in his hand.

A psychiatrist said to me, "He who is tasting fear is tasting chaos, but he who is tasting faith is tasting cosmos." These people were tasting cosmos; life was an integrated and adequate whole. Chaos was over; creation had come. They knew that these creative forces within them were adequate to transform every situation, every problem, every injustice, every opposition—everything—into opportunity. When you know you can do that, then there is no place for fear.

This fear was not mere bravado. It had a quiet dignity about it, the kind that Jesus had, "Now when they saw the boldness of Peter and John, and perceived that they were uneducated, common men, they wondered; and they recognized that they had been with Jesus" (Acts 4:13 RSV). It was the calm that is at the center of a cyclone. It was the calm of creative assurance—assurance that anything can be met and used.

O Jesus, put your creative calm within our bosoms so that we stand in front of everything as it comes and goes in your calm and in your courage. For when we are unafraid, we live. Amen.

AFFIRMATION FOR THE DAY: By my calm courage people shall this day recognize that I've been with Jesus.

HAPPY WARRIORS OR UNHAPPY WORRIERS?

1 Peter 5:7-10

We have seen the sense of calm courage in Acts, as in this passage: "They seized the apostles and made a public show of putting them in prison. An angel from the Lord opened the prison doors during the night and led them out. The angel told them, 'Go, take your place in the temple, and tell the people everything about this new life.' Early in the morning, they went into the temple as they had been told and began to teach." (Acts 5:18-21).

Note: they came straight out of prison and went straight into doing the very thing that had put them in prison, namely, the proclaiming of the good news. They might have said, "Now let's lie low for a while till this opposition dies down." But instead they went back to the same job at the very center of the opposition—the temple. They didn't go to the margin; they went to the center. There they bared their brows and hearts and faced the storm. They didn't do it reluctantly and hesitatingly: "Early in the morning, they went into the temple ." Early in the morning! They couldn't wait for the doors to open; they were chomping at the bit.

The secret was in the commission: "everything about this new life." It was "this new Life" that possessed them. This Life within them made them adequate for this life around them. The only way to get rid of fear is to raise the level of life within so that you can meet life around you, meet it by adequacy.

They didn't try to get rid of fear by reducing their contacts with life, the way of escapism. They got rid of fear by increasing their contacts with Life and then increasing their contacts with life. It was Life against life. And the Life within was more than a match for life around.

This picture of the happy warriors standing in the temple at daybreak, eager for the battle of living to begin is one of the most triumphant pictures in human history. Many of us are not warriors; we're worriers. A lovely hibiscus, sometimes called "The Warrior" was mistakenly spelled "The Worrier." Many of us are just that—worriers. We live on a diet of fingernails. But these people were living on intimate contact with God; amazing courage was the outward result.

O Lord, help me to live so in contact with you in the Spirit that I shall partake of this glorious freedom from fear and anxiety. I accept your poise as mine. Amen.

AFFIRMATION FOR THE DAY: I shall have the at-crack-of-dawn eagerness to face life by God's grace.

THIS FEAR HITS ME IN THE STOMACH

Luke 21:25-26

We are studying the mastery of fear. The early disciples had it, and we may have it too.

The effects of fear are apparent. They touch every portion of our beings. They throw sand in the machinery of living. This appears even in birds and animals. In India I was invited to speak at a garden party in a Nawab's palace. He was fond of chickens and ducks. One duck, an excellent layer, was standing near a table when the Nawab's son suddenly hit the table with a fly swatter. It so frightened the duck that she immediately laid an egg, and in five minutes laid another, and hasn't laid one since! Her fright upset the whole rhythm of her body and made her sterile.

It can do worse. It can kill. King Ferdinand V of Spain was warned by a soothsayer that he would die in Madrigal, so he refused for twenty-one years to visit his own palace there. He became ill in a small village and, learning that its name was Madrigalejo, died of fright in 1516. When "Cholera" came back from touching a city, so the story runs, someone asked him how many he had touched in that city; and he replied, "Twenty thousand, but forty thousand died." When asked how it happened that only twenty thousand were touched and forty thousand died, Cholera replied: "The rest died of fright."

People today are living under that same fear of death. An intelligent and cultured lady, seventy-two years of age, said to me, "I am afraid of death. This fear hits me in my stomach." She had to have an operation because of a tied-up condition brought on by fear. I slowly read this passage to her: "He also shared the same things in the same way. He did this to destroy the one who holds the power over death—the devil—by dying. He set free those who were held in slavery their entire lives by their fear of death" (Heb 2:14-15). "And set free those who were held in slavery . . . by their fear of death"—that meant her! She walked through that verse into freedom. The lifelong bondage was broken. Her internal organs could now settle down to normalcy, no longer tied up with fear. Salvation had extended to her emotions.

O Christ, I thank you that you have met and have conquered all our fears. In you I am free from fear. Help me to stay in you and hence live without fear. Amen.

AFFIRMATION FOR THE DAY: Fear has no part in the life of a Christian; therefore no fears for me.

THEY WEREN'T NATURALLY FEARLESS

John 16:32-33

Just how did the early Christians get such amazing freedom from fear? Originally they were full of fears. They were afraid of their physical safety, for he had to speak to them on a storm-tossed lake, "Why are you afraid, you people of weak faith?" (Matt 8:26). They were afraid of their reputations: "If they have called the head of the house Beelzebul, it's certain that they will call the members of his household by even worse names. Therefore, don't be afraid of those people" (10:25-26). They were afraid of the unknown: "When the disciples saw him walking on the lake, they were terrified, and said, 'It's a ghost!' They were so frightened they screamed. Just then Jesus spoke to them, 'Be encouraged! It's me. Don't be afraid'" (14:26-27). They were afraid of the spiritual world: "Hearing this, the disciples fell on their faces, filled with awe. But Jesus came and touched them. 'Get up,' he said. 'Don't be afraid'" (17:6-7). They were afraid of ultimate failure: "Don't be afraid, little flock, because your Father delights in giving you the kingdom" (Luke 12:32). They were afraid of organized opposition: "The disciples were behind closed doors because they were afraid of the Jewish authorities" (John 20:19).

These disciples, the boldest of whom couldn't stand the gaze of a serving maid, found themselves collapsing with fear: "And all his disciples left him and ran away" (Mark 14:50). Then suddenly they became irresistible apostles, unafraid of anything: life, death, Sanhedrins, Roman authorities. How did it happen? At least three things account for the amazing change. First, they got themselves off their own hands into the hands of God. As long as we are on the basis of self, we feel insecure, afraid. Second, the Spirit moved in, took over, cleansed their powers, and made an inner unity; they felt coordinated and whole. Third, they began to feel that they belonged to a "kingdom that can't be shaken" (Heb 12:28) and to the final victory. Anyone who will go through these three things is invulnerable, secure. Fear has no part or lot in him or her. That one belongs to the Fearless Society—the Society of the Emancipated—which can put its whole weight down free.

O Lord, help me to take those three steps—help me to get myself off my own hands into your hands, and help me to be possessed by the Spirit, and help me to belong to the unshakable kingdom. Amen.

AFFIRMATION FOR THE DAY: I am in God's hands; I am possessed by the Spirit; I belong to the unshakable kingdom.

Three Secrets of Fearlessness

John 16:1-4

We take one more look at the amazing boldness of this society, a boldness that was not merely in the leaders but pervaded the whole. A pervasive faith pushed out fear. Note this:

> So they called them and charged them not to speak or teach at all in the name of Jesus. But Peter and John answered them, "Whether it is right in the sight of God to listen to you rather than to God, you must judge; for we cannot but speak of what we have seen and heard." And when they had further threatened them, they let them go....
>
> When they were released they went to their friends and reported what the chief priests and the elders had said to them. And when they heard it, they lifted their voices together to God and said, "...And now, Lord, look upon their threats, and grant to thy servants to speak thy word with all boldness."...And when they had prayed, the place in which they were gathered together was shaken; and they were all filled with the Holy Spirit and spoke the word of God with boldness....
>
> And with great power the apostles gave their testimony to the resurrection of the Lord Jesus, and great grace was upon them all. (Acts 4:18-21, 23-24, 29, 31, 33 RSV)

Why were they so without fear? Three things arise from the account. First, they were accountable to God and not to people—"to listen to you rather than to God?" They had an unshakable center of loyalty to the Ultimate and the Absolute. When your supreme loyalty is fastened on people and things, you are uncertain and fearful. Second, they were true to their deepest selves—"we cannot but speak of what we have seen and heard." Third, they were true to their calling—"grant to thy servants to speak thy word with all boldness." True to God, true to themselves, true to others: these three things were at the basis of their freedom from fear. They were not playing for safety. Had they been, they would have been unsafe; for anxiety would have crept within. As one novelist has Paul say, "I am afraid of safety"; hence he was safe! Be true to God, to yourself, and to others; and safety will take care of itself; for you are safe when you are unsafe—safe in God.

O Lord, I thank you that I need not fly here and there for safety. I am safe in you whatever happens. For every happening can further me if I stay in you. Amen.

AFFIRMATION FOR THE DAY: I am safe in the purposes of God; outside of those purposes I am unsafe.

THE MASTERY OF INADEQUACY
AND INFERIORITY

1 Corinthians 3:18-23

We come now to meditate upon another mastery found among the people of the kingdom as seen in the Acts—*the mastery of inadequacy and inferiority.*

I said there were three things accounting for the absence of fear in that society: they were true to God, to themselves, to others. But there was another secret of their complete release from fear; they were adequate. Their level of life within was adequate to meet the problems and possibilities before them.

These men and women did not start out with adequacy for the task before them. They were commissioned to undertake the most impossible of tasks, namely, to change the present world order into the kingdom of God, and this in both the individual and society. This was the biggest task ever entrusted to a group of people, anywhere, at any time. Moreover, no group at anytime, anywhere, were more inadequate to the task assigned them.

They were provincial; none of them probably had been outside one tiny country, yet they were to change the world—a world they had never seen. They were uneducated for the most part, yet they were called on to teach the world, including Greece and Rome and India and China, for they were to go "into the whole world and proclaim the good news to every creature" (Mark 16:15). They were without social standing in the society they were supposed to change; they were mere outsiders. They were from a province that was looked down on by the elite of Jerusalem—Galilee. The leaders complained that Jesus taught the people "from Galilee all the way here" (Luke 23:5). He began with the low castes and not with the upper brackets. And finally, they were inadequate as persons. When they began, their level of moral life within was not appreciably higher than the level around them.

Peter, under pressure, could curse and swear and could fight, drawing his sword and cutting off the ear of a servant.

There was nothing—absolutely nothing—that would make one pick this group to remake the world. They add up to inadequacy. What was the secret of their amazing adequacy?

O Lord God, if these men and women became adequate, help me to find their secret; for they were persons like us, inadequate. In Jesus' name. Amen.

AFFIRMATION FOR THE DAY: It is not what I am that is the important thing, but what God is going to do through me.

FROM THE PIT OF NOTHINGNESS

Luke 10:21-22

We saw yesterday that there was nothing in this original group that would make us pick them as the potential saviors of humanity. They were nobodies, but they became somebodies. They could sing in the words of Isaiah, "You yourself have spared my whole being from the pit of destruction" (38:17; NASB has "pit of nothingness").

Nothingness had become "somethingness-plus"! These people who had nothing had everything—enough and to spare for the rest of the world. They lived and preached with an overflow. How did it all happen?

I said they had nothing. That must be modified. They had nothing except receptivity. And having receptivity, they had everything—everything that God had. That was the secret of their adequacy. They knew how to take. And they took all they needed for themselves and all they needed for others.

It is all so simple it is breathtaking. Jesus trained his followers for three years in one thing and only one thing: receptivity. He trained them in how to let go in order to take. The key sentences are these: "Truly, I say to you, whoever does not receive the kingdom of God like a child shall not enter it" (Luke 18:17 RSV), and, "I thank thee, Father, LORD of heaven and earth, that thou hast hidden these things from the wise and understanding and revealed them to babes" (Matt 11:25 RSV). The central characteristic of a child is receptivity. When my grandson, at two-and-a-half years of age, said to his mother, "Electricity is in the telephone wire," he was repeating what I had said to him. He was receptive and hence had something to impart. That spirit—and that spirit alone—is the secret of the passing from a condition of inadequacy to adequacy.

A derelict vessel resisted all efforts to raise it from the mud until someone suggested that it be surrounded by scows with chains attached to them and to the bottom of the vessel, which was done when the tide was out. When the tide came in, it lifted the derelict effortlessly. These people were stranded in moral inadequacy; Jesus taught them to receive the incoming life of God, the Holy Spirit; they did, and life arose effortlessly on this Tide.

O Holy Spirit, I thank you that I do not have to struggle and pull by self-effort. I have only to let go and let you lift me to new heights of power and adequacy. Amen.

AFFIRMATION FOR THE DAY: Anybody can receive who wants to receive. I want to receive.

DISCOVERING OUR OWN POWERS OR HIS?

2 Corinthians 3:4-6

This adequacy in these early disciples was not a discovery of inherent resources within themselves, as some modern emphases assert. Of course, there is some truth in discovering hidden resources within oneself. Most of us are running on half cylinders, calling on half our resources within—mental, physical, spiritual. But the real reason for not using every one of our hidden powers is that what powers we have are not coordinated, not related to anything significant, and hence at war with one another, canceling one another out. Coordination comes from the surrender of ourselves and our powers to something beyond us. That breaks the self-preoccupation of each of our urges and centers them on something beyond each. The only center to which we can surrender is God.

The moment we make that surrender, we attach ourselves to a Source of power beyond ourselves. That puts us in our right place—dependent. But if the end of religion is to tap resources within yourself and develop them, that leaves you centered on yourself—independent. One produces humility and an acceptance of grace; the other produces self-righteousness and pride and a subtle parading of one's own powers. As a consequence there are no powers, just weakness and a parroting of phrases. I have never seen people who talked about developing the hidden resources within who impressed me with having any special powers. They have a philosophy but no fact. It is a verbalism. They become intoxicated with the wine of their own wordiness and think it reality. But it is an unreal world of words. The words become deflated by the pressures of life, and the philosophies won't work. The initial shot in the arm dies down and leaves them with deflated powers and as deflated persons. It is lifting oneself by the bootstraps.

But here in the Acts they were discovering, not their own powers, but God's power. The source and center was in God. That put them in their place—subordinate.

O God, you put us in a dependent place only to make us more perfectly ourselves; for the more we have you, the more we have ourselves. Amen.

AFFIRMATION FOR THE DAY: My eyes are on God and God's resources; therefore I am in my right place—dependent.

ADEQUATE WHEN ATTACHED TO ADEQUACY

1 Corinthians 15:57-58

A religious writer tells of a woman who bought a jeep that was advertised to get you out of any hole; she found that when she got the jeep into sand up to the hub, it refused to get her out. She was angry and disgusted when someone came up and reminded her that there was a fourth gear that she had not used. She used it and got out. The writer insists that there is always that unused fourth gear, the tapping of lower levels of power. A good illustration and something in it, but it is pure humanism and leaves you with your eyes on yourself, hunting for that fourth clutch to pull you out. It is self-salvation.

That is not the atmosphere of the Acts. They were not looking at their own inner resources; they were looking at Christ. They were not introspective; they were receptive. Suppose the electric bulb should say, "Look how I shine; the resources are within me. I'll stand in my own right and be independent. I'll unscrew myself from the bondage of this socket." That bulb would die. It remains a light as long as it is attached and receptive. Suppose the faucet should say, "Look what comes out of me. I'm self-sufficient. I have resources within me. I'll stand in my own right. I don't need to be attached to this pipe." It would be as dry as dry! If the rose should say: "Look at my beauty. I have drawn this beauty from myself. I don't need to be attached to this ugly earth, for I'm heavenly in myself." And suppose it should pull itself loose to be free and lovelier! The result is certain; it would be withered by its self-sufficient pride!

Everything and everybody are dependent, except God. And the more we acknowledge that dependence and become receptive, the more we live; when we become receptive all out, then we live abundantly. We master inadequacy by becoming adequate in God. We are not able but enabled. "In him who strengthens me, I am able for anything" (Phil 4:13 MNT). Note "in him"—in myself little; in him everything! My adequacy is to be adequately adjusted to Jesus.

O Jesus, I thank you that in you I am able for anything. So let me be perfectly adjusted to you, so that I'll be able to be perfectly adequate for anything. Amen.

AFFIRMATION FOR THE DAY: I am adequate for everything because God's adequacy covers everything.

THE SIMPLE ART OF DRINKING

John 7:37-39

We pause a little longer on this matter of receptivity. It is the secret of victory, the only secret I know. Jesus said: "All who believe in me should drink!" (John 7:38).

The difference between believers is this: some just believe, and some believe and drink; they know how to take, to receive, to drink. Hence they never thirst. Some are always thirsty, for they just believe. They assent to Jesus, but they don't assimilate Jesus. Their minds believe, but their hearts do not receive.

I know of a missionary, a very dear friend, who became a world figure. He was leaving India discouraged and beaten. He was ardent and zealous but exhausted; for while he believed, he did not know how to drink. At a zero hour, when he was about to give up and leave India as a failure, he saw this passage—really saw it—"Everyone who drinks this water will be thirsty again, but whoever drinks from the water that I will give will never be thirsty again. The water that I give will become in those who drink it a spring of water that bubbles up into eternal life" (John 4:13-14). The missionary began to drink, began to accept the resources of God and live by them. Instead of leaving India, he went straight into its soul with adequacy and power. He had enough and to spare, and thousands were converted through him. Three young men converted through him became leaders of the Christian movement in India, and one of them led a movement which brought over 200,000 to Christ. I heard him say years ago, "For thirty-five years, I have never had a blue or discouraged hour." Those who know him know it to be true. There was one simple secret: the believer learned to drink.

Now here is the truth about tapping inner resources: "The water that I give will become...a spring." There is no inherent, natural spring—it is a gift—"the water that I give." The gift becomes a gusher. But the resources are not ours. They are a gift, the gift of grace.

O Holy Spirit, you are the source, and we are the channels. It is not our responsibility but our response to your ability. Help us to take and take fully. Amen.

AFFIRMATION FOR THE DAY: Today, not my responsibility but my response to God's ability, that shall be my keynote.

A GIFT PRODUCING SPONTANEITY

1 Timothy 1:3-5

We saw yesterday that adequacy is a gift from above and not a discovery or development from within. If that sounds too imposed, making people the tool of the Divine and therefore mechanical, let us be reminded that the gift produces spontaneity: "but whoever drinks from the water that I give will never be thirsty again. The water that I give will become in those who drink it a spring" (John 4:14). The gift from above produces spontaneity from within. It is not easy to give to people without weakening them, making them dependent. Here the gift makes human beings; instead of weakening them, it awakens them.

That is psychologically sound. For if the attempt is to awaken your own powers, it leaves you self-conscious and hence self-centered; you are the center of your powers. Anything that leaves you self-conscious and self-centered weakens you—"All who want to save their lives will lose them" (Matt 16:25). But the method of Jesus is different; Jesus gives the gift, and you rise from the gift to the Giver in awe and gratitude and love, and that takes you out of self-preoccupation and centers you on Another. You lose your life, and you find it again. So all this modern attempt to discover your own powers keeps you mulling around on yourself, and that is off-center.

The climate of the Acts is gratitude for grace from God and not grubbing for greatness in oneself. That is the emphasis of Jesus: "And behold, I send the promise of my Father upon you; but stay . . . until you are clothed with power from on high" (Luke 24:49 RSV).

Note: "upon you"—not discover it within you; "power from on high"—not from within. That makes your universe God-centered, not you-centered. Again: ". . . but to wait for what the Father had promised . . . you will be baptized with the Holy Spirit" (Acts 1:4-5). You are to wait, not awaken. And you are to be baptized with the Holy Spirit, baptized from without. And again: "Rather, you shall receive power when the Holy Spirit has come upon you" (v. 8). Note "receive power"—not awaken your own powers; and the "Holy Spirit has come upon you"—upon you, not discovered within you.

The climate of the Acts is receiving power, not releasing power.

O Lord, we thank you that this takes our eyes off ourselves and puts them on you. For we know if we look within, we'll be discouraged; but if we look at you, there is adequacy. Amen.

AFFIRMATION FOR THE DAY: I am a human pipeline attached to Infinite Resources, so I'm inexhaustible.

FROM ABOVE, NOT FROM THE SUBCONSCIOUS

Ephesians 2:4-5, 8-9

We must pause another day on the source of our adequacy. It is from above, not from us. "Suddenly a sound from heaven.... They were all filled with the Holy Spirit" (Acts 2:2-4). Note "from heaven... all filled." It was not an uprush from the subconscious but a downrush from heaven. The uprush would have been from the corrupted depths, but this was a downrush from the cleansing heights. It left them, not little gods glorying in their discovered might, but good people glorying in amazing grace.

This put everyone on the same level. If the source is within, only the gifted, extraordinary person is the source of extraordinary gifts. The ordinary are left out. But at the foot of the cross, the ground is level. Here anyone can receive; the highest is open to the lowliest.

Peter puts it thus, "This Jesus... received from the Father the promised Holy Spirit. He poured out this Spirit, and you are seeing and hearing the results of his having done so" (2:32-33). We get the Holy Spirit from Jesus, but he received the Spirit as a gift; therefore, freely receiving, he freely gives. This means that we too, freely receiving, freely give. Like produces like.

And further note: "this Spirit... you are seeing and hearing the results." The "seeing and hearing" points it. It issues as present, operative fact: it is "this." Those who point you within are usually dealing with the verbal; this was dealing with the vital. The word of adequacy had become flesh in the person and the group. Those who point you within point to a philosophy; this points you to a fact. And the fact was turning the world upside down. The philosophy of discovering everything within you does not turn the world upside down; it only turns words inside out.

Peter said to Simon, "You believed you could buy God's gift with money" (8:20)! The modern equivalent is, "You thought you could obtain the gift of God with manipulation—of yourself." Again: "If God gave them the same gift he gave us... could I stand in God's way?" (11:17). The "same gift"—that canceled our superiorities. The latchstring was out to all!

O Lord, how can I thank you enough for your grace so freely and fully bestowed upon us in Jesus? It sends us to the fountain to drink and to our knees in gratitude. Amen.

AFFIRMATION FOR THE DAY: Since this is all of grace, I can take grace and live by grace. I shall.

WHY DO YOU STARE AT US?

Ephesians 4:7-10

If the disciples had been given the modern advice to discover their own resources, they would have been out of the running. They had no resources. Thrown upon their own resources, they had to say, "Why couldn't we throw the demon out?" (Matt 17:19). When the pressure of adverse circumstances came upon them, one betrayed him, another denied him with an oath, and they all forsook him and fled. And even after the resurrection they were behind closed doors in fear. Discover their inner resources? They would have discovered only their own selfishness and impotence and fear. The modern advice would have left them cold.

But when they didn't have to turn to themselves but to this Risen Jesus—who promised them adequacy within in the coming of the Holy Spirit—that was different. It opened a door, upward. Anyone could enter a door of grace. They didn't have to be worthy or specially endowed or even good, just willing and receptive and obedient. Then infinite power was at their disposal.

Then the very thing that modern advice suggests did happen. They did discover their inner resources; they did find a plus added to all they were and did. But the resources were from God within and not within themselves minus God. Had they discovered and developed their own inner resources, they would have looked on themselves as seven-day spiritual wonders; and others would have done the same. And the whole thing would have resulted in spiritual pride, the most deadly of spiritual maladies. Now they could say with the grace-filled Peter, "Why do you stare at us, as though by our own power or piety we had made him walk?...And his name, by faith in his name...the faith which is through Jesus has given the man this perfect health in the presence of you all" (Acts 3:12, 16 RSV). Note the emphatic repetition: "his name, by faith in his name...the faith which is through Jesus." Their eyes and their emphasis were on Jesus, not on themselves. That put them, not on pedestals, but on their knees. It all issued, not in pride, but in power. God had men and women humbly receptive, therefore usable. They didn't specialize in dispensing miracles; they were miracles of grace!

O Lord, I thank you that even a little child can open her or his hands and take a gift. Help me to be as simple as a child and therefore wiser than the wisest. Amen.

AFFIRMATION FOR THE DAY: When people think of me, they shall think of grace; for I shall live as a miracle of grace.

THE SPIRIT-QUICKENED LIFE

Romans 8:9-11

We saw yesterday that the very thing modern advice tells you—discover your hidden resources—actually did take place. They had inner resources beyond their dreams. But those resources were Resources—they were rooted in God within. The Spirit quickened their mortal bodies (Rom 8:11 KJV). Their bodies had power to resist disease, to recover from wounds and bruises, as when they stood around Paul, who had been dragged out of the city as dead, and he arose and went into the city on his own two legs. Then the next day went from Lystra to Derbe (Acts 14:19-21). Amazing vitality! God had given them new wineskins to hold this new wine of the kingdom. Then the Spirit quickened their minds, bringing to their remembrance everything that Jesus had said to them. Their hitherto dull minds were dancing with new truth and insights. The ancient scriptures lived—lived with Jesus as their central theme. Their minds were opened as to what was to be, for they could see the curve of the future in the present. Uncultured people taught the cultured and confounded the wisdom of the wise. "They couldn't resist the wisdom the Spirit gave him as he spoke" (Acts 6:10). They could resist his wisdom but not the Spirit in that wisdom. It was wisdom without any worm of human pride at the core of the apple. It was sound wisdom because it was Spirit-touched wisdom. It was a wisdom that led them to lay the foundations of life securely in the moral foundations of the universe. It was a wisdom that kept them off the odd, the marginal, and the irrelevant. It was sifted wisdom—sifted from legalism, from the local, the passing. It was universal wisdom rooted in concrete fact.

Just how can we account for the fact that a group of provincial people, who had never been outside their own narrow country or outside their own narrow religion, could lay the foundations of life in such broad and universal terms that we are building on them in our complex age? Building on them? We know instinctively that if we don't, we are building on sand and nothing but sand.

O Divine Spirit, touch our wisdom into Wisdom, our being into Being, our ways into the Way, and our very life into Life. In Jesus' name. Amen.

AFFIRMATION FOR THE DAY: My body, my mind, and my spirit shall be Spirit-quickened today.

I've Always Had Tasks I Couldn't Do

Ephesians 3:20-21

We are meditating on the discovery of your resources after the Holy Spirit comes within. Not before. If you try to discover your resources before God moves within, you will discover just what has been discovered in depth psychology: conflict, hidden motives, contradictory urges. But once you are surrendered and receive the Holy Spirit, then that inner chaos becomes cosmos. After the wrong is cleansed away, even the imperfect good is in the process of being made into the perfect good.

"In the same way, the Spirit comes to help our weakness" (Rom 8:26)—not merely our wickedness but our weakness. Our weaknesses throw us back on grace so that our very weaknesses serve us—serve to link us with Almightiness. Those who feel their own adequacies never turn to grace. But those who feel their own inadequacies constantly turn to the Spirit's adequacy. They are bound to, for there is no other open door. People have asked me what is the secret of my life. I have invariably replied, "If there is any secret, it is in these two things: I have kept my prayer life intact, and I've always had tasks I couldn't do."

I knew I couldn't do them; they were too big for my inadequacies. So I've offered my inadequacies to God by surrender and have taken God's Adequacy by receptivity. It is so simple and effective. A very influential woman had put on her tombstone: "She hath done what she couldn't." Well, that's me! I've done what I couldn't, and knew I couldn't, so I've learned to take grace with both hands. When I've stood before kings and governors and hostile audiences and learned skeptics, I've expected God to press the right button within me to give the right answers and to say the right thing. And God always does it to the degree I've depended upon God. "When they bring you before the synagogues, rulers, and authorities, don't worry about how to defend yourself or what you should say. The Holy Spirit will tell you at that very moment what you must say" (Luke 12:11-12). That has been my verse, given years ago, and it has worked—always!

O Lord God, I thank you that I need not live in fretful inadequacy but in fruitful Adequacy. I can live on grace and more grace and therefore always adequate. Amen.

AFFIRMATION FOR THE DAY: God will press the right button within me today in every situation.

SUCH AS I HAVE I GIVE

Acts 15:5, 28

We look, on this our last day of meditation on the mastery of inadequacy, at the way the people of the Acts mastered inadequacy. Note Peter said to the lame man at the Beautiful Gate: "I don't have any money"—that was inadequacy, the most serious inadequacy modern people know. The hell of an empty purse is the deepest hell that modern materialism can conceive. Peter was there. But he walked straight out of that hell of material inadequacy into the heaven of adequacy: "but I will give you what I do have. In the name of Jesus Christ the Nazarene, rise up and walk!" (Acts 3:6). If he had been adequate—had money—he would have tossed him a coin, and that would have ended it. But blocked at the material, he turned to the spiritual, turned to grace, and a deathless deed resulted—the man walked! The blocking became a blessing!

Note again: "Those who had been scattered moved on, preaching the good news" (8:4). The persecution didn't break them; it made them. Blocked here, they broke out there, and broke out into larger and larger opportunity. They were like quicksilver: the more you squeeze it to suppress it, the more you scatter it.

Note again: "Some believers from among the Pharisees stood up and claimed, 'The Gentiles must be circumcised. They must be required to keep the Law from Moses" (15:5). A lovely name for believers—"believers from the Pharisees"! They had no business as believers to belong to the Pharisees. They belonged to Christ! That double allegiance and off-centeredness of a group drove Paul and Barnabas to go to Jerusalem for a clarification of the Christian position. That clarification broke the chrysalis and let the glorious butterfly of the gospel free of Jewish shackles. The opposition turned into opportunity.

Everything that happened brought them out on the victory side of things. From within them there was an expansive push of the Creative Spirit through inadequacy to Adequacy, through emptiness to Fullness, through nothingness to Everything. "We can do all things!" they cried. And they could.

O Mighty Spirit, work within my weakness to transform it into your Strength, within my foolishness and make it into your Wisdom, within my all and make it into your All. Amen.

AFFIRMATION FOR THE DAY: Everything that happens will bring me out on the victory side of things today.

THE MASTERY OF CONFUSION

James 3:13-17

We come now to meditate upon another mastery in the Acts—*the mastery of confusion: mental, moral, and spiritual confusion.*

Think of the setting in which the gospel came into being. Palestine was the crossroads of the nations; everything went through it. Fierce Jewish monotheism prevailed; pagan cults, indigenous in countries around them, seeped in; Greek philosophy and Eastern mystery cults invaded their minds and culture; Roman law and Roman gods came in side by side. How could a faith arise out of that milieu that would be a world faith for all people everywhere? Wouldn't it be weighted down with irrelevancies and misconceptions and moral misjudgments that would snuff out its life or cripple it? What miracle of clarification took place? What was the purifying center of reference that kept the movement steady and clean and adequate?

It wasn't this, that, or the other—it was one thing—the Person of Jesus. Jesus had said, "You are already made clean by the word which I have spoken to you" (John 15:3 RSV). The words that Jesus had spoken to them had cleansed their thought of God from a vengeful Jehovah to God our Lord; their thought of life as a weary treadmill to life as a glorious open vista; their thought of the Law from meticulous legalism to love of God and love of humanity; their thought of clean and unclean food, transferring it from the ceremonial without to the moral within; their thought of marriage as a human-dominated arrangement to a lifelong partnership of one man and one woman; their thought of an exclusive race and class to a community of humanity; their thought of purity as ceremonial to purity that was moral; their idea of atonement by animal sacrifice to the majestic atonement of the Incarnate God giving self in atonement; their conception of earning salvation by works to salvation by faith and self-surrender; their thoughts of overcoming others by force to overcoming by love; their conception of a Jewish kingdom dominating others to a universal kingdom of God. Yes, they were clean through the word he had spoken, the cleanest group our planet had seen. But there was something deeper that was mastering their confusions.

O Jesus, your words are like pruning hooks that cut away the jungle of our overgrown confusions. You are reducing life to its great simplicities and its great clarifications. Amen.

AFFIRMATION FOR THE DAY: I am ready for all irrelevancies to be pruned away. I would be clean through God's Word.

JESUS, THE GREAT CLARIFICATION

1 Timothy 3:16

We saw yesterday that the first step in the mastery of confusion was the words Jesus had spoken to them. But there was something deeper than the words—it was the Word, the Incarnate Word, the Word made flesh, Jesus. He, as a Person, was the center of the clarification from confusion. They had a center of reference—a purifying center of reference—the Person of Jesus. He himself put content and meaning into his words. The divine illustration became the divine illumination. In his light they began to see life.

A Jewish rabbi said, "Take out Jesus from human history, and you cut out the heart." Take Jesus out of Christianity, and you have cut out its heart. Christ would mean nothing, God would mean nothing, the Holy Spirit would mean nothing, the kingdom of God would mean nothing, if Jesus did not put meaning into all of them—the meaning of his own character and life.

When I say Christ, I think Jesus. When I say God, I think Jesus. When I say the Holy Spirit, I think Jesus. When I say the kingdom of God, I think Jesus. The important thing is that if I don't, I put the wrong content in all of these.

Alcibiades says of Socrates: "Somehow the words of others don't affect me much; but yours, even stray fragments passed on inaccurately at secondhand, grip the soul of everyone who hears them and make me ashamed of what I am, so that I know I couldn't live beside you and still be it."* If this could be said of Socrates, it is infinitely true of Jesus. The words of Jesus are guaranteed by the fact of Jesus. The fact of Jesus struck people more than his words. As someone has said, "It was not the principles to which the Jews objected, but the specific application of them in the revolutionary and redeeming figure of Jesus." It is the Person of Jesus that saves Christianity from decay and distortion. He brings it back again and again. The Person saves the system. In him, as the Irish historian W. E. H. Lecky says, there are a principle and a power that are the secret of survival and revival. Rediscover Jesus, and there is revival.

O Jesus, in you the Word became flesh and the flesh became Word. Through your flesh we see the meaning of life. How can we ever thank you enough? We never can. Amen.

AFFIRMATION FOR THE DAY: If I begin with Jesus, I begin; if I don't, I begin to have trouble and confusion.

*No published source was found for this quotation.

THE EARLIEST CREED: JESUS IS LORD

Philippians 2:9-11

Of all the clarifications that have ever taken place in religion at anytime, anywhere, the greatest and the profoundest was in the earliest Christian creed.

Someone has said that all great discoveries are reductions from complexity to simplicity. Error and evil are complex; they have to attempt to stop up all the holes, for there are many. But truth and goodness are simple. On the wall of a superintendent's office in a rubber factory is this motto: "The answer when found will be simple." It always is. But of all the reductions from complexity to simplicity, the greatest and profoundest was in the earliest Christian creed: "Jesus is Lord." Three words, and yet three worlds are in them: heaven, earth, and hell.

This earliest creed is found in these words: "If you confess... 'Jesus is Lord,'... you will be saved" (Rom 10:9). Again: "Every tongue [should] confess that Jesus Christ is Lord" (Phil 2:11). And: "No one can say, 'Jesus is Lord' except by the Holy Spirit" (1 Cor 12:3). But note that this was not the repetition of a creed; it was a confession, a confession of an attitude: "'Jesus is Lord' to me." It was a committal of life as well as repetition of a creed.

How did it happen that this phrase arose out of a fiercely monotheistic people whose central confession was: "Hear, O Israel: The LORD our God is one LORD" (Deut 6:4 RSV)? The people who had repeated, "The LORD our God is one LORD," now found themselves repeating, "Jesus is Lord." Was Jesus doing something that only God could do?

Was his touch upon nature and upon human nature the very touch of God? His impact upon nature and human living was so tremendous that they found their unwilling lips making the most momentous confession that ever fell from human lips anywhere at any time. It was life's central revelation. And the revelation was this: "This Man, who walked our dusty roads, slept upon our hillsides, was crucified on one of our trees, and was laid in one of our rock tombs, was at the right hand of final authority—was Lord and would have the final say in human affairs." That confession was breathtaking.

O Lord, here we are at the crux of human living: this is so or not so. Help us not to make a mistake here; for if we do, then all life will go wrong with it. Amen.

AFFIRMATION FOR THE DAY: Jesus is Lord—of all my thoughts, all my actions, all my relationships, everything.

EVERYTHING ANCHORED TO JESUS

Hebrews 2:7-9

When the early Christians made the confession that "Jesus is Lord," they fastened upon the very center of the Christian faith: Jesus. The center of that faith is not Christ—the excarnate Christ, the universal Christ, but the incarnate Jesus—the Word become flesh. The center of the Christian faith is the incarnation, God's redemptive invasion of us. God became like us that we might become like God.

The whole Christian faith is anchored to Jesus. God is anchored to Jesus. For we know little or nothing about God except through Jesus. Apart from Jesus we look up to God through our own conceptions, but these are usually misconceptions. Through them we arrive at something other than God. But through Jesus we see the Lord, "He that hath seen me hath seen the Father" (John 14:9 KJV). The character of God is none other than the character of Jesus.

Christ was anchored to Jesus. Apart from Jesus, the Christ—the Anointed One, the Messiah—has been misconceived, often as a nationalistic hero or a strange mystic. "I am the Messiah, Christ reincarnated," said a Hindu in the hearing of a British sea captain. The blunt reply was, "Well, if you are, then I'm changing my religion."

The Holy Spirit is anchored to Jesus. We know little or nothing about the Spirit's character unless we see it in the character of Jesus: "[I] will send another Companion" (John 14:16)—"another" like me; "the Holy Spirit...will remind you of everything I told you" (v. 26); "he will take what is mine and proclaim it to you" (16:14). The Holy Spirit is a Jesus-like Spirit.

The kingdom of God is anchored to Jesus. He fixes in his own person the character of the kingdom. The kingdom is the spirit of Jesus universalized. Life is anchored to Jesus. In him we see its meaning and its goal. In him we see life as Life. In him the great clarification took place. When they said, "Jesus is Lord," then everything in heaven and on earth fell into place.

O Jesus, you are the rift in the clouds that hang between me and God and eternity and life. Through you I am the meaning of God, eternity, and life. I thank you. Amen.

AFFIRMATION FOR THE DAY: I glance at other things, but I gaze at Jesus— the center of my universe.

WE ARE DRIFTING INTO HUMANISM

John 17:1-3

We are meditating on the great clarification that took place when the early Christians confessed, "Jesus is Lord." Without that confession, life is under a strange sense of either unfulfillment or being at loose ends. The Hindus have had nine so-called incarnations of God. They are waiting for the tenth—the Nishkalank Avatar, the Spotless Incarnation. They cannot live on the Is; it is all unsatisfactory. They are living on the To Be.

Where groups have taken Jesus as teacher and example but not as Lord, there the key to God slips through their fingers. For them, Jesus as teacher and example takes his place among the other moralists and philosophers who point to truth. But they are not the truth. Jesus never pointed to truth; he pointed to himself and said, "I am the Truth." He never pointed to the Way as a signpost; he simply said, "I am the Way." He did not philosophize about life; he said, "I am the Life." And the amazing thing is that when we try him, it works. He becomes the Way, the Truth, the Life. His ways become the Way. His truths become the Truth. His life becomes the Life. In him we see God. And apart from him, God is vague and uncertain. A member of a Unitarian group said to me, "I wish you would come to our annual convention and help us to get God back into our movement. For we are drifting into humanism." That was interesting and revealing. Here was a group specializing on God and losing God, and here I was specializing on Jesus and finding God. If you lose the Incarnate Jesus, you lose the Excarnate God. If you know the Incarnate Jesus, you know the Excarnate God.

"Jesus is Lord" was the key to the mastery of confusion. When they began to make him Lord of their thoughts, they knew that their thoughts were becoming Truth; when they began to live his life, they knew that this was Life; when they began to walk his ways, they knew that this was the Way. Life burst into meaning everywhere. The universe was a universe and not a multiverse. Life added up to sense—to Sense!

O Jesus, I thank you for the fact that when I know you, I know how to think, know how to feel, know how to act. I just know how to be—blessed, blessed certainty. Amen.

AFFIRMATION FOR THE DAY: I shall approach every subject, every relationship, everything, through Jesus today.

THIS

Revelation 1:8, 17-18

We have been meditating upon the way the disciples walked out of confusion into clarity when they repeated the great clarification: "Jesus is Lord." The emphasis in the Acts is upon "this Jesus."

In Acts 2, the word *this* is used seven times in the Revised Standard Version. There was a "thisness" about the whole thing, not a "thatness." Peter used "this Jesus" three times at Pentecost (Acts 2:23, 32, 36). It was not "that Jesus," pointing to a dead person, but "this Jesus"—alive, present, vital, redemptive, available. And this Jesus was producing "this": "*this* is what" (v. 16); "he has poured out *this* which you see and hear" (v. 33); "when they heard *this* they were cut to the heart" (v. 37) [italics added]. It was the thisness of the message that produced the thisness of response in repentance and new life. In history, if we preach "that" instead of "this," we produce "that" instead of "this" in experience.

They repeated "Jesus is Lord"—not "Jesus will be Lord." He is Lord now of everything. They found him Lord of the past. One of the most helpless feelings one can have is to feel that the past is not past for it invades the present as guilt. Nothing we do can lift that guilt. Only the Divine can lift it and make us as though we had not sinned. Jesus did that. His nailed-pierced hand goes over the past, and lo, it is gone as guilt. It remains only as gratitude for such amazing grace that can, and does, lift the burden of guilt. That guilt belongs to a person that was and is not. "So then, if anyone is in Christ, that person is part of the new creation. The old things have gone away, and look, new things have arrived!" (2 Cor 5:17).

Then they found Jesus was Lord of the present. They could walk up to sin and temptation and sorrow and opposition, look them straight in the eye, and in the name of Jesus walk through them without the smell of fire upon them. Then they found Jesus was Lord of the future. At the center of that future was death, but Jesus had pulled the sting of death, so the future was free of terrors. They could say, "We don't know what the future holds, but we know Who holds the future. Jesus is Lord!"

O Jesus, you are Lord! All things are under your blessed feet. If we will accept that blessed fact and identify ourselves with you, then all things are under our feet. Amen.

AFFIRMATION FOR THE DAY: I face past, present, and future in Jesus; he has mastered all three, so I'm unafraid.

THE THREE WORKING IDEAS

Hebrews 12:1-2

The three working ideas of Acts are: (1) Jesus is alive; (2) Jesus has come within in the Holy Spirit to abide forever; (3) Jesus is Lord, he is at the right hand of ultimate authority.

Stephen, who incarnated the Christian gospel perhaps better than any person in the Acts, sums it all up in these words about Jesus, "But he, full of the Holy Spirit, gazed into heaven and saw the glory of God, and Jesus standing at the right hand of God" (Acts 7:55 RSV). He was Lord of heaven and earth. He illuminated heaven; he illuminated earth. He illuminated sorrow; he illuminated death. He illuminated everything. He was the Great Clarification.

So when they worked out from Jesus to God—to life, to everything—they knew where they were going; they were on the Way! Confusion of thought and act and attitude was mastered. They knew where they were heading. Life was adding up to Sense. Everything in Jesus clicked into meaning. They had found the clue to the jigsaw puzzle of human living. They were through with bypaths and roads with dead ends; they were on the Way with both feet and with the consent of all their being. This was It!

An African American minister said, as he was leaving an Ashram: "I am going from here to read myself full, think myself clear, pray myself hot, and let myself go!" The people in Acts were full, clear, hot, and, therefore, could let themselves go. For they knew where they were going. Jesus was the Alpha—the Beginning; and he was the Omega—the End; the First and Last and In-Between! He was everything.

Of one minister it was said, "Without a problem spake he not unto them." But those people of the Acts were not dealing with problems; they were dealing with possibilities. Life wasn't an impenetrable jungle; it was an open road, and they went dancing along that road knowing it was the Way!

They knew that they knew, were sure that they were sure, and it was all self-verifying. Here was knowledge that was so *knowing* that it turned into Wisdom. Here was faith that had turned into Fact. Life was alive—and how!

O blessed, blessed Jesus, you have turned all my sunsets into sunrises, all my gloom into glory, all my doubts into delights. You are the Great Illumination. Amen.

AFFIRMATION FOR THE DAY: I am on the Way with both feet, with the consent of all my being and with all I have.

THE MASTERY OF NEGATIVE ATTITUDES

Job 2:13; Ezekiel 3:14-15; 4:1-6

We turn now to another mastery—*the mastery of negative attitudes*. Since they had found mastery over confusion and knew what they wanted to do and say, and where they wanted to go, they became positive persons leaving a positive result. They were no longer nay-saying but yea-saying. The world listens to the yea-saying.

I picked up a magazine and read an article by a very able Indian on the question of Christian missions in India. Fully 90 percent of the article was negative. When I got through, I had a sinking feeling in my middle. And more serious still, I found myself saying to myself, "Why should I continue to support financially and morally all this negativism?" His negativism affected my person and my purse! We never follow a negative person.

The one negative person in the Acts was a deeply spiritual man and a very accurate prophet: Agabus. He made two prophecies, and they both came true. One was that a famine would fall on the land (Acts 11:28), and the other that the Jews would "bind the man who owns this belt" (Paul) and imprison him (Acts 21:10-11). Both these prophecies came true. But they were both negative—famine and imprisonment. Agabus seems without further influence in the pages of the Acts. No one can follow long a person who emphasizes the famine and imprisonment side of things, however true it may be. So no one names his son "Agabus." At least I have never heard of anyone doing so. Why? For we lean to the positive, innately so. We want to see beyond famine to fullness, beyond imprisonment to immensities.

The "friends" of Job "sat with Job on the ground seven days and seven nights, not speaking a word to him, for they saw that he was in excruciating pain" (Job 2:13). Ezekiel says of himself, "I came to the exiles who lived beside the Chebar River at Tel-abib. I stayed there among them for seven desolate days" (Ezek 3:15). The "friends" of Job arose after seven days, critical and negative of Job. Ezekiel arose after seven days with deep sympathy and love for the captives. The "friends" of Job dropped out; Ezekiel lives on with power.

O Lord, help me to come out on the constructive side of things. Help me to rescue a positive out of every negative. For I live only as I live positively and affirmatively. Amen.

AFFIRMATION FOR THE DAY: I am a positive person; therefore I shall think, act, and be positive.

THE CRITICS GET CRITICIZED

Matthew7:1-5

Job and Ezekiel each sat seven days and nights before a problem, one of suffering, and the other of the waywardness of a people. When Ezekiel went to tell the captives of their sins, he said, "I went away, bitter and deeply angry" (Ezek 3:14); he was going to blister their souls. But God said, "No, Ezekiel, not yet. You sit where they sit. Learn their problems and temptations firsthand by experience. And then you can speak." So he said, "I sat where they sat" (v. 15 KJV)—and learned their problems from within.

When Ezekiel did speak, there was tenderness in his voice, compassion in his heart. The people knew he understood and sympathized, so they heeded his words. Those words were deep speaking to deep. But when Job's "friends" sat beside him and pondered his suffering, they arose critical and negative. They threw salt in his sores by telling him how evil he must be to have all this evil come upon him. They sat on the judgment throne beside God and handed out God's judgment for him. But in the end God said, "I'm angry at you and your two friends because you haven't spoken about me correctly as did my servant Job" (42:7). So the critics got criticized, the judges judged. Those who sat on Job got sat on. They reaped what they sowed.

> I will punish the men growing fat
>   on the sediment of their wine,
>   those saying to themselves,
>   the LORD won't do good or evil. (Zeph 1:12)

They were colorless and negative—the LORD won't do either good or evil. They suffered from nonexpectancy. Result? They were "growing fat on the sediment of their wine." They were suffering, not so much from the hardening of their arteries as from the "hardening of their categories."

How different the atmosphere of Acts! There life was open, responsive, positive, creative. If they were critical, it was constructive. They took nothing away without substituting ten times as much. If they tore down with the left, they built up with the right.

O God, our Lord, help me this day to belong to those who build: build with appreciation, build with love, build with the positive. Help me to be creative. Amen.

AFFIRMATION FOR THE DAY: When I sit where people sit, I shall rise with love and sympathy and understanding.

TWO CONTRASTING COMMISSIONS

Galatians 1:15-17

There is a very instructive contrast between what Jeremiah conceived to be his commission and what Paul conceived to be his. Jeremiah felt he heard this from God,

> "This very day I appoint you
> > over nations and empires,
> > to dig up and pull down,
> > to destroy and demolish,
> > to build and to plant." (Jer 1:10)

Four items in his commission were negative: "to dig up and pull down," and "to destroy and demolish." Only two were positive: "to build and to plant." He was twice as negative as he was positive. Hence he is called the "weeping prophet," and his sayings are called the "lamentations of Jeremiah." And this is the point; we don't follow him.

But note how Paul conceived his commission in Acts 26:15-18 (RSV). Note the points in that commission.

(1) "Who are you, Lord?" the most important question. It is all begins with your view of Jesus. (2) "I am Jesus whom you are persecuting." Everything you do is done in relation to me. (3) "But"—the interposing of redemption. (4) "Rise and stand upon your feet." Free servants freely give their allegiance and love. (5) "I have appeared to you"—firsthand; (6) "To appoint you to serve." Jesus is Lord; you are surrendered to him. (7) "And bear witness to the things in which you have seen me." The point of witness is "me." (8) "And to those in which I will appear to you"—a continuing revelation. (9) "Delivering you from the people and from the Gentiles—to whom I send you." Freed from your own race, "the people," and from other races—"the Gentiles" (10) "to open their eyes"—receptivity produced. (11) "That they may turn from darkness to light"—light on life. (12) "From the power of Satan to God"—delivered from evil. (13) "Forgiveness of sins"—past blotted out. (14) "And a place among those who are sanctified by faith in me"—significance—"a place"!

O Christ, we thank you for this commission. To this man. Our future hung upon that command and his obedience. We thank you that he was not disobedient. Amen.

AFFIRMATION FOR THE DAY: My sense of mission will move in the realm of the constructive, always.

Turning the World Upside Down

Acts 17:5-8

We noted yesterday Paul's fourteen-point commission. Not one negative point in the fourteen—all positive. No wonder he was a positive person with a positive message and a positive result. He was alive with God and life and destiny, and he made persons and situations live. This is in deep contrast to the man of whom a GI inquired when he returned to his hometown after a long absence: "Is so-and-so alive yet?" And the inhabitant replied, "No, not yet."

Paul was alive and positive, and everyone knew it. This impact was felt a few days after his conversion. "Right away, he began to preach about Jesus in the synagogues. 'He is God's Son,' he declared. . . . They were keeping watch at the city gates around the clock so they could assassinate him. But his disciples took him by night and lowered him in a basket through an opening in the city wall" (Acts 9:20, 24-25). He was a positive man and got positive results and got them immediately. He not only positively changed people; he did something more—he "turned the world upside down." In his positive presentation of Jesus a revolution in thought and act and attitude was taking place. What were some of the positive ways the world was turned upside down?

The revolution was accomplished by seed thoughts, seed actions, and seed attitudes. Nothing is so powerful as a seed. Seeds of the *peepul* (or *pipal*) tree in India, falling into the cracks of a building, will leave the building in ruins. So Paul dropped seed thoughts into ancient structures, and they crumbled.

1. The Jesus that Paul preached reversed the method of revelation. Hitherto it was a verbal revelation—a book, a voice. Now it was a vital revelation—a Life, a Person.

2. Jesus reversed the method of salvation. Hitherto people were doing something for God; while in Jesus, God was doing something for people. Salvation was a gift.

3. Jesus reversed the method of inheriting the earth. Hitherto people tried to inherit it by conquest, by force; and here Jesus was teaching them to inherit it by meekness, by receptivity. The earth belongs to those who know how to inherit it by meekly learning its secrets and obeying its laws—the meek.

O Lord, our hearts are being turned upside down as we contemplate your Son. He reverses all our values; he reverses us. Help us to be a part of his revolution. Amen.

AFFIRMATION FOR THE DAY: I belong to the Great Affirmative. I shall be affirmative in all my thoughts, attitudes, and actions.

THE MAJOR REVERSALS

Revelation 21:5-7

We are looking at the ways the world was turned upside down with the impact of the Jesus whom Paul preached.

4. Jesus reversed the method of greatness. Before Jesus, those who were greatly served were great; and the greater the number of servants, the greater the person. But Jesus reversed that by making those great who greatly served others. That opened greatness to all—not the getters but the givers were great. Jesus himself was an illustration of this. I saw a raja's name upon a marble tablet, and his titles extended four lines. I turned to someone and said, "'you will call him Jesus' (Matt 1:21); one word—'Savior'—was sufficient." I can't even remember the raja's name, but neither I nor the world can forget the name of Jesus!

5. Jesus reversed the method of being defiled. Before he came, you were defiled by "unclean" foods and by touching "unclean" persons and things. But Jesus said, "It's not what goes into the mouth that contaminates a person in God's sight. It's what comes out" (15:11). That which goes into the person is physical, but that which comes out of a person—evil thoughts, evil words, evil acts—comes from the heart and defiles the person. Here he turned purity from the ceremonial to the moral, the greatest moral turn upward that has ever been made in human history and the most effective and decisive.

I sat in a compartment of a train with a Brahman. When I asked if he was going to have his dinner brought into the compartment as I was, he replied that he was going to eat his food in the Brahman refreshment room at the next station. "Are you afraid of my evil eye falling on your food and thus making it unclean?" I asked. He replied: "No, but they tell us if a person of another caste sees you eat, he emits rays different from yours; and it stops digestion." Even this Brahman was feeling the impact of the moral upon the ceremonial and had to defend it on pseudo-scientific grounds rather than ceremonial. The revolution was pressing upon him.

O Jesus, your thought and mind are pressing upon the old things within us and are turning our inner world upside down. We thank you. Amen.

AFFIRMATION FOR THE DAY: I am a part of the greatest revolution that ever touched us, and I shall extend it today.

EVIL A PARASITE UPON THE GOOD

Hebrews 12:1-2

We continue to look at the points at which the preaching of Jesus created a revolution—turned the world upside down.

6. The cross was the revelation of the heart of God. That was new and almost unthinkable to that ancient world. Cicero said, "The very mention of the cross should be far removed not only from a Roman citizen's body but from his mind and his eyes and his ears."* Even to think about the cross would defile the proud Roman. But Jesus accepted the cross as his very own and through it showed the love of God. The cross was hate, and through it Jesus showed love. The cross was sin, and through it Jesus accomplished the healing of sin. The cross was humanity at its worst, and through it Jesus showed God at his redemptive best. To atone for sin through the action of sin is new. To show the best through the worst, that was new and revolutionary. The thought and outlook of antiquity were reversed.

7. Goodness and love are stronger than evil and hate. Evil and hate seem strong, and they are, in the beginning. But they have nothing behind them, nothing except the force of the evildoer and the hater. The universe doesn't back them, sustain them, further them. They are alone in a world of moral qualities. Therefore all evil and hate are doomed to self-destruction. For they have within them the seeds of their own destruction. A target practice by the military has an interesting method of disposal of shots that miss the target. If they don't hit the target, they explode of their own accord. That is what evil and hate do. Give them enough rope, and they will hang themselves. No situation can stay together with evil and hate at its center. There is no cement in sin. You have to throw enough good around evil, enough love around hate, to keep them going. All evil is a parasite upon good; all hate is a parasite upon love. Make evil pure evil, and it will destroy itself. Make hate pure hate, and it will destroy itself. Therefore goodness and love will wear down all evil and hate.

O Lord, I thank you that when I am in you; then the universe approves of me and backs me and furthers me. I have cosmic backing for my way of life. Amen.

AFFIRMATION FOR THE DAY: No parasites tolerated in me today, everything contributive, positive.

*Cicero, as quoted in Phil Moore, *Straight to the Heart of Galatians to Colossians* (Oxford, UK: Monarch Books, 2014), 233 (a footnote cites Cicero's legal defense of Gaius Rabirius in 63 BCE as the source for the quotation).

ON TURNING THE OTHER CHEEK

Matthew 5:43-48

We come to look at the last of the ways in which the preaching of Jesus turned the world upside down.

8. You can conquer by turning the other cheek. This was absolutely revolutionary. On a Roman tomb were these words: "No man ever did more good to his friends and harm to his enemies." That was the approved standard. Jesus reversed that. He said overcome evil with good and hate by love. Conquer by the turned cheek. Is that weakness, or is it power? If we practiced that, would we be everybody's doormat or everybody's temple of refuge?

I picked up a letter that told of a woman who had been changed from a nominal Christian to a real one. She wrote to her daughter:

> Daddy left this morning to take some cattle to the sale, and he didn't come home for dinner. When suppertime came, he still wasn't home. I knew he had met some men, and they were drinking. My stomach started to get upset, my head started aching, and I began to worry, and at the same time I began to get rebellious and angry. As usual, when Daddy pulls this stunt, I went to my bedroom to get ready to leave for a few hours so I wouldn't have to face him or see him. I was seething with what I thought was righteous indignation. I heard the truck drive in and heard Daddy come in and lay down on the front-room floor. Then I looked at myself in the mirror, and my heart said, "Wait, listen!" I knelt down and prayed. I then got up and went into the kitchen and fixed Daddy coffee and supper. I got him up, and we ate together, and I sat there and loved him, rather Jesus and I loved him. Soon Daddy raised his head and said, "You aren't mad! Why?"

And then she added: "Blessed, wonderful Jesus, thou lovest him too, and I pray that soon our marriage will be complete: You, my husband, and I."

The husband probably responded, but if he did or didn't, the victory was already there. The wife had already mastered her resentments and bitterness—. The victory in being a Christian.

The positive was in the process of overcoming the negative.

O blessed Jesus, your ways are our ways—the ways written within us. And when we do your will, we do our own deepest will. We thank you. Amen.

AFFIRMATION FOR THE DAY: Today I shall overcome all evil with good, all hate by love, the world by a cross.

POSITIVE IN THE RIGHT DIRECTION

2 Corinthians 1:19-22

We have been studying the mastery of the negative attitude toward life.

There are strength and power and drive in the positive in contrast to the weakness and indirection of the negative. A tourist came back from England, and all he could talk about was the fact that his hotel window wouldn't open; it was stuck. He couldn't see the greatness of Britain—its democracy, its freedom, its contributions in literature and economic and political morality—all he could see was a stuck window. He and his report were stuck in that stuck window—negative!

An Indian came back from England, and his chief emphasis was on the fact that in an elevator was a sign that said: "Beware of Pickpockets." That one sign held his attention, and he couldn't see the vast honesty of a great people. Pickpockets picked him of the positive and left the negative. So his influence upon his hearers was negative.

But in the Acts the atmosphere was positive. However, it was not positive in general; it was positive in certain particulars. Today there is an emphasis on the positive as the positive. There is no doubt that there is great gain in turning from the negative attitudes toward life in favor of the positive. This emphasis is contained in a song that tells us to accentuate the positive, eliminate the negative.

This is good, but it needs qualification. It is not enough to be positive; you must be in the right direction and for the right things. Otherwise your positive may be positively disruptive. The two most positive characters of Europe in the last generation were Hitler and Mussolini. And they pulled down Europe in ruins around them.

In religion it is possible to be positive about everything and end up in being positively mushy. There must be discrimination about your positivity; for if you back what the universe does not back, you end in collapse, for all your positivity.

O Spirit of Truth, help me to back what you back and approve of what you approve. I would affirm your affirmations, and only your affirmations. Amen.

AFFIRMATION FOR THE DAY: I shall be positive, but I shall discriminate and affirm only what God affirms.

183

NOT-THE-WAY TRIES TO STOP THE WAY

Hebrews 10:22-25

We saw yesterday that our positive attitudes must be discriminating. Positive thinking may be good, provided your positive is good. To be positive for the sake of being positive may end in the negative, for reality doesn't back that positive.

To have faith in faith as some modern emphases advocate may end in collapse, for you may have faith in the wrong thing. And to have faith in faith is to have faith in the wrong thing. Paul, before he was converted, had full faith in what he was doing as the right thing; these Christians were a danger to the national faith and to the nation itself. So he would arrest the heresy in the name of truth. So "[Saul] went to the high priest, seeking letters to the synagogues at Damascus. If he found persons who belonged to the Way, whether men or women, these letters would authorize him to take them as prisoners to Jerusalem" (Acts 9:1-2). Here was positive zeal for the Jewish faith backed by legal authority, yet it ended in Paul's collapse and blindness. Why? He was positively backing the wrong thing. It was a case of Not-the-Way laying hold of the Way and trying to bind it. And that is futile, for the universe was behind the Way, and only the Jerusalem authorities and a zealous Paul were behind the other way. The universe affirmed the one and denied the other. Their positive turned out negative; it ended in blindness and prostration.

Your faith has to be faith in the Way—in Jesus Christ, who is the Way. There you can safely say yes to everything. There you can be positive to the utmost limit, positive with the stops out. For "in him it is always yes. All of God's promises have their yes in him" (2 Cor 1:19-20). Note "in him it is always yes." Out of him it is always no. For Life affirms his affirmations; and since Life does, we may safely do so. In him we can affirm all out.

O Jesus, in you I find the Way. Therefore in that Way I can be affirmative and all-out affirmative. For Reality is behind the Way. I thank you. Amen.

AFPIRMATION FOR THE DAY: My starting point is Jesus; I am affirmative as I move out from him to everything.

ONE SAW INIQUITY; THE OTHER AN INSTRUMENT

Acts 9:10-16

This all-out affirmation that the followers of Jesus found in him put a terrific drive in the Christian movement. It invaded the whole of life with its mighty affirmations. In doing so it cleansed away the hopeless, the negative, the loss of nerve, the morally and mentally collapsed, and brought a new affirmation into human living. Anything and anybody could be redeemed—and was!

Note this: "Ananias countered, 'Lord, I have heard many reports about this man. People say he has done horrible things.'...The Lord replied, 'Go! This man is the agent I have chosen.'" (Acts 9:13-15).

Note "he has done horrible things....This man is the agent I have chosen." One saw an iniquity; the Other saw an instrument! And the positive prevailed—and how! It prevailed over the doubts and fears of Ananias, and he turned to the powerfully positive. "Brother Saul"—his would-be murderer—was a brother, for his positive love turned the enemy into a friend—and more—into a brother. The stricken Saul must have shaken with sobs as he cried, "My God, they're calling me brother! I, who have come down to murder them; they've made me a brother." Then and there Saul was converted, I believe. He was stunned and blinded on the Damascus road, but not converted. Here he saw through human forgiveness the divine forgiveness and entered the gates of Eternal Life.

The yes in Jesus caught on in the soul of Ananias, and he became a yes in his attitudes toward Saul. He went beyond his original commission regarding Saul, for his commission was, "he has seen a man named Ananias enter and put his hands on him to restore his sight" (Acts 9:12). But Ananias went beyond that, and said: "The Lord Jesus...has sent me that you may regain your sight and be filled with the Holy Spirit" (9:17 RSV). Ananias added on his own: "be filled with the Holy Spirit." He affirmed for a murderer the highest that humanity can receive: "be filled with the Holy Spirit."

O Jesus, Redeemer, you are the positively redeeming, for you redeem us from all pessimism and all collapse and give us the highest. Amen.

AFFIRMATION FOR THE DAY: When I follow his affirmations, I shall go beyond them; for he inspires the More.

THE STEPS DOWN AND UP

Acts 26:19-23

We are studying the mastery of the negative by the positive. This is vividly seen in Paul himself. Note his steps down into the negative: (1) "The witnesses placed their coats in the care of a young man named Saul" (Acts 7:58). Here he was more or less passive, allowing them to lay their garments at his feet. (2) "Saul was in full agreement with Stephen's murder" (8:1). Here the passive turned to consent; he inwardly approved of the murder. (3) "Saul began to wreak havoc against the church. Entering one house after another, he would drag off both men and women and throw them into prison" (8:3). Here he became active in his negative attitudes; the inward consent turned to outward act. (4) "Saul was still spewing out murderous threats against the Lord's disciples" (9:1). Here the action became the person. He had committed murder; now he was murder—he breathed threats and murder. The act had become an attitude, had become him. He was positively possessed by the negative.

Then came the flash of light from the face of Jesus on the Damascus road, and Saul's whole false universe of hate and murder tumbled in around him. He became physically blind. Why? Because he was now spiritually blind; he couldn't see his way. So the spiritual blindness was transferred to a physical blindness—a conversion of a spiritual malady into a physical symptom. His negativism was complete. Then the positive, based on Reality, began to set in. Redemption began through love: "Brother Saul." The positive love broke down the negative hate. The physical symptom, blindness, was removed when spiritual insight began to come. Forgiveness invaded him, took away his inner conflicts, and then—wonder of wonders—he was "filled with the Holy Spirit." Now the positive took complete possession of him, and he began to breathe love and good will and redemption. The positive became him. The man who breathed threats and murder began to breathe out the Holy Spirit.

O Divine Spirit, how I thank you for your gracious redemption, willing to come into and take possession of murderous hearts. Take mine. Amen.

AFFIRMATION FOR THE DAY: Today I will breathe in the Holy Spirit, and I will breathe out the Holy Spirit on everything and everybody.

HE LIVES LIKE A CORINTHIAN

1 Corinthians 6:18-20

We have been studying Paul's turning from the extreme negative to the extreme positive. This illuminating sentence tells of the mighty transition: "Right away, he began to preach about Jesus in the synagogues. 'He is God's Son,' he declared" (Acts 9:20). One moment he was persecuting Jesus, and the next moment he was proclaiming Jesus—from the absolutely negative to the absolutely positive. And proclaiming the most absolutely positive assertion that language has ever been called on to make: Jesus is the Son of God! The pendulum had made the full swing and stayed there for the rest of Paul's glorious life.

The great believer in Jesus began to be the great believer in humanity; faith in the Son of Man began to be faith in the sons of men. This faith—that the worst could become the best, that the weakest could become the strongest, that the most down-and-out could become the most up-and-on-top—throbs through the whole of his life and letters and impact. Note this amazing result, and among a people of whom it was said of any low-down profligate, "He lives like a Corinthian." The Corinthian was the lowest watermark of morality, a result depicted in these words:

> Don't be deceived. Those who are sexually immoral, those who worship false gods, adulterers, both participants in same-sex intercourse, thieves, the greedy, drunks, abusive people, and swindlers won't inherit God's kingdom. That is what some of you used to be! But you were washed clean, you were made holy to God, and you were made right with God in the name of the Lord Jesus Christ and in the Spirit of our God. (1 Cor 6:9-11)

That moral and spiritual positive out of that moral and spiritual negative! No wonder a new, solemn joy went through that ancient world that sin and evil had met its match; people could attain to that hitherto impossible thing for the multitudes—goodness!

I saw a public dump that had been transformed into an amphitheater, beautified with glorious flowers and used as a vesper circle: from a dump to devotion, from waste to worship! This had happened in Corinth!

O Christ Jesus, you are the mighty Redeemer of our waste humanity, making filthy rags into writing paper upon which you write your thoughts. Amen.

AFFIRMATION FOR THE DAY: All my contacts today will be redemptive; I'll touch everything with God's touch.

FROM LUST TO LOVE

1 Corinthians 13:1-7

We have been studying the mighty affirmation of the Christian movement.

I looked at one of the most beautiful churches I had ever seen, and the pastor quietly said, "It was made of waste marble gathered from a dump." Waste marble into that! That was happening in the Christian movement in the Acts; the marble from the moral dump heaps of humanity was being built into a beautiful temple for the habitation of God in the Spirit.

I sat with a cultured Christian from the Tonga Islands and heard him tell how a hollowed-out rock that had been used as a receptacle for babies' heads that were to be crushed and offered to the gods had been transformed into a font for the baptizing of babies—from crushing to consecration! That was the mighty affirmation at work.

That transformation takes place today among the cultured. I sat with a devoted and beloved bishop whose life had been spent in Africa. I remembered the story goes that, after his first year in Africa as a missionary he was voted to be sent home, a failure, an impossible person. Then the committee decided to give him another chance provided he would read the thirteenth chapter of 1 Corinthians every day for a year. He did. He was transformed, and the very people who were going to send him home elected him to be their bishop! Now note the lowest statement that could be made about a man—"he lives like a Corinthian"—has been transformed into the highest standard of human living— "he lives like the thirteenth chapter of 1 Corinthians." The lowest lust had become the highest love. The cleansing Affirmative!

No wonder Paul ends the Acts of the Apostles with these words: "They will listen!" (28:28). Those words were a summing up of Paul's mighty faith in humanity: They will listen! His last recorded words in the Acts were words of faith that the Gentiles would respond. And his faith has been justified. We have responded!

O Jesus, we have listened! How could we help but listen when your voice speaks out of Reality to the depths of us? In you, the yes has at last sounded. Amen.

AFFIRMATION FOR THE DAY: If I have lived like a Corinthian, I shall live like the thirteenth chapter of 1 Corinthians.

I WAS ALL TIED UP INSIDE

2 Corinthians 13:1-3

We continue to look at the mighty redemptive affirmation in the Christian impact. It was seen then; it is seen today!

Note this: "I was all tied up inside—fears, resentments, guilt complex, inferiority complex, worries—everything that tied me in a tight knot. God could not get through to me at all. Then came the Ashram. My soul began to emerge, God was getting through to me, and the cleansing process began, and I was a new creature. What a glorious ten years I have had. My teaching is more valuable now, my church work, everything I do now, is done to his honor and glory. I am happy in Jesus."

A psychoanalyst went to a pastor, for he was personally upset. He said, "These people with whom I deal hang on my belt. They call me up at 3:00 am. They make me God. I can't stand up under it." The pastor gave him a copy of *Abundant Living.** Seven pages of it changed him. He found God and release. He had charged fifty dollars an hour to patients, would string them out, and then would bring up another problem just as they were about to get well. Now he charged eight dollars an hour and did a lot of free work. He was getting a lot of insights into Jesus and the meaning of the gospel, an entirely made-over man. He and his patients had been existing on analysis; now he was living on synthesis. Life had been put together on a higher level. There was subtraction, leading to addition and multiplication—a plus.

The positive note is summed up in the Acts in the title given to Barnabas. Before he laid everything at the feet of Jesus, his name was Joseph; and *Joseph* means "one more." He was one more child in the home, one more disciple. But when he gave everything to God, his name was changed to *Barnabas*, which means "Son of Encouragement." He encouraged everybody, was on the offensive of positive, creative love. He embodied the positive and the affirmative and thus the creative.

The Christian movement was a movement of encouragement—en (= within) and courage—courage within.

O blessed Holy Spirit; make me a "son of encouragement." Help me to encourage every good thing and every good person I meet and help me to encourage the possible good. Amen.

AFFIRMATION FOR THE DAY: I am not "one more." I am a plus in God. I shall live by what God builds.

*E. Stanley Jones, *Abundant Living* (Nashville: Abingdon Press, 2014).

DOES THE COSMIC PROCESS
AFFIRM OUR AFFIRMATIVE?

Revelation 21:1-4

Before we leave this mastery of the negative by a mighty positive, we must look at another phase. It is not enough that the individual affirm the positive; *we must feel that the whole cosmic process affirms our positive.* We cannot have a positive in us as persons while the whole historical process affirms a vast negative. We must feel that the sum total of reality is affirming the positive with us. Then and then only do we belong to the affirmative.

But in no other viewpoint except the Christian is there an affirmation of meaning to history and a belief in progress here and now. Only in Christianity did a new kind of hope emerge. In all other systems was a kind of paralysis; nothing new was emerging. We find in Ecclesiastes, which expresses some pre-Christian and sub-Christian themes: "Whatever has happened— / that's what will happen again; / whatever has occurred— / that's what will occur again. / There's nothing new under the sun" (1:9). This vicious circle was found in all ancient faiths.

Scottish theologian John Baillie calls attention to the fact that the circle as the symbol of life arose simultaneously in Greece, India, and China. Life was a circle that turned round on itself in meaningless existence; it got you nowhere. The only thing to do was to escape from this circle into the spiritual and the eternal. There was no escape forward; the only escape was backward or inward or upward. Salvation was escape—escape from the weary round of existence. The devotees' interest was not in the future, for there is no future, but in the changeless eternal world. The Stoics called this the "flight from the world of sense to pure being." Salvation in Hinduism is to get out of this world of karma and transmigration into realization of oneness with the non-personal Brahma. The world process is *maya* (illusion). History was not worth recording, for it had no meaning and no goal; only the spirit counted. Hence all India's literature is philosophy, related to spirit and its emancipation from a material world. Salvation is escape.

O Lord, teach us what you have in mind for us and our world. Help us to catch your mind with joy and offer ourselves as agents of your purpose. Amen.

AFFIRMATION FOR THE DAY: I am on the Way, the Way not to escape but to something Big and Significant.

THE NEW WORD: HOPE

1 Peter 1:3-5

We are studying the mastery of despair—despair as to the universe and life. All the other faiths except Christianity have what John Baillie notes "indifference to the events of the time-series, whether present or future, through steadfast contemplation of the timeless nature of things, timeless reason, timeless beauty, timeless divinity."*

Augustine translates Psalm 12:8 as "The wicked walk in circles." But in the non-Christian faiths, not only the wicked but people as people, the good as well as the bad, walk in circles, getting nowhere in this mundane existence. Only as one escapes into the spiritual does a person get anywhere. That leaves people pessimistic about the world process. There is no hope for it or any hope in it. The only hope is to escape from it. "The wise man is the man who is as much without hope as without fear, the man who is altogether indifferent to what the future may bring!"** Even a new beginning could bring "no ground of hopeful rejoicing since the new round of things would be exactly like the old, witnessing the same process of degeneration, and coming full circle again to the same melancholy end."***

That was the world of thought and idea and outlook into which Christianity burst. Its impact brought a new, vibrant word: *hope*. In almost all literature "hope is regarded as an evil thing. It is *ignis fatuus*, the great deceiver."† In all except this new faith. Here hope emerged. Paul told the Christians in Ephesus that when they were pagans, they had no hope (Eph 2:12). The fact is that nobody had any hope until they got into touch with this new dynamic of hope in the Christian faith.

Jesus never used the word *hope*; to him it was all realization. But when his thoughts and spirit came into contact with the minds and hearts of people, a new hope sprang up. There was a new hope about everything: life, destiny, the future, and the world itself. What was the new thing that brought this new hope'?

O Lord, you have begotten us into a lively hope by the resurrection of Jesus from the dead. When he left the tomb, we arose with him full of hope and cheer. Amen.

AFFIRMATION FOR THE DAY: I am a child of hope. I belong to the deathless hope, hope about life and destiny and people.

* John Baillie, *The Belief in Progress* (Oxford University Press, 1950), 52.
** Ibid., 65.
*** Ibid., 50.
† Ibid., 65.

IN ALL THESE THINGS

Colossians 1:11-14

We have seen that a new hope arose in human hearts with the impact of Jesus upon human spirits and thought. What produced it?

A. N. Whitehead gives a penetrating word: "I hazard the prophecy that that religion will conquer which can render clear to popular understanding some eternal greatness incarnate in the passage of temporal fact."* "Some eternal greatness incarnate in the passage of temporal fact"; that was fulfilled in the greatest temporal fact that has ever been seen in our world, the incarnation of God in Jesus.

That incarnation took place at a definite point in history in a definite person with a definite body. "The Word became flesh." This coming of the Divine into human manifestation tells humanity that salvation is not release from mundane existence but victory and release in the midst of mundane living. Persons and the time process itself can be redeemed in the midst of this world and its processes. Salvation was not escape; it was victory in and through human living as it now is and shall be.

The verses that most vividly show this are these:

> Who shall separate us from the love of Christ? Shall tribulation, or distress, or persecution, or famine, or nakedness, or peril, or sword?...No, in all these things we are more than conquerors through him who loved us. For I am sure that neither death, nor life, nor angels, nor principalities, nor things present, nor things to come, nor powers, nor height, nor depth, nor anything else in all creation, will be able to separate us from the love of God in Christ Jesus our Lord. (Rom 8:35-39 RSV)

In this sweeping passage is the secret in this one phrase: "in all these things." Note the "in." Every other system used other prepositions: "apart from" (Hinduism), "beyond" (Buddhism), "above" (Greek philosophy). Only the Christian faith said "in." Why? Because the incarnation was "in"—not "apart from" or "beyond," or "above"—it was "in." The victory had been wrought within the time process and over the time process and through the time process. It was a victory wrought out in life, and all life began to live!

O Jesus, wherever your feet have trod, flowers spring up in barren places; and hope is born within us with your coming. You are Life, Life, Life. We thank you. Amen.

AFFIRMATION FOR THE DAY: My victory today shall be Jesus. So no escapism, no trying to check out of problems.

* Alfred North Whitehead, *Adventures of Ideas* (New York: The Free Press, 1933), 33.

ON EARTH AS IT IS IN HEAVEN

1 Peter 1:18-21

We noted yesterday the phrase "in all these things" was a key phrase; the victory was "in." Another phrase gave people hope: "Jesus is Lord." It is the oldest and profoundest Christian creed. This phrase penetrated to the very roots of life: "Jesus is Lord, of all life now and hereafter!

Note they did not say, "Jesus will be Lord," for that would have expressed hope. But they said, "Jesus is Lord," and that expressed a fact now. He had met everything, spiritual and material, and had conquered it; so he is Lord here and now. Out of that accomplished fact in history grew up their amazing hope about everything. Their hope included everything, for he was Lord of everything.

The vicious circle of living, the weary round of treadmill existence, had been broken. Life was no longer a circle, turning back on itself forever; it was an open vista—a Way. Life, history, the world, everything had meaning. The prayer—

> Thy kingdom come,
> Thy will be done,
>   On earth as it is in heaven (Matt 6:10 RSV)

—pointed life toward the coming of the kingdom on earth. The earth was to be the scene of final victory, therefore part of that victory. It was not merely a future victory when Jesus would return to reign—he was reigning—Jesus is Lord! Where was the kingdom? In his person. As John Baillie says: "The kingdom is not something yet to come. It came with Jesus Christ." He is the kingdom personalized. In knowing him you "have tasted the excellence of the Gospel and the powers of the coming age."* In Jesus, the victory of the coming age is realized. Not that he will not come again. The Scriptures say he will come in the final consummation of the kingdom. But in the meantime we partake of that final victory. As far as those in Christ are concerned, it has come and is present. They partake of the "powers of the coming age"—realized eschatology. Jesus is Lord!

"He must reign until he has put all [things] under his feet" (1 Cor 15:25 RSV). Note: "reign until"; he is reigning now even when all things are not under his feet. Things not under his feet perish.

O Jesus, you are Lord, Lord of heaven and earth, time and eternity; you are Lord. In that fact we face all life knowing that all that refuses your Lordship perishes. Amen.

AFFIRMATION FOR THE DAY: Today, not only shall I affirm "Jesus is Lord," but everything I do and am will affirm it.

*John Baillie, *The Belief in Progress* (Oxford University Press, 1950), 206.

193

EVERY MAN'S INFINITE, ESSENTIAL PERFECTION

Hebrews 6:1-3

We have been studying the mastery of despair about life and the worldliness. That mastery came through the realization that Jesus is Lord.

It was based on the solid realization that the Incarnate was the Invincible. I say "solid realization," for it was in deep contrast to modern movements that assert humanity's perfection in itself, and all we have to do is realize it. One exponent of this says, "I sincerely believe that the single greatest equipment for foreign missionary work, as well as for all spiritual work, whether at home or abroad is a conception of every man's infinite, essential, God-given perfection."* How this could be equipment for mission work in India is hard to see. There is nothing new in that conception for the Hindu who believes he is already part of Brahma, therefore infinitely and essentially perfect— if he can only realize it! That's the rub—if he can only realize it! I have never seen anybody in East or West who realized that he or she was God, or who was essentially and infinitely perfect. It is the philosophy of a few, the religion of none. For it is based on words, not on the Word made flesh—a fact. It is a philosophical fancy, not a solid fact. No one is God but God, and no one is perfect except God. To tell you that you are God or perfect in yourself gives a shot in the arm by an injection of fanciful wordiness, but it has a letdown, a deflation.

Moreover, it leaves you as the center: I am God; I am perfect. It has no place for self-surrender, only for self-realization. That leaves the self unsurrendered. Nowhere in the New Testament are you told to realize your perfection. Christian faith is too realistic for this romanticizing. You are told to be perfect, to go on to perfection; but nowhere are you told that everyone is perfect now, inherently and infinitely so. That is foreign to New Testament Christianity. It leaves no place for redemption; it has place only for realization. It gives you no Savior. It is salvation by enlightenment as to your essential perfection. That is Vedantic Hinduism, not New Testament Christianity.

O Divine Spirit, I thank you that you can put my feet on the road to perfection; you can mold me stage by stage into the image of Jesus. Amen.

**AFFIRMATION FOR THE DAY: I am a Christian in the making.
I am not perfect, but I belong to the Perfect One.**

* No published source was found for this quotation.

SELF-REALIZATION OR SELF-SURRENDER?

Hebrews 2:6-9

We are studying the mighty positive of the New Testament movement. But it is the positive without jumping the rails into assertions about every person's divinity or inherent perfection. That would not be the Word become flesh; it would be the Word become word, not anchored in the facts. It would lift the whole thing out of New Testament redemption and put it in the framework of alien philosophies. It would make Christianity deal with extravagances instead of extrications. Humanity, according to the New Testament, is neither divine nor a devil. Humanity is made in the image of God, a "little less than God," but humanity has fallen and needs redemption, and grace undertakes that redemption; the end is perfection in the image of Christ. Note the end is perfection—not the beginning. To make perfection the beginning is to fly in the face of the facts, for people are not essentially and inherently perfect, and they know it. Any such assertion is romanticizing in regard to human nature. It is to make people go on a jag from the wine of their own extravagant wordiness, and it ends in a rude awakening when the next morning arrives and they have to face the realities of life with the realities of what they are. And those realities do not add up to perfection.

This takes them away from the emphasis on self-surrender and puts it on self-realization. And it does another thing; it accompanies that self-realization by self-assertion. "I am essentially perfect; therefore I can do wonders, perform miracles. I am divine; therefore miracles are my natural accompaniment." That makes them into a seven-day wonder. But in self-surrender the emphasis throws them back on grace: "I can of myself do nothing; but surrendered to God. God does wonderful things through this unworthy instrument." That makes for open possibilities—infinite possibilities—but it also makes for humility. I am not the center—God is. I am not perfect, but I am in the hands of the Perfect and am being made into the image of that Perfect to the degree that I cooperate.

O Lord, I thank you for this redemption. It puts me into the dust and then raises me to the highest heaven. It creates a humble glorying in grace. Amen.

AFFIRMATION FOR THE DAY: I belong to the Infinitely Perfect, and today I shall become more like Jesus.

BY THE GRACE OF GOD I AM WHAT I AM

1 Peter 1:22-23

We come to our last day in the consideration of the mighty positive of the Acts. For the individual it means life is going to be affirmed until it awakes in God's likeness. It takes humanity as we are—sinful, disrupted—and undertakes to make us as we ought to be—like Christ.

It starts out, not with the disciples discovering and declaring their infinite and essential perfection, but with their humbly receiving the "promise of the Lord"—the Holy Spirit. It doesn't say to the Jewish leaders guilty of Jesus' murder: "Realize your infinite and essential perfection, and all your shortcomings and guilt will drop away." They did say: "Change your hearts and lives. Each of you must be baptized in the name of Jesus Christ for the forgiveness of your sins. Then you will receive the gift of the Holy Spirit" (Acts 2:38). That was realistic, anchored to the facts; it also opened infinite possibilities by grace giving them the Spirit to make them into Jesus' image.

They didn't say to the lame man at the Beautiful Gate, "Realize your infinite and inherent perfection." They said, "In the name of Jesus Christ the Nazarene, rise up and walk!" And Peter added: "You Israelites, why are you amazed at this? Why are you staring at us as we made him walk by our own power or piety [and we may add, perfection]?... The faith that comes through Jesus gave him complete health right before your eyes" (3:6, 12, 16). The eyes of the disciples and of the people were on Jesus as the source of the miracle. They weren't seven-day wonders, dispensing miracles because of their divinity or their perfection; they pointed to Jesus.

And Paul didn't say, "By my realization of my essential and inherent perfection I am what I am"; instead he said, humbly and gratefully: "I am what I am by God's grace" (1 Cor 15:10). That pointed to grace, not to Paul.

So the positive affirms life mightily even unto perfection, but it is realistic. And it affirms the cosmic process as having a goal and end—the kingdom of God on earth. That breaks the paralysis of thought about the individual and opens infinite possibilities for society—the kingdom of God.

O Lord God, it takes away my breath to know that I am under the process of redemption and that redemption is redeeming me into God's image. What a redemption! Amen.

AFFIRMATION FOR THE DAY: I am good only as I surrender to grace and let it operate fully within me.

THE TWO EMPHASES THE PERSON AND THE ORDER

John 1:14-19

We have been studying the mighty affirmations of the Acts. It was the divine positive becoming incarnate in a group. It was life-affirming and world-affirming. It meant the individual was going to be made into the most wonderful image ever seen upon our planet: "It does not yet appear what we shall be, but we know that when he appears we shall be like him" (1 John 3:2 RSV). "Like him"—what a destiny!

But the positive was just as positive about society, the total life. For this world was to be the scene of the coming of the kingdom of God on earth.

It was the fact that the kingdom of God was to come on earth that gave hope and faith about the world and its ultimate meaning and goal. The world was to be redeemed, not rejected. It was to end, not in illusion, but in illumination. If the cross had its head and arms above the earth, the basis of that cross was in the earth, and the earth was to partake of that redemption.

The kingdom of God is the all-embracing conception that gives cosmic and total meaning to life and redemption. In the Acts the kingdom and Jesus are the two emphases: one the Order and the other the Person. Note: "After they came to believe Philip, who preached the good news about God's kingdom and the name of Jesus Christ, both men and women were baptized" (Acts 8:12). Note the good news was not just Jesus, the Person, nor the kingdom, the Order—it was both. Paul had these two emphases also, "From morning until evening, he explained and testified concerning God's kingdom and tried to convince them about Jesus" (28:23). And again: "Paul lived in his own rented quarters for two full years and welcomed everyone who came to see him. Unhindered and with complete confidence, he continued to preach God's kingdom and to teach about the Lord Jesus Christ" (28:30-31). Now note "God's kingdom...about the Lord Jesus"—the Order and the Person.

To preach the Order made religion social; to preach Jesus made religion personal—it was both social and personal.

O Jesus, we thank you that you inspire us anew to preach you and your message. For your message is the kingdom. Help us to get hold of both: you and the kingdom. Amen.

AFFIRMATION FOR THE DAY: The social and the personal shall become one in me, each a part of a living whole.

GOD A HALF-GOD RULING
OVER A HALF-REALM

Matthew 13:37-41

We have seen that the message of the Acts was the Person, Jesus, and the Order, the kingdom. But they were not two messages; they were one.

Jesus started out "preaching the gospel of the kingdom of God" (Mark 1:14 KJV), the only thing he ever called his gospel. And he sent out his disciples to preach the gospel of the kingdom of God. Then he seemed to change his emphasis and began to preach himself. "I am the way. . . . No one comes to the Father except through me" (John 14:6). Which was his message—the Order or the Person? Or did they coalesce and become one? They became one; he used interchangeably "for my sake" and "for the kingdom's sake." He was the kingdom personalized; the Order came to embodiment in him. The Absolute Order and the Absolute Person came together and were one. That meant religion was personal in that it had personal relations with a Person; it was also social in that it had relations with an Order embodied in that Person. It was not now personal and now social; it was both by its very nature. So I do not want a personal gospel or a social gospel; I want one gospel that redeems the total life, individual and social. That is as it should be, for God is not a half-god ruling over a half-realm. God is the God of all life. God's kingdom is a total kingdom.

It also meant that the material and the spiritual were being redeemed. A Chinese leader put it this way, "Where the material and the spiritual are integrated, there is the kingdom of God." The kingdom of God is where the will of God is done on earth in all relationships as it is done in heaven.

When the disciples said, "Jesus is Lord," they knew that the kingdom had come in Jesus. God was not only redeeming by Jesus, God was ruling by Jesus. That made the nature of the kingdom plain; it was love ruling in human affairs, the Christ-like spirit universalized. Some would make out God as redeeming by Christ but as ruling by other methods of a different spirit—force and compulsion. But his redeeming and his ruling are one. For both express his nature as love. The kingdom is love in total operation.

O Lord, we thank you that Jesus reveals you as redeeming through love and as ruling through love. Help me to make love the all-embracing method and atmosphere of my life. Amen.

AFFIRMATION FOR THE DAY: I shall live today as love realized in every thought, attitude, and act.

THE KINGDOM IS THE WAY

Romans 8:29-30

We come to note another aspect of the kingdom, an aspect seldom noted.

"And [Paul] entered the synagogue and for three months spoke boldly, arguing and pleading about the kingdom of God; but when some were stubborn and disbelieved, speaking evil of the Way before the congregation, he withdrew" (Acts 19:8-9 RSV). Note "pleading about the kingdom of God; but when some were stubborn and disbelieved, speaking evil of the Way." Here the kingdom of God and the Way are used interchangeably. But Jesus is called the Way—"I am the way"—yet here the kingdom is the Way. So things equal to the same thing are equal to each other; Jesus and the kingdom are one!

But this shows not only the identity of Jesus and the kingdom but also that the kingdom is the Way written into the nature of things, the way we are made to live. We usually make the Way the way of salvation. It is, but it is more; it is the Way unqualified, the way to do everything—to think, to act, to feel, to be under every conceivable circumstance—for God and humanity, in the individual and the collective. It is the Way. There are just two things in life: the Way and Not-the-Way. The Christian way is always the Way, and the unchristian way is always Not-the-Way. There are no exceptions.

When God made you and me and the universe, God stamped within us the Way—the way we are made to live. We can live against that Way written in us; but if we do, we get hurt. It is our destiny written in us.

The Way of Jesus is the Way of the kingdom, and the Way of the kingdom is our way—the way we are made to live. This passage puts it thus, "God destined us to be his adopted children through Jesus Christ because of his love" (Eph 1:5). We are destined to belong to the Way; and that destiny is written in our blood, our nerves, our tissues, our very make-up. "The kingdom of God is within you"—it is written in the very constitution of our being. The laws of the kingdom are the laws of our being, stamped within our very selves, therefore inescapable. When you revolt against them, you revolt against yourself.

O God, our Lord, we thank you that we have a destiny, the most glorious destiny that can be conceived; we are destined for your kingdom. It is our Homeland. Amen.

AFFIRMATION FOR THE DAY: I shall fulfill my destiny by making the laws of the kingdom the laws of my life.

THE WAY, WHICH THEY CALL A SECT

Matthew 5:17-20

We have seen that the kingdom is the Way. When people got hold of this, it got hold of them. It gave them a mastery over alternatives; there was no other way than the Way!

Note the passages in Acts where the Way is used: "if he found persons who belonged to the Way" (9:2); "publicly slandered the Way" (19:9); "a great disturbance erupted about the Way" (19:23); "I harassed those who followed this Way to their death" (22:4); "This I admit to you, that according to the Way, which they call a sect, I worship...God" (24:14 RSV); "Felix, who had an accurate understanding of the Way" (24:22).

This adoption of the Way to describe the Christian way was amazing. It meant that they had cut down through the jungle of rival claims and had climbed out to a clear way, which turned out to be the Way. All alternatives were gone—they were certain with an invincible certainty.

Now note "according to the Way, which they call a sect" (24:14 RSV). A sect is a section of life, something cut off, not the whole. They called it a sect; Paul called it the Way—the Whole, Reality. From that day to this we have been doing just what Paul's contemporaries did; we make the Way into a sect by making it a way to heaven, a way to save our souls, a way to keep well, a way to success, a way of social custom. Or we make the Way synonymous with our denomination or even synonymous with the church. But the Way is the Way—the way to do everything—all else is Not-the-Way.

Many Christians, and practically all non-Christians, make the Way into a sect by making it a religion—alongside other religions—maybe a little better, but still a religion. But Jesus never used the word *religion*, nor did he conceive of himself setting one religion alongside other religions. He came to set the gospel over against all human need, whether in this religion, that religion, or no religion. He came to set the Way over against ways.

And when you entered this kingdom, you knew instinctively that this was the Way. The quest was over.

O Christ, when our wandering feet touch the Way, there is the thrill of being conscious that this is the thing for which we were born. This is It. We thank you. Amen.

AFFIRMATION FOR THE DAY: I shall not turn the Way into a sect; it shall be the whole—the whole of my life.

HUMAN TOTALITARIANISM AND GOD'S

Daniel 6:26-27

There is a further observation that we must make upon the Way. If the laws of our being and the laws of the universe are the laws of the kingdom, and if the kingdom is the Way, and if that Way is stamped into the nature of things, then the victory is assured. For these laws of the kingdom are self-executing; break them and you get broken automatically.

Then why should we fear alien ways of life? They are doomed to break themselves upon Reality. Take Communism. The issue in the world today is between human totalitarianism and God's totalitarianism—between materialistic, atheistic Communism and the kingdom of God on earth. But Communism has enacted its laws and imposed them on people and situations, and they have to execute them with all the force they have available. But since those human-made and human-executed laws do not fit Reality, they have a frustrating time in making them work. They will ultimately fail; they are bound to.

The laws of the kingdom are not imposed but exposed out of the heart of Reality. Those laws fit us, and we fit the laws. We are made for each other as the eye is made for light. These laws are self-executing; break them and you get broken—automatically. Those who belong to the kingdom have a decided advantage and a decisive advantage, for the kingdom to which they belong automatically executes its own laws; it breaks the breakers. The dust heaps of the centuries are witness.

My prediction is that Communism will break itself upon the very moral universe that it says does not exist. It says there is no objective morality written into the nature of things. Only that is right that gets you to your goal of Communism, a moral opportunism. That moral opportunism will break it from within. For if you use any means to get you to your goal, you will have to use any means to keep yourself in power. There will be no moral cement to hold it together. It will fall to pieces. Force will be used to hold it, and that force will produce counterforce, and the system will perish.

O Lord, we thank you that your kingdom is an everlasting kingdom, and of the increase of your government there will be no end. And we belong to it! Amen.

AFFIRMATION FOR THE DAY: I am aligned to Reality, and nothing can stop me as long as I keep that alignment.

201

TRAINEES FOR THE NEW ORDER

Hebrews 6:17-20

We have seen that the idea of the kingdom of God on earth gave the Christians a mastery over the ultimate hopelessness of human living history has a goal, and that goal is the kingdom of God on earth. That kingdom carne in preview in the society in the Acts of the Apostles and will come in full consummation with the return of Jesus Christ to reign. In the meantime we can be the agents of the coming of that kingdom now. And we can prepare ourselves to be the agents.

Jesus pointed to this preparation in these words: "'Therefore, every legal expert who has been trained as a disciple for the kingdom of heaven is like the head of a household who brings old and new things out of their treasure chest'" (Matt 13:52). Note that important phrase: "trained...for the kingdom of heaven." It visualizes a course of training in the kingdom mentality and outlook and spirit. When you are trained for the army, you have trained out of you what can't fit into army mentality and practice and trained into you the things that do.

Now that was what Jesus expected of us, to have trained out of us all that will not fit into the kingdom of God and trained into us all that will. We were to enlist as trainees of the New Order.

What would that involve? It would mean all pessimism about humanity and the future of humanity and of the world would be trained out of us. The kingdom will come—and come on earth! We are the people with a future—and a future with ultimate victory in it. We belong not to ultimate defeat but to ultimate Victory! And that ultimate Victory is now. Jesus is Lord! Not will be—is! This glorious passage gives that invincibility now: "Therefore let us be grateful for receiving a kingdom that cannot be shaken" (Heb 12:28 RSV). Is the kingdom of God the one unshakable kingdom? Yes! Everything around is shaken and shakable. But the kingdom is not shaken, for it is founded on the foundations of the universe, founded on the rock of Reality. We stand unshaken in the midst of an unshakable kingdom.

O God, our Lord, how can we thank you enough for this unshakable kingdom? We may tremble on it, but it doesn't tremble. It is there, eternally there. Amen.

AFFIRMATION FOR THE DAY: Everything that does not fit the kingdom will be trained out of me today.

REPENT, FOR THE ECUMENICAL CHURCH IS AT HAND?

Ephesians 2:12-18

We come now to our final day on the consideration of the mastery of pessimism about our planet and its future. The future belongs to the kingdom and to those who are trained for the kingdom.

We haven't been trained for the kingdom. We train our ministers for the Methodist ministry, the Episcopalian, the Baptist, the Presbyterian, and so on. But we don't train them for the kingdom. We don't train them to see everything from the kingdom viewpoint and outlook. We are trying to train them to the Ecumenical Church outlook, which is good but not good enough. For suppose you go out and say, "Repent, for the Ecumenical Church is at hand"; what will happen? The people will shrug their shoulders and say, "What's that?" You are confronting people with the relativism of the church instead of confronting them with the absolute kingdom. Note the difference: If I go out and say, "Repent, for the kingdom of God is at hand," you don't shrug your shoulders; you bend the knee! For this is the Absolute, confronting all relativisms with an imperious demand, "Repent, submit, and be redeemed." That viewpoint takes away the tentative, the halfway, and gives us the conqueror's tread.

It makes us vital and fresh. Jesus said, "'Therefore, every legal expert [scribe] who has been trained as a disciple for the kingdom of heaven is like the head of a household who brings old and new things out of their treasure chest'" (Matt 13:52). Now a scribe is the last person you would have expected to bring forth the new. He was a copyist. He created nothing; he copied the past. But even the dry-as-dust copyist becomes creative if he gets hold of the kingdom and is trained in it. Everything is lighted up, takes on freshness and vitality, when you get hold of the Absolute and the Absolute gets hold of you. Then you become trained in receptivity: "let us be grateful for receiving a kingdom" (Heb 12:28 RSV)—receiving! The kingdom does not come by trying or struggling but by surrender and receiving. That opens its powers to all. You don't have to be worthy; you have to be willing. You don't build the kingdom; you receive it—God's highest gift!

O Lord, I thank you that I do not have to build the kingdom; that would mean strain. But I can receive the kingdom, all its powers at my disposal. I thank you. Amen.

AFFIRMATION FOR THE DAY: I shall train myself in receptivity totally. I shall learn to take, to assimilate, to receive.

THE MASTERY OF SICKNESS AND DISEASE

Matthew 4:23; 10:1

The next mastery in the Acts that we will consider is *the mastery of sickness and disease*. The Christian movement has a message for the body. The body is included in Christian redemption. But it is not the central emphasis. Christianity is not a healing cult. Its main business is not keeping the body in repair. Those who make Christianity a healing cult make God serve them, and they and their physical needs are at the center. They try to organize the universe around them as the center instead of God as the center, and that won't work. So the healing cults leave a lot of shattered faith and spiritual disaster in their wake, which greatly overbalance the healing results.

The primary purpose of Christian redemption is to save us from sin and evil and get the ransomed self off its own hands and into the hands of God. Self-surrender is the pivot of the process of redemption. But as a result of this redemption from sin and evil—and the transference of life from self-centeredness to God-centeredness—a great many sicknesses and diseases drop off as a by-product of that redemption. This accounts for the amazing health pervading society in the Acts. But it cannot account for all. Apparently health came (1) through the direct healing of God in dramatic cures; (2) through what Paul calls the giving of "life to your human bodies also, through his Spirit that lives in you" (Rom 8:11); (3) through deliverance from underlying fears and worries, resentments, jealousies, guilt, and self-preoccupation; (4) through right thinking and emotions; (5) through the physician. In these five ways health streamed into the mortal bodies of people.

Note that it was not one of these ways—the direct touch of God upon our bodies—that was the sole channel of healing. It was a combination of all of these. Where one way and only one way is selected—the way of faith producing an obvious miracle—and rigidly held to, in its wake there is strewn the wreckage of faith and unhealed bodies. God cannot be straitjacketed.

O Lord, your heart and your purpose envelop many ways of healing. Help us to discover and use your ways. For you are health, and you will health to your children. Amen.

AFFIRMATION FOR THE DAY: I will have the best body I am capable of having to be used for the kingdom.

GOD HEALS THROUGH PHYSICIANS

Psalm 103:1-5

We noted yesterday the five ways in which God heals. We take them up in reverse order.

First, God heals through the physician. This method is not mentioned in the Acts or in the Epistles except by implication. "Luke the dearly loved physician" is mentioned in Col 4:14, and he is mentioned as one who continued to be a physician, not *was* a physician. Nowhere is medicine derided or are physicians repudiated in the New Testament. Paul says: "Don't drink water anymore, but use a little wine because of your stomach and your frequent illnesses" (1 Tim 5:23). A little wine was prescribed as a physical remedy—true, a doubtful remedy—but in use in those days. The use of remedies is the point.

But while physicians and remedies are not repudiated, they are very marginal in the New Testament. They are not the chief dependence for health. Other forces were at work producing health and healing. But not all diseases were cured. Timothy had "frequent illnesses." Paul had a "thorn in my body," for which he sought the Lord three times and got the reply, "My grace is enough for you, because power is made perfect in weakness." To which Paul replied, "So I'll gladly spend my time bragging about my weakness" (2 Cor 12:7-9). Paul's infirmity was probably sore, running eyes; for he said to the Galatians: "You know that I first preached the gospel to you because of an illness. Though my poor health burdened you, you didn't look down on me or reject me, but you welcomed me as if I were an angel from God, or as if I were Christ Jesus!...I swear that, if possible, you would have dug out your eyes and given them to me" (4:13-15). That the infirmity was a moral struggle with sex—as has been suggested by some who on behalf of an absolutist position in regard to physical healing would like to get rid of Paul's unhealed physical infirmity—has no basis whatever in the New Testament.

While not all diseases were cured in the New Testament, yet this alternative was there: either God will cure the infirmity, or God will give us power to use the infirmity until the final cure in the resurrection, when we get our perfect resurrection body. In either case a real way out.

O Lord, I know that you will cure my diseases now or give me power to take up those infirmities into the purpose of my life and transmute them into higher victory. Amen.

AFFIRMATION FOR THE DAY: I will take all my infirmities to God for cure or for power to use them for higher ends.

IN A MORTAL WORLD THE BODY BREAKS DOWN

2 Corinthians 12:7-10

We ended on the note yesterday that not all diseases are cured in this life. This is a mortal world, and the body was never intended to be immortal in a mortal world. The body sometimes breaks down. And this occurs to those who are saints and who are filled with faith. When one such saint was crippled with pain from arthritis, some absolutists were wringing their hands in agony and wondering where the lack of faith rested—in them or in the sufferer. I commented, "The victory lies in his spirit. He was radiant when he was free from pain, and he is still radiant wracked with pain. The victory of spirit is the real miracle, far greater than any physical miracle of healing." 'The saint said," I would rather have you preach my funeral sermon; for while they would be bemoaning my lack of healing, you would be singing the 'Hallelujah Chorus.'"

When an absolutist position is taken, a great deal of wreckage results. One such absolutist healer himself died of cancer. Another had to leave his healing services in order to go to the Mayo Clinic for an operation for cancer. Another dropped dead of heart failure as he was laying hands on the sick in a healing service.

The flexibility of outlook in the New Testament does not leave behind this wreckage. It is sane and wholesome and sound. These people were amazingly healthy because they had found the Way, and the Way turned out to be the way to live—physically, mentally, spiritually, collectively.

The Whitby, Ontario, Canada, mental hospital probably turns out a larger percentage of cures than any other institution in North America. When asked about the secrets of healthy living, the head of the hospital replied, 'Work and love." If you do not have a creative activity, you're unhealthy automatically; and if you don't love something and someone beyond yourself, again you're unhealthy automatically.

The society in the Acts knew those two things—they were creatively working, and they were creatively loving. Hence they were healthy. Disease germs and functional disturbances simply could not find any lodging in such healthy living.

O Lord God, I thank you that we can be so sound within that disease germs and functional disturbances can find no seedbed within ns. Make us that way. Amen.

AFFIRMATION FOR THE DAY: Today I shall creatively work and creatively love.

RIGHT THINKING AND RIGHT EMOTIONS

Philippians 4:8-9

I mentioned yesterday two things necessary to health: work and love. Karl Menninger, head of the famous Topeka Clinic, gives four things necessary to mental and physical health: creative work, creative play, creative worship, and creative love. He adds to Cabot's list the word "creative."* This is important; if the work, play, worship, and love are not creative, producing something constructive outside self, they bring disease not health. It is the element of self-losing and self-transcending that produces health. If any of these leave you in a state of self-reference or self-preoccupation, they are not fruitful—they are festering.

The deliverance from self-preoccupation found in the Acts is the most disease-freeing influence ever let loose in our world. People began to love God and others instead of themselves, and, lo, their bodies blossomed into health.

A very intelligent woman asked me what was the secret of my abounding health and vitality; and I answered, "I suppose it is grace. I've learned how to receive—to receive Grace into my body and my spirit." She thoughtfully replied, "Yes, but it is also right thinking and right emotions." She was profoundly right. If you depend only on grace and do not look to right thinking and right emotions, then you will be only fitfully, instead of continuously, healthy. Here is where many healing movements break down. They emphasize sudden healing grace but put no emphasis on right thinking and right emotions. They emphasize healing instead of health. It should be both. Jeremiah emphasizes both: "but now I will heal and mend them. I will make them whole and bless them with an abundance of peace and security" (33:6). Health is a continuous state before the healing. And we have no right to ask for healing unless we are practicing attitudes of mind and emotion that produce health.

The effects of thought and emotion reach down into every cell of the body and affect them for good or ill. So much so that doctors say that 50–75 percent of diseases are caused by mind and emotion.

O Christ of the Healing Touch, touch our minds and our emotions and our bodies into health and healing. Make us the best that we can be. Amen.

AFFIRMATION FOR THE DAY: All my thoughts and all my emotions shall contribute to health.

* See Richard C. Cabot, *What Men Live By: Work, Play, Love, Worship* (Houghton Mifflin, 1929).

PERCENTAGE OF DISEASES ROOTED IN MIND AND EMOTION

Psalm 6:2-7

We saw yesterday that mind and emotion can produce disease. A gynecologist said to me, "Probably 90 percent of diseases are either caused by, or at least affected by, mind and emotion." Another doctor put it this way, "Apart from contagious diseases and malignancies, all the rest are caused by mind and emotion."

The effect of emotions is vividly seen in Daniel in these passages: "The king's mood changed immediately, and he was deeply disturbed. He felt weak, and his knees were shaking" (5:6). Again: "Now as for how I, Daniel, felt about this: My thoughts disturbed me greatly. My mood darkened considerably" (7:28). "Then I, Daniel, was overwhelmed and felt sick for days. When I finally got up and went about the king's business, I remained troubled by the vision and couldn't understand it" (8:27). "So I was left alone to see this great vision all by myself. All my strength left me. My energy was sapped, and I couldn't stay strong" (10:8). "My lord, the vision bothered me deeply, and I couldn't stay strong during it. So how can I, my lord's servant, speak with you, my lord? Even now there's no strength in me, and I can hardly breathe (10:16-17).

Human nature in all ages, in all climes, is the same. A heart specialist said to me, "Of all heart diseases 75 percent are caused by mind and emotions." A director of music in a church revealed this, "I didn't know whether I had an ulcer or cancer, or both. But when the pastor was moved, I was well." The inner tensions upset her whole system. A prominent pastor was a lawyer before he entered the ministry; he told me that for ten years before he decided to go into the ministry, he was ill—ill from indecision. The moment he decided to go into the ministry, he was well and has been ever since. The indecision threw functional disturbance into his system. A commanding officer was harsh and tyrannical. He said to a group, "It's all bunk about getting stomach ulcers from temper. I never had any ulcers." And a man in the group replied, "How about your adjutant?" Wrong thinking and emotions do produce spiritual chaos in and around one and, therefore, physical chaos.

O Spirit of God, help me to be the kind of person who shall be healing to myself and others. Help me by word and thought and emotion to spread health. Amen.

AFFIRMATION FOR THE DAY: No ulcerated spirit within me shall cause ulcers to myself or others.

STRESS: THE CAUSE OF ALL DISEASES?

Psalm 94:18-19

We are studying the effect of mind and emotions on the body. A pastor tells of how his mother became physically ill when her son was converted. She was fighting it for herself. Then the mother herself was converted, and the moment she was she became well and happy. A husband, whenever he came near his wife, sneezed ten times. The reason was that his wife criticized and nagged him, and he took this method of warding off her attacks. He went on the offensive! This was all unconscious, of course. Many retreat into an illness as a method of getting out of a difficult situation, "If I were well, I could do it. But I'm not well, therefore I do not have to do it." Illness is a refuge.

An article in the *Reader's Digest* gives the theory that the basis of all diseases is what a doctor called "stress." He became interested, not in specific diseases, but in the possible cause of all diseases—something that lay back of everything. And he fastened on stress. When one is under stress, the glands throw their secretions into the system to maintain the balance of the organism. But if the stress is long continued, then the defense mechanism breaks down, and the balance is not maintained. When that happens, disease may break out anywhere in the body, and that disease may be of various kinds. But the cause back of it all is stress. If that is true, then the maintenance of inner rest and poise is an absolute necessity for health.

A young wife, intelligent and cultured, had over forty allergies. Her marriage was childless. When she found she was going to have a child, every one of those forty allergies dropped away. The cause of them all was inner stress. A young man was called on to interpret my speech in India. He was afraid to try it. So he developed a sore throat as a way out of the dilemma.

O Jesus, you have shown us how to live with ourselves by living with adjustment. Help me to bring every thought and every emotion into adjustment. Amen.

AFFIRMATION FOR THE DAY: My quiet heart shall be without stress or strain this day, settled down in God.

209

HEADACHES THROUGH RESENTMENTS

Ephesians 4:31-32

We spend another day on the effect of mind and emotion on the body. Habakkuk says:

> I hear, and my insides tremble.
> My lips quiver at the sound.
> Rottenness enters my bones.
> I tremble while I stand. (Hab 3:16)

A woman working in an aircraft factory found that she was having headaches continually. She couldn't find anything in home or personal life that could cause it, until one day she realized that she resented having men in greasy clothes take the tools that she passed out. When she faced her resentment and saw how unreasonable it was, her headaches disappeared.

A druggist said to me, "The husband's sin can make the wife ill, and the wife's sin can cause illness in the husband." An Indian youth told me he carried a bottle of water around in his pocket to soak the cloths he had wrapped around his legs. They were always dry and numb. I found he had been accidentally shot while out hunting with a white man. This dryness and numbness developed after that. The accident occurred during the hot, dry season. The dryness made him think subconsciously of the accident, and numbness set in. When the connection was shown, the symptoms disappeared.

A very intelligent and cultured woman, wife of a doctor, made herself and everyone around her miserable by her fear of germs. She cleaned and scrubbed incessantly and was afraid of visitors, afraid they would bring germs into the house. But the biggest disease-breeding germ was right inside her: fear. Fear and resentments and self-centeredness are the seed plots in which diseases germinate and flourish. A pastor who was always ill said that whenever he went into the pulpit, he felt it sinking beneath him. He had been slipping through fear and conflict, and he created this outer symptom of sinking as a symbol of what was taking place within. It was what psychology calls "conversion," a converting of an inner fact into a physical symptom.

O God, you are teaching us your way, sometimes by the hard way. When we won't take your way, we find by hard experience that our own ways upset us. Amen.

AFFIRMATION FOR THE DAY: I rest in the quietness and calm of God; therefore I am well in God.

THE HOLY SPIRIT QUICKENS OUR MORTAL BODIES

Ephesians 4:22-24

We have seen the effect of mind and emotion upon the body. The remedy is simple: surrender! Don't fight these wrong thoughts and attitudes and emotions, for that makes them sit tighter. Don't defend them, for that makes them sit pretty. Bring them up and out and surrender them into the hands of God. That surrender will make a vacant place within you, so the Holy Spirit can move in. And the Holy Spirit within us quickens our mortal bodies (see Rom 8:11 KJV).

The greatest source of health and healing is the Spirit within us bringing to bear stimulating and healing power upon our bodies—from within. This is what I would call the continuing miracle of health: very quiet, very unobtrusive, but very effective. The Spirit stimulates right thoughts, right emotions, right attitudes, and is thus the silent Agent of Health. When we allow it, the Spirit quietly solves our conflicts, coordinates our desires, cleanses our alien thoughts, and makes harmony within; this inner harmony is passed on to the body as health.

Perhaps we've been like the squirrel that a friend of mine saw running up and down a tree in great distress. My friend saw a huge snake hypnotizing the squirrel, his beady eyes fastened on him. Then my friend disturbed the snake, and the eyes of the snake shifted to him. Immediately the squirrel ducked into a hole—safe! When we are assaulted by some hypnotizing sin or wrong attitude, the Holy Spirit disturbs us from within, gets our eyes off the sin onto Jesus, and we are safe.

There was a nurse who, whenever added responsibility was put upon her, always developed an illness. It was a retreat into illness out of responsibility. She came to an Ashram and surrendered this fear of responsibility to God and went back and is now joyously accepting responsibility, and she is well and happy and adequate! Her surrender gave place for the Holy Spirit to move in and replace fear with confidence, inadequacy with adequacy. The Spirit quickened her inner life into health and hence the outer.

O Blessed Spirit, you are the fountain of life and health within. Help me to know how to accept the life and health you are offering. Make me skilled in receiving. Amen.

AFFIRMATION FOR THE DAY: Since the Spirit within is the source of my health, I shall let the Spirit rule within.

ONLY 8 PERCENT REALLY WORTH A WRESTLE

John 14:12-14

We are studying the great source of healing health—the Holy Spirit quickening us within.

The Holy Spirit within gives us power to face our fears and anxieties and thus keeps us free from the illnesses produced by fears and anxieties. Professors at the University of Wisconsin, making a study of fears and worries, found that "40 percent are about things that never happen; 30 percent are about things past help; 22 percent are petty and needless. That leaves only 8 percent really worth a wrestle."* But even that 8 percent need not produce a wrestle. When we surrender them to God, with the aid of the Spirit, we can face them together. We supply willingness, and God supplies power. It is fighting the good fight of faith.

For instance, on the same day, two different women came to me and said they could not speak in public, got all tied up with fear. One got all balled up in a solo once; since then her voice has been cracked and strained.

The obvious remedy is not to fight those fears but to surrender them. Then the words of Jesus will be fulfilled: "Don't worry about…what you should say. The Holy Spirit will tell you at that very moment what you must say" (Luke 12:11-12). The Holy Spirit within is the Counselor, telling you what and how you are to speak. That includes the "how" as well as the "what"—the gesture as well as the gist.

"Man's character is largely built on relationships with some exalted power lying outside himself," writes chief psychologist John A. Blake at the Central State Hospital at Petersburg, Virginia.

> Psychologists have observed that when such a relationship, early acquired and strongly rooted in the depths of humanity's personality in infancy and childhood, is either lost or seriously impaired in later life, a conflict results, manifesting itself in some form and degree of personality disorder.…In such cases one might rightly say [a] man became literally "sick in the spirit.**

Through surrender and the acceptance of the Holy Spirit within, we are no longer "sick in the spirit"; We are "well in the spirit," or better, "well in the Spirit." The Spirit within is the source of our health and well-being.

O Spirit Divine, we thank you that you are the Spirit of Health. In you we are well and whole. As long as we can take and take fully, that wellness and wholeness continue. Amen.

AFFIRMATION FOR THE DAY: I am well in the Spirit, for the Spirit has full and absolute control.

*No published source was found for this quotation, but references online attribute the study to Margaret McCordie at the University of Wisconsin.
** "John A. Blake, Former Greenwood Resident, Quoted in Two National Magazines on Work in Psychology," *The Index-Journal*, Greenwood, SC September 14, 1953, 10.

INDECISION THE CAUSE OF ILL HEALTH

John 14:25-27

The Spirit within helps us to health by helping us decide things. When we listen to the Counselor, then we decide things and get off the horns of dilemmas and, hence, are well persons. Raymond Lull was a great missionary when he really surrendered. But for some time he was upset because he was undecided. When about to get on board ship to sail to do missionary work among the Saracens, he pulled back at the last minute and let the ship sail without him. He became ill, with a high temperature. He got on another ship, but they put him off when they saw he was ill. Then he got on a third ship; when it actually got out of the harbor, his fever left him. He was well—well because he was really surrendered to being a missionary.

The wife of a college president was laid up for a year with a bad heart. It all began as self-pity and developed into resentments about a certain senator. "Why doesn't somebody kill him?" she asked. She almost went into a spasm when he came back into headlines in the newspapers. She began to be irritable toward her husband, and as a consequence he began to be irritable toward her. Everything was tied in knots. Then she surrendered this inner resentment to God, she inwardly relaxed and was well. The Spirit within helped her to right relationships and hence to health.

A man, who had ulcers for years, could get no insurance. The ulcers were gone in a week after he read *Abundant Living* and surrendered his fears and resentments. The doctors were puzzled. He now has forty thousand dollars' worth of insurance. Above all he is a happy, useful, untied man. The Spirit within brought health through deliverance.

Another man said to me, "I had glaucoma of the eyes, with only a short time of sight left. You counseled and prayed with me, and out of that I found peace and a surrender of the will that has only recently brought an amazing result. On last examination about a month ago the doctor found the tension entirely gone—negative." Clearing up the inside through the Spirit means clearing up the outside, and that means health and glorious well-being.

O Spirit of God, teach us how to let go of any clinging fold within that may keep us from you and hence from health. Help us to cut the last strand that holds us to ill health. Amen.

AFFIRMATION FOR THE DAY: I shall make the best decisions in the light of my best knowledge and leave the results with God.

AUTHENTIC CASES OF HEALING

Psalm 116:6-14

We are studying how God heals us through the indwelling Spirit when we surrender to God. Here is a testimony: "When I came to this Ashram, I was a coughing, fever-ridden, tubercular person, hemorrhaging and with a cavity in the left lung. Now I've been pronounced 'well-arrested,' do all my own housework, run two houses, raise two sons, belong to a prayer group, and teach a Sunday school class. My husband was a heavy drinker, bordering on alcoholism. Our home was on the verge of collapse. Today peace and love prevail, and we have been blessed financially beyond our fondest dreams."

Here is another: "I am the lady who attended my first Ashram last summer and forgot my cane. I have never needed or used that cane to this day. When I went to Green Lake, I had several nervous disorders; in a short time I was free from all of them. I also deserted my selfish way of living. I have never had such happiness, joy, and peace as I have experienced since July 9. My days have been so full and interesting."

And still another: A woman came to the Ashram with headaches and throbbing "like bubbles in my brain." They made her sleepless. The doctor gave her pills to be used whenever these spells came on. She kept them in her handbag. At the Ashram she put them away. She said, "Yesterday the headaches got so bad I said to myself I would have to take one. As I was about to open the bag, a Voice said, 'I wouldn't take that if I were you.' I put it back, and my head stopped throbbing, and I've been well ever since!"

Here is a similar case: "I told you of having suffered for years with psychomotor seizures; each felt as if a bomb had exploded in my brain. I felt as if I had taken the bombing for America. I read your books and began to know Christ really. I am living a transformed life. My seizures are gone. I'm well."

Most of these have been cases of functional disorders. Does God heal cases of structural disease? Yes!

O God, your healing extends to us, to the total us. For you are out to rid us of every evil of body, mind, and spirit. You are out to make us whole, every whit. Amen.

AFFIRMATION FOR THE DAY: There is no functional disorder of which I cannot be free now if I will cooperate with God.

A PERSONAL TESTIMONY

Psalm 84:5-7

We have seen that God can and does heal functional ailments; can and does God cure structural diseases?

The answer of the Acts is a positive yes. The man at the Beautiful Gate was lame from birth (3:2); Dorcas was dead (9:37); the father of Publius lay sick with fever and dysentery, and Paul laid hands on him and healed him (28:8). These were structural diseases.

Today we find structural diseases being healed. A woman had a cyst on an ovary, and as it was growing; the doctor decided on surgery. There was special prayer for her in a healing service. She went back from the Ashram, prepared to undergo the operation; but when the doctor examined her again, the cyst was gone. Another woman with a similar cyst asked for special prayer and then forgot all about her ailment and began to seek the Holy Spirit. She found him; and with the Spirit she found healing; when she showed herself to the doctor, he said no operation was necessary as the cyst had disappeared.

I have told how, at the beginning of my ministry, I was suddenly healed and became strongest in the place where I was weakest, namely, in nervous energy. This healing was apparently functional. May I tell one that was apparently structural? Several years ago I was about to go on a round-the-world evangelistic trip and had a routine checkup at the mission-board medical department. They found sugar. They suggested a more thorough checkup, and that was done at Atlanta—a sugar-tolerance test. It did not turn out too well. The doctor there gave this verdict: "You have a mildly severe case of diabetes. It won't get any better; it will probably get worse, and it will hasten your deterioration." Which was lovely news! When this report got to the mission-board doctor, he called me up from New York, two days before I was to fly to Japan, and said: "If you were a regular missionary of the board, I wouldn't let you go. But if a diabetic specialist in St. Petersburg will permit you, we'll accept his decision."

O Lord, we thank you that you are master of disease, all disease. Help us to open the depths of our beings, physical and spiritual, to your healing grace. Amen.

AFFIRMATION FOR THE DAY: Since I can have all the healing I can take, I take all the healing I need.

A MINIMUM OF STRAIN WITH A MAXIMUM OF RESULT

Psalm 66:16-19

We left off yesterday with the mission-board doctor suggesting that if I were a regular missionary of the board, he would not let me go to Japan. I am a regular missionary of the board; but since I pay my own way, I can do as I like. The diabetic specialist said, "You have a marginal case. It can be controlled by diet." I wondered how I could keep to a diet traveling to seventy-three cities in Japan in three months!

But the Lord's assurance was clear: "You go. In Me you are well and whole. And there will be a minimum of strain with a maximum of result." When I asked how I should know I am well and whole, God replied, "The test tube." That was specific. For two months after my arrival in Japan the test tube was not clear, so I had to walk by faith. Then in April 1953, the test tube cleared, and it has been clear ever since. When I had a thorough checkup at the Lahey Clinic under the president of the American Diabetic Association, he said, "You not only are fine; you are extraordinarily fine."

As to the "minimum of strain with a maximum of result" that too proved true—gloriously true. I was speaking from two to five times a day for three months and traveling between times, and I came out at the end without exhaustion—even felt fresh. I finished a book I was writing, though I had only thirty-five weeks of the fifty-two when I began. And there was a maximum of result. In three months, 36,000 people, from high officials down signed cards to become Christians. It was perhaps the most fruitful three months I've ever had in forty-seven years of evangelistic work. There was literally a "minimum of strain with a maximum of result."

But we cannot ask for healing unless we are doing our part in having continuous health. My prescription for continuous health is (1) exercise—I take it the last thing before I go to bed; (2) right habits—I go to bed at a decent hour; (3) right thinking and emotions; (4) grace. These four things have been the basis of my marvelous health at seventy—abounding health!

O Lord God, I thank you that you will good health for us; if I get in line with your will and purpose, I can have all the health I can use. Help me to get in line. Amen.

AFFIRMATION FOR THE DAY: Since my health is my wealth, I shall take God's health and make it my own.

THE MAIN EMPHASIS ON REDEMPTION FROM SIN

Psalm 73:23-26

On this last day of the discussion of the mastery of disease, let us sum up the New Testament attitude.

The healing of disease is a part of the application of the gospel to life. Jesus came to banish evil—all evil. The evil of the mind is error; the evil of the emotions is suffering; the evil of the body is disease; the evil of the soul is sin. Disease is not the will of God; it is an enemy to be banished. God does not send disease except as we break God's laws, and disease results as a by-product.

But the curing of disease is not the main emphasis or the working force of the New Testament. Jesus cured disease, but he asked people to keep it quiet. He did not want to be known primarily as a healer. He was a Savior: "You will call him, Jesus because he will save his people from their sins" (Matt 1:21). Most of our healing would come as a by-product of our being saved from the sins of resentments, fear, anxiety, self-centeredness, and guilt. That is the major emphasis of the gospel.

Even in the Acts, healing is mentioned only seven times in twenty-eight chapters. The emphasis was not there. It was on proclaiming the good news in Jesus Christ as redemption from sin and evil. Everything else was on the margin. And in the whole of the Epistles from Romans to Jude healing is mentioned only five times. (These references are to the RSV.) The main emphasis is elsewhere. When we bring healing of the body from the margin to the center, we throw the gospel out of balance.

There is one thing I must mention before closing this discussion. Part of the healing must await the final cure in the resurrection when we get a resurrection body. Not all diseases are cured in this life, for we live in a mortal world where the body breaks down sometime or other. But God will do one of two things: Either God will cure the disease now, or God will give us power to use the infirmity till the final cure in the resurrection—not bear it but use it. In either case it is a way out. God is out to cure disease—all disease—either now or in the final cure.

O Lord God, we thank you that by cooperation with you we can be willing and adequate for any job we have to do. We can count on you now for all we need. Amen.

AFFIRMATION FOR THE DAY: I can have health enough for my lifework if I get that lifework from God.

THE MASTERY OF SADNESS AND GLOOM

Psalm 63:5-7

We come now to note another mastery in the Acts: *the mastery of sadness and gloom*. There is an amazing joy in the pages of the Acts. It was a joy that came not by isolation from sorrow and trouble but by insulation. In the midst of a world that was breaking down and hence filled with sadness and gloom, these people had an amazing joy.

Going through a swamp that had a green, slimy mold upon it, a man saw a patch that was clear and fresh. Upon investigation he found that down beneath that spot was a bubbling spring, which pushed back the green slime. That is what happened in the Acts. They found a deep, bubbling spring of joy within themselves; and they pushed back the surrounding slime of sadness and gloom and showed a clear spot in history of an amazingly clear and crystal joy.

The reason for this astonishing joy was simple: their inner lives had been cleared of conflicts, resentments, fears, self-preoccupations, and guilt. These are all killjoys. When you get rid of them, joy spontaneously springs up within. You don't have to try to have a good time; you just have one—have one constitutionally.

Many people have to invent newer and newer ways to have a good time. It is a symptom of an irrepressible sadness down underneath.

Fully surrendered Christians don't try to have a good time; we just have one. Biblical scholar J. Rendel Harris (1852–1941) says, "Joy is the strength of the people of God; it is their characteristic mark."* If there is no real joy, there is no real Christianity. For Christianity is life set to music. It is doing everything for fun. And you do everything for nothing. You love God for nothing; you love others for nothing. You serve God—for nothing. Peter said to Jesus, "Look, we've left everything and followed you; what will we have?" (Matt 19:27). That showed how pre-Acts and sub-Acts his faith was. He was looking for a reward, something added to what he had. But the reward was there— Jesus! After the coming of the Holy Spirit, the disciples didn't talk of a reward; they had it within.

O Divine Spirit, having you within, what lack I? Nothing—nothing in heaven or on earth. For heaven can only be a prolongation and intensification of This. Amen.

AFFIRMATION FOR THE DAY: I will be as happy as I am holy, as glad as I am good, as peaceful as I am pure.

* No published source was found for this quotation.

NEVER ASSOCIATED GOD WITH JOY BEFORE

Psalm 59:16-17

We are looking at the mastery of gloom and sadness in the pages of the Acts.

A cultured woman who had a Roman Catholic background underwent a real spiritual conversion, and she exclaimed, "Strange, but I never associated God with joy before." God was the Unbroken Silence, awesome and apart, or the Stern Lawgiver, demanding obedience or else! But God as Joy—well, only those who know God know!

A letter came to me that said, "I have had it in every way imaginable as far as temptations, trials, burdens, physicians, psychologists, and parsons are concerned. I've had psychotherapy, logotherapy, bibliotherapy, and just rockin' in the sun. The experiences of the last two years would fill a book and bore you to distraction. Today after despairing of ever attaining release, it finally happened. The best part was not as a storm or a quiet stealing into the heart; it came to me like this: Dark curtains round me are lifting; cleansing winds of heaven are blowing over and around me; cool, sweet water is flowing in; now there is neither pain nor great joy. Just a solid, steady calm and him—he is here!"

That last phrase was the secret—"he is here!" Where God is, there is no gloom; and where God is fully, there Joy is fully, for God is Joy!

A committee went to the station to meet their new rector, whom they had never seen. They walked up to a man they thought might be the rector, and asked, "Are you our new rector?" He shook his head sadly and said, "No, it's dyspepsia that makes me look this way." When I ask some people if they are happy, and they reply that they are, then I suggest that they notify their faces. You didn't have to tell these early Christians to notify their faces, for their faces notified others that they had found a deep spring of Joy within. The people couldn't account for this Joy except on the basis that they were drunk. Peter replied, "These people aren't drunk, as you suspect" (Acts 2:15); "as you suspect"—they were drunk with God and hence with Joy!

O Joy that seeks me through pain, I dare not close my heart to you. Help me to accept you and thus to accept your Joy. For I cannot have you without Joy. Amen.

**AFFIRMATION FOR THE DAY: If "joy is the strength of the people of God,"
then joy shall be my strength today.**

A DRUNKENNESS THAT MAKES YOU MORE SOBER

Psalm 40:1-3

We saw yesterday that the disciples were drunk, but not as was suspected; they were intoxicated with a divine Joy. As the most joyous person I have ever seen, "Mary," puts it, "This is a drunkenness that makes you walk straighter, that makes you dress neater, that makes you more refined, that makes you more sober." And it may be added, "that makes you think straighter." A crooked person can't think straight, an unhappy person can't feel straight, and a tangled-up person can't walk a straight road. Peter said to a sorcerer, "Will you never stop twisting the straight ways of the Lord into crooked paths?" (Acts 13:10). A crooked person makes a crooked universe around him. A straight person makes a straight universe around her. That is the deep source of joy; life makes sense and adds up to intelligence and meaning and goal. Out of that fact Joy springs automatically. For no one can be happy in a meaningless universe. Only when the universe has a key, an unfolding plan, can one skip along life's way with dancing feet and dancing heart.

A lineman of a telephone company, when asked why accidents took place, replied, "If we could get people inwardly cleared of conflicts and sins, we could practically abolish accidents in industry. The greatest problem in a lineman's work is forgetfulness. And forgetfulness is caused by inner unhappiness and conflicts." The fact is that inner unhappiness and conflicts are the chief cause of confusion in the world. We project our inner unhappiness upon our surroundings and disrupt them. If you won't get along with God, you can't get along with yourself; and if you can't get along with yourself, you just can't get along with anybody else. These people in the Acts were getting along with God, therefore with themselves, therefore with others. Life was set to music. "Mary" says: "I do wish I could share all the joy in my heart with her. She deserves it, and I have enough for ten people." Enough for ten people; joy was bursting its seams and spilling over on everybody and everything.

O Joyous Jesus, let me open my heart to your Joy, for I walk in a sad world. Help me to spread love and joy about wherever I go, for I have enough and to spare. Amen.

AFFIRMATION FOR THE DAY: My strength is the strength of ten because my heart is pure, therefore happy.

EVERYTHING HAS A NEW TASTE

Philippians 4:4-7

Jesus spoke of salt that had lost its savor (see Matt 5:13). A great many live in a savorless universe, a universe without taste. The Christian faith not only puts meaning into life, it puts taste into life.

Here was a woman who was about as distracted and upset a person as I have ever seen outside a mental hospital. I could do little except try to quiet her. But "Mary" "loved her into the arms of Jesus." She saw in the face of Mary what she wanted. And she found it! One moment she was one kind of person, and the next moment she was another. She wrote one of the most beautiful letters I have seen, and it included these words, "Everything has a new taste when you are a Christian, doesn't it?" It does!

A man who was once grumpy made his surrender to Christ in an Ashram, and put it this way, "I always woke up with reluctance and afraid to meet the day, and said to myself, 'Good Lord, it's morning!' Now since I've surrendered, I run to the window and joyfully exclaim: 'Good morning, Lord!'" these people in the Acts were saying just that, for Jesus was a sunrise to them. In him all their sunsets had turned to sunrises. They greeted life with a cheer and a song!

Bishop Arthur Moore called a man standing at the train station to the car window and said, "Is anybody in this town enjoying religion?" The man replied, "Them that's got it is." That's it. These people had religion; or better, religion had them, had them all over, and they were enjoying it all over. One man hadn't seen another man for many years. The second man said, "Why, you don't look any worse than you did then."

The neighbors of the disciples saw a radical and profound difference. They had struck Joy!

Somebody has said, "Joy is always found on the other side of the cross." At the cross you are cleansed of a thousand conflicting desires and emotions; thus cleansed, your heart sings. But it can only sing as it is clean. Sin is sad, for sin has nothing behind it backing it. But goodness is glad, for the sum total of reality is behind it.

O Divine Spirit, relate me to God fully and wholly, and then my life shall have music deeper than the music of the spheres. I shall out-sing the morning stars. Amen.

AFFIRMATION FOR THE DAY: I belong to the People of the Glad Heart, and today I shall be a good illustration.

I HAVE NO PROBLEMS

1 Peter 1:6-8

It is said in the Gospels: "At that very moment, Jesus overflowed with joy from the Holy Spirit" (Luke 10:21). When this is so, you are not dependent on your surroundings for joy; the springs are within.

The joy of the Acts is of that kind, "They had them beaten. They ordered them not to speak in the name of Jesus, then let them go. The apostles left the council rejoicing" (Acts 5:40-41). Rejoicing in what? Nothing around them; it was within them. Another revealing passage, "But the Jews... stirred up persecution against Paul and Barnabas, and drove them out of their district. But they shook off the dust from their feet against them, and went to Iconium. And the disciples were filled with joy and with the Holy Spirit" (13:50-51 RSV). There is a difference between "filled with joy" and "filled with the Holy Spirit"; the joy subsides, the Holy Spirit abides. The Holy Spirit is the abiding root of which the joy is the fruit. The Holy Spirit, when we surrender, is always in the subconscious but sometimes emerges into the conscious as joy. When the joy is not always there as a bubbling joy, it is always there as peace. Peace is joy seated with hands folded, serene and calm.

I described the amazing joy of "Mary" in my book *Growing Spiritually*, detailing how she went through an accident in which she and her family were smashed up and her husband killed—went through on wings and without a tear. Mary is the bubbling, radiant type. A woman of an opposite type met the same experience in the same way. A month after her husband was killed in a motor accident, Iva came to me and said,

> I have no problems. I am living in glory. Apparently God took over my subconscious and worked through it. People said I was in a shock, and I would come back to sanity. But if this is insanity, I want it to continue! It's a miracle, for I am not naturally this kind of person. I've been the type who is seeking and anxious, and here I've found I am calm and composed. It is a miracle.

She too went through tragedy on wings and without a tear. So the joy of the Holy Spirit won through different temperaments with the same result.

Blessed Spirit, you are the spring of my joy. Therefore I can have joy amid the joyless, ease amid the peaceless, and victory amid the vanquished. I thank you. Amen.

AFFIRMATION FOR THE DAY: I have no problems, for all my problems are possibilities—possibilities for victory.

I LAUGH DOWN WHAT I DON'T GET DONE

1 Peter 4:12-14

The amazing joy throbbing through the pages of the Acts was seen vividly in Philippi. The Philippian church was born out of pain turned to joy. Paul and Silas sat at midnight in an inner prison with backs bleeding, hands and feet in stocks, and "were praying and singing hymns" (Acts 16:25). One can understand the praying, for almost everyone prays when we get in a jam; but singing hymns—well that showed an incorrigible joy that bubbled up amid those impossible surroundings. This is about as pure a spring of joy that has ever risen from the depths of human living on our planet. It was a happiness that wasn't dependent on happenings.

It wasn't a joy that went up like a rocket and came down like a stick. It stayed up. For when Paul wrote his letter to the Philippians, he was in jail again; and in the brief letter he mentions joy twelve times (in the RSV). This church was born out of pain that became joy, and this letter was written out of an imprisonment that became a greater joy. So when he spoke in this context, they knew that his joy had scars on it. But they were radiant scars.

This power to transform everything into joy is found today in lives surrendered to God. Note this: "I think I told you at the Ashram how I thank out weariness. After my last class I lie down, relax and touch lovingly and thankfully every experience where God has worked through me clearly and well. I touch little gracious things that have happened. I laugh down what I don't get done. If I got all things done, I'd be out of work tomorrow. These blessed tips of thought refresh me so thoroughly that I get up like new." Note "I thank out weariness. I laugh down what I don't get done." Here is the secret of joy: "thank" and "laugh." The thankful heart pours out in its thanksgiving the dregs of unhappiness. It is a cleansing stream. And the power to laugh is cleansing. "Why don't you get ulcers because of all this criticism?" a friend asked. I replied, "I've learned to laugh, to laugh at everything, especially at myself." Joy, Joy, Joy!

O Blessed Fountain of Eternal Joy, help me to drink deeply of you this day, so that I shall never thirst, never thirst for the lesser joys. This is It. This is It. Amen.

AFFIRMATION FOR THE DAY: I shall become so joyous that I will be Joy, so peaceful I will be Peace.

STILL HAD THAT WONDERFUL SMILE

Isaiah 62:3-5

We have looked at this pure spring of joy bubbling in the pages of the Acts. And that pure joy is bubbling now!

"Mary" is a direct spiritual descendant of these joy-filled people of the Acts. I described her going through an accident in which her husband was killed, and going through it on wings. It is one thing to go through it that way once, but would it happen again? Wouldn't there be a deposit of fear in the subconscious that would come out in another accident? She did have another accident, in which an experienced driver was driving her car; and when the car in front suddenly stopped, her car crashed into it, smashing the radiator and putting the car out of commission. After the crash, the driver looked over his shoulder to see how she was taking it, and he said, "I'll be blessed if she didn't still have that wonderful smile!" Her subconscious was held by Joy, and her smile during the accident was the sign that the within was intact!

This Joy comes out in comparatively small matters too. When there was company for dinner, "Mary" dropped a chocolate cake she was taking out of the oven—dropped it on the floor because of a burnt finger. She took it laughingly to the guests and served it as it was! Nothing had happened, was her comment. And that is the point; nothing had happened! The within was intact, held by Joy!

"Mary" has an amazing power to impart this joy to others. She says, "It's wonderful to see God give people a spiritual transfusion through you. They come with blue lips and pale faces. They go away with a glow and a glory, your very life poured into them." "Mary" knew and they knew that the life poured into them was not her own but God's! Her spirit is seen in the following: We were standing at the gate of an airport waiting for our plane to be called. The wind was cold. She gaily said, "Lean up against the wind and let it warm you." When you can wring warmth out of a north wind, you are incorrigibly happy and resourceful. You are joyous in spite of.

O Blessed Lord, I thank you for this Joy unspeakable and full of glory. I thank you that now I can joy out all sorrow, all opposition, all pain. In Jesus' name. Amen.

AFFIRMATION FOR THE DAY: I am happy with God's Happiness and joyous with God's Joy. What can life do to me?

THE MASTERY OF RESENTMENTS

1 Thessalonians 5:14-18

We have looked at the mastery of gloom and sadness in the Acts. One reason was this, previously quoted, "Joy is always found on the other side of the cross." You go to the cross and are cleansed of all resentments, all hates, all inner conflicts. Then Joy comes automatically. Cleansing and cheerfulness are cause and effect.

This is in real contrast with so much of modern somber religion in which the length of the face is supposed to tell the strength of the grace. A visitor in a Scottish home happened to be there on the Sabbath. There was nothing to read except the Bible; all the other books were carefully put away. He read the Bible at length and then asked his host if it would be all right if he took a walk outside, and his host replied, "Yes, provided you don't enjoy it." The people in the Acts enjoyed living because living was enjoyed; joy had penetrated living to its depths. Some people were puzzled about Rufus Moseley, a saint of the South, jiggling his hands and his whole body when he talked; so I said, "His outer jiggling is a symptom of an inner jiggling. His brain cells are dancing with joy at the wonder of Jesus and the constant surprises that meet him at every turn, and this outer semi-dancing a manifestation of an inner dancing—the two sides of one fact!"*

Someone put it this way—J-O-Y—Jesus first, Others second, Yourself third. When that combination is put together in that order, you're bound to have Joy. But if you have something else first, other than Jesus—for instance, resentments and anger—then you are bound to be joyless. The greatest killjoy is resentment. It eats at our joy like a cancer. Let us look now at *the mastery of resentment.*

There is an amazing absence of resentment among the early Christians. In the pages of the Acts there isn't one single syllable of revenge or asking God to deal harshly or even justly with enemies. It is the most retaliation-absent account that has ever been written, for it depicts a society out of which all except love had been eliminated—a society of no inner hurts.

O Spirit of God, we thank you that you cleanse us from all inner bitterness and fill us with nothing save love. We open our hearts to you. Amen.

AFFIRMATION FOR THE DAY: My soul is too glad and too great to be the enemy of any person or even to hold resentments.

* For more about Rufus Moseley, see J. Rufus Moseley, *Manifest Victory: A Quest and a Testimony* (New York: Harper & Bros., 1941). E. Stanley Jones provided one of the forewords for the book.

MEETING A WRONG WITH A WRONG

Matthew 5:38-41

The highest watermark of spiritual religion in the pre-Christian stage is the Psalms. Yet the spirit of resentment and bitterness creeps into them:

> LORD, remember what the Edomites did on Jerusalem's dark day...
> a blessing on the one who pays you back the very deed you did to us!
> A blessing on the one who seizes your children
>   and smashes them against the rock! (Ps 137:7-9)

The prevailing attitude in that ancient world was tit for tat—you do this and I do that—an eye for an eye and a tooth for a tooth. Life was on the legal level.

This spirit of revenge is seen when the disciples asked Jesus if they should call down fire from heaven on the Samaritan village that refused to allow them to enter because "he steadfastly set his face to go to Jerusalem." The Samaritans were wrong in their fierce prejudice against anyone going to Jerusalem. That was race prejudice pure and simple. But the disciples were also wrong in answering a wrong with a wrong. They tried to soften that wrong and give it a religious flavor by saying it would be from heaven, therefore with a divine sanction upon it. And they quoted a sanction from the prophets, "as [Elijah] did" (Luke 9:51-54 KJV). So this spirit of tit for tat was still in religion up until the coming of the Holy Spirit. There it died out in the fires of a burning love for everybody—even enemies.

Outside this circle of cleansing fire, where Christianity was faint in its effects, we see that same spirit creeping in. In the birth stories about Jesus was one that said a boy ran into the boy Jesus and knocked him down, and Jesus said, "Thou shalt fall and never rise again." And the boy fell dead.* That is so palpably false to the spirit of Jesus that it would be like introducing a cancer into healthy tissue. Before the Old Testament, revenge was unlimited. If a man knocked out your eye, you would get two if you could. The Old Testament limited the revenge—one eye for one eye. Jesus abolished revenge; evil was to be overcome with good.

O Lord, I thank you that I am being taken hold of by a Love that knows no revenge or even resentment, but would overcome hate by love, the world by a cross. Amen.

AFFIRMATION FOR THE DAY: Resentments are banished from not only my acts but my very thoughts.

* See *The Infancy Gospel of Thomas* (c. 185 CE), 4:1.

THE LAMB WAS ON THE THRONE

Matthew 5:43-48

Jesus said to his disciples, "Go! Be warned, though, that I'm sending you out as lambs among wolves" (Luke 10:3). Of all the helpless pictures this is the most helpless and most hopeless: "lambs among wolves." They haven't a ghost of a chance to survive, for they weren't even grown sheep that might run away, but lambs that could give neither fight nor flight—a symbol of complete helplessness. Yet when the book of Revelation closes, it depicts the Lamb upon the throne. The lambs had conquered the wolves! The Lamb was on the throne, the ruler! How did that happen?

It wasn't chance. It was the manifestation of a superior force, the power of love. Not a passive love but a positive, outgoing love that took the offensive. When Jesus said that, when smitten on one cheek we are to turn the other, that was not a wet-rag type of passivity; it was a daring moral boldness. For when a person hits you on one cheek, you seize the moral offensive, turn the other cheek, and say to that person, "This too, please." The person smites you on the cheek, and you smite that person in the heart by your daring moral courage. You knock the weapons out of his or her hands and use your weapon of love. You do what "Mary" suggests, "There is nothing that I can do for them but love them with love unlimited." The disciples loved with love unlimited. And to the degree that they loved with love unlimited, they conquered with conquest unlimited. A new power had been loosed in the world—love unlimited.

This love unlimited broke down barriers between classes and races and between personal and corporate enemies. It was the great solvent. There is neither a whisper of prayer or desire for revenge on enemies nor the slightest sign of resentment. Is this their attitude, "Now, Lord, take note of their threats"—and punish them and protect us? No!—"and enable your servants to speak your word with complete confidence" (Acts 4:29). They asked not for revenge but for the power to preach and to love. No wonder such love won the multitudes, for it was new, a brand new thing in that love-absent world. They coined a new name for it: *agape*, a divine love.

O Lord, give me in this generation the power to love everybody and everything and help me to love and keep on loving though the objects of the love do not receive. In Jesus' name. Amen.

**AFFIRMATION FOR THE DAY: I shall love everybody today
with love unlimited, the loveless, the unlovely.**

227

I Do Not Frustrate the Grace of God

Romans 12:19-21

Had the disciples allowed resentment to invade them even the slightest, it would have blocked and canceled all that grace had planned. Paul, misunderstood and misrepresented, battered and badgered, could have let some self-pity and resentments invade him; and that would have canceled everything. But he could say, "I do not frustrate the grace of God" (Gal 2:21 KJV). I do not cancel it by my attitudes. Many do.

An Indian pastor tells how he sat by the lake in Sat Tal in the Himalayas, "I looked at the lake for an hour and enjoyed the beauty of nature. I asked, 'Are you, O God, beautiful too?' And I couldn't answer my own question. I further asked, 'Why don't I enjoy you, O God, the way I enjoy nature?' And I found the answer: there are resentments in my heart, and I have exaggerated the offense." He blocked the grace of God by resentments.

Another Indian, this time a bishop, tells how he set aside an evening for prayer for the Holy Spirit. As he prayed, the matter of a grudge he held against a man came up. This was blocking the prayer for the Holy Spirit. Tears flowed as he prayed for this man. As he prayed for him, release came, and he was filled with the Spirit. His life since then is showing the fruit of the Spirit, an ordinary man doing extraordinary things.

I was about to go into a situation that had baffled me. It was all tied up with resentments and clashes. As I sat writing in a plane, the Lord said, "Lay aside the writing; I want to talk to you about this situation. You are to go into it with love and nothing but love, no matter what happens." I promised I would. To my surprise, two members of the group came to me beforehand and asked forgiveness for their attitudes. Barriers began to fall. Difficulties cleared up, and there were no problems. Love dissolved them.

O Lord, I thank you that I need not fight my resentments; I can surrender them. And when I surrender them, you take them over and make me over. Amen.

AFFIRMATION FOR THE DAY: No resentments shall be the seed plot for spiritual weakness within me.

I LOVE YOU, BUT I DON'T
LIKE CERTAIN THINGS

2 Corinthians 6:4-10

We are studying how to master resentments. Don't fight them. That brings them into the focus of attention, and whatever is in the focus of attention becomes power. "Whatever gets your attention gets you." And don't suppress them. That only makes them work in the subconscious as uneasiness and conflict.

Suppressing resentments is like canning spoiled fruit; you try to preserve what can only putrefy.

Someone has defined a resentment or grudge as the "taking of stinging nettles into your bare breast, hoping this will make the other fellow scratch." You punish yourself hoping this will punish the other.

A daughter told how her mother literally "blew her top." Her mother and father hated each other. The father was to retire soon. The mother, resenting the fact that he would then be at home all the time, became more and more resentful. She had a cerebral hemorrhage and died, killed by her own resentments. The death of some people through resentments is not so overt; it is covert. When we take resentments into our bosoms, we take death—slow or sudden. When Jesus met Paul on the Damascus road, he did not try to conquer him by threats of punishment. He asked, "Saul, why are you harassing me?" (Acts 9:4). There was no syllable of resentment or threat of punishment.

That simple, plaintive question broke down the resistance of Paul, who replied: "Who are you, Lord?" Note that he used the word "Lord," for this absence of threatening showed him a new type of power. It set the pattern of the kind of reaction that this new faith would show, the reaction of love to everything and everybody. That laid the foundation for Paul's emphasis. Christianity was after the pattern of Christ.

A man told me he had held resentments against a man for twenty years. He took a cue from *Abundant Living*, went to the man, and said, "I love you, but I don't like certain things about you. I'm sorry I've had these resentments." The resentments were dissolved, and the two men became fast friends.

O Lord, I thank you that your love and my resentments cannot live in the same heart. I let the resentments go, for I want you more than anything else. Amen.

AFFIRMATION FOR THE DAY: Every minute I hold anger or resentments, I miss sixty seconds of happiness.

The Bitterness Poisoned Him

Hebrews 12:12-15

We continue to look at the mastery of resentments. A woman was a puzzle and a problem to the doctors. They could find nothing physically wrong, yet she was dying. She could assimilate nothing; everything she ate came back, rejected by her system. The doctors called in a minister and said, "There is something there that we cannot touch. See if you can find out what it is." He found it was a deep-seated resentment, a bitter hatred against a woman who had been going around with her husband. "I could tear her limb from limb," was the bitter outburst. He gave her several of my books and marked the places where I spoke of resentments and their effects. She saw she was wrong and surrendered the resentments through prayer. Three days later when she sat in church, she waved to the doctor, her face radiant. She was a well woman in spirit and in body. The doctor pronounced it a miracle; it was a miracle of grace.

A businessman was worked on by pastor after pastor to get him to become a Christian and join the church. No response. One day a pastor got to the bottom of his hardness. He told of how his wife had walked out on him over a trivial difference and had never returned. The bitterness over this poisoned him. He could not and would not forgive. Then in prayer he gave it all up. He appeared in church; and before the minister had stopped speaking, he came to the altar and made his confession and joined the church on the spot. He is now a useful, victorious Christian.

A wife was tied in knots with resentments against her mother-in law and other in-laws, because the house they all lived in was not divided so she and her husband could have a life of their own. She was just as bitter against her husband for not dividing it. Her stomach was tied in knots and her nerves bad. But the stomach and the nerves were perfectly good; they were being badly treated. For the stomach and the nerves are made not for ill will but for good will. The wrong messages were going over the nerves; the nerves were good.

Gracious Lord, help me to send the right messages over my nerve wires so that they will send health, not illness, to the rest of my body. In Jesus' name. Amen.

AFFIRMATION FOR THE DAY: My nerve wires will carry nothing but messages of love today.

I DISTINCTLY REMEMBER FORGETTING THAT

Acts 28:17-19

We have seen the mastery of resentments and anger in the Acts. The root of that power to master resentments was in the forgiveness these Christians found through Christ. Forgiven, they forgave. Here is an example out of India: A drunkard became a Christian and settled down to honest work. At the season for reaping he was attacked by bullies, who reaped his fields, cut off his fingers with an axe, and left with the harvest. The Indian YMCA secretary, who had been the means of his conversion, showed him the money that had been collected by an aroused public to help him prosecute; the bullies were known. He looked at the bags of money and then at his fingerless hands, and said: "Sir, you have been a Christian all your life, and I accepted Jesus not long ago. But when I accepted him, I promised to follow in his footsteps. You told me that when he was crucified, he didn't say, 'Father, punish them'; but he did say, 'Father, forgive them; for they know not what they do.' So, just as my Master forgave his enemies, I must forgive mine; for they have done this in the ignorance of their hearts. They did not know anything better."

Wherever the spirit of Christ is, there is an absence of resentment and bitterness, whether among the early Christians or among the Christians of today. Unlimited forgiveness characterizes real Christianity. Clara Barton was asked about a cruel thing done to her, "Don't you remember that was done you?" She replied: "I distinctly remember forgetting that."*

The souls of these Christians were too glad and too great to be the enemy of any person. British artist Sir Edward Burne-Jones has painted the picture of a knight who met an enemy who had done him a cruel wrong. As the hot blood mounted within him, thirsting for revenge, he saw Jesus' figure on a wayside cross. He dismounted and knelt, praying that the wild lust for revenge would be crucified, when Jesus came down from the cross and kissed the lips of this faithful servant; the enemy passed unharmed**—the mastery of revenge.

O Jesus, you are the forgiveness of God. You give that forgiveness freely and fully. Help me to take that forgiveness and give it freely and fully. Amen.

AFFIRMATION FOR THE DAY: As they arise, I shall bury all my resentments and hurts at the foot of the cross.

*William E. Barton, *The Life of Clara Barton: Founder of the American Red Cross*, vol. 2 (Boston: Houghton Mifflin, 1922), 345.
** "The Merciful Knight," http://www.leninimports.com/edward_burne_jones.html, accessed March16, 2017.

THE MASTERY OF MANY THINGS

Philippians 3:13-16

We come now to another mastery in the Acts—*the mastery of the many things on behalf of the one.*

This mastery is seen in these two contrasting passages: "Jesus knew the dispute that occupied their minds" (Luke 9:47 MNT), and "Paul was occupied with preaching" (Acts 18:5 RSV). In one case the question of personal prestige and position occupied the minds of followers of Jesus; the ego and its interests were at the center. In the other case the question of preaching Jesus was the center of interest; the ego was on the edges, and the sharing of Jesus was at the center. The results of these centers of interest were obvious. In one case the disciples canceled out their own power. The boy possessed with demons had a better case of demon possession than they of God possession, and they could not get the demons out. In Paul's case he had a better case of God possession than the people had of demon possession, and the demons came out. The difference was in what occupied the center.

What an amazing thing to occupy the minds of his disciples as Jesus walked steadily to the cross—their own selves! Jesus had not moved in to take perfect possession as yet. He was there, but their unsurrendered selves pushed past him and took over the center. They were divided personalities. But in the case of Paul, Jesus held the center; and Paul's self and its desires were on the margin. He could say, "I do this one thing" (Phil 3:13); and the disciples before Pentecost could say: "These forty things we dabble in."

The person who cannot say, "I do this one thing," has to say, "These many things I dabble in." That person's soul forces are not fused into one; she or he is a dabbler instead of a doer. The Holy Spirit cleanses from conflict as well as from contamination. The scattered rays of the sun, not concentrated, set nothing afire; but when they are brought through a burning glass and concentrated at one point, they set that point ablaze. Paul set that ancient world on fire, for his soul was a burning glass.

O Holy Spirit, I become receptive to the rays of your power, and I concentrate them upon my task. Help me to set on fire everything I touch. Amen.

AFFIRMATION FOR THE DAY: I am going over my life to eliminate the bad for the good, the good for the better, the better for the Best.

HE DID MANY THINGS

Mark 6:18-27

One of the tragic illustrations of a man being given to the many things instead of the one is Herod: "For Herod feared John, knowing that he was a just man and an holy, and observed him; and when he heard him, he did many things, and heard him gladly" (Mark 6:20 KJV). Note "he did many things"; he tried to do many things in lieu of doing the one thing he should have done: give up his brother's wife. The great refusal of Herod to do that one thing was the cause of his downfall; for the unsurrendered thing, Herodias, moved in and took possession of him and caused him to murder the man he respected most—John—to murder him and his own conscience. The many things could not atone for the one thing.

A superintendent of schools gave permission for a speaker to speak in a high school. But after a certain microscopic opposition began from a very marginal splinter group, he changed his mind and canceled the address. Then to cover the cowardly caving in, he took refuge in an irrelevant section of a statute of the state. When asked about it, the superintendent, who was also a deacon, said, "Well, you see I wear two hats—one my Christian faith and the other my school superintendency. Now I'm wearing the latter." That "two-hat" theory of life left him a moral blur, and his leadership in each sphere was nil. Willa Cather emphasized this when she wrote, "Listen, my friend. No man can give himself heart and soul to one thing while in the back of his mind he cherishes a desire, a secret hope, for something very different."*

When you step into the Acts, you feel the atmosphere of single-mindedness, of people who have been cleansed of incompatible desires, who know where they are going and are on the Way with both feet! They went places. In a hesitant world they knew no hesitancy; in an uncertain world they had an invincible certainty, knowing that the sum total of Reality was behind them. It is no wonder that they won!

O Spirit Divine, fuse all my life forces into a burning unity in the fires of your passion. Make me glow with a singleness of purpose and the fire of your love. Amen.

AFFIRMATION FOR THE DAY: I am through with contradictory desires and motives; I'm a single-minded person.

*Willa Cather, *Shadows on the Rock* (Canada: Alfred A. Knopf, 1931), book 3, §5.

THIS IS NOT PREACHING; IT IS REVELATION

Luke 4:17-19

We are looking at the mastery of the complicated and a reduction of life to the simple. The account says that the Pharisees tempted Jesus to speak "about many things" (Luke 11:53). Many ministers are tempted to speak "about many things"—of everything except the one thing they are sent to speak of—Jesus! Or as someone has said, "We speak *about* Jesus instead of being his spokesman."

As "Mary" was listening to a devoted preacher of Jesus, she heard Jesus say to her: "Listen, ears, this is not preaching—it is revelation." The face of Jesus was being unveiled—people saw him—it was revelation!

In contrast to this, note the caption of a Whitney Darrow cartoon that showed two ministers conversing in a comfortable, luxurious library. Said the older man to the younger, "Drawing upon my not inconsiderable experience, Andrews, my advice to a young man ambitious of preferment in our calling is to steer clear of two subjects— politics and religion."* Many preachers follow that advice!

A senator voted for a bill that went against his convictions, and when a friend took him to task, he said, "But you don't know how many pressures are brought upon us." The friend replied, "Pressures, man, where were your inside braces?" The early Christians had inside braces—the Spirit within! The Spirit within made the pressures from without seem trivial. This was the pressure of the Almighty on them, from within!

Someone experimented with the strength of a growing squash. It was harnessed with pulleys and it lifted over a thousand pounds in growing! Its fiber became as tough as wood. These Christians were growing through the indwelling Spirit, and they lifted the world in their growth. They overturned systems and religions. The inner dynamic toughened them in their tasks. They were no longer tender-minded; they were tough-minded. There can be no growth without singleness of purpose!

O Christ of the single heart and the single eye, make me single-purposed, driving toward a single goal—the kingdom. Then I shall have drive. Amen.

AFFIRMATION FOR THE DAY: The braces within me shall be greater than the pressures upon me.

* We are unable to verify the quotation directly, but the cartoon appeared in the May 28, 1949 issue of *The New Yorker*.

Wanting Three Tabernacles

Isaiah 58:6-11

We have been studying the mastery of the many things and the giving of oneself to "this one thing."

Upon the Mount of Transfiguration, Peter suggested that there be built three tabernacles: one for Jesus, one for Moses, and one for Elijah. Moses represented the Law, Elijah the prophets, and Jesus the new revelation. Peter wanted to put them all three on the same level. A cloud came down upon them as he said this. Whenever you try to divide your inner life by competing supreme loyalties, a cloud will descend on you automatically. The divided life is the clouded life.

But this very cloud was cleansing, for from it came a voice, saying, "This is my Son whom I dearly love.... Listen to him!" The Law and the prophets were fulfilled in Jesus. "When they looked up, they saw no one except Jesus" (Matt 17:5-8).

That outer clarification became an inner clarification when the Spirit came upon them and in them. All else had been pushed to the margin, and Jesus had taken the center; the many were mastered by the One! That was the greatest mastery that had ever taken place in human history. Religion would be centered in the incarnate Jesus. Everything would start from him and return to him for reference. That gave them singleness of purpose and a central drive. They cut through the hesitant many on behalf of the One.

When Paul at Mars Hill spoke of many things—good things but not the Thing—he failed. He left a blur at Athens: no church, no epistle left behind. What an epistle he could have written to that center of learning! But he preached good views instead of good news. When he went to Corinth, he saw his mistake and there "decided to know nothing among you except Jesus Christ and him crucified" (1 Cor 2:2 RSV). There he left a church and two great epistles.

No one can be strong and go far unless that person goes to his or her knees and clarifies purposes and vision. When Jesus fills that person and her or his horizon, then the person begins to go places, for the person knows where he or she wants to go and stops trying to run to opposite goals at once.

O Lord God, send a cloud upon me if my vision is not clear, so that I can emerge from that cloud seeing no one save Jesus only, for he is my universe. Amen.

AFFIRMATION FOR THE DAY: My love for Jesus shall eat up the lesser loyalties, absorb them.

THE MASTERY OF THE SECONDHAND

Romans 8:1-2

We now take another step in mastery—*the mastery of the secondhand*. The early Christians not only centered on the One—on Jesus—they centered on a firsthand Jesus. We can see the difference between the firsthand and the secondhand in the account of the seven sons of Sceva who were exorcists and undertook to cast out evil spirits at secondhand:

> There were some Jews who traveled around throwing out evil spirits. They tried to use the power of the name of the Lord Jesus against some people with evil spirits. They said, "In the name of the Jesus whom Paul preaches, I command you!" The seven sons of Sceva, a Jewish chief priest, were doing this.
>
> The evil spirit replied, "I know Jesus and I'm familiar with Paul, but who are you?" The person who had an evil spirit jumped on them and overpowered them all with such force that they ran out of that house naked and wounded. (Acts 19:13-16)

The man who had evil spirits had a firsthand experience of evil spirits, and these seven men had a secondhand experience of Jesus, "In the name of the Jesus whom Paul preaches, I command you." The firsthand mastered the secondhand, and they fled. That always happens; the firsthand inferior will always master the secondhand superior. If Jesus is to be power, then it must not be by a repeating of his name at secondhand—the Jesus who is real to somebody else—he must be real to you. Secondhand religion is always overpowered by firsthand evil. The comparative impotence of the church is caused by the secondhand nature of its religion. Its religion is in creeds, in rituals, in books, in services, in prayers; but it is not a fountain of firsthand living experience of Jesus. As "Mary" says: "They preach Jesus, but don't preach Jesus available." Jesus is never available if you are preaching a secondhand Jesus. It must be out of one's own depths to the depths of the other person. Only that which comes from the heart can reach the heart. Only one loving heart can set another heart aflame. In the Acts these people were not guides pointing woodenly to a way; they were men and women who were joyously walking the Way and recounting the wonders of it at firsthand. No wonder multitudes pressed into the Way to accompany them!

O Spirit of God, take the dimness of my sight away and let me see this Jesus face to face, so that his fire may catch fire in my heart and set me aflame. Amen.

AFFIRMATION FOR THE DAY: My religious experience will be firsthand, straight out of the heart of God.

WE HAVE HEARD FOR OURSELVES

John 4:39-42

We continue to look at the mastery of the secondhand.

Many preachers are in line of the succession of the sons of Sceva, "By the name of the Jesus whom Fosdick preaches, the Jesus whom McCartney preaches"; this is religion in quotation marks. It was said of one minister that when he began to preach, he turned to one side and made a gesture with his two hands about a foot apart and then turned to the other side and made the same gesture. When somebody asked him why he did this, he replied: "I am doing this because what I am about to say is in quotation marks"; the sermon was someone else's sermon! It was secondhand preaching and of course produced secondhand Christians—Christians groping amid the half-lights, ready to be pushed here and there with the more impressive quotation.

When years ago I asked Sarojini Naidu, the poetess and patriot of India, about socialism in India, she replied, "Well, socialism is still in quotation marks in India." It was ideas imported from abroad; it wasn't firsthand and indigenous. That was years ago. Now socialism is no longer in quotation marks in India; it is rooted in the soil and soul of India. Nothing is power that is not personal and firsthand.

The people of the Samaritan village passed from the secondhand to the firsthand in these words, "They said to the woman, 'We no longer believe because of what you said, for we have heard for ourselves and know that this one is truly the savior of the world'" (John 4:42). It was no longer a mediated faith; it was an immediated faith, nothing between.

The greatest necessity of the church today is the conversion of secondhand Christians into firsthand Christians, the conversion of people who are walking in half-lights to people who walk in full light. "Whoever follows me won't walk in darkness," said Jesus (John 8:12); and he might have added, "nor in half-lights either." They can be "in the light in the same way as he is in the light" (1 John 1:7).

O Jesus, you are the light of the world, not the half-light of half the world. Help me this day to break through halfwayness into full light and full life. Amen.

AFFIRMATION FOR THE DAY: I shall walk in the light as he is in the light and have perfect fellowship with him.

WITH UNVEILED FACE

Jude 24-25

We are looking at the mastery of the secondhand in religion.

Here is a potent passage: "Right up to the present day the same veil remains when the old covenant is read. The veil is not removed because it is taken away by Christ. Even today...a veil lies over their hearts. But whenever someone turns back to the Lord, the veil is removed" (2 Cor 3:14-16). "Whenever someone turns back to the Lord, the veil is removed"; when you get to the Lord, not to the system or the creeds or the ritual built up around God but really to God, then the veil is removed.

Veiled minds and hearts are the breeding grounds for doubts and fears and defeats. The veiled becomes the vague, and the vague becomes the victim. Veiled religion is powerless, without contagion and without growth.

But this is unveiled religion, "All of us are looking with unveiled faces at the glory of the Lord as if we were looking in a mirror. We are being transformed into that same image from one degree of glory to the next degree of glory. This comes from the Lord, who is the Spirit" (v. 18). "With unveiled faces"—veils of struggling and trying to be good, veils of taking our faith from others and echoing them, veils of half surrenders and half allegiances, veils of double-mindedness—these are all taken away, and we stand face to Face, "looking...at the glory of the Lord." The glory of the Lord is not a half-lighted-up Jesus, but the real Jesus in all his glory and power. Result? We are "transformed into that same image from one degree of glory to the next degree of glory." A firsthand Jesus produces firsthand Christians made into his own image. And everyone can see it! A boy of fifteen said of a certain Christian, "You may question his words and his arguments, but you can't question his face—his face is the face of one who has lived with Christ through the years—it shows."

And this is added to this Scripture passage: "This comes from the Lord, who is the Spirit." It is the result not of trying but of gazing into his face, for the Lord at whom you gaze becomes the Spirit within you. You look at God and then find that the Holy Spirit is within, working in you what God does himself.

O Lord at Whom I gaze, become within me the Spirit who makes the miracle of the changed countenance and the changed life; take utter and complete possession. Amen.

AFFIRMATION FOR THE DAY: I gaze this day with unveiled face and heart into God's face, and will be made more like Christ.

THE MASTERY OF JEALOUSY

Galatians 5:19-21

We come now to consider another mastery that emerged in the Acts—*the mastery of jealousy.*

Jealousy appeared among the disciples before the coming of the Holy Spirit; there was a dispute among them as to which one was greatest. Jesus dealt with this in amazing clarity. He took the driving urge for greatness and redeemed it—there is a place for ambitious people in the kingdom—"Whoever wants to be great among you will be your servant" (Mark 10:43). The urge for greatness is right now become great by becoming the servant of all. He turned the urge from being egocentric to being other-centric. That saved the urge and the person and made them both contributive.

Then he went on to say, 'Whoever wants to be first among you will be the slave of all" (v. 44). If you are to be great, you must be a servant of all; but if you are first, you must be the slave of all. The degree of greatness is determined by the degree of self-giving: a servant and you are great, a slave and you are first. Ambition was redeemed by harnessing it to the lifting of others. It was no longer a jostling for position and treading on others in the upward climb; it was a stooping to lift everybody in sight and in the process growing tall yourself as a by-product. This kind of greatness tended to erase the possibility of jealousy; you can't very well be jealous of a person who doesn't want anything except to get under everybody in sight and lift them. This method of Jesus is perfect; it redeems the urge for greatness and diminishes the possibility of jealousy as a result of that greatness.

That is why jealousy dropped out of the relationships of these Christians. They weren't suppressing it; they just didn't feel it, for they were out to serve everybody from the lowest to the highest. That principle and practice would eliminate jealousy from any society and from any heart to the degree that it is put in operation.

O Jesus Master, you told us how to be great and showed us the way; you obeyed your precepts, and we are, as a result, at your feet. Amen.

AFFIRMATION FOR THE DAY: I am the servant of all; therefore, there is no reason for jealousy within me.

A Mental Cancer, Jealousy

James 3:13-16

There was opportunity for jealousy in the Acts, but it didn't appear. For instance, when Paul and Barnabas started out, it was Barnabas and Paul: "Appoint Barnabas and Saul" (Acts 13:2). But it soon became "Paul and Barnabas" (v. 43) or "Paul and his companions" (v. 13). But there was no whisper of jealousy that the older man was jealous of the younger, who was taking precedence. They were both slaves of all and as such were both "first" inherently, without trying to be first. Greatness without jealousy became the settled condition.

There was jealousy in the Acts, but it was outside the Christian group: "The high priest, together with his allies, the Sadducees, was overcome with jealousy. They seized the apostles and made a public show of putting them in prison (5:17-18). And: "When the Jews saw the crowds, they were overcome with jealousy. They argued against what Paul was saying by slandering him" (13:45). They were fighting in the name of religion, defending principles and religion, but underneath, jealousy was the motive.

Jealousy comes out in all sorts of ways today. A little girl would wake up at night screaming with pain in her legs. This was after her little baby brother came. She wanted love and attention. Her mother, seeing what the trouble was, gave the little girl extra attention and love; and the pains ceased.

This is found in all ages. A woman said in a meeting, "I'm on the road to recovery from a cancer—a mental cancer—jealousy."

A little girl looked at the picture of a place where her younger sister had gone for a vacation and remarked, "Looks like a horrible place." She was jealous that she didn't go. But when she herself went later, she thought it was a wonderful place. Jealousy spoils everything it touches; it makes a beautiful place into a horrible place, makes lovely people into horrible people, makes friendships impossible and kills love. Jealousy is a cancer.

O Lord, let me tolerate no jealousy. Help me to think of everyone with love, a positive, outgoing love. And help me to get under everyone and boost them. Amen.

AFFIRMATION FOR THE DAY: Jealousy is the vice of the small-souled; I shall be big with love.

JEALOUSY COMES OUT IN PHYSICAL SYMPTOMS

Luke 19:37-40

We saw yesterday how hidden jealousy breaks out in symptoms quite different from the disease. A little boy developed deafness when a new baby arrived. His mother, a wise woman, saw what was happening and gave the boy special attention and love, and the deafness disappeared.

What are we to do when we find jealousy eating at the heart of our happiness and our usefulness? Don't fight it; that only drives it into the subconscious. Bring it up and out into the open and surrender it to God. This is how one very useful woman met her feeling of jealousy.

"Thank you for the sermon on surrendering our 'word.' My 'word' was *jealousy*, jealousy of a fellow worker. I gave it up when I started for the Ashram; and when I did, something happened with the fellow worker. When I returned, this woman, who irritated me with her superiority, came in and sat down across from me and said, 'I wished for you yesterday. I was talking with one of the teachers who is having a struggle in his inner life and has many problems, and I felt you could help him solve them.'" Jealousy was gone out of her heart and out of her relationships.

After you have surrendered the jealousy, go one step further and keep saying all the nice things you can about the person you have been jealous of. And let all your thoughts of that person turn to prayer.

A man described how he and the other men who worked on commission in a store would criticize one another, especially if one sold more goods than another. That was self-defeating, for it made them all sell fewer goods; the customer would unconsciously sense the undertone of hostility in the place and buy less. Jealousy is a cancer, eating at our happiness and our effectiveness. So root it out of your thoughts before it gets a foothold. Once in, it becomes the spring of action and emotion. Consent for God to take it out, and cooperate in keeping it out.

O Jesus, give me the heart that knows love and only love for everybody. Help me to love those I do not like, and then I'll probably like them. Amen.

AFFIRMATION FOR THE DAY: As love casts out all fear, so love will cast out all jealousy in me.

241

THE MASTERY OF GUIDANCE

Isaiah 26:7-9

We come now to another mastery in the Acts—*the mastery of guidance.*

Guidance is at once the most precarious and the most precious thing in the Christian life. I say *precarious*, for you can go wrong following "guidance." Some do. A pastor's life was a wreck, his credentials surrendered and his home life broken, because he followed "guidance," a wrong relationship with a woman. He got his wires crossed, mistaking the voice of his sex emotions for the voice of God. "I thought I was following the guidance of God," he said as he viewed the ruins. While there are casualties now and then in guidance, and its direction and fruit must be carefully watched and scrutinized, nevertheless the casualties of living unguided lives are infinitely greater. The wreckage of not living by God's guidance is so vast that we scarcely notice it, for it is commonplace. All the troubles and wreckages in the world have one root: not living under God's guidance. So the occasional wreck that takes place in mistaking God's guidance should not scare us away from the infinite possibilities of life under God's guidance.

God has a plan for every life. When God made you, God made you different. God has not made anyone like you and never will again. God destroyed the pattern. You are unique and have a unique contribution to make. You are important in the scheme of things. The one supreme business of life is to find God's plan for your life and live it. Having a life plan from God gives you a backbone upon which all the bones of your life are fastened, all cohering in the central plan that holds them all together in meaning and purpose. Most people go through life spineless and disjointed. No central plan organizes their lives and directs them toward a single goal. They live a hand-to-mouth existence of opportunism. Hence they leave nothing but a blur. They live aimlessly and then stumble into the arms of death, and it is all over tragedy.

O Lord, teach me to know your will for my life and then teach me to work it out with all my ransomed being, giving the utmost for the highest. Amen.

AFFIRMATION FOR THE DAY: When God guides, God provides— provides everything for carrying out that guidance.

TWO SECRETS OF POWER

Isaiah 30:20-21

The secret of power in the Acts is twofold: First, these Christians fully surrendered to God and through that surrender were enabled to accept the gift of the Holy Spirit. That enabled the Holy Spirit to come into immediate contact with the human spirit, heightening all its powers and adding a plus to everything. Second, these heightened powers were under divine control and were working out a plan, a life plan. Without following divine guidance, the Holy Spirit's power in their lives would have been canceled or frustrated. Without this divine guidance, life is like a hose with the water running to waste. Guidance directs the water of the hose where it is needed.

The disciples made some mistakes in guidance, but the mistakes taught them to turn to truer guidance and overrule their mistakes. They made a mistake, I believe, in deciding on a successor to Judas. First, they put forth two men and asked God to choose between them. They gave God no leeway; they tried to tie God's hands. God didn't want either of the men; God wanted Paul. Second, they took a wrong method of guidance; they cast lots. That was the first and last time they used that method. The God of law and order can't be made into a Cosmic Juggler, making chance lots fall in the right way. "I have taken a chance in the sweepstakes; and if you will pray that I win, I will give half the proceeds to your church," said a man to me in India. I replied, "I will pray that God will give you sense enough not to waste your time, your money, and your character on lotteries." I called out to a drunk as he staggered unsteadily across the street, "Look out; you're going against the red light!" He waved his hand and said, "God always takes care of his children," and walked on!

The disciples learned their lessons; guidance moved from the outward to the inward, from chance events to obedience to the voice of God under moral law.

O Holy Spirit, teach me to hear your voice and to distinguish between it and the voice of my desires. And help me to obey when I know, risking my all. Amen.

**AFFIRMATION FOR THE DAY: God's guidance is always
into greater character and greater effectiveness.**

GUIDANCE FROM THE OUTER TO THE INNER

Isaiah 40:11

The guidance in the Acts moves from the outer guidance of events—wet fleece, lots, sacrifice through fire—to the voice of God within the soul. But that voice was not independent of or apart from human intelligence. Sometimes where the intelligence could not be a part of the decision, the voice was direct and immediate and imperative. But mostly the Holy Spirit's voice and the human intelligence coincided and were one. This statement, "It has seemed good to the Holy Spirit and to us" (Acts 15:28 RSV), is the high-water mark of guidance. Yet even that was not free from marginal irrelevance. For instance, the account says, "For it has seemed good to the Holy Spirit and to us to lay upon you no greater burden than these necessary things: that you abstain from what has been sacrificed to idols and from blood and from what is strangled and from unchastity" (vv. 28-29 RSV). The two items "from blood" and "from what is strangled" were practices of the Jews, which they tried to pass over into the Gentile world as universal practices. They failed. The RSV margin note says, "Other early authorities omit *and from what is strangled.*" It was quietly dropped out. It was local and temporary and not universal. Yet the guidance not to put the Jewish yoke of circumcision on the Gentile Christians was right. It was so right it could stand the marginal irrelevance introduced and still be right.

Sometimes the guidance of the Spirit was a no. "Paul and his companions traveled throughout the regions of Phrygia and Galatia because the Holy Spirit kept them from speaking the word in the province of Asia.... They tried to enter the province of Bithynia, but the Spirit of Jesus wouldn't let them" (16:6-7). But that no was in order to guide them to a larger yes. For the closed doors into Asia meant an open door into Europe; the man of Macedonia called them to Europe and to us. God never closes one door without opening a bigger one. "I just love red lights," said the overflowing "Mary." Why? "Because he gives me a red light in order to give me a bigger green." God's blockings are God's blessings—always—if we know how to take them.

O Lord, I know that your red lights are only in order to guide me to a more glorious green. Help me to take gladly your prohibitions in order to take your possibilities. Amen.

AFFIRMATION FOR THE DAY: If I am blocked today, I shall look around to find the larger open door.

WAS PAUL WRONG?

Isaiah 42:16

We come to consider the puzzling case of Paul's guidance about going to Jerusalem. The account says:

> Compelled by the Spirit, they kept telling Paul not to go to Jerusalem....
>
> [Agabus] came to us, took Paul's belt, tied his own feet and hands, and said, "This is what the Holy Spirit says: 'In Jerusalem the Jews will bind the man who owns this belt, and they will hand him over to the Gentiles.' When we heard this, we and the local believers urged Paul not to go up to Jerusalem....
>
> Since we couldn't talk him out of it, the only thing we could say was, "The Lord's will be done." (Acts 21:4, 11-12, 14)

Just what was the will of the Lord there? Were the disciples at Tyre and Agabus wrong when they told Paul through the Spirit not to go? It seems to me they were right. But Paul had a fear of safety, and they were asking him to play safe. He tells the Ephesian elder how he felt:

> Now, compelled by the Spirit, I'm going to Jerusalem. I don't know what will happen to me there. What I do know is that the Holy Spirit testifies to me from city to city that prisons and troubles await me. But nothing, not even my life, is more important than my completing my mission. This is nothing other than the ministry I received from the Lord Jesus: to testify about the good news of God's grace. (20:22-24)

Nothing more noble and beautiful in literature, the revelation of a completely dedicated soul. Yet I wonder if the disciples at Tyre and Agabus weren't right; they were warning him by the Spirit not to go. But his strong point—his willingness to be a martyr—made him plunge ahead through the red lights. He disobeyed but disobeyed honestly. And God turned this honest disobedience into victory. The glorious account of Paul's trials before the tribunals, the amazing mastery of the man amid the storm and the shipwreck, and his work at Rome; it all turned out gloriously. But we don't know what more glorious things might have happened had he not gone. God turned second best for Paul into victory.

O Lord, I know you have a first will and a second will for us. If we miss your first, you offer a second. Help me to take your first, always. Amen.

AFFIRMATION FOR THE DAY: I am walking with the lights today, everything under God's guidance.

THE MASTERY OF LEGALISM

Romans 3:20-26

We come now to consider another mastery in the Acts—*the mastery of legalism*.

Jesus had to put the gospel into the framework of a people whose religion was a vast legalism. The center of that faith was the Law. That Law, which was good, degenerated from Law to laws. To the central core of moral Law they added innumerable ceremonial laws. Soon the ceremonial laws took precedence over and obscured the moral Law. Jesus struck at this when he said:

> How terrible it will be for you blind guides, who say, "If people swear by the temple, it's nothing. But if people swear by the gold in the temple, they are obligated to do what they swore." ...You say, "If people swear by the altar, it's nothing. But if they swear by the gift on the altar, they are obligated to do what they swore." You blind people! (Matt 23:16-19)

All that confused and irrelevant legalism, which resulted in an *outwardism*, of which the Pharisee was the perfect example, had to be replaced by a "new covenant, not based on what is written but on the Spirit, because what is written kills, but the Spirit gives life" (2 Cor 3:6). The people of this new covenant "weren't written with ink but with the Spirit of the living God. You weren't written on tablets of stone but on tablets of human hearts" (2 Cor 3:3). The new law was written within. The outwardism was replaced by an *inwardism*, which became the law of love. The spring of conduct was not in duty but in love. "Love God and do as you like" became the expression of a love that would make you like what God loves; and you would do it out of love for God.

As Jesus had to replace the first covenant—which had become a legalism—with a new covenant—which was the law of love—so he had to replace the Jewish Sabbath with a new kind of Sabbath. The old Sabbath was so overburdened with intricate and impossible and irrelevant restrictions that Jesus couldn't redeem it. So he replaced it by a Christian Sabbath with a new basis and outlook.

O Christ of the Discerning Heart, we thank you that you are the Great Emancipator, freeing us from the irrelevant little to the relevant big. Amen.

AFFIRMATION FOR THE DAY: I shall base my life, not merely on the restrictions of law, but on the release of love.

THE JEWISH SABBATH REPLACED
BY THE CHRISTIAN

Matthew 12:1-8

We saw yesterday that Jesus found the Jewish Sabbath so overladen with irrelevancies and trivialities and burdensome restrictions that he had to replace it with a Christian Sabbath, with a new content and outlook. The Jewish Sabbath couldn't be redeemed, so it was quietly displaced.

Jesus gave advance notice of this, "The Human One is Lord of the Sabbath" (Matt 12:8). To drive home his lordship, he proceeded to break the legal bondage that had been built into the Sabbath. This was one of the reasons they crucified him.

The idea underlying the Sabbath—one day's rest in seven—was right and had to be preserved. But the system built up on that idea had to be discarded, and a new vehicle of expression had to replace it.

A new content had to be put into the Sabbath. What better content than the day of the resurrection, the first day of the week? The old Sabbath commemorated the first creation; the new Sabbath commemorated the new creation. The old Sabbath commemorated the fulfillment of God's creative life in nature; the new Sabbath commemorated God's creative Life in human nature. The first Sabbath was overlaid by legalism, so the new Sabbath would start not with legalities but with Life, the glorious resurrection Life of Jesus. "Jesus is Lord" was applied to the Sabbath; he changed it into his own image and conception. How? By decree? No, that would have spoiled it; for again it would have become a legalism depending on his command. We would have taken his words of change and made them into a new legalism.

He did something better. He inspired people to begin a new day with a new content: "On the first day of the week, when we were gathered together to break bread" (Acts 20:7 RSV); "On the first day the week, each of you should set aside whatever you can afford from what you earn so that the collection won't be delayed until I come" (1 Cor 16:2). A new practice and a new principle grew up; a new Sabbath resulted.

O Jesus, your ways and your wisdom are always right. We thank you for saving the Sabbath for us with the glorious content of the resurrection. Amen.

AFFIRMATION FOR THE DAY: I belong to the most triumphant day—the resurrection—I shall illustrate it.

TWO THINGS TRANSFERRED
TO THE NEW SABBATH

Galatians 4:8-10

We saw yesterday that alongside the Jewish Sabbath there grew up the Christian Sabbath; the one commemorates the first creation and the other the second creation, the resurrection. And into that new Sabbath, commemorating the new beginning, were put new meanings and practices.

One of the new practices was to break bread. "On the first day of the week, we were gathered together to break bread" (Acts 20:7 RSV). Now the breaking of bread was not the partaking of an ordinary meal, for the account says, "And when Paul had gone up and had broken bread and eaten" (Acts 20:11 RSV); the breaking of bread was different from the eating. It was the same as that found in Acts 2:42 (RSV): "And they devoted themselves to the apostles' teaching and fellowship, to the breaking of bread and the prayers." Obviously the breaking of bread was the Love Feast, a distinctly Christian rite. This was transferred to the first day of the week, the Christian Sabbath.

The second religious act transferred to the Christian Sabbath was the taking up of contributions: "On the first day of every week, each of you is to put something aside and store it up...so that contributions need not be made when I come " (1 Cor 16:2 RSV). "Store it up" meant obviously to put it into the common treasury, the church treasury; so there would be no collections taken when Paul came.

So the Love Feast and collection were transferred to the Christian Sabbath and gradually everything else connected with Christian worship. The transition was made from an impossibly legalistic Jewish Sabbath to a Christian Sabbath, and it was done not by a verbal command of Jesus but by a vital urge of the Spirit. The new wine of the gospel had to be put into the new wineskins of a Christian Sabbath. The change was not made by a Roman Catholic pope as some claim; it was made in the pages of the Acts by the Christian insight that the old Sabbath could not contain the new meanings; so under the guidance of the Spirit, the new was adopted. And how grateful I am that it was! The new has the life of the resurrection within it.

O Blessed Christ, you are gently putting aside the outworn old and replacing it with the glorious new. Help me to accept the new with gratitude. Amen.

**AFFIRMATION FOR THE DAY: Since I belong to the expansive new,
I shall lay aside all the outworn old in my life.**

READY TO VANISH AWAY

Hebrews 8:10-13

The germ of the use of the Christian Sabbath—instead of the Jewish—was to be found in the fact that as soon as the resurrection took place, the disciples, seeing the absolute importance of this event, began to meet on that day straight off. The account says:

> It was still the first day of the week. That evening, while the disciples were behind closed doors because they were afraid of the Jewish authorities, Jesus came and stood among them. He said, "Peace be with you." (John 20:19
>
> After eight days, his disciples were again in a house....Jesus entered and stood among them. He said, "Peace be with you" (v. 26)

Jesus met with them on the succeeding first day of the week (eight days later would be the first day), thus accustoming them to meet with him on that blessed day. The revolutionary change was made in an evolutionary way. That was wise; for if it had been by a verbal enactment of Jesus, it would have precipitated a violent controversy between the old and the new. Now the transition was not verbal but vital. Then was fulfilled this verse "When it says new, it makes the first obsolete. And if something is old and outdated, it's close to disappearing" (Heb 8:13).

The old Sabbath was obsolete, for it was not usable. It can't be used today, not universally. For the Jewish Sabbath was from sundown to sundown. Now in parts of the world, as in Norway, the sun in certain periods doesn't go down at all, or for just a brief portion of a day. So those who insist on the Jewish Sabbath as binding on Christians are forced to change the letter of the Jewish law by making the Sabbath go from six o'clock to six o'clock. But that gives away the case. If you don't take a legalism entirely, you don't take it. Moreover, if you can change it in one aspect, why can't the whole thing be changed to a more suitable day with a Christian content in it?

We have a day now that fits our gospel. The most important day in our calendar is the day of the Resurrection. What better way to commemorate it than by the Christian Sabbath?

O Jesus Christ, we thank you that we have found a day with content, the most glorious in the world. Help us to make that day worthy of that glorious fact. Amen.

AFFIRMATION FOR THE DAY: I cannot really take the Christian Sabbath without taking its content—the Resurrection—I do, wholly.

THE MASTERY OF THE OLD BY THE NEW

Matthew 9:14-17

This leads us to a new mastery—*the mastery of the old by the new.*

The gospel of Jesus was set in the midst of a people who held tenaciously to what they felt was a God-inspired and God-given system, a system so important to them that they said that if the people of Israel would keep the whole Law for a day, the Messiah would come. The Messiah came, and instead of keeping the whole Law, he substituted for it a new Law. How did he do it? The pivot upon which the whole thing turns is this verse: "Don't even begin to think that I have come to do away with the Law and the Prophets. I haven't come to do away with them but to fulfill them" (Matt 5:17).

What an amazing way to get rid of something that was imperfect and inadequate! He didn't say, I'll wipe the slate clean, and we'll begin all over. He picked out the good and fulfilled it, and the irrelevant dropped off as a dead leaf. Someone has said, "You cannot overthrow a wrong thing unless you recognize the good in that thing—the good that makes it float—then when you have recognized the good, you can strike at the bad." Jesus did even better than that, for he recognized the good and fulfilled it with such wondrous meanings that the people saw their relevant old as so beautiful that they simply did not want the irrelevant old. It dropped away in the light of this new.

Jesus didn't say a word against animal sacrifices as atonement for sin, but he did something better; he went to the cross, gave himself for sin, and in the light of this divine sacrifice animal sacrifices dropped away.

How did he get rid of the 3,600 burdensome commandments held by the Jews? Fight them? Oh no, he picked out two: "you must love the Lord your God" and "you must love your neighbor." Love to God and love to people, and when the people looked at them as illustrated in Jesus, they knew that the other commandments were irrelevant, and they dropped away. The glorious new pushed out the fading old. He didn't fight the old; he fulfilled the good in it, and the other dropped out.

O Jesus, your wisdom shines upon us and illuminates our footsteps. In your light we see light. And your light never fades; it shines more and more to the perfect day. Amen.

AFFIRMATION FOR THE DAY: I shall pick out of the passing old the good that makes it float and redeem it.

BUT A NEW CREATION

Matthew 15:10-20

We saw yesterday how Jesus got rid of the obsolete old by rescuing any good that lay in it and fulfilling it. The old dropped away.

He got rid of the Old Testament as a final revelation by inspiring people to write a New Testament. In the light of the New, the Old was seen to be only a preparation for this glorious New. He didn't destroy it; he fulfilled it.

He got rid of clean and unclean food by a simple statement, "It's not what goes into the mouth that contaminates a person in God's sight. It's what comes out of the mouth that contaminates the person" (Matthew 15:11). What comes out of the mouth comes from the heart, and that is where the contamination is. The simple transference from the ceremonial to the moral made the whole system of clean and unclean irrelevant. It faded out.

He got rid of the rite of circumcision as the distinguishing mark of belonging to the people of God by making it to be of the heart, resulting in changed character and life. He inspired Paul to put it in these words, "Being circumcised or not being circumcised doesn't mean anything. What matters is a new creation" (Gal 6:15). Not the ceremonial putting off of the old but the putting on of the morally new—a new creation—that was the important thing.

This could be brought up-to-date and applied to our situation by the fact that, just as circumcision was the outward sign of a Jew, so baptism by water is now the outward sign of a Christian. In doing so, have we substituted a new legalism for the old? A new outwardism for the old outwardism? Yes, unless we take baptism for what it is—a rite that may lead you to the Redeemer. But if it stops you at itself and makes itself the issue, it is not beautiful; it is idolatry. You are not saved by a rite; you are saved by a Redeemer. So this passage could be translated, "Being baptized or not being baptized doesn't mean anything. What matters is a new creation." Cornelius and his group received the Holy Spirit before baptism, the people of Ephesus after. None *at*. That is important—very.

O Jesus, we thank you for baptism, but we thank you more that it is in your name; it leads us to your feet. You are the end and therefore the issue. Amen.

AFFIRMATION FOR THE DAY: I shall illustrate the new creation in all my acts and thoughts, and witness to it.

APPLICATIONS OF FULFILLMENT

Revelation 21:22-27

We pause another day on the mastery of the old by the new. The old outwardness in praying became the inwardness of the closed doors, praying to the Lord who is in secret. The praying was thus not aimed outward toward people to be seen of them; it was aimed upward toward God and resulted in spiritual communion with God, a spiritual act.

Fasting was not outward to be seen by people; it was inward of the spirit, fasting not merely from the demands of the flesh for food but from all its pressing desires—from sex cravings and sex thinking—fasting!

The old aggressive attitude toward other nations, resulting in periodic wars, was now fulfilled and became a loving aggression, carrying the good news to every tongue and people. The aggression of hate became the aggression of love. The aggressive spirit was redeemed to higher ends; it was fulfilled.

Fierce allegiance to the nation was now lifted and fastened upon the kingdom of God, a new Society of the Redeemed. These people were enlarged in the enlargement of the unit of loyalty, universalized, in fact.

Their allegiance to a Book became an attachment to a Person. For the early Christians had no Book as yet. But they had a Person. That made religion, not obedience to a Law, but the living out of a Life from the letter to the spirit. When they did get the Book, these words took them by the hand and led them beyond the words to the Word made flesh, the Person.

All the old died out like a seed dies—dies to live as flower and fruit—not destroyed but fulfilled.

What Jesus did for the Jewish system, he does for every system. He doesn't destroy it; he fulfills it by gathering up its good and letting the old drop away, irrelevant and unwanted. The New is the Creative New.

O Jesus, my Lord, you are not only the Savior of our souls but the Savior of the good found anywhere, making it into the better and the best. I thank you. Amen.

**AFFIRMATION FOR THE DAY: I shall not sigh over the passing old;
I shall sing over the coming New.**

THE MASTERY OF INGROWN ATTITUDES

1 Timothy 1:3-5

We come now to a new mastery—*the mastery of ingrown attitudes*. These Christians were turned from the spiritually ingrown to an outward moral and spiritual offensive. From the very moment of the coming of the Holy Spirit, they were released from self-preoccupation and turned toward sharing this new life with others.

This was important, for the coming of the Holy Spirit brought such a deep joy that they appeared to be intoxicated. That joy could have been a snare. It could have caught them in the tangle of being taken up with their own inner happiness and joy. It could have resulted in their going around in circles, revolving around their own states of soul and mind. It didn't. Their joy had within it the quality of love, and that love turned their interests outside themselves. It was the joy of sharing. Had their joy lacked love, the movement would have degenerated into an ecstatic movement, revolving around its own inner states.

This is an essential difference between the realization of Brahma on the part of the Hindu and the realization of God on the part of the Christian. The Hindu tries to realize his oneness with Pure Being, which is lifted above relationships. Hence those who are supposed to have realized Brahma are themselves objects of wonder and pilgrimage. People go to them; they don't go to people. They are not outgoing; they are lost in the ecstasy of their own inner realization of God. There is no love at the basis of this realization, for the God they realize is *sat* (being), *chit* (intelligence), and *ananda* (bliss). But note there is no quality of love, for love would attach one to life, and in this realization all attachments are broken.

This trying to find Brahma ends only in trying, for there is no such being as Brahma. Hence it is a philosophy but no finding. I have never seen anyone who impressed me as realizing Brahma.

But these people at Pentecost were invaded by the God of love revealed in Jesus, invaded by and filled by him. Love became the center of their experience, hence their sharing.

O Jesus, Revealer of the Love that lies at the heart of things, when I find you, I find Love and nothing but Love; hence I can give love and nothing but love. I thank you. Amen.

AFFIRMATION FOR THE DAY: I belong to the self-giving Christ; I cannot therefore be anything but a self-giving Christian.

HOLDING THEIR SPIRITUAL PULSES?

John 7:37-39

We noted yesterday that it was love—redeeming love—at the heart of their experience of God that made the disciples outgoing instead of ingrown. An ingrown spiritual experience is as bad as an ingrown toenail. One sets up a physical festering and the other a spiritual festering. The validity of a spiritual experience is determined by its vitality. Does it have enough vitality to be redemptively contagious?

One of the most striking things about the experience of God in the Acts is the complete absence of any sign of the ingrown. This group did not sit around holding their spiritual pulses, analyzing themselves, and holding séances to see if God would appear by their techniques. God in the Holy Spirit was in them; they knew it. And God was not playing hide-and-seek with them; the Spirit came to abide with them forever. The only way they could get God out was to sin God out. With the fact of God fixed, they went out to witness. The Holy Spirit was given on the condition that they be witnesses: "You will receive power when the Holy Spirit has come upon you, and you will be my witnesses" (Acts 1:8). And the special work of the Holy Spirit is this: "he will bear witness to me; and you also are witnesses" (John 15:26-27 RSV). So the very nature of the experience of the Holy Spirit was a witnessing experience.

This meant that their inner experience was a base of operation; it was not the end. That was psychologically sound. It freed them from self-preoccupation and made them outgoing. Any religious experience is sick if at the end you are preoccupied with yourself. One of the supreme dangers of psychoanalysis is that it keeps the analyzed person preoccupied with self, sometimes a year or two years or more. That very self-preoccupation would create a neurosis if you didn't begin with one. Analysis? Yes, but just enough to find the facts. And they can usually be found in a comparatively short time. Then on to the synthesis that comes through self-surrender to God. And then, on to the sharing of that experience of God with others. Then the person is psychologically sound in the self and creative with others. That person is on the Way!

O Lord, I thank you that your plan of redemption is sound for me and for others; it is sound. And when I work it out, the sense of soundness spreads through me. Amen.

AFFIRMATION FOR THE DAY: Love lifted me, and love lifts me out of myself, free to serve.

EXPERIENCE BECOMES EXPRESSION

Luke 8:36-39

We have noted that the experience of the Holy Spirit and the sharing of that experience were one. The second chapter of Acts begins with the description of their being filled with the Holy Spirit and ends with the statement: "The Lord added daily to the community those who were being saved" (Acts 2:47). One would have thought that chapter would have been taken up with the description of what happened inwardly when the Holy Spirit came within them. There is a complete absence of that. Instead, there is this revealing statement: "They were all filled with the Holy Spirit and began to speak" (2:4). The moment the experience became experience it became expression. And because it became expression, it became deeper experience. For expression deepens impression. Nothing is ours until we share it. If a person or movement is not evangelistic, it will soon cease to be evangelical. If Christianity is not a contagion, it will soon cease to be a conception.

But note that while the second chapter of Acts speaks of addition—"The Lord added"—the rest of Acts speaks of multiplication; the addition became multiplication. "And walking in the fear of the Lord and in the comfort of the Holy Spirit it was multiplied" (9:31 RSV). Many churches are growing precariously by addition—birth of children, people moving in. But unless the addition becomes multiplication, unless the people added become contagious themselves, it is less than Christian.

One of the greatest churches in America in my estimation is the Hollywood Presbyterian Church. The meaning of that great church is summed up in the motto on the wall of the meeting hall for youth, "To know him, to help others to know him." To know him as personal Savior and Lord in a firsthand living way; to help others to know him in a firsthand living way; these two things sum up the meaning of our Christian faith. They are the alternate beats of the Christian heart. They mean inflow and outgo, receptivity and response.

O Lord, I thank you for the rhythm of your salvation; it provides for my needs and the needs of others, and it provides for them equally. I thank you. Amen.

AFFIRMATION FOR THE DAY: Today I shall make "to know him, to help others to know him" a living fact in me.

CAME NEAR UPSETTING THE TABLE

1 Thessalonians 1:5-8

In one of my quiet times this came: "Know Me; receive Me; illustrate Me; give Me." That sums it up. The first is to know Christ as your own, personal Savior and Lord. The second is to receive God's daily divine invasion of you. The Spirit wants to come deeper every day. The third is to illustrate Christ, to become a pocket edition of him. And the fourth is to give Christ.

A big businessman, recently in the kingdom, said that the "reason people do not share is because they have nothing to share." The moment he got something personal, he began to share it with his wife, his secretary, his business personnel, his social associates.

Sometimes the sharing takes place by humbling ourselves. A woman and her husband were scarcely speaking, each afraid to give in to the other. The woman surrendered to Christ and gave up her resentments. When she returned from the Ashram, a place of spiritual retreat, she got up and prepared her husband's breakfast. Before she always let him do it. Softened by this, he asked, "What did you learn at the Ashram?" She replied, "The first thing I learned was to begin with myself. Before this I've always begun with you. I've been wrong in my attitudes." And she got on her knees to him and said, "I'm sorry. I've been all wrong. Forgive me." He came near upsetting the table in dropping on his knees beside her. He said, "No, I've been as much to blame as you, and more. Forgive me." They both surrendered themselves to God and each other; and a new, joyous era began in that home.

The place to begin dealing with others is to begin with yourself. The confession of your own sin creates the consciousness and conviction of sin in others. And it makes it easier for others to confess their sins. Confession begets confession. "Mary," in asking people to come to the altar, left the pulpit and knelt on the congregation side of the altar, not on the inside as ministers do; and the congregation flocked to kneel beside her, all broken up by her simple confession of need.

O Lord, melt my pride and stubbornness and help me to confess people into the arms of Jesus. Maybe people will follow me on the road of confession to the foot of the cross. Amen.

AFFIRMATION FOR THE DAY: Since confession begets confession, I shall be open to confess anything Jesus prompts me to.

THEY HAVE AN ENTHUSIASM
AMONG THEMSELVES

Colossians 1:3-7

We are studying the fact that there was a simple and profound mastery of the ingrown in the Acts. The doors of life began immediately to swing out. They were releasing themselves and in the process were released from themselves.

I was talking to the head of a great university, a skeptic; in discussing the religious life of the university, he remarked about a certain religious group, "They have an enthusiasm among themselves." That was revealing. They were ardent in their getting together, in their loyalty to their faith; but it was "an enthusiasm among themselves"; it didn't get beyond the circle. It was all like a dog chasing its tail and getting nowhere.

One of the most influential Christians in this country was "Brother Bryan" of Birmingham, Alabama. The grateful citizens put up a monument to him in the center of the city.* The traffic flows around that monument, which shows Brother Bryan kneeling in prayer with his face lifted to the sky. That man prayed himself and his Lord into the life of a great industrial city; they voted him the most useful citizen of their city. The story goes that one time he sat listening to a speaker who was expounding how to do evangelism effectively. Brother Bryan grew restive under the flow of words and ideas; he went out of the meeting, across the street, sat down with a workman who was eating his noonday lunch, and led him to Christ on the spot. He felt that the way to do evangelism was to do it. The theory was the practice. The fact is that the thing we believe in is the thing we practice. If we don't believe in a thing enough to practice it, then we just don't believe in it. The only way to do evangelism is to do it. Francis, a simple villager of India, learned to read through adult literacy, and this led him to the Bible. In one year, one-hundred-one were baptized through him at Christmas, and fifty-three more were ready at Easter. He gave his witness, and the Holy Spirit did the rest, for the Spirit witnesses to our witness.

O Spirit Divine, open my lips and my heart to give my witness. For if I hold my peace, the stones will cry out, the hard, bare facts will speak. Amen.

AFFIRMATION FOR THE DAY: If I do not witness, I will soon have nothing to witness to.

* See the statue and learn more about the Rev. James Alexander Bryan, "Brother Bryan," at http:// bbmission.com/history/, accessed March 17, 2017.

AN OLD TATTOOED WOMAN
WON A THOUSAND

Acts 8:4-8

We ended yesterday with the emphasis that evangelism is not for the specialists; it is for the Christian as a Christian. When I was in Formosa, I was told that during the war an old tattooed grandmother, a member of the head-hunters, was converted and immediately began to convert others. The Japanese tried to stop her work, but the people carried her on their shoulders up into the mountains, where she continued her witnessing and converting. When the missionaries returned at the end of the war, they found she had won over a thousand of these head-hunters to Christ; and they had erected their own churches and were self-propagating. When the missionaries arrived among them, though they had been starved during the war, their first question was not about food but, "Do you have any Bibles in America? Could you get some for us?" They were hungry for the Bread of Life. An old tattooed woman, her own heart aflame, set the mountains aflame.

If an old woman can do it, then a child can do it too. A little boy of ten said, "Mother, I think I saved the soul of a policeman today." "How?" asked the mother. "Well, he was so nice to me in taking me across the street that I said, 'You're so kind, you're like a Christian. Are you one?'" Whether or not the policeman became a Christian, the little boy was more of a Christian by sharing his faith.

"Genie and I went to see a neighbor, and in half an hour we had prayed her into the arms of Jesus," said "Mary." This same Mary had been talking all day to people and leading them into conversion. At eventide she came into the hotel, and a man opened the door and asked, "How are you?" He got the unexpected reply, "Converted." She was so full of it that it simply overflowed spontaneously. She says of people entering conversion, "It is wonderful to see the light go on in their eyes." It is. And when you see the light go on in their eyes, you get the reflection in your own.

O Lord Jesus, let me be so full of the spirit of conversion that out of the abundance of my heart my mouth may speak. And may it speak with clarity. Amen.

AFFIRMATION FOR THE DAY: Everything I say and do and am shall cry "Converted!" to everyone I meet today.

A BUTCHER KNIFE AND THE WAY

Acts 16:25-34

We continue to look at the mastery of the ingrown through turning life into outgoingness in evangelism. I was talking with a man who told of a reporter investigating crime in this country. At the end of the investigation, in which he laid bare the crime situation in some of our cities, the reporter was so depressed by what he had found that he committed suicide. He had no inner resources to match these outer conditions, so he simply backed out of life through self-destruction. The people in the Acts, finding in the Holy Spirit inner resources, were able to walk into life with all its evil and sin and call it to repentance and conversion.

This tragic dilemma is seen in this case: A woman who was an alcoholic had a daughter, who after examination, was told that she had cancer. The shock to the family circle was terrible. The husband said to the wife, "This has come upon us because of the way you are living." It angered her, so she left and went to her parents' home and told what the husband had said. The parents said, "Well, maybe your husband is right." This made her more furious. So she went back home and found her husband gone. She decided to commit suicide; tried to do so with some electric gadgets and failed. She then took the butcher knife, determined to slit her wrists. She took the knife into the living room and laid it down on a book in order to gain time to get up the nerve to end things. She noted the title of the book, *The Way*, one I wrote.* She began to thumb through it, was arrested by it, and began to read it. In the midst of reading she dropped on her knees and surrendered her life to Christ and was converted on the spot. Her alcoholism dropped away; she became an entirely new person, and is on top of her world and its tragedies.

The coming together—of that butcher knife and *The Way* on the same table—represent dramatically the human alternatives: the way of self-destruction through despair or the way of self-surrender to the Deliverer. It is the way of the slit wrists or the nail-pierced hands, suicide or salvation.

O Jesus, you are standing at the crossroads of human life. Help us to take not the ways to dead ends but the Way, the Way of release and freedom and victory. Amen.

AFFIRMATION FOR THE DAY: Today I shall illustrate the Way and not the way of escape.

*E. Stanley Jones, *The Way* (Nashville: Abingdon Press, 2015).

WE CANNOT BUT SPEAK

Acts 14:1-7

We continue this week to look at the mastery over ingrownness by the outgoing spirit of sharing. The whole of the Acts is one recital after another of this redemptive pressure on individuals, cities, and civilizations. If God had redemptively invaded the world in Christ, then the people, touched by this invasion, began to invade redemptively the situations around them. Freely they had received, so freely did they give. Like was producing like. Love begat love.

If the last spoken word in the Acts is "They will listen!" (Acts 28:28), then the last recorded act is: "Paul lived in his own rented quarters for two full years and welcomed everyone who came to see him. Unhindered and with complete confidence, he continued to preach God's kingdom and to teach about the Lord Jesus Christ" (vv. 30-31). The Acts are acts of evangelism from first to last. Here are men and women on fire. The pages are ablaze with a consuming passion to share.

Wherever the authentic Christian spirit is found, there is the same passion to share. John Richardson, an Indian Christian on the Nicobar Islands, located between India and Burma, was put in jail by the Japanese when they captured the islands during the war, because he wouldn't side with the Japanese. His son was taken out and shot, and they set the date on which he was to be shot. But he refused to knuckle. On the day appointed for his execution, he heard the footfalls of his executioners. But the Japanese said instead, "Japan yesterday made peace, so you are free." His courage and steadfastness so impressed the islanders that about ten thousand of them became Christians, nearly the whole population. Then the man who had offered his head for his convictions was ordained bishop of the islands.* The words *martyr* and *witness* are the same. The early Christians and authentic Christians of today witness even though it means martyrdom—literal or social or economic or political martyrdom. "We can't help speaking about what we have seen and heard" (Acts 4:20), is the divine compulsion within people. If we hold our peace, the stones—the hard, bare facts of life—will cry out; for people need conversion and need it everywhere.

O Holy Spirit, if I hold my peace, uneasiness seizes me. If I declare the good news, I feel a sense of well-being and joy. This is what I am made for. Amen.

**AFFIRMATION FOR THE DAY: This divine compulsion will impel me
to share what has been shared with me.**

*The details of this story have not been verified, but see M. D. Srinivasan, *Sons of the Light* (Indian Society for Promoting Christian Knowledge, 1962).

EVANGELISM IS INHERENT

Acts 19:18-20

We continue our study of the mastery of ingrownness and inhibitions. With the impact of the Spirit of Christ upon the human consciousness there was an immediate reaction into outgoingness. This extends from the highest to the lowest.

"Mary" was used of God to help a girl through to release; she unconsciously used the correct psychological approach, though she knows little of technical psychology. The girl was on the verge of a breakdown, living on coffee and nerves. This day Mary told her to leave her long face at the door, and she would be going away with a new one. For five hours she poured out her troubles, and Mary listened. The girl said, "But this isn't getting on your nerves, is it?" "No," replied Mary. "It is necessary to get it all up and out." Then Mary finally said, "Now that you have told me all this, do you think you are ready to get to the real thing?" The girl broke down and told her. Then Mary went out of the room and left her with a picture of Christ. She told her to give her answer to him. She did. Then Mary returned and in simple prayer took her the rest of the way to victory. This girl in turn is on fire and winning others. Anyone who is sincere can do this work.

Our evangelism may be by word, and it may be by life. A college student was crossing the campus to his roommate after a wretched debauch. He happened to look up and saw through a lighted window the oldest and best-beloved member of the faculty writing at his desk. He knew the professor would be busy writing something he believed would help the world, this in deep contrast to the way he himself had spent the evening. The thought smote his heart. Then and there he turned over a new leaf and began to write on it the record of a useful, dedicated life. Tertullian tells us that most of the converts of his day were won not by reading the scriptures but by watching how the Christians lived and died. "If there were more like him, there'd be less like me," said a man with a debauched face as he pointed to a Christian.

O Christ, take such possession of me that I will show by my very looks that I have looked into your face and the reflection lingers. Give me a Christian face. Amen.

AFFIRMATION FOR THE DAY: Since evangelism is inherent in my being a Christian, it shall be inherent in all I do today.

LACK OF AN INNER PUSH

Acts 20:1-2

We saw yesterday that our faces can be the message of our evangelism. "Mary" was standing in a railway station, her face as always glowing with the love of God, when a redcap came up to her, removed his cap, stood looking at her. and then said: "Ain't you religious?" "Well," said Mary, "I belong to Jesus." He commented thoughtfully, "I thought so." Then they talked about Christ.

Conversion may take place through a spoken word. I listened to a radiant Christian tell how she was ashamed and filled with inferiority because of a broken home. But she listened to a radio address, knelt before the radio, and was soundly converted.

I am writing this in Oklahoma near where George Wade, a very contagious Christian, was converted in a chamber-of-commerce meeting of all places! As I spoke at the meeting, he felt his need, he said, and opened his heart then and there to the love of Christ, was soundly converted, and showed the fruits of it the balance of his useful days.

A doctor said to me, "Many people are failures because of the lack of an inner push from someone in the moment of crisis." Well, that inner push can come through the word or the silent influence of a life.

Some have that spiritual contagion, and some do not. I saw in an atomic plant a Geiger counter pass over a glass pond in which there were small turtles. Nothing happened when it was passed over some of the turtles; but every time it came to one little turtle, there would be sparks and noises from the machine. That turtle was radioactive. Some Christians are like that; they are radioactive with the Holy Spirit, and you feel the sparks of the Spirit when you get near them.

But some are dead; nothing outgoing coming from them. The society in the Acts of the Apostles was radioactive with the Holy Spirit. People felt that here was something different from the dead forms of religion. Here was religion with a spark.

O Holy Spirit set me afire with the fire of you. Let me emit love and only love, faith and only faith, joy and only joy, peace and only peace. Amen.

AFFIRMATION FOR THE DAY: I shall be radioactive with the Spirit today, and people will feel the contagion.

FOUNDATIONS OF PROGRESS IN CONVERSION

Acts 26:12-18

We are meditating on the outgoing contagious love inherent in Christianity.

When the constitution of India was being drawn up, it was debated hotly as to whether the sentence, "The right to profess, practice, and propagate one's faith is guaranteed to the individual," should be put in. The government rejected two hundred amendments that tried to soften or do away with the word *propagate*. Although for the most part non-Christian, it said, "No, the Christians believe it is an inherent part of their faith to propagate it, and we shall respect that right." It is an inherent part of our faith to propagate it. That faith is not practiced unless it is propagated.

It can be propagated in very simple ways and yet, oh, how effective! Sarah Chakko was one of the great women of India and of the world, president of Isabella Thoburn College, the oldest women's college in Asia, and vice president of the World Council of Churches. She told, two days before she died, how a prayer I had had with her in a crisis in her early days of teaching was the turning point of her life and responsible for her becoming president of the college. I told that story at a meeting a few days after her death, and the president of a great agricultural institute, Henry Azariah, stood up and told how, when he was a student, he was all confused and uncertain. He went to see me in his father's compound; and as we talked at the junction of two roads, I said to him, "Henry, you are at the crossroads of life. Let Christ have you." As we prayed, he surrendered his life to Christ. "That decision was the basis of my becoming head of this institute," he said. Dr. Gideon stood up and said, "If I am president of Ewing Christian College, it is because of a decision I made while a student in one of the meetings Stanley Jones conducted in Delhi. I was all upset and at cross-purposes. But that decision straightened out my life and brought me to this position." When we lead others to Christ, we start influences that will never stop.

O Christ, inspire me this day to put my hand on the shoulder of some wavering person and lead that person to you. For we all need you, inherently. Amen.

AFFIRMATION FOR THE DAY: I shall not pass anyone today who needs me; maybe a college president is in the making.

COLLEGE PRESIDENTS AND OUTCASTS

Acts 5:27-32

We saw yesterday how three college presidents of three great institutions traced their coming to those positions through an initial conversion. We must add two more. The wife of Principal Muherjee of St. Stephen's College in Delhi was one of the most effective women in northern India. She was led to Christ the same night that Dr. Gideon made his decision. One more: the head of the Saharanpur Theological Seminary in north India made his decision as a student in a similar series. So the heads of five of the most influential Christian institutions in north India all trace the beginnings of their spiritual life and subsequent positions to a simple conversion.

These illustrations are among the educated and influential. Take some simple outcaste Christians and see the same spirit at work. The Arya Samajists, a fanatical Hindu sect, persuaded the grain merchants and shopkeepers not to sell any food to the outcaste Christians or to give them any employment. They picketed the Christians' homes, not allowing them to get food or employment for six weeks, trying to starve them into signing their names that they were no longer Christians. To this they added threats. The boys and girls in Christian schools gave up a wheat cake from each meal and sent it to feed these picketed Christians. The Aryas tried to drive the pastor away. He would not budge. This all so touched a Hindu member of the legislative council, he told the Hindus that if they didn't stop this boycott of the Christians, he would undertake a fast to death until they did. They relented and lifted the boycott. The Christians were holding a prayer meeting in thanksgiving for the strength given to them to hold out, when in the semidarkness they heard the flutter of wings, heard it twice. A lantern was brought; no birds were there. They concluded God had sent the Holy Spirit like a dove in approval for their witness. Why not? At any rate the Hindus drove out the Aryas and honored the Christians for their stand.

O Holy Spirit, whether by sound of fluttering wings or by the silent influences within the heart, give your power and approval to me that I may witness faithfully. Amen.

AFFIRMATION FOR THE DAY: I need no sound of fluttering wings; my own heart's love impels me to share.

AT THE END OF MY ROPE

Acts 8:35-40

This impulse to share Christ is endemic in those who know him. "Mary" got into a train at a late hour to go home after speaking in Chicago. The coach was full, so she went into the diner. The men were sitting around drinking. Seeing that "Mary" was "different," one of the men asked her where she had been and what she was doing. She replied, "Speaking." "On what?" "On religion." With that they all covered their glasses with their newspapers. "Oh no," said "Mary," "this has nothing to do with that." That let down the tension, and they said, "Go on and tell us about it." Soon everybody in the dining car was crowding around her. "How did you get this?" one asked. "At the foot of the cross," she replied. "Well, how did you get at the foot of the cross?" And she replied: "At the end of my rope." "Hurry up," one of them said. "You only have three quarters of an hour to finish this before we get to our station." For two hours not a drink was ordered, and they listened breathlessly as a simple country girl full of the love of Christ told how it can and does happen. "The best two hours of my life," said a soldier boy back from Korea. They had seen the real thing incarnated.

Mary got hold of a leading manufacturer and his wife. Let him tell his story:

> I haven't been very good to God. Many times I have hurt him and his cause. For a long time he has been knocking at my door, but for some reason I could not or would not open it all the way, occasionally a small crack but nothing more. And then came Mary, and she didn't waste much time. She asked, "Bill, have you really surrendered to God, surrendered everything?" I had to tell her I had not. I had a secondhand religion. God has never been very real to me. Perhaps the reason is found in a book I picked up giving a recipe for being miserable: "Think about yourself; talk about yourself; use 'I' as often as possible; mirror yourself continually in the opinion of others; listen readily to what people say about you; expect to be appreciated." As I read that, I knew it fitted me. So God wasn't real.

O God, my Lord, help me to take down all the barriers to reality in my life. Help me to let you have me, really have me, all the way, all the time. Amen.

AFFIRMATION FOR THE DAY: This sharing of Christ will be an expression not of duty but of love; I love to talk about him.

MINE HAS LEFT ME WITH ANSWERS

2 Corinthians 1:20-22

We continue the story of the conversion of a leading manufacturer:

> Last night I couldn't sleep very well; and usually if I wake up at night, my mind
> jumps into a kettle of boiling candy. Last night it didn't. God kept waking me
> up and telling me all the things he wanted me to do; and, believe me, it was
> quite a list. Right at the top was: "Seek ye first the kingdom of God." I am still
> not sure enough of myself to say that I really have it for keeps, but I do know
> I am on the Way and with God's help I will stay there.

He is on the Way with both feet. And a simple country girl helped him to it. Any-body can do it.

You don't have to be a saint to be a witness; for you're not witnessing to yourself or to your attainments—you're witnessing to Christ. And don't argue with people; witness. A man who was very argumentative tried to argue with "Mary." She said nothing. When he was through, he said, "Aren't you going to answer me?" "No," said she, "for I was just thinking what a wonderful person God is going to get when he really gets you." He was disarmed! Another, a liberal put up all his objections and questions; and Mary quietly answered at the close, "Your way has left you with questions; mine has left me with answers." Give that answer through witnessing!

Someone has said that the Acts of the Apostles is simply an exposition of the one sentence, "Rather, you will receive power when the Holy Spirit has come upon you, and you will be my witnesses in Jerusalem, in all Judea and Samaria, and to the end of the earth" (1:8). Two things and two things only with Acts: the coming of the Holy Spirit and the consequent witnessing in the Spirit's power in larger and larger circles. So there are just two things here: receiving power and witnessing with power. All else is "filling."

And today, all else is "filling." All our services, all our prayers, all our spiritual exercises, have one goal in view: to receive power. And the end of receiving power is to witness with power. If it doesn't, then it is all "faultily faultless, icily regular, splendidly null."* It ends in witness, or it is worthless.

O Jesus my Lord, help me to receive power, to receive it with all the pores of my being open. Then help me to give it in witness and to give it all out. Amen.

AFFIRMATION FOR THE DAY: To receive power, to witness with power, these are the alternate beats of my heart.

* Alfred Lord Tennyson, *Maud* (1855), pt. 1, §2:6, in Charles W. Eliot, *English Poetry III: From Tennyson to Whitman*, The Harvard Classics, vol. 42 (New York: P. F. Collier & Son, 2909–14).

THE MASTERY OF THE HUMAN DILEMMA

Acts 2:37-39

We come now to look at one of the central masteries of the Acts—*the mastery of the human dilemma.* That human dilemma is expressed in these words: "When the crowd heard this, they were deeply troubled. They said to Peter and the other apostles, "Brothers, what should we do?'" (2:37).

This question gathers up in itself all the cries that have been wrung from the heart of humanity since the dawn of creation as we find ourselves caught between the moral imperative and our own wrong actions. The crowd saw, as in a flash, that in being a part of the crucifixion of Jesus, they had sinned grievously, were off on the wrong track, and had run straight into God.

That dilemma is universal. We feel guilty. We have run up against a strange imponderable, the moral law; and we can't get by it or around it or under it or over it; we are right up against it. It is inexorable. We can't bribe our way past it, nor can we earn our way past it by our worthiness, for we haven't any worthiness, nor do we know where to get it.

The different religious systems are varied attempts to answer that one question, "What should we do?" The answer of the Hebrews was to be found in this question and the answer: "How can young people keep their paths pure? / By guarding them according to what you've said" (Ps 119:9). The answer was keep the Law. The rich young ruler ran to Jesus, fell at his feet, and asked, "Teacher, what good thing must I do to have eternal life?" Jesus pointed him to his own answer, "Keep the commandments." He wanted the young man to see the inadequacy of his own answer. He saw it and said, "I've kept all these. What am I still missing?" (Matt 19:16-20). He knew instinctively that even keeping the Law left him with a sense of bondage. "What am I still missing?" If keeping the Law left one with that sense of inadequacy, what would the breaking of the Law mean? Both in the keeping and in the breaking of the Law the conscience was restless, for it was guilty. The Law gave the knowledge of sin but could not and did not show the way to release. It had no answer.

O Lord, you have put this strange thing called conscience within our bosoms. Help me to find the answer to its demands. For you have an answer. Amen.

**AFFIRMATION FOR THE DAY: The Law makes me guilty,
but Love makes me guiltless through redemption.**

THE ANSWERS OF BUDDHISM AND HINDUISM

Ephesians 4:1-6

We saw yesterday one answer to the human dilemma "What shall we do?"—the answer of Judaism—and we found it inadequate.

The answer of Buddhism is quite different. It doesn't deal with the fruit; it goes to the root of the guilt, desire. It is desire that brings forth action, and it is action that makes the wheel of existence turn round, and it is the wheel of existence that brings forth birth after birth. So cut the root of desire, and that will stop the action, and the stopping of the action will stop the wheel of existence from turning round. Then you go out into that passionless, actionless state called *nirvana*, the state literally of the snuffed-out candle. "Is there any existence in nirvana?" I asked a Buddhist priest in Ceylon. He replied, "How could there be? There is no suffering in nirvana; hence there can be no existence." The answer of Buddhism is sweepingly radical. It would get rid of the problems of life by getting rid of life itself. It would get rid of our headaches by getting rid of our heads. The answer is too radical and very ineffective. For in trying to get rid of desire, you create another desire, the desire to get rid of desire. Besides it can't be done. For the only possible way to get rid of one desire is to replace it by another desire, a higher desire. Buddhism produces many seekers but no finders. It puts people on the eternal quest.

The answer of Vedantic Hinduism is different: When you find yourself asking the question—"What should we do?"—you are asking the wrong question. Don't try to think of what to do; think of realizing, of realizing your identity with Brahma, God. You are a part of God; as such there is no sin, no suffering; it is all *maya*, or illusion. In this realization you are lifted above all action and its fruit in guilt; you are emancipated. The trouble with this answer is that it is the philosophy of a few and the religion of none. As a religion it simply doesn't work. In my long experience of India I have never found anyone who convinced me that he had found it. It was assertion.

O God, our Lord, you are saving us with hard refusals, hedging our way here and hedging it there with futility until we find the Way. I thank you. Amen.

AFFIRMATION FOR THE DAY: I shall illustrate the Way and not some way to futility.

OTHER PROPOSED WAYS
OUT OF THE DILEMMA

John 14:1-6

We are looking at the various answers to the human dilemma, "What should we do?" We come to another answer, the answer of the ordinary Hindu. It is the answer that would pile up good deeds to overbalance the bad deeds, and thus the balance to one's account would get one out of the dilemma. You are saved by a good deed. This is the answer not only of the ordinary Hindu but also of the ordinary person in the West, "I'm not so bad; I do a lot of good deeds."

The fallacy of this is obvious. If one does good deeds the balance of his or her days, with a perfect record—no missteps, no departure from the moral law—it still wouldn't touch the fact that the person has broken the law and has sinned against God and therefore broken a relationship. All our good deeds cannot cancel that guilt and restore that broken relationship.

Our Roman Catholic friends have an answer that is strangely like the Hindu answer, that we must do so many penances for so much guilt. These penances are usually the praying of so many prayers. But penances are a degradation of New Testament repentance. Repentance is a turning from, and penance is atonement for. The difference is profound. Penances are a kind of religious magic; they wipe out the sins by their repetition. The prayers are degraded in the process. And in the end they encourage repetition of the sins, since they can be atoned for by further penances. A low standard of morality is usually to be found where penances are the answer.

Then there is the answer of the Muslim, strangely akin to the above. That answer says: Go through the prayers five times a day; fast on required days; repeat the Koran, especially the creed—"There is one God, and Mohammed is his prophet"; go on pilgrimages. Do all this and your sins are cut off. This answer is faithfulness to a religious system. But it is a faith; it does not turn into fact. The Muslims believe but do not illustrate. They are still on a quest. I have never seen one who impressed me as having found the answer.

O Divine Redeemer, redeem us from ways that lead to dead ends and frustrated hopes. Lead us from the ways to the Way, the Way that is self-verifying. Amen.

AFFIRMATION FOR THE DAY: When people see Christians, they must think not of question marks but of exclamation points.

THERE IS NO DILEMMA

Acts 18:14-17

We come now to a modern answer to the dilemma, "What should we do?" The modern answer says, "Go to church." This answer is good; but if it stops there, it is not good enough. It may result in a spiritual stalemate, a secondhandedness in religion, with the feeling that there is something between. It leaves one walking in a fog of dimness and uncertainty and a feeling of being just this side of. Unreality is the climate. Half lights, half realizations, half salvations, half assurances—these are the things that leave half satisfactions.

In the Acts going to church was not the means of salvation; it was the result of salvation. They just couldn't stay away, for Christ was there! To stay away was to miss him. There is another modern answer to the dilemma, "What should we do?" It is the answer of pagan psychiatry: "There is no dilemma. Religion has created a false sense of guilt. Forget the guilt by forgetting the religion. Live free. Don't suppress your desires; for if you do, a complex is set up." This appeals to many, for many modern people are more afraid of a complex than we used to be afraid of hell. This answer may help people who have a false sense of guilt and a false sense of religion. But other than that corrective, it is false advice and leads to greater conflict and confusion. I have never seen anybody helped by that advice. On the contrary, I have seen the opposite. The moral law is a fact; and you can't wave it out by technical terms, however learned they may sound. It just doesn't budge. Moreover, I not only have not found one single person helped by that advice; I have not seen one psychiatrist who gave that advice who wasn't also in conflict, a problem dealing with problems. One person who had gone through a long course of analysis on a pagan basis said at the end, "I was abnormally maladjusted; now I'm normally maladjusted." With God left out you're just that—abnormally maladjusted or normally maladjusted—but you're maladjusted! For God is the center of all adjustments.

O God, our Lord, adjusted to you, I'm adjusted to everything; out of adjustment to you, I'm out of adjustment with everything. I bring all into adjustment with you. Amen.

AFFIRMATION FOR THE DAY: I do not ignore or deny the moral law; I obey it by the power of redeeming love.

DISCOVER YOUR OWN PERFECTION

Romans 7:21-25

There is another modern answer to the human dilemma, "What should we do?" It is the answer of so-called "new thought" in its various guises: "You don't have to do anything. Just discover your latent resources; all the answers are within you. Discover yourself and in doing so you discover your own perfection, even your own divinity." That answer is not new; it is as old as Vedantic Hinduism, and as morally powerless. It gives you an initial shot in the arm by an injection of overexpanded wordiness about infinite power and infinite perfection. But like all boosts not founded on fact, this boost ends in a bust, in a reaction of deflation as one bumps up against the realities of human living.

This emphasis on perfection and divinity within is a reaction against the worm-of-the-dust emphasis. But this reaction has created just as many problems. Humanity is neither a worm nor a wonder; humans are sinful beings with infinite possibilities through grace. That last—through grace—is important, for it gets your eyes off yourself and puts them on God. That breaks the tyranny of self-preoccupation and releases you from being self-centered. You are self-centered, even if you are occupied with discovering your own innate perfection or innate divinity. Anything that leaves you centered on yourself is off-center. It breaks the law of finding yourself by losing yourself. And that is fatal. All movements that live on grace live. All movements that live on self, even if they spell it with a capital—Self—perish. They simply don't fit the facts.

We turn with relief from these half answers to the Christian answer, voiced by Peter, "Repent, and be baptized every one of you in the name of Jesus Christ for the forgiveness of your sins; and you shall receive the gift of the Holy Spirit" (Acts 2:38 RSV). Is this the answer to the human dilemma, "What shall we do?" Or is it like a coin that has been in circulation so long that it is slick and smooth and without any distinctive characteristics? Is it outworn and outgrown? Or is it as up-to-date as tomorrow morning? It is eternal Freshness.

O God, your answers come from eternity and last for eternity, for they meet eternal needs. Help us as we begin the unfolding of your answer and help us to follow. Amen.

AFFIRMATION FOR THE DAY: The answer people see in me shall be as fresh as the morning dew and as sparkling.

REPENTANCE IS A CHANGE OF MIND

Matthew 3:1-2, 7-10

We now turn to the answer given by Peter to the human dilemma, "What should we do?" The first step in the answer is "repent." Now note he didn't say, "Do penances"; he said, "Repent" (Acts 2:38 RSV; the CEB has "Change your hearts and lives"). Is there a difference? A very profound and decisive one. In doing penances you try to atone for what you have done by what you are now doing, namely, penances. That puts your eyes on the wrong place, you. Repentance is different. It is literally *metanoia*, a change of mind or change of outlook or viewpoint. You've been looking at the wrong place: your interests, your prestige, your happiness, yourself. Now change your viewpoint in life. Look at God, the kind of God revealed in Jesus; see that you've not only broken God's law but wounded God's love. Look at yourself and your sins in the light of that love. How do they look? Does it make you change your mind about them? Does it make you want to throw them away and begin all over again? Do your sins become intolerable in the light of what you see in the face of Jesus? Does this make you sorry to the point of not only remorse but renunciation? Do you fling them away and empty your hands so you can take the gift? If so, you're ready for the next step.

The next step is: "Be baptized every one of you in the name of Jesus Christ." In other words, confess outwardly what has taken place inwardly. Baptism stands as an outer confession of an inner allegiance: "in the name of Jesus Christ." You belong to him outwardly now as well as inwardly. But suppose that you have already been baptized, then what? Well, confess it publicly by word as baptism was a confession by act. "If you confess with your mouth 'Jesus is Lord,'...you will be saved" (Rom 10:9). The confession of Jesus, not the mode of confession, is the important thing. It may be by act—baptism, or by word—confessing Jesus is Lord. The confession is the crux. It is the outward revealing of a change of mind. The outward expression deepens the inward impression. Before yourself and the world you come clean.

O Jesus, I have gone through the greatest catharsis, the changing of my mind and the changing of my position before the world. I'm cleansed. Amen.

AFFIRMATION FOR THE DAY: I have changed my mind, not someone else's, and I've changed it wholly.

272

FORGIVENESS AND FILLING

Titus 3:3-7

We come now to look at the last two steps in the Christian answer to the human dilemma, "What should we do?" The first step was a change of mind—"Repent"—and the second was a change of stand before society—"be baptized…in the name of Jesus Christ" (Acts 2:38 RSV); own outwardly your allegiance to him. Inwardly and outwardly you're his. Result? Two things.

First, "for the forgiveness of your sins." That is the biggest boon that can come to a person, barring none. For forgiveness rights your relationship with God, with your past, with yourself, and with your fellow humans, with life! And you didn't earn that forgiveness by your penance or good deeds, or by the fact of your own divinity or perfection; you gained it by grace, by unmerited goodness. Result? Your mood is gratitude, not pride of achievement or pride of innate perfection; you're at the feet of the Crucified Redeemer. Love possesses you, and you want to share that love. Your life is turned outward in loving service to express that gratitude. Psychologically that is sound; it ends with you in the place where you ought to be, outside yourself.

But that inner self, emptied of self, is now ready to receive the Divine Self, the Holy Spirit. Second, "and you shall receive the gift of the Holy Spirit." God's highest gift—Godself, the Holy Spirit—is now freely given. Note "given"—it is not earned or discovered within—it is a gift from on high. Now you do find God within. But the mood is not: How wonderful I am! I've discovered my own perfection and the divine within. The mood is: How wonderful God is to give me such a gift! It's all of grace. Now you're at the place where "new thought" begins. You've been along the road of purification from self and sin by sin and self-surrender. Now God can give with both hands. And can give God's highest—Godself. Now I possess the Divine—by Grace, and am on the road to perfection—by Grace. Now "I am what I am by God's grace" (1 Cor 15:10). I skip and dance along life's way and sing of grace. I'm out of the human dilemma, and how!

O Jesus, you are Grace. I am melted in gratitude. My heart is a fountain of grateful tears. For Grace lifted me, and Grace filled me with God. Amen.

AFFIRMATION FOR THE DAY: Grace relieved me; Grace redeemed me; I shall talk and sing of nothing but Grace.

MASTERY OF NON-CARING IN GENERAL

Romans 1:18-21

We have studied the mastery of the ingrown. We have applied it to outgoingness in evangelism. We take another step and apply it to *the mastery of non-caring in general.* The moment people come in contact with Jesus, they began to care; so much so that Baron Karl von Hugel, the Roman Catholic layman, defined a Christian as follows: "A Christian is one who cares," a very profound definition. Where Christ is not, people do not care.

When the blind man called after Jesus, the disciples told him to keep quiet; he was disturbing things. But Jesus stopped and asked them to call the man. Then they ran to him and said: "Get up! He's calling you."(Mark 10:49). They weren't interested in him until Jesus was. They followed his interest. We have been doing that ever since.

An Indian Christian doctor told me he came across a woman by the roadside with a crowd around her as she was giving birth to a child. It was a *tamasha,* a show to them. He took the woman and the child into his hospital. But not a person in that crowd would help. They didn't care. This same doctor told me of another case of a man lying with a broken leg, with a crowd standing around looking, no one doing a thing. He had to pick him up and take him into his hospital, and nobody would help. They did not care. He told another story of a woman lying on the road hurt, and the bystanders were doing nothing. A Christian woman came along, took her in her *tonga* to the hospital, and gave her some money. She cared.

I visited a school for the blind and saw the loving care and patience given to the students. The Hindu head of industrial schools, a government representative, said: "Only Christians will do this work." The government could not get teachers for these schools. Christians are people who care; and the more Christian they are, the more widely they care and more deeply. When they are truly Christian, they care for everybody, even enemies. I asked an old lady, of one-hundred-one years, her recipe for long life, and she answered, "Take care of others and let God take care of you." That was perfect; take care of others first and then let God take care of you second.

O Lord, put in me the spirit of caring, of utter caring for everybody, everywhere, and at all times. For in doing it to them, I do it to you. I know that. Amen.

AFFIRMATION FOR THE DAY: I belong to the People who Care; I shall be a good member.

THEY CARED WITH PRODIGAL LOVE

Matthew 27:3-4

We are studying in the mastery of non-caring. When Judas threw down the thirty pieces of silver before the high priests and cried that he had sinned in betraying innocent blood, they replied with a sneer, "What is that to us? That's your problem" (Matt 27:4). Sin doesn't care. The Christian does.

In Acts 27, in the account of the shipwreck, the sailors attempted to get off in a boat to save themselves, leaving the passengers to perish. Paul thwarted their attempt, thus saving the whole company and the sailors. He cared about everybody, for he was a Christian.

This spirit of caring runs through all of Acts as an undertone. They cared for the sick, and healed them. They cared for the guilt-laden, and preached good news to them. They cared for enemies, and prayed for them and loved them. They cared for slaves, and freed them. They cared for the outcasts, and brought dignity to them. They cared for the alien, and made family of them. They cared for those of another color, and brought them into a kingdom that was colorblind. They cared for the unclean, and loved them into cleanness, wholeness, and fellowship. They cared with prodigal love. They knew the truth of these lines:

Say not that in life's flow and ebb
    Your brother need not your behoof;
For in this wondrous human web,
    Through his life's warp runs your life's woof.

And if it's good, or if it's bad,
    Both you and he are in the loom,
For fair or foul, for sad or glad;
    You both will share a common tomb.*

Only they changed that and made everyone share, not a common tomb, but a common glory. They didn't merge themselves downward to humanity; they got people to come up to them in God. They shared what they had—God. And that infused hope and life into the withered views of hopeless people. This shower of caring went over parched souls and bodies, and in its wake spring up life and hope.

O Jesus, you are the Divine Refreshing, and you bring times of refreshing from the presence of the Lord, for you are the Infinite Caring. We thank you. Amen.

AFFIRMATION FOR THE DAY: In a loveless situation I shall love, and where needed most shall love most.

*Lorin Webster, "The Web of Life," *Chips from a Busy Workshop* (Boston: Gorham Press, 1919), 51.

A DIFFERENCE OF LORDSHIP

2 Corinthians 5:11-15

We are studying the mastery of non-caring. In 391 CE, a monk named Telemachus leaped into the arena among the human gladiators in Rome and was stoned to death by the spectators; however, his martyrdom stopped the inhuman gladiatorial shows. He was a Christian, and he cared.

Writer Basil Mathews (1879–1951) tells of a young medical missionary in Mesopotamia who was attending to a young Arab whose life was at stake. He could be saved only by a blood transfusion from a healthy man. The family was informed; but the father, brothers, cousins, all refused to be lanced to give their blood, even to their own kin. The doctor saw only one way to save that life, and he took it. He lanced his own body and gave his own blood. A window was opened in the spirit of those watching Arabs. New light poured in. They were amazed. This was something that had never come into their lives before. From that day that doctor was able to do what he would with those Arabs, and no man dared harm a hair of his head.* The difference was not a difference of race. It was a difference of lordship. It was the difference between Mohammed and Jesus Christ. Christ cared, and those who follow him care. And the closer they follow him, the more they care.

A college student in India felt the plight of the rickshaw pullers in a hill station. He became a rickshaw puller himself and stayed with them in their miserable huts. Their lot became his. No wonder the government chose him to be labor commissioner in the new government. He was a Christian, and he cared.

An American pilot had to bail out of his burning plane; as he floated down, a German fighter circled around him. He thought his hour had come and folded his hands in prayer. The German saw this, folded his hands in the same way, waved to him, and flew off. They were both Christians, and they cared. At the end of the war this pilot sent a thousand dollars to help the Germans. The caring begot caring. One loving heart sets other hearts aflame. Christians care.

O Jesus, let my heart catch the passion of your heart. May I begin to care and care for everybody, everywhere. For if this spirit of caring dies, we sink and become animals. Amen.

AFFIRMATION FOR THE DAY: If I care for those who care for me, what do I do more than others?

*No published version of this story was located.

THE SECRET OF THIS CARING?

Ephesians 4:31-32; 5:1-2

What is the secret of this caring on the part of the Christian? Its roots are deep, deep in the very nature of our faith. In depicting the last accounting, Jesus is shown saying to those on his right: "I was hungry and you gave me food...a stranger and you welcomed me...in prison and you visited me" (Matt 25:35-36). The righteous replied, "When did we see you hungry and feed you?" (v. 37). And the Master replied, "When you have done it for one of the least of these...you have done it for me" (v. 40). He was hungry in their hunger, bound in their imprisonment, and lonely in their being a stranger. In other words, when we care for them, we care for him. No deeper motive for caring could be conceived; to care for the least is to care for the Lord.

And to hurt the least is to hurt the Lord. When Paul was arrested by the risen Jesus, "he heard a voice asking him, 'Saul, Saul, why are you harassing me?'" And when Paul asked, "Who are you, Lord?" he received the reply, "I am Jesus, whom you are harassing" (Acts 9:4-5). To hurt them was to hurt him. This gave action universal significance—every act was significant beyond the immediate act to that immediate person—it touched God, the universal Lord. This makes morality more than morality; it makes it spirituality. To have relationships with an act is to have relationships with a Person. Morality is not merely related to an impersonal law; it is related to a Personal Life. To break a law is to wound Love.

This universalizes the incarnation of Jesus. He was incarnated once in Palestine, but he is incarnated again in a sense in every person. To do it to them is to do it to him. "I have stopped slamming doors to show my resentment against people, for I find I'm slamming the door on Jesus," said an awakened Christian. That gives significance to every person and to every act toward that person.

That makes all life vascular; cut it anywhere and it will bleed with the blood of the Son of God. To be at enmity with any person is to be at enmity with him. To love anyone is to love him. To care for anyone is to care for him. No wonder the Christians cared! They had a motive for caring, the profoundest motive imaginable.

O Jesus, I see you in the hungry eyes of every little child; I see you in the sick, in the sinful; I see you everywhere. I kneel in awe and reverence. Amen.

AFFIRMATION FOR THE DAY: Jesus will meet me today in the person of someone in need; I must not miss him.

URANIUM ONCE ON THE SCRAP HEAP

Ephesians 4:17-24

We now turn to note the results of this caring. The caring was curing. For whenever one goes astray, it is usually because that person thinks nobody cares. Those who deal with alcoholics say there is seldom—or never—a cure unless the alcoholic feels that somebody cares. This new faith of Jesus put cosmic caring at the heart of the universe. God cares. The universe is friendly; it cares. And deeper, it is redemptive. That threw a friendly framework around every single human problem. The universe is not vast indifference; it cares. That tipped the scales in the direction of hope, hope for everybody. A great many things that are very useful to us were once thrown away as waste material. More and more will people discover that what we now consider waste will be put to useful and glorious purposes. We see the same thing arising in the Acts of the Apostles. A temple of God was arising, the most beautiful society our planet has seen; and that temple was being reared out of waste material, human lives that were on the scrap heap of society. People who were on the scrap heap—either through their own sins and follies or through the sins of society—as slaves were now being rescued, reshaped, and growing into a temple for the habitation of God in the Spirit.

I've been told that uranium was once thrown out on the scrap heap as worthless. The substance that is at the basis of atomic energy once considered of no use! And now that very castoff substance is to be at the basis of the energy that will transform the world. That is what was happening in the Christian movement. People who were the nobodies were now the centers of the energy that was transforming the world. It was the miracle of the nothing becoming everything, of the powerless becoming power. In this new kingdom, the little child played with infinite forces; of such belonged the kingdom of God. The meek, the submissive, those who knew how to accept, were inheriting the earth; it was theirs. And how!

O Lord, I thank you that you are taking the things that are not and bringing to naught the things that are. You are revealing these things to babes. I thank you. Amen.

AFFIRMATION FOR THE DAY: I shall be careful today, for everyone I meet has valuable potentialities.

JESUS THE REDEEMER OF WASTE MATERIAL

Ephesians 5:3-10

We saw yesterday that uranium, the substance at the basis of atomic energy, was once thrown out on the scrap heap as worthless. It was thought by Indians on the Malabar Coast to be useful only to weight their coir rope and make it heavier, so it would sell for more money. A German, looking at this strange, heavy, black sand coiled into the strands of coir rope, wondered what it was. He discovered it was uranium sand, went to India, developed the sand, and made a fortune. Uranium used for the purposes of cheating! Uranium used for the purposes of obliterating cities! One day we will look back on both with horror. We are going to take this substance that was used for either scrap or base purposes, and we are going to transform the world for everybody, everywhere. A new world was in waste material, or material prostituted for low ends!

Jesus took the Zealot, a man who wanted to rebel against Rome by force, and harnessed his revolutionary zeal to the greatest revolution of all, the kingdom of God. He took the sex urges of Mary Magdalene, which had brought seven devils of lust to live within her, cleansed these urges, cast out the devils, and harnessed her urges to the new creation—the creation of new hopes, new loves, newborn souls. He took the "sons of thunder," James and John, tamed their tempestuous tempers, and harnessed these drives toward kingdom goals. He took the man Peter, who was anything but rock, and turned him into a rock on which civilizations are built. He took the female sex (concerning whom the Jew thanked God that he was not born a woman, a leper, or a Gentile), cleansed her of inferiority, and made her the greatest depository of the spiritual life of the centuries. Jesus took his greatest persecutor, Saul, transformed him into the man who could write the most beautiful thing on love that has ever been written—the thirteenth chapter of 1 Corinthians—and thus made love the greatest thing in the world. The man of hate set love at the center of virtues and illustrated it in himself. Jesus was the redeemer of waste materials.

O Jesus, how can I thank you enough that took me—a "child of waste"—and redeemed me and set my life to music, a discord become a concord? Amen.

AFFIRMATION FOR THE DAY: Today I shall probe into souls and look for pay dirt for the kingdom.

A SOCIETY OF CARING

Acts 11:27-30

We are looking at the results of caring. Bishop Alfred Robert Tucker (1849–1914), before he became a bishop in Uganda, was on the way to becoming a great artist. One day he was painting a picture of a poor lost woman, struggling in the street with sleet and wind beating in her face and a little baby at her breast. When he finished the picture, suddenly the thought came to him: "God bless my soul, how can I be so busy with the picture of a lost woman instead of going to preach the gospel to those who are really lost?" From that moment he consecrated himself to bearing his bold and brave witness in the remotest parts of the earth to those who would hear him.* He turned from pictures to persons. Why? He was a Christian, and he cared.

As a student, George Washington Carver (c. 1864–1943) was interested in painting. His teacher at Simpson College said to him, "George, what your people need is improved agriculture." It was a call. He reluctantly yet resolutely put his artist's materials in the bottom of a trunk and began to apply himself to agriculture. It is said that he added fifty million dollars to the agriculture of the South. Out of the lowly sweet potato he produced one hundred fifty commercial products; out of the lowly peanut, three hundred commercial products. I said to him, "Dr. Carver, you and I are in the same great business. You're discovering wonders in peanuts, and I'm discovering wonders in people, both of them wrapped in strange wrappings." He cared, and because he cared, the world is richer for his living.**

This spirit of caring is the greatest redemptive force that has been loosed upon our planet. It was the natural atmosphere of the amazing new society in the Acts. They cared: for the sick and healed them, for the needy and fed them, for slaves and freed them, for the despised and lifted them, for the sinful and showed them the cross, for women and lifted them to equality with men, for children and set them in the midst of human interest, for the old and cared for them, for enemies and prayed for them, and, when they were hungry, fed them. They cared and therefore conquered, conquered by caring. The future is in the hands of those who care.

O Jesus, your caring is contagious. Your deepest caring, your prayer, "Father, forgive them," sends us to our knees, gets us at the depths. Help me to care that way. Amen.

AFFIRMATION FOR THE DAY: I belong to the fellowship of all who love, in the service of all who suffer.

* See Arthur P. Shepherd, *Tucker of Uganda: Artist and Apostle 1849–1914* (London: Student Christian Movement, 1929) at https://www.wdl.org/en/item/9947/, accessed March 18, 2017.
** For more on George Washington Carver, see http://www.tuskegee.edu/about_us/legacy_of_fame/george_w_carver.aspx, accessed March 18, 2017.

THE MASTERY OF CRITICISM
AND CRITICAL ATTITUDES

Matthew 7:1-5

We come to another mastery in this new society—*the mastery of criticism and critical attitudes*. The caring that these people had was caring that extended to people they didn't like.

One looks in vain in the pages of the Acts for the carping, critical spirit. There was the positive pointing out of wrong in people and situations, but they pointed out this wrong in love. It was redemptive, not critical. There is a difference. For criticism is usually motivated by jealousy, by a sense of inferiority, by egotism, that would try to lift itself by putting down the other person, by finding fault with others to cover faults in oneself. But in love, pointing out evil is motivated by concern for the other person. You love enough to help. If you didn't care, you would keep quiet and let the person go on hurting himself or herself.

When love gets low, criticism gets high. I find in myself, whenever I get out of touch with Christ, I begin to be critical of others. But when I am in living touch with Christ and therefore filled with love, then that love hides a multitude of sins. I feel sorry for people rather than critical of them.

When someone asked Rufus Moseley, a saint of the Southland, what he thought about a certain man, he replied, "I'll talk to God about him and let you know." When asked later, he replied, "The Lord said, 'You talk about me.'" That was a perfect reply, for it was the manifestation of a perfect attitude. He had his eyes on Jesus instead of on people. When Peter said to Jesus (pointing to John), "Lord, what about him?" He replied, "What difference does that make to you? You must follow me" (John 21:21-22). A perfect reply, for we are not following Christians; we are following Christ. We can always let our full weight down on him. As I write this, I am interrupted by someone who is a fine person but who is being kept out of the kingdom of God by the faults of Christians. I could say to him what Jesus said to Peter, "What difference does that make to you? You must follow [Jesus]." It's the only safe thing.

O Jesus, I thank you that I can always put my full weight down on you. When I look at you, I cannot think of the faults of others; I see my own. Amen.

AFFIRMATION FOR THE DAY: Today I shall glance at the faults of others and gaze at the goodness of Jesus.

PROSECUTOR'S STAND OR WITNESS BOX?

Romans 2:17-23

We are looking at the mastery of criticism. Going around and picking motes out of peoples' eyes doesn't sharpen our eyes; it dulls them to our own faults. For the attitude becomes: I must be good; look at the bad I am finding in others. But that is a fallacy; for by finding the bad, you become the bad. Always finding the bad is itself a bad attitude.

A minister preached a sermon on "The Mistakes of Stanley Jones." I saw him the next day at a ministers' meeting and asked him how many were converted the night before, as he preached on my mistakes. I told him I had twenty-five converted while he was preaching about me. How many did he have? He looked embarrassed and managed to say in defense, "Well, I have to fight the devil." I replied, "Good. But be sure he doesn't invade you while you are fighting him."

When we are on the prosecutor's stand, we are not in the witness box. If we are denouncing others, we are not announcing Jesus. Our business is to be, not the judge of all the earth, but the bearers of the good news of Jesus. Only God is good enough and wise enough to decide people's destiny. He has never committed to us judgment on people; he has committed to us the privilege of bearing the good news. So I preach the gospel and leave judgment with God. That is simpler and safer. "For with the judgment you pronounce you will be judged," said Jesus (Matt 7:2 RSV). So the one who is dispensing judgment is laying it up for herself or himself.

We have such partial knowledge of people and their motives that we are in no position to judge them. A little boy looked through the keyhole of an operating room and saw a doctor cutting a patient. He said to the son of the doctor, "Your father is a very bad man; I saw him cutting up people." We don't know the why of people's actions, so we are in no position to judge them. Only God knows that. So we must go out to love up the good in people and love down the bad. If we fail, we are better for having tried, for we give out love and become love.

O Jesus, you are wisdom; when I take your way, I find it better for me. I become born of the qualities I give out. Help me to give out love and only love. Amen.

AFFIRMATION FOR THE DAY: Today I shall give out love and only love and if not received, then more love.

YOU HAVE ME DOING EVERYTHING

John 21:15-22

In living contact with Jesus the mood of life changes. You find yourself going out in love to everybody. The critical attitude toward life and people is dissolved when we get into living fellowship with Christ. Where there is communion with Christ, there are no critical attitudes toward others. We don't become blind to their faults, but love sees why the faults are there and pities and longs to help. Love makes you understanding. As "Mary" puts it, "I don't want to be understood as much as I want to be understanding." Then she adds to someone who had helped her, "You have been like a catalytic agent to me. You have me doing everything without you doing anything but believing in me." That last phrase is the secret of helping people: "believing in me." Those who believe in Christ believe in people, and in believing in them "have [them] doing everything."

That was the secret of the lack of criticizing people in early Christianity; they believed in people, not for what they were, but for what they could be and would be in Christ. They were thinking, not of where people were, but of where they were going. They loved them into loving, believed them into believing, and lived them into living. They passed on a blood transfusion of faith and love into the withered lives around them. They were people of construction rather than of criticism. No movement can live on the criticism of others. It dies of its own negativism.

This is particularly true of Christian movements. The spirit of criticism in a Christian movement is so alien to that movement that it eats like acid into the souls of those who hold it and soon destroys the movement. The criticizers get criticized; the biters get bit. A girl heard that if you wished a wart off yourself onto others, yours would disappear; so she wished the wart on her hand onto the nose of her sister and found to her dismay that one came out on her own nose! Criticism criticizes the criticizers!

O Jesus, help me to find good in everything and everybody; and where I cannot find it, help me to produce it by my love and faith. May I love love out of the loveless. Amen.

AFFIRMATION FOR THE DAY: I will look on everybody and everything through the loving eyes of Jesus.

MASTERY OF CRITICISM OF
FELLOW CHRISTIANS

Psalm 15

We come now to a particular application of the mastery of criticism—*the mastery of criticism of fellow Christians*. Of the people of a certain South Sea island it was said facetiously that they maintained a precarious living by taking in one another's washing. Some Christians maintain a precarious spiritual living by washing other Christians' clothes, mostly in public. One such minister used to send a prominent fellow minister a telegram every Sunday morning, denouncing him. As his wife was about to die, she called him and said, "I am afraid we have been on the wrong track." As this minister told what his wife had said, he rolled in an agony of remorse on the floor of a minister's study. Criticism had come home to roost—and how!

Paul was severe on this type of departure from the Christian Way, "Who are you to judge someone else's servants? They stand or fall before their own Lord (and they will stand, because the Lord has the power to make them stand)" (Rom 14:4). This penetrating statement offers this warning: You may be condemning someone whom the Master commends; "the Lord has the power to make them stand." Then you and Christ are at cross-purposes over this person.

The Christian Way is simple: Christ is our Redeemer and our Judge; we are the beings redeemed, but not judges. That makes every Christian look on fellow Christians with a redemptive look. Every Christian belongs to Christ, and anyone who belongs to Christ belongs to everyone who belongs to Christ. Christ as the loving center holds everyone in love around that center.

Now when we slip off of Christ *as* the center and begin to revolve around doctrines *about* Christ as the center, then we will be divisive. We are then revolving around our opinions instead of around a Person. The Person unites; opinions about the Person divide. If I say, "What do you believe?" we go apart; if I say, "Whom do you trust?" we are together—one name upon our lips, one loyalty in our hearts.

O Christ, you are the center and you are the circumference. If we have you, we have everything. Help us to have you by having your attitudes toward everybody. Amen.

AFFIRMATION FOR THE DAY: All my rising criticisms of people will turn to prayer for them.

IS CHRIST DIVIDED?

1 Corinthians 1:10-13

In the pages of the New Testament the Christians were one. They all belonged to one Church with local manifestations. When separate sovereign groups began to spring up in Corinth—one around Paul and his emphasis, another around Peter, and a third around Apollos—Paul was outraged and cried, "Has Christ been divided? Was Paul crucified for you?" (1 Cor 1:13). They had slipped off the center—Christ—and began to be centered in good men instead of the God-Man. And that is always and everywhere divisive. For if you separate from others on the basis of this doctrine or that doctrine, this emphasis or that emphasis, you have to defend yourself against the others who do not hold your position. By its very nature it is divisive.

Only Jesus is the Truth. Since we imperfectly comprehend him who is the Truth, what we hold is truths about the Truth. Someone has put it this way: God has let down a rope from heaven for us to take hold of; that rope is Christ. But we have taken the end of that rope and unraveled it into strands. One group takes hold of the strand of a particular mode of baptism, another of a particular type of bishop, another of a particular doctrine such as justification by faith, another of a particular ritual, another of a particular emphasis such as holiness, another of a particular attitude toward man, and so on. Each thinks they have the Truth, when all they may have is truths about the Truth—the Truth in the rope—not the strand. And we will be surprised that, when God pulls up that rope, a lot of other people holding to their strands will come up too.

Jesus prayed that "they will be one just as we are one" (John 17:11). How is God one? Undifferentiated union? No. There are Lord, Son, and Holy Spirit; each with his own name, identity, and function and yet fundamentally one. Then if we are one the way God is one, we are to have a union of diversity, some form of federal union. That points the way to a union not of compromise but of comprehension. Such a union is possible and is possible now.

O Jesus, we thank you for your prayer clarifying the kind of union we are to have, a union around you but with varying emphases on other things. Amen.

AFFIRMATION FOR THE DAY: Since I am one with everyone who belongs to Christ, I shall act that way today.

ONE FLOCK, MANY FOLDS

John 10:11-16

We are studying the mastery of non-caring as applied to those who belong to the same flock but are in different folds. Jesus said there was to be "one flock, with one shepherd" (John 10:16). That is possible under federal union: one flock—the Church of Jesus Christ in America, but numerous folds—the Lutheran branch of the Church of Jesus Christ in America, the Nazarene branch, and so on.

To change the figure, just as the fingers of the hand have a separate existence and yet are united in one hand, so we could have branches of the one church united in a federal union. Then there would be union with freedom—union in hand and freedom as fingers. Federal union gives union and yet freedom under that union. In order to have union, it is not necessary to tie up the fingers and merge them into one unwieldly finger. The fingers, while free, are united in the hand, organically united. They can act as a single organism. So federal union is organic union with a federal structure. The idea that we must be one undifferentiated union in order to be united presents a false picture.

The Indian *chakor*, a species of partridge two and a half times the size of the American partridge, is now being stocked in many states. A doctor, who raised them as a hobby and had a thousand in various pens, said that they would fight one another if one group was put into the pen of another group. But if both groups were put in a third pen, they would live together, amicably. If any denomination tries to absorb the rest, it will be resisted. But if all are put into a new structure—a federal union—then they will live together amicably. The principle of federal union worked among the American colonies, making them one nation; it will work in making Christians one people and yet with freedom.

O Christ, you are drawing us closer to you and to one another. When we find one another, we will find you. For where two or three are together in your name, there you are. Amen.

AFFIRMATION FOR THE DAY: I'm bound to all my fellow Christians, but I'm free to live my life with Christ.

CHRISTIANS ARE THE MOST UNITED BODY

Mark 9:38-41

We are looking at the possibility of mastering our differences in a higher unity around Christ. In him we are one. Anybody who belongs to Christ automatically belongs to everybody who belongs to Christ. It is inherent. We do not have to seek unity; we only have to express the unity we now have. Christians are the most united people on earth and the most divided—united in Christ and divided in the expression of Christ.

We are making progress in getting together. We have outgrown some manifestations of a few generations ago. In the mountains, a hymnbook was found in which was this hymn:

> I'd rather be a Baptist and wear a smiling face
> Than be a dirty Methodist and fall away from grace.
> I'd rather be a Methodist and talk about free grace,
> Than be a hard-shelled Calvinist and damn near half the race.

They set that to music and sang it!

In front of a church is a big billboard with this inscription on it: "This is the only church authorized by God to represent Jesus Christ in the world." We laugh at these manifestations of impossible arrogance parading as the Christian faith. But the fact that we can and do laugh at them measures the distance we have come. There was a time when people took these arrogances seriously. Now they are an appendix on the body of Christ. Another sign on a church expresses where we are going: "Out of the world of many into the world of one."

The following conversation gives the growing climate of our church life. A United Brethren member said smilingly to a group, "Well, hereafter in heaven we are all going to be United Brethren"; and a Quaker, or Friend, said quietly, "Well, if we are to be United Brethren hereafter, why not be Friends now?" We may not be members of the Society of Friends, but we can be friends now and are becoming more and more so. The Spirit of God is brooding over the chaos of our divisions and is bringing out of it a cosmos of a united church.

O Christ, your prayer that they may be one is being answered, and your Spirit is breaking down the things that divide us, for we are seeing the things that unite us. Amen.

AFFIRMATION FOR THE DAY: I shall be a principle and a power for unity in every situation I am in today.

THE MASTERY OF PRAYER

Luke 11:1-13

We come now to consider another mastery, an important one—*the mastery of prayer*. The mastery of the art of prayer is life's most important mastery. It can be summed up in one sentence: If we know and practice the art of prayer, we know and practice the art of living; if we don't know that art, then we don't know the art of living. To pray is to penetrate, to penetrate through this physical encasement into the spiritual world of light and power and to live within this physical encasement by that spiritual light and power. We live in two worlds at once: the physical world interpenetrated by the spiritual and lifted to a new level of life. We can live literally by resources not our own; we can live by Another.

But while prayer is life's most wonderful resource, it can be twisted and turned into all sorts of things. First, into a formula. A minister's wife expounded at length on the beauty of the prayer book they used, and then added, "Do you really think that God answers prayer?" She thought of prayer as a formula but not as a fact. Does God answer prayer? The answer is that, just as God has made an open universe contingent upon our action—so that things won't be done unless we do them, God has left certain things open to prayer—things that won't be done unless we pray.

This is a universe of law and order, yet it is an open universe; things can happen within this universe if we decide to do them. The spiritual universe is also one of law and order and an open universe, open to cooperation with God for new things to happen. These are things that God wants to happen, but God can't let them without our cooperation. Prayer is cooperation with God, cooperating in carrying out unfinished creative purposes. God wants us to help finish an unfinished universe. So in prayer, we do not have to overcome God's reluctance; we only have to cooperate with God's highest willingness. Anything that ought to happen can happen to the one who prays. That person has linked with divine purposes and has, therefore, divine power at his or her disposal for human living. The person of prayer is the person of power.

O Lord, I thank you that I am not at the mercy of a universe without heart and without purpose. I am aligned to you, and therefore anything right can happen. Amen.

AFFIRMATION FOR THE DAY: I am determined to learn the art of prayer, so I'll make prayer my life climate today.

THEY DID THE MOST INCREDIBLE THINGS

Luke 9:28-31

We saw yesterday that laws govern prayer as laws govern the universe. What are they? The people in the Acts evidently were guided by them, for they did an incredible thing. It was not telling lame men to walk and dead people to arise; it was infinitely more incredible. It was nothing less than accomplishing in a short space of thirty years something that philosophers and lawgivers and moralists had attempted for ages with little success. They lifted humanity onto a new plane of living and introduced into society the basic changes, upon which humanity has lived ever since. They did the most difficult thing that has ever been done. And they did it with incredible ease, without strain and without drain; for they didn't do it; they let God do it through them. They did it through prayer.

Then we turn to the exciting adventure of seeing just how they used prayer and just how they did not use it. For this didn't just happen. It happened because they put themselves in line with God's purposes.

The Acts of the Apostles gives an account of the use of prayer that is the cleanest, the sanest, the wisest, and the most powerful ever seen on our planet—yes, ever. There isn't a misstep in regard to prayer in the whole account or a missed emphasis. It is all sound, as sound as a bell.

First of all, they had seen prayer in Jesus. Jesus had cleansed prayer for them. After he cleansed it, he used it and used it mightily. In three great crises he prayed. First, at his baptism, and as a result the Spirit descended upon him "like a dove." Prayer brought the Holy Spirit. Second, he prayed at the transfiguration, and as a result he stood transfigured. Prayer made him luminous, showed what the material can be. Then third, he prayed when he was accomplishing the end for which he came, the atonement for sin. When he prayed, "Father, forgive them," God could forgive because Jesus was dying for them that they might be forgiven. He answered his own prayer by making it possible for God to forgive.

O Jesus, your life was behind that prayer, your life laid down. Therefore, you did the incredible; you redeemed a race. We are at your feet; you have us wholly. Amen.

AFFIRMATION FOR THE DAY: I shall do incredible things through prayer, for I do not do them. He does.

289

PRAYER FOR ONE THING: THE HOLY SPIRIT

Luke 24:45-49

We saw yesterday that the people in the Acts showed the sanest and most effective use of prayer that has ever been seen. Let us study how they used it and learn their secret.

First of all, we find them starting out as a group in prayer and praying for one thing: the Holy Spirit. "All were united in their devotion to prayer, along with some women, including Mary the mother of Jesus, and his brothers" (Acts 1:14). They were not praying for their safety, for their loneliness now that Jesus was taken away, for revenge upon their enemies who had crucified Jesus, for their needs to be met, for the power to perform miracles—none of these. They were praying simply for the Holy Spirit. And for the Holy Spirit unconditionally. They weren't praying that the Spirit might come and make them a success or give them power to do miracles or even to witness; they prayed for the Holy Spirit and the Spirit alone. And in order for the Holy Spirit to take them over unconditionally, they surrendered unconditionally. They wanted the Spirit for nothing but himself.

That is the purest form of prayer known. And they did this as the first step, off the bat, as it were. They didn't grow into this purified form of prayer; they began with it. That struck a note, set a standard. Prayer was not primarily for things—for success, for healing, for power—prayer was a person wanting a Person. Prayer was wanting that Person so much that they were willing to surrender everything, including themselves especially, if only that Person would come in and take over. The Holy Spirit did, and how! "They were all filled with the Holy Spirit" (Acts 2:4). The hands of God were untied; God could do anything, everything, for people who didn't want anything except for God to come in and take over.

What a corrective to a great deal of modern praying, which makes prayer into a success cult, a healing cult, an ego-expanding cult! All this is making ourselves the center; we're using God. Prayer is prostituted. People try to capture the holy to serve them. Here God is the center. Humanity is surrendered to God. That is the right relationship. Anything can now happen.

O God, my Lord, I thank you that you have set our faces in the right direction, toward you. Give me yourself and only yourself, and then all I need will come as a by-product. Amen.

AFFIRMATION FOR THE DAY: My praying today shall be for the highest object, for the Holy Spirit.

THE KINGDOM FIRST: ALL ELSE ADDED

Matthew 6:28-33

We noted yesterday that the disciples began their prayer life on the center; they prayed first and foremost for the Holy Spirit and not for things. They got off on the right foot; hence they went far.

But there was another fact to be noted in praying for the Holy Spirit; each prayed for the Spirit to come not upon that person alone but upon the individual and the group. Had it been individuals praying for an individual coming of the Holy Spirit, it might have been a covered desire for uniqueness in spiritual power. In other words, it might have been all in the service of the ego. But here they prayed for each and all; they prayed together "with one accord." What each wanted individually, each wanted for all. This canceled out egoism and socialized the experience of the Holy Spirit. Yet it deeply individualized it, for the person is more personalized when transcending self and thinking of others. We find ourselves when we lose ourselves.

Did this praying for the Holy Spirit preclude their praying for their own needs— material needs? On the contrary, those needs were met. Shared goods were "distributed to anyone who was in need" (Acts 4:35). They fulfilled that saying of Jesus: "Desire first and foremost God's kingdom...and all these things will be given to you as well" (Matt 6:33). They got the supreme value straight and sought it—the kingdom of God—and all their lesser needs were met; food and success and self-development were added.

But if they had begun by praying for their need of food or success or self-development first, as many modern cults suggest, then they would have missed the highest, and the lower would not have been guaranteed.

A great many use prayer as a means to their ends. If you pray, you'll get this, that, and the other. That is using God, making God a means to our ends. "I have been using Christ, making him a means for me to get what I wanted," said a minister's wife. She saw she was off center. She surrendered her self-centered self, and hence, her self-centered praying found Christ, and with him, everything she needed. Prayer in the Acts began with God and ended with everything.

O Holy Spirit, I want you and you alone. All else can wait or never come at all. But I cannot do without you. In you I have everything and more than everything. Amen.

AFFIRMATION FOR THE DAY: I shall try not to use Christ but to let him use me today.

NOT FOR SAFETY BUT FOR BOLDNESS

Philippians 1:12-14

We have seen that prayer in the Acts began at the right place, not for things but for the Holy Spirit. As time goes on, I find myself praying less and less for things and more and more for God. For if I have God, I have everything—yes, everything—I need and more.

When we note the next instance of specific praying in the Acts, this too is significant: "And now, Lord, look upon their threats, and grant to thy servants to speak thy word with all boldness" (4:29 RSV; CEB has "complete confidence"). Here again, prayer was not for their needs but for the needs of others; they prayed for boldness to witness to others. God was first, others were second, and they were third. Prayer breaks the tyranny of self-preoccupation, absorbs you with God, and makes you interested in others. It is freeing. And it is inherent.

In finding the Holy Spirit, self-surrender was the first condition: no surrender, no Spirit. So self-surrender being inherent, the first thing that happened was shifting the basis of life from self to God. You become God-centered instead of self-centered. And the moment you are God-centered you are other-centered; for God is love, and love is interested in others. You follow God's interest, and God's interest is in others. So the prayer is for boldness to witness to others. This is all following a pattern, root and fruit.

Had their prayer been initially for their own needs and for self-development, they would have prayed for their safety in view of the threats. But they were afraid of safety. They were in an adventure with God, an adventure of love. God had loved them into loving, and their own safety was unimportant. They wanted not safety but souls. So the doors of prayer turned out, not in. It produced a healthy mindedness. They were not morbid would-be saints, concerned with their own mental and spiritual states. They were bearers of good news, and the only thing that mattered was to bear it. A Hindu said at the close of one of my addresses, "If what the speaker has said isn't true, it doesn't matter. But if it is true, then nothing else matters." Nothing else mattered to them, for they knew it was true, so true it was Truth.

O Christ, we have looked into your face in prayer, and now we cannot rest until we share the blessed vision of what we have seen. We pause to see more in order to share more. Amen.

AFFIRMATION FOR THE DAY: I shall pray not for safety but for boldness in witnessing to my Lord.

BROTHER SAUL

Acts 9:10-19

We continue the mastery of the art of prayer in the Acts. The next place we find an instance of prayer is when the apostles had sent Peter and John to the Samaritans, "where they prayed that the new believers receive the Holy Spirit" (Acts 8:15).

This instance of prayer is in the direct line of the kind of prayer that emerged in Acts; it was a prayer for others. And the highest prayer for others, that they might receive the highest gift God had—the gift of Godself, the Holy Spirit. This was significant. Had this spirituality been the type I have seen in India, it would be more interested in being objects of wonder at the spirituality developed than in imparting it to others. In other words, it is a development of the self and as such is self-centered. But self-giving was at the heart of the divine gift of the Holy Spirit, and hence they caught the contagion. They wanted to give the highest since they had found the highest.

The next place prayer is mentioned is when Ananias goes in to the stricken Saul, lays hands on him, and prays: "Brother Saul, the Lord sent me— Jesus...so that you could see again and be filled with the Holy Spirit" (9:17). Again the same outgoing type of prayer for others and this time for an enemy, and infinite compassion is in the prayer: "Brother Saul." Turning an enemy into a brother through love! Moreover, as we have noted, Ananias went beyond the original commission of Jesus to him "that he could see again," and added on his own, "and be filled with the Holy Spirit." He wanted his former enemy to share the highest he had—the Holy Spirit.

The next instance of prayer is when Peter went into the death chamber of Dorcas and "knelt and prayed. He turned to the body and said, 'Tabitha, get up'" (9:40). Again, here was prayer reaching even beyond death to the spirit world. Prayer can do anything, anywhere, provided it is linked to the loving, redemptive purposes of God. If it is linked to the self and its selfish purposes, it goes nowhere except in futile circles, round and round on itself.

O Lord, I thank you that you have put laws into our freest act, the act of prayer. When we obey those laws, we touch life everywhere with your power. I thank you. Amen.

AFFIRMATION FOR THE DAY: I shall touch everything redemptively through prayer this day.

LAST INSTANCES GATHERED UP

Ephesians 6:18-20

We come now to gather up the remaining instances of prayer in the Acts. "Peter went up on the roof to pray....He saw heaven opened up and something like a large linen sheet being lowered" (Acts 10:9-11). Here prayer was the instrument through which the Jewish prejudices of Peter were broken down, and he saw there was no ceremonial cleanness or uncleanness of anyone before God. He accepted people as people. Prayer here brought one of the most important revelations that ever came to humankind and laid the basis for human development everywhere. Here again prayer was outreaching beyond the self.

Another instance of prayer was this: "While Peter was held in prison, the church offered earnest prayer to God for him" (12:5). Here prayer was not for the safety of those praying that the persecution might not strike them, but for him whom it had struck. It was outgoing and altruistic.

A striking instance of prayer going out to others is this: "As they were worshiping the Lord and fasting, the Holy Spirit said, 'Appoint Barnabas and Saul to the work I have called them to undertake.' After they fasted and prayed, they laid their hands on these two and sent them off" (13:2-3). This was the mightiest outreach of prayer ever seen; for it touched the ends of the earth, even to us, through Paul and Barnabas, the missionaries.

An illustration of how prayer might have been turned to self-concern, but wasn't, is this: "Around midnight Paul and Silas were praying and singing hymns to God, and the other prisoners were listening to them" (16:25). Had Paul and Silas been praying for their own release, the prisoners would not have been listening to them; that would be what was expected. But here the prayer was so set to victorious joy—"singing hymns"—that the prisoners were drawn to it with amazement. Another instance: "'we remember the Lord Jesus' words: "It is more blessed to give than to receive." After he said these things, he knelt down with all of them to pray" (20:35-36). Note "to give than to receive"; with that emphasis he knelt down and prayed. When his life was in danger, he prayed that they might think more of giving than receiving. Prayer was outgoing still.

O Lord, how I do thank you for the wonderful love that pulsates through all this praying. Turn my prayers from festering inwardness to healthy outgoingness. Amen.

AFFIRMATION FOR THE DAY: My praying shall be the outgoing of my love to others and to him.

CONCLUSIONS REGARDING PRAYER

Philippians 1:3-5, 9-11

We must pause a little longer to look at the last two instances of prayer in the Acts and to draw our conclusions.

"The angel said, 'Don't be afraid, Paul! You must stand before Caesar! Indeed, God has also graciously given you everyone sailing with you'" (Acts 27:24). Even here the thought was not for Paul's personal safety but for his witness before Caesar. And the deliverance for witnessing included giving him the safety of his fellow passengers. Again prayer was outgoing, thinking of witnessing and of the safety of others.

The final instance is this:

> Publius' father was bedridden, sick with a fever and dysentery. Paul went to see him and prayed. He placed his hand on him and healed him. Once this happened, the rest of the sick on the island came to him and were healed. They honored us in many ways. When we were getting ready to sail again, they supplied us with what we needed. (28:8-10)

This last instance is revealing: prayer was for others, for this healing, still outgoing.

In the Acts, prayer had been redeemed. From being a self-concerned act of getting benefits for oneself, it became the agent of glorious redemption. Everywhere prayer was love in action through God. People were reaching out through God to touch others redemptively. In the process, prayer itself was redeemed. It was turned out instead of in; except in one instance, when they prayed for the Holy Spirit for themselves. Then we can pray all out for ourselves. For if the Spirit comes, he takes over the self. Prayer then is not for us but for One, to control and guide and use the self.

Then is there no place in prayer for our own personal needs? Is that ruled out? No, they are provided for, but indirectly. Note the last thing said about Paul praying for the sick of the island was, "they supplied us with what we needed"—the last thing was that their needs were all met—"what we needed." That brought them out at the place Jesus had promised: "Desire first and foremost God's kingdom ... and all these things will be given to you as well" (Matt 6:33). "All these things" come as a by-product of seeking the kingdom first. This is the right order.

O Jesus, you have guaranteed our needs if we seek the kingdom first. Then help me to get first things first. If my eye is single, my whole body will be full of light. Amen.

AFFIRMATION FOR THE DAY: I shall seek God's Spirit for my spirit so that my spirit may be given to others.

THE POWER OF THE LORD WAS WITH HIM TO HEAL

James 4:3-6

We pause to gather up today the lessons we have learned about prayer.

Prayer in the Acts is psychologically sound. I quoted in another book the saying of Adler the psychiatrist, "I suppose all the ills of human personality can be traced back to not understanding the meaning of the phrase 'It is more blessed to give than to receive.' "* Also the statement of Karl Menninger that if one feels a nervous breakdown coming on, he should go across the tracks and find someone who needs him and do something for him. Both are saying that breakdowns come from self-absorption; health-mindedness comes from other-absorption.

Then prayer in the Acts is absolutely sound. Instead of leaving them absorbed in their own mental and physical and spiritual states, it was continually pushing them out and making them absorbed in others.

That made them healthy-minded. Moreover, it made it possible for God to guarantee their needs. God cannot guarantee the needs of the self-absorbed, for that would fix them in their self-absorption; they would be God-guaranteed in their self-absorption. That would cut across the whole meaning of the gospel, which is self-release.

But prayer, which is often advocated today as a means of curing oneself of one's own ills, can be wholly wrong. It can add to one's self-preoccupation, using prayer for one's own purposes. Prayer has therapeutic, or healing, value only if it loosens you from self-preoccupation and gets you interested in something beyond yourself.

When Jesus spent all night in prayer to the Lord, the next morning the "power of the Lord was with him to heal" (Luke 5:17 RSV).

The all-night prayer meant the all-morning power and power to heal in two directions. It kept him whole and made others whole. Our needs are automatically guaranteed if we let prayer carry us beyond ourselves. The self is lost in others and found in itself.

All this prayer and personal soundness in the Acts is perfectly unselfconscious. They knew no psychology as such; but they knew the Person, and the Perfect Person made them whole.

O Jesus, I do thank you that the soundest psychology comes from knowing you, for you are mental soundness itself. Then let me take your attitudes, and I shall be every whit whole. Amen.

AFFIRMATION FOR THE DAY: I shall be perfectly unselfconscious in my praying for others; it will be natural.

*See E. Stanley Jones, *Abundant Living* (Nashville: Abingdon Press, 2014).

THE MASTERY OF ENFORCED IDLENESS

Luke 11:9-13

We now turn to another mastery in the pages of the Acts—*the mastery of an enforced idleness.*

We have been noting how prayer turned the early Christians to amazing outgoing activity. "Mary" expressed this when she said, "Prayer seems to work in reverse with me. Instead of making me quiet, it injects into me an amazing vitality. I feel as though when I come out of prayer, I want to do something about everything." That expresses the heightening of one's vitality through prayer.

But there's another side to life; we are often forced into physical inactivity we cannot control. Can there be mastery then? If there is mastery of activity, can there be mastery of inactivity?

In the pages of the Acts inactivity is of two kinds: chosen and imposed. The chosen inactivity was seen in the disciples waiting for ten days for the coming of the Holy Spirit. If Jesus had said "go," he had also said "stay" and "wait." For ten days they did nothing but stay and wait. They might have been champing at the bit, eager to be off to tell the good news of his resurrection, but it would have been half-baked if they had. For not only were they to tell of his resurrection; they were to illustrate it. They were to be an illustration as well as an illumination. People were to feel the resurrection through these resurrected lives. So the best thing they ever did was not to do. For ten days they were quiet and receptive. "You will receive," said Jesus; and they had to learn that art of receiving before they knew the art of giving. For ten days they lifted their chalices to heaven to be filled with the wine of the Spirit; and when they put these chalices to the parched lips of humanity, they were full to the brim. We rush out fussily without any staying and waiting, and we put empty cups to parched lips. The passage "who works for those who wait for him" (Isa 64:4 RSV) expresses the fact that to wait is to work. For then we work with resources not our own. There is a divine plus added to all we do and say. The disciples learned that the greatest working is not working—it is receiving. Then our work is not fussy activity but fruitful creativity.

O Jesus of the mountainside, help me to expose my inmost being to the incoming of your Spirit. Then my doing will be a doing, plus. My love will be a loving, plus. Amen.

AFFIRMATION FOR THE DAY: I shall live with the windows of my spirit open to the highest God has for me.

THE TEN DAYS THAT CHANGED THE WORLD

Acts 1:12-14

We are considering the mastery of enforced idleness. The disciples chose to wait ten days for God's reinforcement within. They were the most important ten days of human history. They were "The Ten Days That Changed the World." For it changed them. The greatest service a minister can give the congregation is to wait in the silence and listen to God. When pastors listen to God, then people will listen to them. William A. Quayle describes it thus:

> When this preacher comes to a Sunday in his journey through the week, people ask him, "Preacher-man, where were you and what saw you while the workdays were sweating at their toil?" And then of this preacher we may say reverently: "He opened his mouth and taught them, saying"; and there will be another though lesser Sermon on the Mount. And the auditors sit and sob and shout under their breath, and say with their helped hearts, "Preacher, saw you and heard you that? You were well employed. Go out and listen and look another week; but be very sure to come back and tell us what you heard and saw."*

That would not be preaching; it would be revelation.

Then choose to be idle. Choose to do nothing but receive. Choose to loaf in God's presence and then you'll be forever busy in God's service.

Scottish philosopher Thomas Carlyle (1795–1881) said: "Hold your tongue for a day and you'll talk sense forever."** Be silent to God for a day, yes, for ten days if necessary; and you'll be vocal and vital for God forever.

Someone has spoken of the "expectant silence of prayer." The silence spent in God's presence becomes expectant, expectant of love and power—yes, of God's very self—to come within and make that within all glorious. When we fast from our activity, we feast upon God's creativity. Then our activity becomes creativity. We lift one hand to God to receive and stretch out the other hand to give. Then when we give, we give nothing less than God. For we have found nothing less than God.

The enforced idleness of ten days at Pentecost were the most pregnant ten days in human history. The higher destiny of a race was in the womb of those hours. A new age was born.

O Holy Spirit, you who are Creation, help me to receive in the silence your creative power and love. I cannot go empty-handed into an empty world. I await your fullness. Amen.

AFFIRMATION FOR THE DAY: I shall be a person of the Silence before I shall be a person of speech.

* William A. Quale, *The Pastor-Preacher* (New York: The Methodist Book Concern, 1915), 371.
** No published source was found for this quotation, but see *Thomas Carlyle's Collected Works*, vol. 29, *Latter-Day Pamphlets* (London: Chapman and Hall, 1870).

TWO CIVILIZATIONS BORN
OUT OF TWO MEDITATIONS

Luke 18:1; 1 Thessalonians 5:17-18

We saw yesterday that the ten days of chosen idleness before Pentecost were the most important and humanity-changing days in human history. Without them all the ages would have been different, and empty.

Another chosen idleness was of the greatest importance: "I didn't go up to Jerusalem to the men who were apostles before me either, but I went away into Arabia" (Gal 1:17). This has an importance that is not obvious at first sight; if Paul had gone straight to Jerusalem to the apostles, their stamp would possibly have been upon him. But they had hesitations about the Gentiles, which might have infected Paul and kept him from being an apostle to the Gentiles. A spiritual authoritarianism was gathering around the apostles, which was setting them apart and above in unnatural aloofness. Paul was saved from that. He gained his authority not by his position but by his service. Then the apostles separated the spiritual and the material by saying they would give themselves to prayer and to the ministry of the Word and would turn over the material to others. Paul kept them together, "You yourselves know that I have provided for my own needs and for those of my companions with my own hands" (Acts 20:34). The material and the spiritual were parts of a living whole with Paul. That was the kind of faith he propagated, and that is the kind of faith we received from him.

Paul went away to Arabia and there in the silence got his gospel as a firsthand thing from God. It would not be a secondhand echo of the supposedly great. So Paul's gospel could be called "my gospel," a gospel mediated through his surrender. Arabia became an emancipating retreat. There God talked to Paul vertically, not merely horizontally through others. In the deserts of Arabia two men meditated—one, Mohammed, who meditated about God without Christ and came out at the place of Allah; the other, Paul, who meditated with Christ as his starting point and came out to God, our Lord. Two civilizations were born out of those meditations, the Arab Muslim civilization and the Christian civilization.

O Lord, I see that my silences count. Help me to know the art of listening, of listening to you. Out of those silences may I come with power and love, to love people to you. Amen.

**AFFIRMATION FOR THE DAY: Perhaps out of my meditations today
some new movement will be born.**

MASTERY OF PRISON IDLENESS

Daniel 6:10-13

We have seen the mastery of two idlenesses; and now we look at a third, this time an unchosen idleness—the idleness of imprisonment. In prison Paul could say, "Brothers and sisters, I want you to know that the things that have happened to me have actually advanced the gospel" (Phil 1:12). His imprisonment really did advance the gospel, far beyond his immediate conception, for he says, "Most of the brothers and sisters have had more confidence through the Lord to speak the word boldly and bravely because of my jail time" (v. 14). But a far greater result than inspiring the brothers and sisters to preach more boldly came out of Paul's imprisonment: his deathless epistles. They have touched the ages and still mold our thinking and acting.

Paul might have chafed at the seeming lack of providence on the part of God, a providence that allowed injustice to prevail and to lock him behind bars. There he was shut off from his beloved preaching. But one of the best things that ever happened was to stop Paul from preaching and to get him to writing. His preaching might have died with him. But his epistles live on. So when his sight was cut off by prison walls, his insight deepened; he poured this deepened insight into immortal literature. God's blocks were blessings. God blocked him here to make him break out there.

When we are in God's will, we may be blocked on a certain level, but only for God to shift the gears to put us on a higher level. All God's downs are ups if we know how to use them. Everything is favorable to the Christian if we stay in God's will, for being in God's will is the victory. No one is defeated if in God's will, no matter what happens around him or her. God's allowing Paul to be imprisoned was really God's method of freeing Paul. For in his epistles, written in prison, he has roamed the centuries free to bless and guide. The enforced idleness was a reinforced effectiveness. Christians don't bear frustrations; we use them, turning frustrations into fruitfulness. Blank walls turn into open doors into victory.

O Lord, I thank you that walls need not be my worries. The only thing that matters is the spirit behind those walls. Give me the spirit that roams the earth free. Amen.

AFFIRMATION FOR THE DAY: All my blockings today shall become diversions to higher usefulness.

THE HUMAN LOG

2 Corinthians 4:17; 12:10

We note mastery over another enforced idleness—the idleness of illness. Paul says, "You know that I first preached the gospel to you because of an illness. Though my poor health burdened you, you didn't look down on me or reject me, but you welcomed me as if I were an angel from God, or as if I were Christ Jesus! Where then is the great attitude that you had? I swear that, if possible, you would have dug out your eyes and given them to me" (Gal 4:13-15).

Here Paul was thrown aside through an illness, probably badly running eyes; but this being thrown aside was the occasion of his preaching the gospel to them. The idleness of illness became the opportunity for preaching. The Galatian church and the Galatian epistle came out of an illness. The running eyes that compelled him to lay up in Galatia also made it possible for him, through the Epistle to the Galatians, to move into the centuries.

A modern and dramatic illustration of this is found in Walter Callow, sometimes called the "human log." he is so helpless he cannot even brush a fly from his face. His arms are helpless, both legs are gone, and he is totally blind. And yet he is one of the most useful men in Canada. He has a suite of offices at the big Camp Hill Military Hospital in Halifax. His own room is a hive of industry, where his secretary answers telephone calls all day long. In this hospital room we make the spirit of Christ live.

He has invented a bus to care for invalids, a wheelchair coach that takes shut-ins to football games, to special events, to entertainments. He has four of them in operation every day, and they are all free. He says of himself, "I could be a lot worse; I want to thank God that at least I can talk and think. I want to repay him, for I believe that after a man dies, they will ask only one question: 'What did he do for others?' "* John Fisher of the Canadian Broadcasting Corporation says: "Walter Callow is the biggest man I know. Beyond the sheets two lips move, and that is all. But inside that paralyzed frame is a heart absolutely dedicated to others." His body cut down to almost nothing, his spirit is free to roam and bless.

O Jesus, I thank you that nailed to a cross and helpless, you put your arms around a world and saved it. Help me to make my crosses redemptive too. Amen.

AFFIRMATION FOR THE DAY: My infirmities shall throw me back on grace for healing or for power to use them.

* See http://www.waltercallow.ca, accessed March 20, 2017.

THE MASTERY OF NARCOTICS

Proverbs 20:1; 23:31-33

We now look at another phase of mastery in the Acts—*the mastery of narcotics and pick-me-ups.* When you look through these amazing pages, you find an almost complete absence of that which occupies so much of modern life. Much modern life is an attempt to stimulate jaded nerves and minds and bodies. People are run down and need a pick-me-up. Or if they don't need a stimulus, they need a sedative, something to allow them to sleep. I am told that five million people depend on sleeping powders to put them to sleep every night; stimulation by day and sedatives by night, the vicious circle.

Yet in the pages of the New Testament there is only one mention of a physical pick-me-up: "don't drink water anymore, but use a little wine because of your stomach problems and your frequent illnesses" (1 Tim 5:23). And that wasn't a pick-me-up; it was wine used as a medicine, of doubtful efficacy at that. Here is a society free from all stimulants and pick-me-ups. Had they found something that took the place of these extraneous stimulants? Yes. Paul puts it in these words: "So by all the stimulus of Christ" (Phil 2:1 MNT). Was Christ the stimulus that stimulated the total person—body, mind, and spirit—and made outer stimulants unnecessary and absurd? Yes. His impact upon our lives stimulates them and makes them their best, plus. His thinking stimulates our minds until they nearly pop with newness; his love stimulates our emotions until we want to put our arms around the world and love it to him; his will injects a new energy and decisiveness into our wills until we want to do something about everything. Our whole beings are heightened by his impact.

I feel sorry for anyone who has to turn to narcotics for stimulus or for sedatives. The moment I see such a person, I know that, if he or she is a follower of Christ, the following is far off—secondhand—so far that the stimulus of Jesus does not get to the person vitally and satisfactorily. The narcotic, whether it is liquor or tobacco, says to the world, "I need a substitute for Christ." One isn't gaining from Christ what one needs, or these substitutes would drop off like a dead leaf, unneeded.

O Christ, you are my all-sufficient stimulus. You silently bombard every cell of my being with life and power. In you I am alive, alive to my fingertips. Amen.

AFFIRMATION FOR THE DAY: All my powers are at their highest and best through the stimulus of Christ.

I HAVEN'T GOT THE GUTS TO DO IT

Galatians 5:19-21

We are thinking on the mastery of stimulants. Unless there is something structurally wrong with a person, when a stimulant would be medically necessary, all taking of narcotics and pick-me-ups is a sign of mental or spiritual or character weakness. They are crutches for lame ducks, and self-defeating, for all pick-me-ups end in let-me-downs. We call them hangovers. The beverage makes you average, and below.

Irving Hoffman in the *Hollywood Reporter* puts it this way:

> If you are a married man who absolutely must drink booze, start a saloon in your own house. Give your wife $20 to buy a gallon of whiskey. There are 123 ounces in a gallon. Buy your drinks at retail from your wife. When the first gallon is gone, your wife will have nearly $60 to put in the bank and $20 to start business again. If you live ten years, buy all your whiskey from your wife, and then die with snakes in your boots, your wife will have enough to bury you respectably, bring up your children, buy a house and lot, marry a decent man, and forget all about you.*

There is more truth than humor in that!

A friend of mine asked a fellow church member why he wasn't in church for the last two Sundays; didn't he like the preacher? "Oh, yes, I do. I like him immensely. The fact is that when I hear him preach, I feel like going home and uncorking every bottle I've got in the cellar and pouring out the stuff. But I haven't got the guts to do it, so I stay away from church on Sunday." One touch of Christ at firsthand; and he'd walk up to that problem and master it. But bottles had him bottled up, less than a man.

A woman surrendered herself to Christ, rose from her knees, opened her purse, handed me her whisky flask, her gold cigarette case, and her sleeping tablets all at one time, and said very simply: "I don't need these now." And she didn't. She had the Real Thing, so the artificial dropped away. It isn't smart to drink; it's weak, an escape mentality, dodging out of problems into insensibility. It's a fool's business, and don't let it fool you into being a fool.

O Christ, you lift me up, and there is no letdown afterward. In you I am up and always up. In you I find a satisfaction with no worm eating at its heart. I thank you. Amen.

AFFIRMATION FOR THE DAY: I shall obey the laws of health and then depend on Christ alone for stimulus.

* No independent source was found for this quotation. It was published in the 1955 edition with permission from Irving Hoffman.

I SMOKE BECAUSE IT HELPS A BUNION

Hebrews 12:1-2

For many years I seemed to be a voice in the wilderness against the evils of smoking. Now powerful voices are being lifted against it. A leading statistical scientist told the annual meeting of the American Cancer Society that the evidence connecting cigarette smoking with both lung and heart disease is overwhelming. Results of investigations in both Britain and America, carried on independently, could be placed one on top of the other, and they would almost exactly coincide; they both say that cigarette smoking causes cancer. Now the tobacco people are frantically trying to find a safe cigarette. The only safe cigarette is an abandoned cigarette.

And it can be abandoned provided one wants to abandon it. To want to abandon it will mean to give up alibis and rationalizations.

Three ministers were talking about why they smoked. One said, "It soothes my nerves so I can think better." Another said, "I use it because it makes me sleep better." They turned to Dr. S. Parkes Cadman and asked him why he smoked, and with a twinkle in his eye he said, "I smoke because it helps a bunion on my right foot." He knew and they knew that they smoked because they were hooked by a habit, an unnatural habit that created an artificial demand for repetition, a demand they could not break.

But one can break it by the grace and power of Christ. In one of my books I noted the story of George Fox saying to William Penn, when Penn asked whether, as a Quaker, he should wear a sword, "Wear it, William, as long as thou canst." I said in comment: "Smoke as long as you can as a Christian." A friend read that comment and said, "That stuck in my mind. One day I said, 'I can't smoke any longer as a Christian.' I had smoked three or four packs a day for thirty years, I quit just like that. There was no struggle; the desire left me, and I was free." When the will was really decided, the power of Christ reinforced that weakened will—an Almighty will—worked in his will. Anyone can be free provided he or she wants to be free more than to smoke. The tipping of the will is important.

O Lord, help me to tip my will in the direction of freedom, not bondage. I would be free. I will to be free. And now I know that all your power is behind my will. Amen.

AFFIRMATION FOR THE DAY: I need be the slave of nothing, absolutely nothing, if I am the slave of Christ.

I Don't Want That Now

1 Corinthians 9:24-27

We saw yesterday that when we link our will with God's will, we can have the mastery of smoking.

A woman had smoked heavily for twenty years. She was a physical wreck, weighing a hundred pounds. She asked me to pray for her healing from physical disease. We went to the chapel together and prayed. As she went to her room, she mechanically reached for a cigarette, drew back, and said to herself, "I don't want that now. I will later." But she didn't want it later. The desire was gone. And with the dropping of smoking her various ailments dropped away, and a year later she was the picture of health, having gained twenty-five much-needed pounds. When we prayed for her physical health, God answered by delivering her from the basis of her ill health, the smoking habit. This points to a much-needed lesson: I question whether anyone has a moral right to ask for health if he or she is holding to any habit that produces ill health.

A friend writes, "I smoked three packs a day. I handed it over to Jesus, and he took it away like that. I didn't even desire it anymore. Then I knew this was a miracle." And it was!

Some try the harder way, on their own. A friend went into a drugstore and saw a woman whisper to the druggist and saw him shake his head. After the woman had gone, the druggist said to this friend, "Did you see that woman whisper to me? Well, she was the eighth person who has come in here this morning asking for a drug that makes people sick when they smoke. She had been to every drugstore in town, she said, trying to get it. But we can't keep it in stock since the newspapers have carried the news about the proved connection between smoking and lung cancer." So the women who caved in under the propaganda that it is smart to smoke are now smarting under their smartness in following the herd into this expensive, foolish, and health-undermining habit. But there is a way out for everybody; surrender to Christ and cooperate with his power.

O Christ, I thank you that nothing, absolutely nothing, need master me except your love, if you are within me and I willingly cooperate with you. Amen.

AFFIRMATION FOR THE DAY: "All things are lawful,...but I will not be brought under the power of any" (1 Cor 6:12 KJV).

THE MASTERY OF COMPLEXITY

Philippians 3:13-16

We come now to look at another mastery in the pages of the Acts—*the mastery of complexity.*

Life is getting more and more complex for the modern person; it is a tangled web of events and pressures and ideas crowding in upon the soul and mind from everywhere. The soul of modern humanity is the focus point for all that happens everywhere. Our ancestors were the focus point of the happenings of a town or village. We are the focus point of a world. Through the radio and television and the newspapers everything is dumped into our minds daily, even hourly. If we yield to this complexity, we become complex, which is a euphemism for becoming inner chaos. Modern humanity is suffering more from complexity than from apoplexy.

But life can be reduced to simplicity. The early Christians knew this and lived in it. Perhaps the answer is a waving of the hand and the objection, "Well, life for them was simple. They lived in a simple age; therefore they could be simple." But their very Christianity got them into complexity. They didn't retreat into inner states of mind and enjoy God. Their very love of Christ drove them into the needs and problems of others. This is illustrated in this passage from Paul:

> I received the "forty lashes minus one" from the Jews five times. I was beaten with rods three times. I was stoned once. I was shipwrecked three times. I spent a day and a night on the open sea. I've been on many journeys. I faced dangers from rivers, robbers, my people, and Gentiles. I faced dangers in the city, in the desert, on the sea, and from false brothers and sisters. I faced these dangers with hard work and heavy labor, many sleepless nights, hunger and thirst, often without food, and in the cold without enough clothes.
>
> Besides all the other things I could mention, there's my daily stress because I'm concerned about all the churches. (2 Cor 11:24-28)

Life not complex for Paul? It was more complex because he was a Christian and therefore compelled by love. Yet listen to this, "I have learned to be content in any circumstance" (Phil 4:11). An inner contentment and quiet simplicity amid this complexity! That is mastery indeed!

O Lord, I, too, can have the quiet, undisturbed heart amid a disturbed world. I find it at the center of your will. There I am in serenity and simplicity. Amen.

AFFIRMATION FOR THE DAY: My heart shall be a deep pool of quiet calm amid the swirling events of today.

I KNOW BOTH

Philippians 4:11-13

We saw yesterday Paul had mastered complexity; amid everything he lived contented. The rest of the passage quoted is, "I know the experience of being in need and of having more than enough; I have learned the secret to being content in any and every circumstance, whether full or hungry or whether having plenty or being poor. I can endure all these things through the power of the one who gives me strength" (Phil 4:12-13). This is one of the most amazingly masterful passages ever written. It wasn't literature; it was life, not fancy, but fact. The wonder of it is that he could be contented in both plenty and hunger, abundance and want, abounding and being abased. Some can be content in hunger, want, abasement—the ascetics—world-renounced. Others are content in plenty and abundance—the aesthetics—world-loving. If you can take only one or the other, you are weak and vulnerable. Paul could take both. If prosperity came, he took it; he could stand it. If penury came, he could take that too. If compliment came, he took it; he could stand it. If criticism came, he could stand that too. He was invulnerable from either side.

Why? For a simple reason. His life was centered not in plenty or penury but in a Person. Come plenty or penury, the Person was still there and centrally there. The roots of Paul's life were in Christ. Plenty and penury were on the margin; Christ was at the center. Therefore Paul was centrally happy in Christ. His happiness was dependent not on happenings but on relationships with an eternal Person.

In these passages he lets us see the center of his rejoicing: "We rejoice in our hope.... We rejoice in our sufferings.... We also rejoice in God" (Rom 5:2, 3, 11 RSV). The last was important and the secret of the other two; unless you can rejoice in God, and in God alone if necessary, you cannot rejoice in hope, for you'll be afraid God won't be sufficient if this or that is taken away. And you cannot rejoice in sufferings, for the God-joy is insufficient. If health and wealth and the world are stripped away, and God alone remains, we must be able to rejoice or we are vulnerable. "All my springs are in you" (Ps 87:7 RSV). When they are, let a drought of anything come, then we are not thirsty for something we do not have.

O Jesus, I thank you for saying, "Whoever drinks from the water that I will give will never be thirsty again" (John 4:14). I thank you for the never-thirsty life. It's wonderful. Amen.

AFFIRMATION FOR THE DAY: I shall drink and drink deeply of the Fountain that never runs dry—God.

I AM ABLE FOR ANYTHING

John 14:12-14

We are meditating on the mastery of complexity. We have seen that Paul had found the secret. The secret was in Christ, "in him who strengthens me I am able for anything" (Phil 4:13 MNT). In things, in attitudes of people, in property, in physical well-being, we are not able for anything. We are dependent, very. In him we are independent of whatever happens.

A college president told me of an interview he had with me twenty years before. He had at that time a deep sense of inferiority because of his father, who had brought disgrace upon the family. He said I told him that in the genealogy of Jesus there was this item: "David was the father of Solomon, whose mother had been the wife of Uriah" (Matt 1:6). Your Jesus had that background in his family history; he became the Savior of the world. I reminded him that, not where we came from, but where we were going was the important thing, that we could have a new heredity from God; therefore we were no longer inferior. He said when he took that thought, his inferiorities dropped away. He became the president of a college, able and transforming others. He was emancipated from the inferiorities of being in a family tradition, for he was "in him." That made the difference.

In the Epistle to the Ephesians the phrase "in him" or its equivalent is found thirty-one times. Being in him brought security and significance and independence of things and happenings. So Paul belonged to a secret society, and the password was "anything"— "able for anything." When you can say that password, you pass on into being in Christ. There is absolute security. For you are "able for anything." You can take prosperity, or you can take adversity; you can take anything and make it into something higher. Then you can realize the meaning of the motto "Not somehow but triumphantly."

You don't muddle through this business of living; you go through it triumphantly. Everything is grist for your mill, for you can take whatever happens and make it serve.

O Lord, I thank you that I have found the secret of living not somehow but triumphantly. In you I am able for anything. I really know how to live. Amen.

AFFIRMATION FOR THE DAY: Not what happens to me but what I do with it after it does happen is the important thing.

THE MASTERY OF WAR

Psalm 46:8-11

We move a step forward in our study of the mastery of life—*to the mastery of war.* The early Christians mastered the central plague of life on our planet: war.

As we read the history of the early Christian centuries, there is an entire absence of war, of preparation for war, and deeper, of the dispositions that produce war. They mastered war. How?

By a very simple method, so simple it is breathtaking. They renounced war and, deeper, the attitudes that produce war. They went out armed only with love, love for everybody, including enemies. They had no enmity; hence they had no enemies. It was a simple way to get rid of enemies; have no enmity, and you have no enemies!

"Yes," but the reply is made, "you have no enemies as far as you are concerned, but the enemy still has enmity, and therefore will wreak that enmity on you whether you have enmity or not." True, but the Christian still has this answer, "Do your worst; I will overcome your hate by my love, your evil with my good, your world by my cross. I will match my power to suffer against your power to inflict suffering. I will wear you down by my spirit—my soul force—against your physical force. I will conquer by turning the other cheek, by going the second mile, by loving my enemies." That sounded absurd, and it was, except that it worked and against the most brutal military empire of that day, the Roman Empire. They conquered Rome, by love! They were thrown to the lions, nailed to crosses, soaked with oil and burned as torches to light brutal festivities. But all the time something was happening within the souls of their torturers; they were being tortured by an awakened conscience. And they succumbed; Rome not only ceased torturing Christians; it adopted the very faith it persecuted. Love was stronger than hate, and soul force was stronger than physical force. A new power was loosed in the world, the power of Christian love. And when that power of love was kept pure, it was invincible. It swept everything before it, and would do the same everywhere, even in this age, if it was kept pure and if it was really tried.

O Christ, we thank you that not merely are you the Prince of Peace; you are the Plan of Peace. Your way works if we dare work it. Give us faith in you. Amen.

AFFIRMATION FOR THE DAY: I may not be able to get rid of war, but I shall create peace in my surroundings.

WE CANNOT KILL A MAN
FOR WHOM CHRIST DIED

Isaiah 2:2-4

We are studying the mastery of war.

For the first three centuries, no Christian went to war, and no Christian became a soldier. Or if he was in the army when he was converted, he resigned. It was felt to be incompatible with the Christian way. "We cannot kill a man for whom Christ died" was the basis of their refusal to go to war.

Then came the great change. After the conversion of Constantine, no one but a Christian could get in the army. The cross was inscribed on the war banners. War was made in the name of the cross. It was naturalized within the Christian system, and yet not quite. There has always been the feeling that the whole thing is wrong, and this among the very ones carrying it on, especially among them. They loathe it. The only warlike ones are the comfortable ones past conscription age who carry on war by substitution—substitution of the younger generation for themselves—war by proxy.

Now, since we couldn't take the way of our faith, we are confronted with a terrible dilemma. We have believed in force and leaned on it to settle our disputes, and now God has put us in a corner. With the discovery of atomic energy, such force has been put into our hands that we are appalled. God is seemingly saying, "You put your faith in force; I'm going to let you see into the heart of an atom. You wanted force, and now I'm giving it to you. But—and this is the terrible point—if you use it again, you will destroy yourselves." That is the terrible dilemma; we got what we wanted—force—but if we use it, we annihilate ourselves. For no one can win an atomic-energy war. Both sides will be ruined, probably in twenty-four hours. Some may crawl out of the ruins as survivors but nobody as victor. So after a long bloody march through the warring centuries we're back again where the early Christians started. They started with the renunciation of war. We, too, have come out at the same place, the renunciation of war. They did it by their faith; we have to do it by our fate. But war must go, or we go.

O Christ, you have been eternal patience, yet you are terrible too. For you have the hand of grace and the hand of judgment. We are now under the hand of judgment. Amen.

**AFFIRMATION FOR THE DAY: I am under the law of love,
and today I shall not violate it.**

THE HUMAN OUTLINE IN THE GRANITE

Isaiah 11:6-9

We saw yesterday that God has two hands: the hand of grace and the hand of judgment. If we won't take from the hand of grace, we have to take from the hand of judgment. The early Christians took from the hand of grace and walked out of war into freedom and love. We are taking the hard way, from the hand of judgment.

I have stood three times since World War II at the place where the first atomic bomb fell in Hiroshima, Japan. Each time I have stood there with a group of Japanese Christians; we have bowed our heads in prayer that no Hiroshima will ever happen again to anybody anywhere, and dedicated ourselves to peace. Nearby the Japanese have enclosed with an iron railing a very significant relic of that awful death flash. On the granite steps of what was a bank building there is the outline of the figure of a man seated. Around this outline the granite has been bleached white by the flash. But the man left his outline clearly defined in the original dark color of the granite. His body kept it from being bleached. All that was left of the man was his dark shadow in the granite. It looks like a fossil in the granite.

Is that symbolic? If we use the atomic bomb in a third world war, will we annihilate humanity; and then will visitors from Mars, searching through the ruins of what was once our proud civilization, come across the dark outlines of a man with the granite bleached around him? Will that dark outline be the only trace left of humanity upon the earth? And will the visitors shake their heads and say, "Atomic war did it"? Overdrawn? Yes, of course; but there is just enough truth in it to make us pause and think and renounce war by compulsion as the early Christians did by choice. It is not a question of whether we will renounce war; we shall have to or perish. The question is whether we will do it by compulsion or by choice. For thirty years I have renounced it by choice because of my Christian faith. I am not sorry I have.

O Christ, I thank you that you are always right; the ages being witness. And you were never so right as in this business of war. We are being forced to your mind. Amen.

AFFIRMATION FOR THE DAY: The seeds of war, conflicts within me, shall have no part in me today.

GOD'S WORD FINAL IN SCRIPTURE

James 3:14-18; 4:1

Before we leave this mastery of war, we must look at an objection: Do not the scriptures at least in some places approve of war? In some places they do. But what places? In the Old Testament and in the book of Revelation in certain passages.

But the Old Testament is not Christianity; it is that period of preparation for Christianity. Christianity is Christ. Revelation was progressive until it culminated in that final and perfect stage, Christ. He said, "You have heard that it was said.... But I say to you," making his own word final even in Scripture. At two places he reversed the old attitudes: "You have heard that it was said, *An eye for an eye and a tooth for a tooth.* But I say to you" (Matt 5:38-39). And "You have heard that it was said, *You must love your neighbor* and hate your enemy. But I say to you" (vv. 43-44).

He reversed the eye for an eye attitude and hating the enemy attitude. But we have reversed his reversals, saying, "Look what they did. We must give them what they gave—an eye for an eye. We must hate our enemy." With what result? Have we got rid of our enemies by hating them? No, we have produced more, for like produces like; hate produces hate. Two hates never made a love, never have and never will.

The early Christians were simple and direct: We refuse to hate. We have been loved by God when we were enemies, and we will love our enemies into friends. If not we are the better for loving. If we are killed, so what? We don't have to live; we can die. And in dying we live forevermore. It worked, and won! They were invincible as long as they kept to their principles.

Incidentally, when the early missionaries to Europe translated the Bible into the Teutonic language, they left out the books of Kings and Chronicles; for they said the Teutonic tribes were already addicted to war. If you want corroboration for war, don't go to the Gospels, the Acts, or the Epistles; for their stand is clear as a bell: "Put the sword back into its place. All those who use the sword will die by the sword" (Matt 26:52). The ages have been a commentary on this: Warlike nations have perished, invariably.

O Jesus, your Word stands. When we stand with it, we stand; when we depart from it, we fall. Help us to take from the hand of grace, for your grace is our safety. Amen.

AFFIRMATION FOR THE DAY: Today I shall affirm all Jesus' affirmations and reverse none of his reversals.

312

THE MASTERY OF DISHONESTY AND LIES

Ephesians 4:22-25

We must now consider another mastery—*the mastery of dishonesty and lies.* Perhaps this should have come sooner in our study, for this mastery is basic. If dishonesty and lying in all their forms are not mastered, then nothing is mastered. All spiritual attainment and all spiritual exercises are automatically canceled. For the test questions concerning a person's character are these: Will that person lie? Are there any circumstances under which that person will tell a lie? Is he or she trustworthy? Can that person be trusted when there is no eye upon him or her except the eye of conscience? If these questions cannot be answered with a straightforward yes, then all else is vain— and more—it is dangerous. Dishonest religion is more dangerous than dishonesty, for often the religion makes the dishonesty float, keeps it alive longer—but only longer, for in the end it sinks.

Acts is the cleanest record of honesty and truth ever described. The one departure from truth and honesty—the case of Ananias and Sapphira—was visited with immediate judgment; they fell dead. And they fell dead not by a stroke from God but by a stroke from within; they died of apoplexy. The moral atmosphere was so tense that the moment they departed from it, they had heart failure.

The moral atmosphere of many churches is so flabby that any departure from truth and honesty wouldn't register on a cardiograph! For instance, a minister was preparing to preach a sermon attacking a fellow minister. A friend asked him, "Have you ever heard him?" He had to confess he hadn't. "Ever met him?" "No." Then the friend told him about this minister he was about to attack, how God was using him, and that if, as he had planned, he took random statements from the minister's sermons and quoted them out of context, he would be distorting the facts. When the friend was through, the minister replied, "Perhaps what you say is true, but I've already written my sermon, and I have to deliver it." He was a defender of the truth, by lies! In a certain country, a commission was appointed to stop rampant bribery. One recommendation was that if anyone was caught at bribery, the person had to restore the amount of the bribe. If the person wasn't caught, he or she was ahead; and if the person was caught, he or she wasn't behind! A flabby moral atmosphere!

O Christ, you make our consciences acute. Your honesty sharpens our awareness of dishonesty. Help me this day to expose my conscience to your mind. Amen.

AFFIRMATION FOR THE DAY: All my attitudes and actions and words shall speak the truth and nothing but the truth.

TWO CASES OF COMPROMISE

James 3:6-12

We are looking at the mastery of dishonesty and lies, which is vital. Lord Salisbury (1830–1903), asked the qualifications necessary for a judge, replied, "The first thing is integrity. And then it would be of some advantage if he knew some law."* That is the atmosphere of Acts.

Besides the case of Ananias and Sapphira, there were two other compromises with truth, and both got Paul in trouble. One was: "Knowing that some of them were Sadducees and the other Pharisees, Paul exclaimed in the council, 'Brothers, I am a Pharisee and a descendant of Pharisees.' ...These words aroused a dispute between the Pharisees and the Sadducees, and the assembly was divided" (Acts 23:6-7). It was a wise maneuver to divide the council and get the Pharisees on his side, but it was a wrong emphasis. For him to say "I am a Pharisee" was to call attention away from the central fact of his life; he was primarily a Christian and had outgrown his Pharisaism. He had counted all things loss to gain Christ, and Pharisaism was one of them. To try to divide the council by an irrelevance wasn't up to Paul, and it only got him into a riot. Compromises end in collapses.

Another instance of a compromise and collapse was when the Jerusalem leaders said to Paul:

> "Brother, you see how many thousands of Jews have become believers, and all of them keep the Law passionately....You must therefore do what we tell you. Four men among us have made a solemn promise. Take them with you, go through the purification ritual with them, and pay the cost of having their heads shaved. Everyone will know there is nothing to those reports about you but that you too live a life in keeping with the Law." (21:20, 23-24)

But Paul didn't "live in in keeping with the Law"; he was under grace. To do this was to repudiate everything he said in Galatians. But he compromised to please the Jewish leaders. It did no good and led to his arrest. It was not this Paul speaking, "We reject secrecy and shameful actions. We don't use deception, and we don't tamper with God's word. Instead, we commend ourselves to everyone's conscience in the sight of God by the public announcement of the truth" (2 Cor. 4:2).

O Jesus, you are Truth and make us love truth. Help us to renounce all hidden, devious ways, and speaking the truths openly, commend ourselves to every person's conscience. Amen.

AFFIRMATION FOR THE DAY: Not only shall I renounce dishonesty and lies; I shall replace compromise with truth and honesty.

*No published source was found for this quotation. Robert Gascoyne-Cecil, 3rd Marquess of Salisbury, served as prime minister of the United Kingdom 1895–1902.

GOD WILL NOT PULL DOWN GOD'S STANDARDS TO OURS

Matthew 22:15-18

We have been looking at the mastery of dishonesty and lies. Jesus is relentless. He will not pull down his standards to ours; we must come up to his. He saves us by hard refusals. You cannot find the Holy Spirit without complete honesty, and you cannot keep the Spirit without it. So you are held at the center. The highest goes if there is any lowering of standards. But the Spirit goes only in awareness, calling attention by that lack of awareness of God's presence to the departure. God is ready with forgiveness and restoration the moment we become honest again.

The head of a state university told me of a graduate who wrote that he would have to return his degree, for he cheated in an examination, and the degree was a badge not of honor but of shame. A trustee suggested that the returned degree be framed and posted as a warning to other students. "No," said the president, "that degree is in my safe, and no one will ever know about it." Then the president wrote the graduate, inviting him to come and see him and stay at his home. He came with his wife and was the honored guest of the president for a week. And the degree was never mentioned. That is a beautiful picture of what God does: God forgives, forgets, and restores us to fellowship, the run of God's house is ours!

However, if there is a basic dishonesty, it will come out in our looks, in our attitudes. Ruskin in *The Stones of Venice* describes a statue, high up in a church, which to the outward eye was finished with exquisite skill; but if you climbed up and examined it closely, you had a rude shock, for its back, hidden from the spectator's eye, was left in a rough state. It was the work of a man who cared only for outward appearances. Ten years later that man was banished from the city for forgery.* There was a flaw in his character that ran all through. "Nothing is hidden that won't be revealed" (Matt 10:26). A student about to be caught cheating in an examination swallowed the paper from which he was copying, turned sick, vomited it up, and was caught. "Nothing is hidden." The mastery of dishonesty and lies is basic, and the early Christians had it. We too can have it.

O Jesus, give me the unsullied honesty of your character. Wash my lips and my heart from all untruth. Make me as pure from dishonesty as a violet under the open sky. In your name. Amen.

AFFIRMATION FOR THE DAY: At the center of my faith is a perfectly honest Person; I shall be like him.

*John Ruskin, *The Stones of Venice*, vol. 1 (New York: John B. Alden, 1885), chap. 1, §§41–43.

THE MASTERY OF PREJUDICE

2 Kings 5:10-14

We consider now another mastery—*the mastery of prejudice*—a much-needed mastery.

The disciples began as one of the most prejudiced of peoples. They were reared in an atmosphere of exclusiveness: racial exclusiveness, social exclusiveness, religious exclusiveness. Added to this Paul had the self-righteous exclusiveness of the Pharisee. Yet in ten days of waiting and receiving, all these walls of exclusiveness and prejudice went down, and they faced life with open-mindedness and openheartedness. What had happened? The Spirit of Truth had come; and as Jesus said: "When the Spirit of Truth comes, he will guide you in all truth" (John 16:13). The Spirit of Truth was guiding them in all truth, all beauty, all goodness everywhere.

This complete openness of spirit and mind is summed up in this amazing passage: "All belongs to you; Paul, Apollos, Cephas, the world, life, death, the present and the future—all belongs to you; and you belong to Christ, and Christ to God" (1 Cor 3:21-23 MNT). Never was there such absolute freedom to possess and appropriate. All things belong to you: all great teachers—Paul, Apollos, Cephas; all great facts—the world, life, death; all time—the present and the future; all things belong to you! What was the secret of this freedom of spirit? Strangely enough, it was found in a complete narrowness: "you belong to Christ." Then belonging to him, everything belongs to you! Strange way to make us free, isn't it? Christ binds us in complete submission to him and then turns us loose! With one point of the compass resting in him, the other point could sweep as wide into truth as it could go! Sure of the center, you are free to appropriate the circumference.

Then what is the secret of our prejudices? We are not sure of the center; hence we nervously have to keep off anything new and untried. Unsure people are prejudiced. Many white people, unsure of themselves, are prejudiced against people of color; many Americans, unsure of America, are prejudiced against foreigners; many Christians, unsure of their own faith, are prejudiced against Christians who hold any differing view.

O Jesus, you are the Savior; then save us from walls that shut others out and shut us in. For we want to live by open faith instead of a closed-in fear. We are to live in sunlight. Amen.

AFFIRMATION FOR THE DAY: Since I belong to Christ, then anything good, beautiful, true, from anywhere belongs to me.

ABSOLUTELY NOT, LORD! I HAVE NEVER

Matthew 9:10-13

We have been looking at the mastery of prejudice. When Peter was about to have his spirit opened to receive Gentiles as equals, he cried, "Absolutely not, Lord! I have never..." (Acts 10:14). That is the classic statement of a classic attitude, old fears holding up a protesting hand against the new. Suppose those fears had prevailed? Peter would have strangled himself and his influence. The rest of his days would have been spent trying to justify the unjustifiable. He would have been on the defensive instead of the offensive—noncreative.

As a boy I was prejudiced against beets; I didn't like the smell of boiled beets, so I wouldn't touch them. Every time they were put on the table, I had to justify my prejudice; so I would exaggerate the smells that were and create them where they weren't. Then one day I tried eating some beets, holding my nose in the process. I found they were not bad; then as prejudice died completely, I found they were delicious. Every time I eat them now, I thank God for the death of Old Man Prejudice!

A woman said to a friend, "Stanley Jones is a Communist." "How do you know?" asked the friend. "Why, he has written a book on it," she replied decisively. She hadn't stopped to inquire on which side of the question I had written the book *Christ's Alternative to Communism*. The title shows! Her mind was completely closed. Another woman, who said I didn't believe in the virgin birth of Jesus, came to hear me; I happened to say I didn't believe in Jesus because of the virgin birth, but I believed in the virgin birth because of Jesus. The miracles didn't carry Jesus; he carried them. But this woman was a diehard and died hard, "Did you notice he didn't say he believed Jesus was born of the Virgin Mary; he only said he believed in the virgin birth?" She lived by chewing on the dry bones of prejudice and was upset when her dry bones were being taken away.

But when we have learned how to receive from Jesus, we have learned how to receive from all his followers—everywhere. Everyone is our possible teacher if we lose our prejudices, even the prejudiced can teach us not to be prejudiced!

O Spirit of Truth, guide me into all truth wherever found, for it only points me to him who is the Truth. I lay my prejudices at your feet. Turn them into possibilities. In Jesus' name. Amen.

AFFIRMATION FOR THE DAY: Everything and everybody shall teach me something today, for I shall be openhearted and open-minded.

WHAT ARE YOU GOING TO DO, SCOLD ME?

Luke 4:24-30

We are considering the mastery of prejudice. We get hold of a portion of truth about a thing and not the whole truth, hence the prejudice. For instance, the Jews who came to see Paul in Rome said, "But we think it's important to hear what you think, for we know that people everywhere are speaking against this faction" (Acts 28:22). They made two mistakes in sizing up this movement. They wanted to know what Paul's views were. They thought he was presenting good *views* when he was announcing good *news*. Then they looked on the Way as a way; they spoke of "this faction" as representing a section of life and not the whole. They did not comprehend what it was all about. Our prejudices are rooted in half knowledge.

I am writing this in Florida, where I have just put up a birdhouse, hoping that a mockingbird will come and occupy it, for a cat got the last nest it built in the shrubbery. The story goes that an expert builder of birds' nests gathered the birds together and taught them how to build a nest. The eagle and the crow learned that sticks were required, flew off before getting further instructions, and made a nest of sticks. The swallow heard that mud is required, flew off, and made his of mud. The mockingbird stayed till all the instructions were in and made a perfect nest.

Stay in the presence of Jesus, long and often. Look into his face, feel his love, catch his mind, and you will know him as the Truth. Then you will go out to find truths everywhere and in everyone, but you will see them pointing in a certain direction, to him who is the Truth. Then you will be unafraid, for every truth takes you by the hand and leads you to him. As you love everybody, you will be led to him who is Love. An elderly lady stopped an alcoholic in his car and asked him to come in. "What are you going to do, scold me?" he asked. "No, love you," she replied. Today he and his family are church members. She had looked into the face of Jesus and then looked into the face of an alcoholic and loved him into loving Jesus. She didn't see prejudices; she saw possibilities and loved them into being.

O Jesus, your love went to everybody, everywhere. Help me to follow your love and love everybody, everywhere. In doing so, we see the unseen and make the unmade. Amen.

AFFIRMATION FOR THE DAY: I belong to creative love, therefore, I shall create newness everywhere through love.

NEITHER DID HIS BRETHREN BELIEVE IN HIM

John 1:43-46

We will spend one more day on the mastery of prejudice.

Jesus loves especially those who are the object of prejudice, for he was the particular object of prejudice. Note these sayings about him: "Can anything from Nazareth be good?" (John 1:46).—prejudice against his hometown. "Why [does he] eat and drink with tax collectors and sinners?" (Luke 5:30).—prejudice against his associations. "He's never been taught! How has he mastered the Law?" (John 7:15).—prejudice against his lack of schooling. "He throws out demons with the authority of Beelzebul" (Luke 11:15)—prejudice against the power working in him. Everywhere he turned, he met prejudice—even in his own home: "because even [his brothers] didn't believe in him" (John 7:5).

How did Jesus overcome these prejudices against him? By going around defending himself and nervously explaining? No, he dissolved them by his unquenchable love and his luminous words. People came to mock and stayed to pray. When the rulers sent soldiers to arrest him, they came back without him and said: "No one has ever spoken the way he does" (John 7:15). They heard the Person and forgot their prejudices. He didn't rebuke; he revealed. And people saw and knew they saw. "People may doubt his words, but they cannot doubt his face," said a fifteen-year-old of a certain minister. Jesus did that; one look into his face and prejudices dropped away.

So if you are misunderstood, don't try nervously to explain. Only little people are always explaining and excusing. "Never explain; never complain," a man had embroidered on a pillow that he carried with him. "To excuse yourself is to accuse yourself" is a saying I heard first from an Indian lawyer. A man said of Rufus Moseley, "The first time I heard him, I thought he was 'off.' But the second time I heard him, I knew I was 'off.'"

A member of the secret police of India told me after a meeting, "I came here to spy on you; I stayed to find Christ." So our attitude toward prejudice should be infinite patience, infinite love, and infinite understanding; and if that doesn't work, we should pray, "Father, forgive them; for they know not what they do."

O Christ, your love breaks me down and breaks me up. If I come to you to find flaws in you, I go away beating my breast and saying, "God, be merciful to me a sinner." Amen.

AFFIRMATION FOR THE DAY: My prejudices are buried; my faith and expectancy from God and people are alive.

THE MASTERY OF SHYNESS

Jeremiah 1:6-10

We must look at another mastery in the Acts—*the mastery of shyness*. There seems to be an almost complete absence of shyness in the Acts. It was probably there, but it was mastered. It is seen in this reference: "God didn't give us a spirit that is timid but one that is powerful, loving, and self-controlled. So don't be ashamed of the testimony about the Lord or of me, his prisoner. Instead, share the suffering for the good news, depending on God's power" (2 Tim 1:7-8).

Timothy was bothered with timidity and shyness; he was somewhat ashamed of testifying to his Lord and was ashamed of Paul as a prisoner. The result of this was a self-concentration that probably produced emotional upsets, especially stomach upsets, "Use a little wine because of your stomach problems and your frequent illnesses" (1 Tim 5:23). He was sick because he was shy. For shyness is a symptom of something deeper—self-consciousness. The shy person is always thinking about the self: What do people think of me? What will they say about me? That drives the shy person in on self and hence into shyness. What is the remedy?

Paul said he had it, and it was this, "But I am not ashamed, for I know whom I have believed, and I am sure that he is able to guard until that Day what [I have entrusted to him]" (2 Tim. 1:12 RSV [margin note]). Paul says, "I am not ashamed"; he had got rid of shame and shyness and timidity. How? By fighting it, clenching his teeth, and saying, "I will be brave"? No! He adds, "For I know whom I have believed." He took his eyes off himself and put them on Jesus. The Christ-consciousness cured the self-consciousness. He didn't say, "I know my weaknesses; I'll eliminate them by trying harder." He did say, "I know whom"; to know him was the remedy. Not to know about him but to know him. To know about him is secondhand; to know him is firsthand. Secondhand knowledge of Christ will not cure you of self-consciousness and its consequent shyness, but firsthand knowledge of him will. Secondhand knowledge is information; firsthand knowledge is transformation.

O Christ, help me to center my mind and my love on you instead of on myself. When I look at myself, I am a problem; when I look at you, I am a possibility. I look at you and live. Amen.

AFFIRMATION FOR THE DAY: I shall master shyness by becoming absorbed in Jesus and the wonder of his love.

I AM SHY AND TIED UP

Mark 4:37-41

We are looking at the mastery of shyness and self-consciousness. Paul said to the timid Timothy that he was not ashamed because he knew whom he had believed, and he was able to guard what Paul had entrusted to him. The remedy for shyness and introversion was twofold, "I know whom," and, "I am sure that he is able to guard what [I have entrusted to him]" (2 Tim 1:12 RSV [margin note]). What had Paul entrusted (or "committed" KJV) to him? This thing, that thing, the other thing? No, Paul had committed himself to Christ. In other words, he had made a self-surrender. The self-surrender had cured self-consciousness. He got himself off his own hands into the hands of Christ. That broke the tyranny of self-preoccupation and self-interest and gave him a Christ-preoccupation and a Christ-interest. As a result, his shame and his shyness dropped away. He was absorbed with Christ. He talked about him, thought about him, and loved him; and as a result he forgot himself. His timidity was gone.

If you have to talk about yourself, think about yourself, be preoccupied with yourself, then of course you will become automatically timid and shy. For you'll be conscious of your own shortcomings. But surrendered to Christ, your center is Christ, your love is Christ, and your message is Christ. Then you have something to talk about and something worthwhile to talk about. Shyness and timidity are swallowed up in a new passion to talk about him.

At interview time, an African American college youth said to me very seriously, "I'm invited to these nights where we can meet the girls, but I don't know what to say when I meet them. I am shy and tied up."

I answered, "You're not in love with any of them, are you?" He slowly replied: "No, I don't believe I am." I replied, "That's your trouble. When you really fall in love with one of them, you'll know what to say; it will say itself." That leads us to the center of the problem of shyness and timidity in religion: it is that you've never really surrendered yourself to him. When you do, you'll love him; and if you love him, you'll talk about him. Sam Shoemaker says: "If you're shy in religion, you're shy of religion."*

O Christ, if I do not talk about you, the stones will cry out; the hard, bare facts will cry out. Take my shyness and set it ablaze with you. I surrender it to you. Amen.

AFFIRMATION FOR THE DAY: I am free from shyness, for I am free from myself; Christ has me, has me wholly.

* No published source was located for this quotation, but see Samuel M. Shoemaker, *Confident Faith* (New York: Revell, 1932).

THE HOLY SPIRIT PUTS BACK MY SHOULDERS

1 John 3:1-3

We pause to look at another source of timidity and shyness—a bad heredity. Many people are shy and timid, with a feeling of inferiority because of what their ancestors were or their parents are. The past lays a crippling hand on the present.

But in this new movement, with redemption at its heart, the thing that mattered was not what you came from but where you were going.

The Christians were more interested in destination than in origins. They belonged to the future, not to the past. They were not interested in ancestors; they were ancestors, beginning a new race of the redeemed. The redeemed were redeemed from bad ancestry. Jesus was loving people back from the pit of nothingness. The nobodies were becoming the somebodies.

A new heredity had come into being. People traced the new heredity straight to God. They were children of God and were therefore the equal of anyone. A new blood had begun to flow within them, the blood of the Son of God. They partook of it in the Communion and felt its emancipating power. They could not look down on themselves, for God looked on them lovingly as his sons and daughters. And more, the Holy Spirit dwelt within them and emancipated them by doing so. They were host to the Highest; how could they belong anymore to the lowest? They didn't. Rufus Mosely once said, "The Holy Spirit puts back my shoulders."* He does. The Spirit strengthens the feeble knees and says to them of a fearful heart, "Be strong."

In the genealogy of Jesus were characters none too reputable. But he began a new heredity so wonderful that we cannot think of what lay back of him, we think of him. He becomes so luminous we cannot think of the dark spots in his past. We don't think of his blood—his heredity; we think of his blood—his redemption. He started a new heredity. So can you. If your fathers were questionable, your Lord is holy. If your brothers are tainted, your Elder Brother is "without sin." You begin a new life from him, your immediate spiritual Ancestor. Then off with inhibitions, timidity, and shyness; you are a child of God!

O Jesus, you stiffen my backbone, give nerve to my every endeavor. In you I am able for anything. So in you I face life and face it unafraid. I am free to be in you. Amen.

AFFIRMATION FOR THE DAY: I trace my life not backward but upward. I am a child of God. What else?

* No published source was found for this quotation, but see J. Rufus Moseley, *Manifest Victory: A Quest and a Testimony* (New York: Harper & Bros, 1947).

THE MASTERY OF OLD AGE

Psalm 92:12-15

We come now to consider *the mastery of old age*, a very needed mastery, for civilization in the West is fast becoming a civilization of old people. With the average length of life at sixty-five years for men and seventy for women,* the mastery of old age is a pressing necessity. It is also imperative if life is not to end for a majority of humanity frayed and frustrated at the end, instead of finished and fruitful.

For many, old age is a burden instead of a blessing. I am writing this in Florida, where the aging and the aged gather to spend their last days. These represent the economically well off for the most part, those who are able to pick up the home environment and put their roots in the sandy soil of Florida. And the soil is sandy, in many ways. For people who have come here to build castles in the air on the foundation of fact have found disillusionment and frustration, except for a certain group. Those who have a sufficiently vital faith and experience of God can—for the most part—stand the shock of transplantation and retirement. I say "for the most part," for many of these have difficulty in being compelled to do nothing significant. They keep busy trying to be busy. And they try to impress that fact upon you. But you can see it is a battle, a battle with trivial nothingness and just living on till the end. There is no mastery of old age except in rare cases. Even people whose lives have been spent in the religious limelight find it difficult to adjust to the shadows. Perhaps they have lived by limelight instead of by the Light.

But when I turn to the New Testament, I find there is no battling with oncoming age. Paul serenely awaited the coming of the end, busy with significant things and fruitful, especially fruitful, up to the last. What was his secret? And what was the secret of this whole society that could mention old age only twice, and both of these constructive and positive? They weren't whining about old age; they were winning through old age.

O Christ, you are the same from age to age, ageless; make me the same. For in my body I belong to a decaying world, but my spirit is ageless in you. I thank you. Amen.

AFFIRMATION FOR THE DAY: My roots are not in the time process but in the eternal process, so I live in eternity—now.

*As of 2015, these figures increased to approximately seventy-six for men and eighty-one for women. See https://www.cdc.gov/nchs/data/hus/hus15.pdf#015, accessed March 21, 2017.

PRIMARILY TO MAKING A LIVING INSTEAD OF GIVING A LIFE

Ecclesiastes 7:8-10

We ended yesterday with the question as to why there were no problems, only possibilities, about old age in the New Testament. The two references are these: "*Your elders will dream dreams*" (Acts 2:17), and "Paul—an old man" (Phlm 9). There is the reference to Timothy not to enroll a widow who is under sixty years of age (1 Tim 5:9), which would be about eighty with us, considering the average span of life then and now.

Now what was the secret? It was very simple. They never considered retiring at a certain age and sitting down and doing nothing. They were primarily Christians and bearers of the good news. They carried on their occupations to support themselves while they were doing that. And they kept them up as long as they were physically able. When they were not, the church took them over; so they could continue bearing the good news. Now anyone who hasn't that as the central purpose of life feels lost and frustrated when retired from ordinary occupation, for that person has given himself or herself primarily to making a living instead of giving a life. The primary purpose is material; and when that goes, the spiritual is not strong enough for a person to carry on without frustration, hence a vast feeling of upset. The secret is simple: Build into your Christian life now, while you're at work, a controlling purpose—the purpose of bearing the good news—of being a lay evangelist in some form or other. You cannot think of Wesley retiring at a certain age; he was busy up to the end, saying to everybody, everywhere, "I commend my Savior to you." No wonder his last words were, "The best of all is, God is with us." You cannot think of Paul retiring at a certain age and sitting down enjoying himself. His last words were these, "I'm already being poured out like a sacrifice to God, and the time of my death is near. I have fought the good fight, finished the race, and kept the faith. At last the champion's wreath that is awarded for righteousness is waiting for me" (2 Tim 4:6-8). Nothing more beautiful has fallen from the human pen about old age; it is mastery.

O Spirit Divine, make my every cell alive with you, and then I shall be perpetually rejuvenated. Then my body will be the adequate vehicle of your grace and power clear up to the end. Amen.

AFFIRMATION FOR THE DAY: I shall live today in two worlds at once, and the eternal world will be more real than the temporal.

THEY SHALL BRING FORTH FRUIT IN OLD AGE

Acts 2:16-18

We come now to see others who have mastered old age when there was a central purpose in life. If the central purpose of one's life is sharing Christ, then there is no reason that purpose cannot be intact and fruitful up to the very end.

One of the most useful men I ever knew, head of a council of churches, was led to Christ by an old African American who put his feet upon the Way. After five sermons by Alexander Whyte, delivered expressly to lead a doctor to Christ, had failed, an old woman led that doctor to Christ. I mentioned the old tattooed grandmother who led a thousand to Christ among the head-hunters of Formosa. When I asked an old man of eighty in Japan what his occupation was, he replied, "Winning people to Christ." He and an old lady went out together to call on people and win them. Another man, head of a meat market, instead of retiring, cut down the hours he gave his business to four, and gave four hours a day to Christ and the church. He won an average of two hundred people to Christ each year for four years. Before he began this work, he had a bad heart; but afterward he forgot all about his heart, and it settled down to normalcy. He had been giving it "attention pains." He didn't know how to speak in public, but he could sit down with people and lead them to Christ.

A woman belonged to a family in which, for forty-nine generations, one member spent life in a wheelchair. She was the one to do that in this generation. But she got hold of *Abundant Living* and saw the possibility of breaking this trail of invalidism. Since then she has helped eight thousand mentally challenged children in her very famous schools. She feels the old invalidism pulling her back as it takes her two hours to get up in the morning and get going! But the point is that she gets going, and how! She decided she would destroy the vicious idea that one member of each generation had to spend life in a wheelchair. She saw children in need and walked out of a wheelchair to serve them, and is radiantly happy. You can walk out of the confines of old age into usefulness if you begin to "see visions."

O Creative Spirit, create in me the divine impulse and power to create. Long after my body is under the law of decay, my spirit can be under the law of creation. I thank you. Amen.

AFFIRMATION FOR THE DAY: I shall beat out the invading physical wrinkles by the inward ardency of my youthful spirit.

THE HEAVENLY FRISKY

Isaiah 65:17-20

Let us note one or two things more on the mastery of old age. One who mastered old age, Rufus Moseley, said he had found what he called the "heavenly frisky." As I was about to speak to an audience in a YWCA in Japan, I was introduced to the president. She was eighty-two, but her face and spirit were both beautiful and very young. Our bodies sag because our minds are sagging. We are not discovering new truth and insights. Rufus Moseley said to me, "I have a very young man down on the inside of me." His playful joy persisted through several years of painful arthritis. He was happy when he was well and when he was ill—just plain happy—inherently so.

A minister prayed a very simple prayer, "O God, hit us on the head and wake us up," and sat down. It was a good prayer. Or maybe God is waiting for us to do what someone wisely suggested, "If you find your brain getting caked and set, take it out and jump on it." Give yourself shock treatment—personally administered—and then believe that God can rejuvenate you.

"True, I am worn; / But who clothes summer, who is life itself? / God that created all things can renew."* God can and does if we let him. Let us remember we can make up in quality what we lack in quantity as we get older.

> If, however, they remember that as the sun nears the west their shadows may lengthen and increase, they may well cease vain regrets. There is nothing more beautiful and nothing that has greater power of winsome attraction than the influence of a matured Christian life, the shadow of one who is nearing the end of the journey.**

I mentioned an old lady of a hundred who gave her recipe for growing old gracefully, "Take care of others and let God take care of you." I repeat that as it is important; for if you think of yourself first, you will grow old miserably instead of masterfully. If we think first of ourselves, then God will let us take care of ourselves and decay in the process, for we have tied God's hands.

Dear Lord, I open the windows of my spirit to your breath. Breathe into me your divine invigorating power, so that I may be remade in every portion of body, mind, and spirit. Amen.

AFFIRMATION FOR THE DAY: Since my bodily forces are on the downgrade, my spiritual forces will be on the upgrade.

* Robert Browning, "Paracelsus," *The Complete Works of Robert Browning* (Boston: Houghton Mifflin, 1899), 52.
** J. Stuart Holden, "Unconscious Influence," *Record of Christian Work*, vol. 27 (East Northfield, MA: W. R. Moody, 1908), 724.

I Don't Want to Lose the Accent

Titus 2:2-5

We look for one more day on the mastery of old age. We saw yesterday this was a joint affair, not all God, not all ourselves, but both. I was talking to an old lady of one-hundred-four who was bright and spry and alert. She had been a missionary in Burma. She told me that very day she read aloud to herself her Burmese Bible, for, she said, "I don't want to lose the accent." She would probably need it in heaven to carry on conversations with her Burmese friends!

This God-and-humanity togetherness for the mastery of old age is seen in the covenant God made with me. A year ago God said to me, "I'm going to give you the best ten years of your life." One of those years is gone, and it has literally been the very best. So I expect the next nine to be the same—or better. Then when I get to the end of these ten years, I am going to ask for another extension, another best ten years! Then the Lord added this, "As long as you have anything vital to give, I'll keep your body in repair so you can give it." I loved that! That put me on my toes. For why should God keep my body in repair if I have nothing vital to give? If that day should ever come, I hope God will let my body break down—suddenly—like the "One Hoss Shay."*

Just a year ago I was supposed to retire. I wrote the mission board, "You, of course, have to retire me according to the rules, at seventy. You may retire me as a missionary of the board. But you cannot retire me as a missionary and as an evangelist. That goes on. And goes on clear up to the very end." There wasn't a bump as I passed the line of the retiring age. I go on with my work at home and abroad. How long? Until the boiler bursts!

This necessity of having something vital to give throws me back not on reserves but on resources. As an old man says in Tagore's words, "I am getting old now so I depend more on the wind than the oars—my sails are set."** So are mine. I must catch the breezes of heaven—so more prayer. I must depend more on God—so more faith. I must do as God bids me—so more love. I must know God's power, or mine fails—so more grace. Every day an adventure with God!

O Lord, I thank you for this adventure into adventurous living. There is a tingle in every nerve and a flush in every cell your power is pervading me. I let it, wholly. Amen.

AFFIRMATION FOR THE DAY: I let the presence of the Spirit renew every cell, revive every fatigue, reinforce every power.

* "The One Hoss Shay," also known as "The Deacon's Masterpiece," is a poem by Oliver Wendell Holmes Sr., written in 1858.
** Rabindranath Tagore, as quoted in T. Cecil Myers, *When Crisis Comes* (Nashville: Abingdon Press, 1967), 133.

THE MASTERY OF INDECISIVENESS

Luke 9:57-62

We must now look at another mastery—*the mastery of procrastination and indecisiveness.* With the coming of Jesus things turned from the indecisive to the decisive. The Jews were looking for a Messiah sometime. That sometime became now; the hope-to-be had become the *is.* All the confusions and hesitations and speculations and prophesying precipitated into a concrete fact, the fact of Jesus. God acted decisively in Jesus. Since God had acted; people must act. Paul put it this way, "God overlooks ignorance of these things in times past, but now directs everyone everywhere to change their hearts and lives" (Acts 17:30). The issues had been cleared; there was only one issue: Jesus. You were with him or against him. To be with Jesus, you were with God; and to be against him, you were against God.

This decisiveness on the part of God as revealed in Jesus passed over to the disciples. The Acts of the Apostles is the most decisive book ever written. There wasn't a hesitation anywhere in the Christian movement. There were hesitations in the Acts, but all of them were in the environment surrounding the disciples; they were not in the disciples. Here they are: "When they received this news, the captain of the temple guard and the chief priests were baffled and wondered what might be happening" (5:24). That was the religious world. Here was the official world: "Felix became fearful and said, 'Go away for now! When I have time, I'll send for you'" (24:25). Here was the Roman world: "The jailer called for some lights, rushed in, and fell trembling with fear before Paul and Silas. He led them outside and asked, 'Honorable masters, what must I do to be rescued?'" (16:29-30). And the confusion of multitudes was seen in this: "Meanwhile, the assembly was in a state of confusion. Some shouted one thing, others shouted something else, and most of the crowd didn't know why they had gathered" (19:32).

In the midst of all this confusion and indecisiveness look at the Christians! They cut down through all that confusion with decisiveness as a knife cuts through cheese. They knew whom they believed, where they were going, and were sure of the power to get there. They belonged to the Great Decisiveness.

O Jesus, Master—you who set your face steadfastly to go to Jerusalem—help me to face everything with the same blessed decisiveness. Take the wobble out of my will and mind. Amen.

AFFIRMATION FOR THE DAY: I belong to the Great Decisiveness, so I'm through with indecisive wobbling and weakness.

PUT IT OFF AND GET AN ULCER

James 1:5-8

When we turn from that ancient setting, we find the same indecisiveness and procrastination. Five million people in America decide their lives by the stars, by astrology. Because they haven't nerve enough to make their own decisions, they let the stars do it. Or they read their fortunes in slot machines, a nickel a revelation! They go to fortune-tellers at so much a reading. They depend on games of chance. "Win a lot of money," I heard one woman say to another as they parted, as casually as saying good-bye.

What is the result of all this hesitation and refusal to decide? It is seen in a motto on the wall of a radio station: "Don't do it now. Put it off till tomorrow, and get an ulcer!" This indecisiveness resulting in procrastination is registering itself in our minds and our bodies. Nervous diseases are on the increase alarmingly.

The Christian has a new vocabulary: "straightway," "immediately," "at daybreak," "now." Someone asked a friend of mine if he would have a cup of coffee, "Yes or no?" The friend answered, "Never." A principle had been decided antecedent to that particular cup of coffee, so the "never" covered that question and all questions down the line. That is what happens to fully surrendered Christians; we have a principle embodied in a Person; and when an issue comes up, we decide it in the light of that principle: "Would Jesus approve?" That puts simplicity and nerve and decisiveness into the Christian make-up. It makes for strength of personality.

Whenever we lose touch with Christ and begin to look around before we decide, we become indecisive and weak. On the one hand, I talked to two men in two days: One, a man who had been an evangelist and was strong enough to win hundreds to Christ. He got out of touch with Christ, began to compromise, and then said, "I am a weak, scared mouse." Another, an alcoholic, kept saying: "I suppose so," "You may be right," "Perhaps," but no decisive words. On the other hand, someone saw "Mary" and asked, "What's happened to you? When I saw you last, you were a scared rabbit. What's happened?" She answered in one word: "Jesus"—he made the difference!

O Jesus, you are the difference. Surrendered to you, our weak wills become steel; our confused minds become clarified; our confused emotions come single-pointed. Amen.

AFFIRMATION FOR THE DAY: Strengthened with might in the inner core, I am able and ready and adequate for anything, yes, anything.

THE MASTERY OF OPPRESSION

Psalm 72:1-4

We must now look at another glorious mastery—*the mastery of oppressive circumstances and oppressive authority.*

The early Christian movement was caught between two millstones of oppressive authority: the authority of its own religious hierarchy, which controlled secular authority; and the authority of the empire of Rome. And these two millstones ground the Christians into flour, which became the bread of God to feed the nations. How did it happen? What was their secret?

This clash with oppressive authority is seen in these words:

> After calling the apostles back, they had them beaten. They ordered them not to speak in the name of Jesus, then let them go. The apostles left the council rejoicing because they had been regarded as worthy to suffer disgrace for the sake of the name. Every day they continued to teach and proclaim the good news that Jesus is the Christ, both in the temple and in houses. (Acts 5:40-42)

The clash with authority was clear-cut and decisive, and their response was just as clear-cut and decisive. And they, who were underneath, came out on top. How?

The answer is simple. They lived under two authorities—the political and the spiritual—and decided the spiritual was supreme and ultimate and final. They would bend the knee there and nowhere else. They also lived under two regimes at once: one of insolent authority, the other the kingdom of God. So they decided to live in the internal climate and let the outer climate do what it would. They would live as much as possible on the outside without compromise, and for the rest they would live within. There they were safe.

That is the only possible remedy in many circumstances. Life is intolerable and impossible without. Therefore, the only thing to do is retreat within, build up a world of your own under God, and then move out from that secure inner citadel, working into the crevices of outer circumstances as best you can. This is important, for you mustn't stay within, else you become ingrown and unsocial. You must work out from your inner security to the outer insecurities with God's grace and power. Do your best and leave the rest.

Dear Jesus, life can become hard and cruel when we have to live alongside or under oppression. You know, for you went through it. Teach us your secret. In your name. Amen.

AFFIRMATION FOR THE DAY: In every situation I cannot change I shall build up an inner world where I shall live with God.

NOT SOMEHOW BUT TRIUMPHANTLY

Matthew 5:10-12

There are those who have to live in homes where there is the silent pressure of incompatibility or alcoholism or unfaithfulness or constant nagging. There are three remedies: one is to run away; another is to retreat completely within. Both are defeatist. The third is the one I suggest, namely, to retreat within and secure one's base by full surrender to God and by keeping a quiet time. Then go out into the crevices of the outer life and function as much as possible there as a dedicated Christian. Does that mean just muddling through?

No, it means "not somehow but triumphantly." Everybody has to live life out under limitations. No one has a clear field, for other human wills are involved.

Jesus had to live his life out under limitations and oppositions, and in the cramping environment of Nazareth. But the account says, "Jesus matured in wisdom and years, and in favor with God and with people" (Luke 2:52). He didn't bear his limited environment; he used it as emery stone to burnish his spirit and mind. He got through "not somehow but triumphantly." The cramping cramped him forward.

When he went into the wilderness, he did not just get through the temptations; he got through triumphantly. He went into the wilderness "full of the Holy Spirit," but he came out "in the power of the Spirit" (see Luke 4:1-13). Mere fullness turned to power under stress and temptation. He came through "not somehow but triumphantly."

Again, it is said, "On the night on which he was betrayed, the Lord Jesus took bread" (1 Cor 11:23). He turned a betrayal into a sacrament. The betrayal passed away; the sacrament lives on. He made the betrayal into a bestowal, a bestowal of life through a sacrament. He went through the betrayal "not somehow but triumphantly."

The supreme place to see the principle at work is the cross. There he went through it "not somehow but triumphantly." "It is finished," he cried (John 19:30 RSV). He didn't say, "I am finished," but "It is finished"; the thing he came to do, namely, to redeem humanity by his death that was finished. He got through "not somehow but triumphantly."

O Jesus, our hearts burn and yearn to make every untoward happening into a toward happening, toward victory and fruitfulness. By your grace I can do it, and will. Amen.

AFFIRMATION FOR THE DAY: All my circumstances this day shall be emery to burnish me for kingdom purposes.

OPENLY AND UNHINDERED

John 15:18-25

We are looking at the mastery of oppressive circumstances and authority. The book of Acts incarnates the spirit that went through "not somehow but triumphantly." Christians invariably came out on the victory side of every circumstance. When the circumstance oppressed them, it only oppressed the glory out. Acts ends in a most unsatisfactory way, unlike the usual novel—with a success ending of the triumph of the hero—but with Paul in semi-imprisonment, a soldier watching him in his own rented house. But even there is this quiet ending, "he lived there two whole years at his own expense, and welcomed all who came to him, preaching the kingdom of God and teaching about the Lord Jesus Christ quite openly and unhindered" (28:30-31 RSV). Of all things, it ends with the word "unhindered"! For seven descriptive chapters is the account of Paul's life and activity under nothing but hindrance. For four-and-a-half years he was a Roman prisoner and more than hindered at every turn, yet the account ends with the word "unhindered." How could Luke write that? It is absurd!

But was it? The thing Paul lived for was not physical freedom but freedom to preach. If the gospel was free to be uttered, he was free. The end of his life was accomplished. So this tame ending was a triumphant ending. He came through "not somehow but triumphantly."

Paul had one purpose in life. He utters it in these words:

> And now...I am going to Jerusalem, bound in the Spirit, not knowing what shall befall me there; except that the Holy Spirit testifies to me in every city that imprisonment and afflictions await me. But I do not account my life of any value nor as precious to myself, if only I may accomplish my course and the ministry which I received from the Lord Jesus, to testify to the gospel of the grace of God. (Acts 20:22-24 RSV)

Note "if only." What befell him didn't matter; but what befell the gospel, with which he was entrusted, did matter. And as the curtain goes down on this amazing human drama, we see the Grand Old Warrior fulfilling his life purpose "quite openly and unhindered." He got through "not somehow but triumphantly."

O Lord Jesus, I thank you that my life cannot finally be blocked, not while I am in you. For you make oppression into opportunity. Finally, "unhindered" is your word. Amen.

AFFIRMATION FOR THE DAY: Little things that happen to me by the way are unimportant if only my life purpose is fulfilled.

LET THE NORTH WIND WARM YOU

Romans 8:35-39

We are considering how to get through everything that happens by using everything that happens. We have seen the marvelous spirit of "Mary" and her triumphant way of meeting everything. We were standing at an airport, the north wind cold, and Mary remarked in her cheerful way, "Lean up against the north wind and let it warm you." That is exactly what she does, leans up against every biting adversity and makes it warm her inner spirit. She confesses her failures and sins and has people weeping over theirs; she makes the north wind warm her.

Some Indian women are physically the straightest and most erect women of the world. Why? They bear burdens on their heads, so they have to walk erect; the burdens become a blessing. The north wind warms them.

The Japanese I have encountered are the rosiest-cheeked people of the world; the babies' cheeks fairly glow with rosiness. Why? Well, there is little heat in their houses, so they have to become inured to the cold. Their cheeks are rosy as a result, the north wind warms them.

Again I have found the Japanese to be a strong-limbed people. Why? Well, in wearing clogs, which stand three or four inches off the ground, they seem to fall forward at every step. But that tipping forward tightens the muscles of their legs and makes them sturdy-limbed. The strain and clumsiness of their walking make for strong tendons and muscles; the north wind warms them.

The arrow is used around the world to guide people to the right path. Japan uses it, but with one barb instead of two. Everywhere, what was originally used for destruction in war is now used to guide the uncertain to their destination. The arrow has been converted from destruction to construction. We are now making the north wind warm us. I am writing this in Japan, and the farmers are busy pruning the fruit trees. It leaves the trees naked and bare. But this north wind of apparent cruelty will warm them into summer fruitfulness. Everything serves those who serve Christ.

O Lord, I thank you that if I know how to set my sails, all winds, including adverse winds, drive me to my goal. I belong to the incorrigibly victorious. I thank you. Amen.

AFFIRMATION FOR THE DAY: I can rescue out of every fell circumstance and happening a victory and a strengthening.

THE MASTERY OF THE LACK OF A MYSTICAL TEMPERAMENT

Acts 5:31-32

This leads us to consider another mastery—*the mastery of the lack of an especially mystical temperament*.

There are many who would shrug off all I have been saying with the words, "Yes, all this is beautiful but beyond me. It's for some people—people with mystical natures—but I'm not mystical and I suppose that shuts me out." They say this with a sigh.

But that distinction is foreign to the Acts of the Apostles. This highest gift of God was not given to especially mystically endowed people; it was given to the garden variety of humanity and given to them equally. There is no artificial distinction between the mystically endowed person and the non-mystically endowed person in the Acts. That distinction was never thought of or planned for. A person as a person could and did receive the highest gift of God—the Holy Spirit—and could and did receive the Spirit equally, according to the degree of surrender and obedience. There were no other conditions except surrender and obedience. The blocks came by choice—by will—not by any inherent incapacity to receive the Highest.

The old "election" was based on the will of God. God elected some to salvation, and others God rejected. This has faded out; it was killed by the kind of God seen in Jesus. It was impossible to believe that the God and Lord of the Lord Jesus Christ could or would do that. This election of some and rejection of others apart from anything except the arbitrary will of God was largely founded on three chapters of Romans, 9–11. But these three chapters are almost entirely concerned with the Old Testament. It was an attempt of Paul to fit in his Christianity with the Old Testament conception of God. It just didn't fit in; "*I loved Jacob, but I hated Esau*" (Rom 9:13), and this before they were born! "Mary" remarked, "Jesus wouldn't have said that." No, this was the old speaking. Paul leaves off his Christianity at the end of the eighth chapter and resumes it with the twelfth. These three chapters were a digression and have caused infinite confusion.

O Lord, I thank you that your love takes us all in and takes us all in equally. The only thing that blocks is our response. Help me to have no blocks anywhere at any time. Amen.

AFFIRMATION FOR THE DAY: As a person I am elected by grace to receive the highest God has for any person.

THE CHOICE IS ALWAYS OURS

Acts 10:43-47

We have seen that the old election was based on the attempt to graft Old Testament conceptions onto the New or to change the figure, to put new wine into old wineskins. But the new wine of God's pure, unlimited love in Christ burst the old wineskin of a partial God who loved people partially. The idea has been quietly discarded.

A new election has taken its place, based not on God's will but on our incapacity to receive. This is more widespread. People shake their heads sadly and say, "Well, this isn't for me. I wish it were. But I suppose I'm just not made that way." This lays a dead hand on all our seeking and expectation and consequent finding.

And it just isn't true. There are no inherent blocks to the receiving of God's highest gifts except those we make by our own choices. The choice is always ours. I am persuaded that everybody is constitutionally made for God. The psychology of Victor Frankl of Vienna (1905–1997), says that the God urge is just as definitely a part of human nature as the self urge and sex urge and the herd urge. If you suppress the God urge within you, there will be set up a complex or neuroses exactly in the same way as if you were suppressing the self urge or the sex urge. This naturalizes the urge for God and puts it at the center of all the urges as the supreme urge. If that urge is unfulfilled, then we are unfulfilled. This was said long ago by Augustine in the oft-quoted sentence: "You have made us for yourself, O Lord, and our hearts are restless until they find their rest in you." Frankl's psychology would say the same only he would change the "are restless to "have a neurosis," intensified!

The Acts of the Apostles, antedating both, gives not the mere doctrine of equal possibilities in all people for the finding of God; it goes further and shows the fact of all people receiving equally the Holy Spirit. "They were all filled with the Holy Spirit" (Acts 2:4), the one hundred twenty, including the women. These were tested disciples. But the "Holy Spirit fell everyone who heard the word" (10:44). These were untested Gentiles.

O Jesus, through you a new all-ness comes into being; your arms are open to all who come. "Come unto me, all ye" (Matt 11:28 KJV). That puts the latchstrings out, even for me. Amen.

AFFIRMATION FOR THE DAY: I am open to the Highest, for the Highest is open to me.

NONE EXCLUDED EXCEPT THOSE WHO EXCLUDE THEMSELVES

Acts 19:1-6

We saw yesterday that there were none who were excluded except those who excluded themselves. The promise is explicit: "You will receive the gift of the Holy Spirit. This promise is for you, your children, and for all who are far away" (Acts 2:38-39).

The blocks are within us, and they can be reduced to two: lack of self-surrender and lack of receptivity. Some may be so tied up emotionally and mentally that they cannot make an intelligent self-surrender. Here counseling and psychotherapy can help clear the blocks to intelligent and emotionally free self-surrender. But that is about all counseling and psychotherapy can do; they cannot give the final cure unless they lead to self-surrender to God. They may help one to sufficient mental and emotional freedom to allow surrender to God. But the end is the surrender and receptivity, not the process of psychotherapy. One is a means; the other is the end.

Apart from these emotionally and mentally tangled people, all men, women, and young people can receive anything God has for them, especially the Holy Spirit, the gift of Godself.

Here are two letters received from two different types of men: one an airman in the Army and the other a leading businessman. The airman: "Have just finished reading for the second time your book *How to Be a Transformed Person.* You see, I was so mixed up in my mind, soul, and body that I needed a book like yours to explain and more or less lead me to see the light. I'm in. What a wonderful, joyous, indescribable feeling! To think it took so long. Trying to have my cake and eat it too." The businessman: "Probably no one is ever quite satisfied with his relationship with God. I certainly am not; but at least now it's real, not something I have heard or read. I see more clearly right and wrong—they are more nearly black and white and not grays....Things have happened in our plant, in the church, in social contacts—things are different."

One based it on feeling—"what a wonderful feeling!"—and the other on things that had happened through him. Both vital and valid.

O Lord, I thank you that you do not come in the same way to all, but you come in the way we need you. When you come, we know. Amen.

AFFIRMATION FOR THE DAY: Not only am I open to the Highest; I am receiving the Highest, for the Highest is receiving me.

THE MASTERY OF PERFECTIONISM

Mark 4:26-29

We come now to a new mastery and a necessary one—*the mastery of perfectionism.*
One of the greatest dangers to the developing spiritual life is to set up goals that are
unattainable and then go into a tailspin of depression and self-condemnation if these
goals are not reached, and reached to perfection. The goals set up in the New Testament
are high goals, the highest ever placed before the mind of humanity, namely, that we are
to be perfect as the Lord in heaven is perfect and that we shall be like God for we shall
see God as he is. That was for the individual. For the individual and society there was
to be nothing less than the coming of the kingdom of God on earth as it is in heaven.
No higher goals were ever set for the individual or for society. Both of them are perfect
goals. Then why didn't they result in perfectionism? There is not one trace in the pages
of the New Testament of paralysis and frustration resulting from what we have come to
look on as perfectionism. Why? Because Jesus wisely put into his teaching the idea of
gradual growth as well as sudden obtainment. The Holy Spirit came suddenly on them,
and the kingdom is to come suddenly, yet in all this was an emphasis on the little things
and on the next steps. The perfection was undergirded by gradualism.

"Whoever is faithful with little is also faithful with much" (Luke 16:10). This is
vastly important and saved the early Christians from expecting suddenly to leap into
perfection. They were Christians in the making, and they would never feel that they
were "made." When the sign was put up at Gibraltar: *Ne Plus Ultra* ("nothing beyond");
when Columbus discovered America, it was changed by simply rubbing out the *Ne* and
making it *Plus Ultra* ("everything beyond"). That is the way of the Christians. To us
there is everything beyond. For the more we see, the more we see there is to be seen. All
our "perfections" turn to imperfections in the light of Jesus' countenance. Yet it isn't a
paralysis; it is a prod. We have seen what we ought to be.

*O Lord, we thank you that in the light of your countenance we see and the seeing
turns to seeking. Your perfection judges our imperfection yet sets us afire to find.
Amen.*

**AFFIRMATION FOR THE DAY: I shall not be so intent on distant goals
that I shall be unfit for the next step and the little task.**

THE SURRENDER OF THE SEVEN KINGDOMS

Luke 14:25-33

We are studying the mastery of perfectionism, the spirit that, when it can't do everything to perfection, ends in paralysis and usually in doing nothing. Jesus insisted we be faithful in the little and then the larger will come to us. That is very healthy. No sudden jumping into everything; prove yourself in the little, and the next larger will be awaiting you.

Ivan Pavlov, the great scientist, at age eighty-seven, gave advice to youth regarding three necessary things: (1) "Gradualness." Don't be in a hurry. Take each day as it comes, step by step. (2) "Modesty." Do not be proud; be humble in the presence of fact. (3) "Passion....Remember that science demands from a man all his life....Be passionate in your work and in your searchings."*

Science comes along and confirms the gradualness of Jesus. Even full surrender of all there is involved gradualness. The surrender is once for all and complete as far as that moment is concerned, but one soon finds that in giving all there is an unfolding of all.

Jesus demands our all. So a full surrender is inherent. The whole of the seven kingdoms must be surrendered: (1) the kingdom of race, (2) the kingdom of class, (3) the kingdom of the nation, (4) the kingdom of religious loyalty, (5) the kingdom of money, (6) the kingdom of family, (7) the kingdom of self. The last kingdom we surrender is the last of the seven, self.

But in all these kingdoms we find, even after a full surrender, areas keep cropping up that have not yet been surrendered. We surrendered all we knew at the time, but fuller knowledge and light show further areas to be brought under his sway. So no one can say, "I have surrendered all"—full stop. The best that one can say is, "I have surrendered all I know." That makes for an all-ness as well as gradualness. It sends us on toward perfection, yet saves us from perfectionism. It is stimulating and saving. It prods us but saves us from paralysis.

O Jesus, your wisdom is so wise, and your stimulus is always a stimulus to a further sanity. I can follow your mind safely and all out. I thank you. Amen.

AFFIRMATION FOR THE DAY: I surrender all I know and all I don't know. When the don't-know is revealed, it is revealed as surrendered.

* Ivan Pavlov, "Bequest of Pavlov to the Academic Youth of His Country," *Science*, 83, no. 2155 (April 17, 1936), 369. (http://science.sciencemag.org/content/83/2155/369, accessed March 21, 2017).

NOW I'M JUST CUTTING DOWN A TREE

Matthew 13:31-33

The power to put up with one's own imperfection and live with it is inherent in the Christian mastery.

I have always disliked hearing played back a recording I have made. I skip it every time I can. For I know I'll hear my haltings, my hesitations, and my mistakes of grammar and thought and expression liberally sprinkled throughout. Then I've said to myself, "Stanley Jones, you do nothing perfectly, for you are an imperfect person. Therefore you've got to learn to live with your imperfect self doing an imperfect work. But God accepts you as you are; now you accept yourself and love yourself in spite of your imperfection." And I'm learning that lesson.

A Hindu businessman came to an Ashram in Sat Tal. We had a conference together afterward, and he said, "I went away walking on air, not touching the earth." That hour together cemented our hearts. But the next day as we marched back in procession, he was marching with me. As we sang the processional, he was out of tune. But the group and I absorbed his out-of-tuneness by a louder in-tuneness, so we marched along without a break. We loved him and accepted him in spite of his being out of tune; for we knew if he stayed long enough, he would catch the tune. He was expressing his newfound joy, expressing it badly, but the point is that he was expressing it. We took the intention of the tune. It was perfect love but not perfect expression of that love.

A man was found cutting down a tree. A neighbor asked him what he was doing, and he replied: "I'm building a house." "Aren't you too old to begin to build a house?" "Well, if I had to lay the foundation, pour the concrete, saw the joists, make the window frames, put on the roof and paint it, then it would be too much. But today I'm just cutting down a tree." And soon he would have his house! "Sufficient unto the day is the evil thereof" (Matt 6:34 KJV), and sufficient unto the day is the opportunity thereof is a way to live that works.

O Christ, you have broken up our tasks and our days into workable portions; help me to do the next little thing in a big way. Then everything will be big. Amen.

AFFIRMATION FOR THE DAY: Every little task today shall be done under the eye of Jesus, in the power of Jesus, and for the love of Jesus.

THE WIDOW'S MITE

Mark 12:41-44

We are dealing with the mastery of perfectionism. We have seen that the way to overcome perfectionism is to be willing to do the next thing at hand and do it well. This passage expresses that attitude: "Do whatever you would like to do, because God is with you" (1 Sam. 10:7). In other words, don't wait for special guidance to do special things; but do the thing at hand and do it in God's name, for God is with you. For whatever you do, you'll do it under divine guidance; for God is with you, guiding you to do the little things in a big way.

I have received many gifts in my life, gifts that have been undeserved and that have moved me. But the smallest gift ever received had the greatest significance, the gift of a "widow's mite." It was from the wife of the president of a large international bank. She had a coin collector watch the coin auctions for a year until he found an authentic "widow's mite"—the coin the widow threw into the treasury—her all. Jesus, seeing it, said she had given more than all the rich throwing in their gifts. This coin was minted in the year 76 BCE and has eight rays on one side and an anchor on the other, the smallest copper coin in use at that time. Just the tossing in of a copper coin was a small event, yet two thousand years later we are looking for that coin, or a similar one, for it had deep significance; out of her love for God she threw in her all. The little became the big, for it was big with meaning (see Mark 12:41-44).

That is the atmosphere of the early Christians. They were doing little things in a big way. And we can't forget them. Eternal meaning was in every single happening. Their actions were seed actions. The group at Antioch "laid their hands on Barnabas and Saul and sent them off" (Acts 13:3), and lo, we feel today the impact of this smallest of acts. If it hadn't happened, we and our whole civilization would have been different. It was a "widow's mite" of an act that was big with destiny. Nothing is small when it is done in Christ and for him.

O Christ, you began as a babe, and you have ended on the throne of the universe. Help me not to despise my Nazareths, for they too may be big with destiny. Amen.

AFFIRMATION FOR THE DAY: Since every happening today may be big with eternal meaning, so I shall do everything as unto Christ.

THE MASTERY OF TRYING TO CHANGE OTHERS FIRST

1 Peter 4:17-19

We now pass on to another mastery—*the mastery of trying to change the world and others first.*

Note that I said the mastery of trying to change the world and others *first*, not the mastery of trying to change the world and others. We are to do that. That is a part of our Christian task, and it is inherent. The big and important question is: Where do we begin?

The disciples didn't fall into the snare of beginning with others; they began with themselves. They didn't start out trying to change the world; they began to change themselves. If they had begun by attempting to change the world, they would have been meddlers; but they began with themselves and became messengers.

The waiting for ten days to settle their own spiritual problems first was one of the wisest moves in history. Those ten days changed the people who were to change the world and made them witnesses instead of moralists. They told what had happened to them, and those who heard them wanted what they saw and heard.

Jesus emphasized this place of beginning when he said, "Why do you see the splinter that's in your brother's or sister's eye, but don't notice the log in your own eye?...You deceive yourself! First take the log out of your eye, and then you'll see clearly to take the splinter out of your brother's or sister's eye" (Matt 7:3-5). Note "first take the log"; begin with yourself, and then you will see clearly to help your brother or sister with his or her problem.

There is nothing more pathetic than to see people with inner conflicts working for world peace. Or people who have no inner integration trying to integrate others; they are cases dealing with cases. I said to a group of social case workers, "Aren't many of you cases dealing with cases, problems dealing with problems?" They burst out laughing, knowing it was so! And it was all very ineffective. A psychiatrist who is full of conflicts dealing with the conflicts of others is tragic. The disciples took hold of the right end of the stick, themselves!

O Jesus, your unerring finger has touched our deepest need, our need to start with ourselves. Then we talk and live with power, for we illustrate. Amen.

AFFIRMATION FOR THE DAY: Everything shall begin with me.
I change all in me in order to change all I come in contact with.

SUCCESS IN EXAMINATIONS GUARANTEED

Galatians 6:1-S

We are studying the mastery of beginning at the wrong place, others. The only effective place to begin anything is with you. The Word has to become flesh in us before it can become power through us. I am more and more persuaded that no one can help another except through sharing what has become vital to him or her—not good advice, but the good news that it works.

I saw a sign on a school in India that specialized in coaching students for their examinations. The sign said: "Success in examinations guarateed"; the guarantee didn't guarantee them against their own misspelling! It wasn't very inviting!

Always the illustration becomes the illumination. The disciples were ineffective in getting evil spirits out of people until they got rid of their own evil spirits of self-seeking pride and self-righteousness. When they got the evil spirits out of themselves, they began to get them out of others.

So don't try to save the world or our circumstances or even your family—begin with yourself. Go over everything in your own life that could possibly block the power of God getting through you to others. Surrender those blocks to God. Then share with those around you in ever-widening circles your victory. Then your work for others will be that of, not a moralistic whip, but a loving witness.

You will remember the question of Peter to Jesus about John, "'Lord, what about him?' Jesus replied, ... 'What difference does that make to you? You must follow me!'" (John 21:21-22). The first thing Jesus directed Peter's attention to was Peter.

When Peter got straightened out, that would automatically help John. But Peter was asking first what the other man was going to do instead of what he was going to do. Begin with yourself, said Jesus, and the other man will catch it by contagion. Then we will not be preaching to people—always an irritation, but we will be sharing with people—always an inspiration. It is the only method that will work.

O Lord, I thank you that you have started us at the right place, ourselves. Now heal us at the heart, and then we'll have something for healing other hearts. Amen.

**AFFIRMATION FOR THE DAY: Remember, O soul of mine,
that it is only one loving heart that can set other hearts aflame.**

WHAT IS YOUR NAME?

Genesis 32:22-30

We spend one more day on the mastery of beginning with others. In the case of Jacob there is a vivid account of what happens to others when we begin with ourselves. Esau was coming to meet Jacob with four hundred men, to avenge himself upon his brother for stealing his birthright. The night before the meeting, Jacob wrestled with an angel all night. The angel asked him the key question, "What's your name?" and Jacob confessed that it was *Jacob*—the supplanter—the supplanter of his brother. When he got out the old name, he found a new one—Israel—for he was a new man (Gen 32:27-28). When this new Jacob met the oncoming Esau, a strange thing happened: "But Esau ran to meet him, threw his arms around his neck, kissed him, and they wept" (Gen. 33:4). How did that happen? A man with blood on his horns, ready for vengeance, was now weeping on his brother's shoulder. How did that happen? Very simple: Jacob began with himself, and a changed Jacob changed Esau.

A big businessman was changed by the surrender of himself to God and passed from a secondhand faith to a firsthand faith. He writes:

> I have often remarked to my Sunday-school class that I felt I wasn't contributing much because all I said was out of a book. But last Sunday what I said was not out of a book; I think God told me what to say. When I finished, a girl came up and said, "Where did you get the material for that lesson? Did that come out of a book?" I told her it didn't. She replied, "I knew it! You can always tell, and it sure made a difference."

It surely made a difference in the Acts, for here was the difference between the stagnant pools of discussion about laws and the bubbling springs of a shared life. Nothing reaches the heart that does not come from the heart. To preach and to witness out of the overflow are the only effective preaching and witnessing. Anything less than this reaches the head but not the heart.

O Jesus, we lift to you our empty cups. Fill them with yourself and your power, and then we will be able to lift those filled cups to the thirsty lips of others. Amen.

AFFIRMATION FOR THE DAY: I go filled to the empty, joyous to the joyless, victorious to the defeated, loving to the loveless.

THE MASTERY OF LONELINESS

1 Kings 19:9-12

We come now to see another mastery—*the mastery of loneliness.*

This is a much-needed mastery; for while life today is apparently thrown together by modern communications, yet there remains a central loneliness in modern humanity. Thrown in with everybody, people feel they don't belong to anybody. All the news of the world is poured into people's minds; they see the scenes of the world on television, yet for all that they feel alone. As Heindricks, an eminent Canadian sociologist, says: "The machine has created loneliness in the modern world. The loneliness of the modern man has been aggravated by the soullessness of the machine."*

These people are lonely: the old man who has lost his partner, the immigrant who has not been made to feel at home in her adopted country, the adolescent with acne, the shy person, the traveling salesperson, the unemployed, the new person moving into a community, the guilty. Loneliness is now a social phenomenon. One recent book is entitled *The Lonely Crowd.* Being thrown with people doesn't necessarily take away loneliness.

Heindricks says: "My chief memory is drunken men and women from Friday night through Sunday in lumber camps."* Alcoholics Anonymous is helping the person who has become so anonymous that the person turns to drink. An African American secretary showers love on a horse she has bought because she is lonely. It is the shy, timid persons who fill our hospital beds.

> I, a stranger and afraid,
> In a world I never made.**

Is there an answer to this basic loneliness? The early Christians seem to have found the answer. There is not a line that expresses loneliness in the Acts. Long periods of isolation, long imprisonments, ostracisms aplenty; yet there is a basic sense of being not alone. They found the secret of being at home anywhere and of being with Christ everywhere.

O Jesus, I thank you that with you I need never, never feel lonely or afraid. You remove that basic sense of loneliness and make me feel I'm wanted and loved. Amen.

AFFIRMATION FOR THE DAY: I am at home everywhere, for I am at home in God, and God is everywhere.

* No published source was located for these quotations.
** A. E. Housman, *The Collected Poems of A. E. Housman* (New York: Henry Holt and Co., 1965), 111.

NOBODY BUT ME AND JESUS

John 16:31-33

We are considering the mastery of loneliness. What was the secret of that mastery in the Acts, and what is the secret today?

It is simple and very effective. Jesus said, "Lo, I am with you always, even unto the end of the world" (Matt 28:20 KJV). And they found that he was! He had changed his presence for his omnipresence. People didn't have to go to Palestine to see him; they dropped into the silence of the heart, and lo, Christ was there. The God revealed in Jesus was personalized. He was not mere vague force; he was a Person, a Person with whom you could talk and have him talk to you in unmistakable terms. I can testify; I know Jesus better than I know any other person in the world. And he knows me better than anyone else in the world knows me, and he still loves me. Someone called to an African American woman standing in a cabin door and asked, "Auntie, who lives there?" The answer came back, "Nobody but me and Jesus." That blessed woman knew a secret, a very great one.

A Chinese friend, Dr. Lo, was traveling with me, and he said that once when he was lonely in America, he turned to his Bible, and the first verse his eyes fell on was this one, "Lo, I am with you always." He felt Christ calling him by his first name. And he did, and does.

People say to me, "You're a traveler around the world, and you get home a couple of weeks a year. Don't you ever get lonely?" My answer is, "Well, I suppose I do live without a home. I feel sympathy for the man who put a label in the lid of his suitcase: 'God bless our home.' My home is a suitcase. Yet I've never had a discouraged or lonely moment in thirty-five years. Why? Well, I know he is with me. And I can turn to him anytime, anywhere, and commune with him." It works. He has guaranteed that his presence will not be a-coming and a-going; he puts it, "even unto the end of the world." He gives a guarantee against loneliness. This motto expresses it: "Without him, not one step over the threshold; with him, anywhere." Then every place is home and every meal the Bread of the Presence.

O Jesus, your loving presence surrounds me, envelops me, makes me at home anywhere, everywhere, and at all times. What more do I need? Nothing! Absolutely nothing. Amen.

AFFIRMATION FOR THE DAY: I can never drift beyond his care;
I can never be where he is not. I am safe and at home, in Christ.

TWOFOLD ANSWER TO LONELINESS

Matthew 28:16-20

The Christian answer to loneliness is twofold. One part of the answer is that Jesus promised he would be with us always to the end of the world. And this becomes a fact; he is with us, not only to the end of the world, but to the ends of the world. I have been in almost every country; and lo, there he was, intimate, personal, and always loving. One is never lonely because never alone. This is real; not merely is it remembering Jesus, it is realizing Jesus. He is closer than any being on earth can possibly be. He is in the deep within. So at any moment I can drop within the silence of my heart and talk with him as friend with Friend. It is a perfect cure for loneliness.

But if your Christian faith is institutionalized—centered in an institution—instead of being internalized—centered in the within—then when you are removed from the institution, you feel cut off, alone, lonely. But when it is internalized, the internal is always with you; and he is in the center of that internal. Hence you are never lonely.

The other side of the Christian answer is that when you get in touch with this living Jesus within, his love within you makes you interested in and loving toward others. That makes others in turn interested in and loving toward you. Your friendliness produces friendliness; hence you always have friends, and these friendships tend to keep you from being lonely.

Someone asked a girl if she didn't get homesick while at camp, and she replied, "I really didn't have time, for I was so busy keeping the other girls from being homesick that I didn't think about being homesick myself." The love of Jesus does just that; it lifts you out of thought of yourself and makes you interested in others, and thus it cures you of loneliness. The self-centered are invariably the lonely. When you are Jesus-centric, you become other-centric and hence free from self-centeredness and free from loneliness. The remedy for in-grownness is outgoingness. Love is outgoing. Jesus creates love and thus cures loneliness.

O Jesus, come in to flood every portion of my being with love and more love for everybody and everything at all times and everywhere. Then will my heart sing of the Eternal Presence. Amen.

AFFIRMATION FOR THE DAY: My cure for my possible loneliness today is to go out and try to cure the lonely with my love.

THE MASTERY OF ALWAYS BEING RIGHT

James 5:13-16

We now consider a new mastery—*the mastery of always being right*. It was a few minutes after midnight; the old year had gone, and the new year had already begun. A pastor said to me as we walked away from a watch night service, "I should have changed that first part of the service and given you more time for the closing. I'm sorry." I laughed and said, "You're safe. You'll have a wonderful year. You have learned the art of saying, 'I'm sorry.' You know how to live." One of the most important things in life is to learn that you don't have to be always right. And you don't have to defend yourself. You can say, "I am sorry. I was wrong."

Paul didn't hesitate to say he was wrong. "Those standing near him asked, 'You dare to insult God's high priest?' Paul replied, 'Brothers, I wasn't aware that he was the high priest. It is written, *You will not speak evil about a ruler of your people*" (Acts 23:4-5). Here Paul reversed himself. His bad eyesight may have kept him from seeing it was the high priest. In any case, he said he was sorry. And he grew bigger in saying it. Only small people are always defending themselves and trying to prove themselves right. Big people feel a central rightness and can therefore put up with marginal mistakes. But small people are not sure of a central rightness; hence they have to try to hold the line at every marginal issue lest their smallness be revealed. They are always right and therefore always wrong.

The more perfect you are, the more you can put up with imperfection in others. Jesus is so perfect that he puts up with imperfections and covers them. A singer was marvelous at times but sometimes jumped the tune. His wife was a wonderful pianist. Someone came up to him at the close of a meeting and said, "You must have missed your wife at the piano tonight. She certainly covers your mistakes." Jesus does just that. He is so perfect that he covers my imperfections. When I get off tune, he lifts his voice higher so people will hear his voice, not mine. Love covers mistakes.

O Christ, I am at your feet. Your covering of my faults converts me from those very faults. So my defenses are down. I defend nothing but your amazing love. Amen.

AFFIRMATION FOR THE DAY: I shall not be afraid to reverse myself on many things, for I am centrally right in him.

I NEVER SAY I'M WRONG

1 John 1:5-10

We are looking at the mastery of always being right. Protestantism was never greater than when it put up a monument in Geneva, Switzerland, saying that Calvin and his associates made a mistake and committed a great sin in burning Servetus. Here Protestantism condemned itself and said, "I am sorry." It was never bigger than when it said those simple words. I know people who, if they just once said, "I am sorry," would be different people.

A switchboard operator said to the superintendent of a hospital, "I never say I'm wrong." "Oh," said the superintendent, "I say it a dozen times a day." Result? She arose to the superintendency of the hospital, and the other woman was caught at the level of a switchboard operator.

A lady ran a flower shop; a gentleman acquaintance of hers furnished the money to open it. Because of her experience and ability she was to run the shop, and he promised her a half interest in the business. Years passed, and the business grew and was a success. She put in long hours of hard work and drew a small salary. Whenever partnership was mentioned, he put her off. He became ill, and someone gave him a copy of *Abundant Living*. The nurse phoned the woman to come to the hospital as he wanted to see her. He broke down in tears on her arrival and said he had wronged her these many years. He sent for an attorney, drew up the papers, and gave her half interest in the business. He was bigger and better for saying, "I am sorry." And now he could live with himself and others.

Scientists now say that there is a substance in tears that kills cancer germs. There is something in a tear of penitence that kills pride, kills self-righteousness, kills sin in general. Nothing is as beautiful as a tear of penitence on the face of a penitent. Heaven bends low to look on the beauty of it. For that teardrop opens the resources of grace and floods the soul with pardon and reconciliation.

If you live by defense, you live by fear. But if you have nothing to defend, you live by faith. You melt the defenses of others when you let down your own. It works.

O Christ Jesus, give me the spirit that acknowledges when I'm wrong, for I want to get rid of all wrong. To defend the wrong is to harbor it. I want to be free, so make me free to acknowledge. Amen.

**AFFIRMATION FOR THE DAY: I shall not be on the defensive.
I shall be on the offensive of love, love to everybody and everything.**

IF WE WALK IN THE LIGHT

Acts 19:18-20

Usually the Lord gives me a key verse for the year, a verse around which life can revolve. On New Year's morning, God gave me this one: "If we walk in the light, as he is in the light, we have fellowship with one another, and the blood of Jesus his Son cleanses us from all sin" (1 John 1:7 RSV).

Our business is to live to the highest light we have, which is Jesus, "as he is in the light." The touchstone in any situation is: Is this according to Jesus? Does it fit into his mind and spirit? Would he approve? If not, then our "light" is darkness.

But it is not always easy to tell whether Jesus would approve, whether it does fit into his mind and spirit. There may be a lot of good in a thing and some evil. A congressman told me of sitting down and adding up on one side the good and on the other side the evil, in a measure to be decided, and he added: "I have to decide it. I can't run out on it. I can't dodge it. But I know I'm not making a clear-cut decision between good and evil. It's not all black and white, it's often gray. What do you do then?" My reply was, 'Well, walk in the highest light that you have; and then if you have made a mistake, the 'blood of Jesus his Son cleanses us from all sin.'" He covers the sins and mistakes that you honestly make in deciding in half-lights. And the word "cleanses" is present continuously; he continuously cleanses from all sins. These mistakes honestly made do not break the fellowship—"we have fellowship one with another"—between Christ and us and between us and others. The fellowship persists, for he provides for a continuous cleansing. So the cleansing is once and for all, yet it is continuous.

So you do not have to be always right. We are all only Christians in the making. We blunder and stumble. But when we stumble, we stumble forward. When we fall, we fall on our knees. "Daddy," said a little boy who had walked many blocks holding on to his father's finger, "you had better take hold of my finger, for I'm getting tired." His very tiredness threw him into greater security. Everything furthers us when we are his, for he loves us in spite of our blunders.

O Jesus, your grace is a continuous wonder to me. You are so stern, holding me to the highest, and yet so tender, stooping to my lowest. You are Grace and more Grace. Amen.

AFFIRMATION FOR THE DAY: If I have to decide in half-lights today, I shall do my best and leave the rest.

RESPONSIBLE FOR ALL WE KNOW AND ALL WE MIGHT KNOW

Romans 8:1-8

Does what has been said about the mastery of not always being right open the door to indulgences, giving excuses for half-Christian living and providing for failure and sin? The answer is an emphatic no!

Let us go back and look at the passage: "If we walk in the light, as he is in the light" (1 John 1:7 RSV); that is clear and decisive. A Christian is one who is responding to all the meanings found in Jesus; walking in all the light to be found in him. The moment we refuse to walk in the light as seen in Jesus, there the light ceases. We begin to walk in darkness. Only the person who is living up to the light that he or she has is getting more light.

I say "the light that he or she has," but we are responsible also for the light that we might have. We should be eagerly open to more and more light, for new light breaks out from the person of Jesus all the time. "[The Holy Spirit] will take what is mine and proclaim it to you" (John 16:14); the work of the Holy Spirit is to unfold an unfolding Christ. Revelation is progressive, fixed in the historic Jesus but unfolding in the universal Christ. The Holy Spirit makes you see that there is more to be seen. That puts you on the tiptoe of opening expectancy. If you sin against the light that you have, there is one penalty; you get no more light. In other words you cease to grow; you deteriorate. The punishment is in the person. You are the payoff.

But the moment we begin to obey again, begin to "walk in the light, as he is in the light," then the fellowship one with another begins, and the blood of Jesus Christ begins to cleanse again. The blood of Jesus cleanses those who walk in the light, and only those. When we refuse to walk in the light, he automatically shuts off the cleansing—and the fellowship. But the person who is honestly walking in the light has fellowship and cleansing even though that person blunders and sins while walking in the light. If God sees the central intentions are right, God forgives and cleanses marginal mistakes and sins. God is not a mote picker; God is a maker of men and women.

O Lord, I thank you that you are not the all-seeing eye, looking for my weakness and blunders. You are the all-saving Lord, loving me in spite of my failures. Amen.

AFFIRMATION FOR THE DAY: I shall walk in all the light I have today, and then in the added light I shall glow.

STEPS IN FINDING THE HOLY SPIRIT

Ephesians 1:11-14

We have been studying the masteries introduced into the individual and society by the coming of the Holy Spirit. These masteries have not been read into the account; they are inherently there and very much more besides. And they have not expended themselves; they are still at work leavening society.

Then the question arises: How does one receive the Holy Spirit?

This is the most important question that can be asked in religion. I am going to outline the steps as I see them. You take them as I outline them; and at the end you may be in possession of the Spirit, or better, the Spirit may be in possession of you.

First, *the end purpose of God's redemption is to give you the Holy Spirit.* The end purpose is to give you Godself. All else is preparatory—the incarnation, the atonement, the resurrection—all are preparatory. Moving into the inside of us in intimate personal relations is the end view of the Divine Lover. Being Love, God could not stop this side of personal intimate contact with the loved one. All that happened *without*, in history, was in order that this might happen *within*, in experience. Everything converges upon this. If we fail to find the Holy Spirit, we fail to fulfill that for which we are made, and we fail to fulfill God's intention.

Second, *the Holy Spirit is primarily a believer's gift.* When the disciples received the Holy Spirit, they were believers. The account says, "Jesus said this concerning the Spirit. Those who believed in him would soon receive" (John 7:39). Note "those who believed in him would soon receive," a believer's gift. When we came to the Christ, in the first coming we wanted forgiveness, reconciliation. We knew little or nothing about asking for the Holy Spirit. But now that we are children of God and are sure of our standing in God, we want to enter our birthright, which is nothing less than the Holy Spirit. In the new birth we received a measure of the Spirit; now we want more, we want to receive the fullness of the Spirit. We want to possess the Spirit; or better, we want to be possessed by the Spirit. We want more of what we have.

O Spirit Divine, I am made for you. My spirit is made for you. When I find you, I find the end for which I was made. I want to fulfill my destiny. Amen.

AFFIRMATION FOR THE DAY: I shall not annul the grace of God.
What grace offers, I shall take with both hands.

FURTHER STEPS IN RECEIVING THE HOLY SPIRIT

1 Thessalonians 4:3-8

We are considering the steps we are to take in receiving the Holy Spirit.

Third, *having come so far along in redeeming you, will God now pull back and hesitate or refuse to give you the crowning gift, the gift of the Holy Spirit?* If so, that would reverse God's character and purpose, for God is driving for this very end. God is driving according to the divine nature as Love, for Love yearns for the object of its love. All the other steps were taken in order to take this crucial step—to step inside us.

Fourth, *there are no blocks on God's side; they are all on our side.* If you have not received the Holy Spirit, then do not look at God to find the blocks; look within yourself, the blocks are there. There is only one person who can keep you from receiving the Holy Spirit, and that one person is you.

Fifth, *the biggest block is a lack of self-surrender.* Invariably I find that this is the real block. We give this, that, and the other; but we don't give the self. Or if we give, we don't give up. We give with strings attached, "I'll give this if God will do this." No, there must be no ifs or buts. It must be clear-cut surrender. And I mean surrender.

I have tried to find a better word, *commitment*, for instance. But *commitment* would seem to imply that your hands are still on the gift. In *surrender*, your hands are not on the gift; they are raised in surrender. God has the gift of yourself, irretrievably. From henceforth the basis of your life is not you but Christ. For you live in Christ, not yourself. That change is not make-believe, it is fundamental. Now you are not your own. Your knees bend in obedience at one place and one place alone, Christ. This is not conditional. Whether I receive or don't receive, Christ has me. And has me for better or worse, to sink or swim, to live or die; I'm in his hands forever. I've burned my bridges behind me.

O Jesus, my Lord, you manage me better than I can, so I give myself not grimly but gladly. It is a happy yielding up of all I am and have. Amen.

AFFIRMATION FOR THE DAY: Myself on my own hands is a problem and a pain; myself in the hands of God is a possibility and a power.

I ENDORSE THIS WITH ALL MY HEART

John 7:37-39

We continue to look at the steps in finding the Holy Spirit.

Sixth, *having come so far along with God, shall I pull back and spoil it all by refusing to give that last thing, myself?* No, I do give that last thing, myself! Since God is not merely giving me this or that but is giving the Divine Self, how can I answer that divine self-giving except by my own self-giving? I cannot ask for God to give all to me if I give things to God, things but not myself.

Most Christians are canceled out, not because they don't give, but because they don't give all. They give, but they don't give up. Yet how gladly we should offer our all in exchange for God's all! It will be the most sensible thing we've ever done. A sacrifice? Nonsense. The sacrifice is to withhold, for then you are sacrificing your spiritual effectiveness, your spiritual joy, your very self. Only as we lose our lives, do we find them. We are obeying a spiritual law that works with mathematical precision.

Seventh, *and since I "receive the promise of the Spirit through faith" (Gal 3:14), I now take this gift of God by faith.* Faith is receptivity toward God. Faith is not a talisman that brings certain things because of the faith. Faith is an attitude toward God that makes it possible for God to work. If God gave to us without our faith, it would mean imposing something on us without our cooperation. Faith is cooperating with God. It is saying yes to God's yes, affirming God's affirmations.

A man gave a check to a minister in financial difficulties. When the minister took it to the bank, the cashier asked him to endorse it. So he wrote on the back of it, "I endorse this with all my heart." Faith writes across the promises of God, "I endorse this with all my heart." A woman brought to me one of my books and, instead of asking me to autograph it, asked me if I would endorse it. I wrote, "I endorse this book," and signed my name. Faith, by endorsing God's promises, cashes in on them.

O Christ, your promises are your character extended in open invitation. So when I have faith in your promises, I have faith in your character. I endorse your character with all my heart. Amen.

AFFIRMATION FOR THE DAY: "Faith is an affirmation and an act that bids eternal truth be fact."*

*No published source was found for this quotation, which is widely attributed to English poet Samuel Taylor Coleridge (1772–1834).

I WILL STOP SEEKING AND BEGIN TO PRAISE

Mark 11:20-24

We are taking the steps in receiving the Holy Spirit.

Eighth, *I will act as if the Spirit were there.* The Holy Spirit will reveal himself in his own way. Faith is acting as if it were done and launching out upon it as a working hypothesis. It is life lived assuming that what God is in character God will perform in the concrete. God's nature is to give the highest; then God will give me this, the gift of the Holy Spirit. When I do this, I am not running contrary to God's nature; I am coinciding with it. I am not overcoming God's reluctance; I am laying hold on God's highest willingness.

And I will not lay down the method of manifestation. The coming of the Holy Spirit may be as gentle as the coming of the dawn or as a rushing, mighty wind; it may be the settling of a conviction within my mind and heart that will take complete possession. To me the Spirit came like gentle waves of refining fire, cleansing and filling my being. But there is no standard way of the Spirit's coming; it suits each need.

Ninth, *I will not look at myself, nor will I look around at others; I will look at Jesus—and thank him.* If you look at yourself; you'll be discouraged; if you look around, you'll be distracted; if you look at Jesus, you'll have peace and quiet possession.

Tenth, *I will stop seeking and begin to praise the Spirit for what he has given and will give.* The seeking attitude is sometimes tense and anxious; the praising attitude is relaxed and receptive. The praising doesn't say that you have everything, but it does say that you are on the Way! It says "thank you" for what you have, and then that thanksgiving is open expectancy for what is to come.

Now that you are in possession of the Spirit, remember that you don't possess the Spirit; the Spirit possesses you. You are not going to use the Spirit; the Spirit is going to use you! The surrender meant a surrender to get the Spirit and now surrender to the Spirit's purposes. You are aligned to those plans and purposes.

O Divine Spirit, I thank you for your coming. My heart is your home forever. We will work life out together—my willingness, your power—what an adventure! Amen.

AFFIRMATION FOR THE DAY: Since I do not possess the Spirit but the Spirit possesses me, I shall leave him in full control.

THE GIFTS OF THE SPIRIT

Romans 12:3-8

We have been studying about receiving the Holy Spirit. But the receiving of the Holy Spirit is not an end in itself; it is a receiving in order to live out life under the direction of the Spirit. The Spirit comes in and takes control and direction of the life forces within and the life activities without. Life is lived now in the Spirit.

According to Paul, the Spirit brings certain gifts: "There are different spiritual gifts but the same Spirit; and there different ministries and the same Lord; and there are different activities, but the same God who produces all of them in everyone. A demonstration of the Spirit is given to each person for the common good" (1 Cor 12:4-7). There are mentioned these gifts: wisdom, faith, healing, performance of miracles, prophecy, the ability to tell spirits apart, different kinds of tongues, interpretation of the tongues. He ends by saying, "All these things are produced by one and the same Spirit who gives what he wants to each person" (v. 11). To the list he adds helpers and administrators (see v. 28).

From this it is clear that there are many gifts but one Spirit, and Paul urges that we seek the highest gifts: love and prophesying (which is not foretelling but forthtelling the good news). The Holy Spirit is the gift for all, but divides the gifts according to the Spirit's will, for the collective good. To pick out one of these gifts and say, if we do not have this gift, we do not have the Holy Spirit, is to cut across this passage. Paul urges that we "earnestly desire" (v. 31 RSV) the two highest gifts: love and prophesying, the power to witness effectively. They are the safest and most needed gifts.

But the greatest work of the Holy Spirit is not merely to introduce new gifts but to cleanse, heighten, and use many of our old inherent powers. The person who has executive ability can now use that ability for the kingdom, and that ability will be heightened by the Spirit. The person who can sing will now sing with a new quality. "Mary" said, "The one thing I can do is love. It is the easiest thing I do. So now Jesus just takes hold of my capacity to love and heightens it. I love everybody and everything." And how!

O Holy Spirit, I place at your disposal every power and every faculty. Take hold of each and cleanse and control and use all I have, all the time and in all possible ways. Amen.

AFFIRMATION FOR THE DAY: All my capacities shall be controlled capacities, and they shall be heightened capacities.

THE LORD GOD HAS SENT ME
AND GOD'S SPIRIT

Luke 4:17-19

We are looking at the mastery of our capacities and faculties by the Spirit. This Spirit control makes sacred all occupations if they are morally legitimate.

Businesspeople come under the head of "administrators." They can be in business for God. How? The application is simple: They are in business to supply their own needs; and after those needs are met, all the rest belongs to the needs of others. The criterion of one's own needs? This: One has a right to as much of the material as will make that person more mentally, morally, spiritually, and physically fit for the purposes of the kingdom of God. Beyond that is luxury, therefore with no blessing of God on it. The individual will then be dealing with dead wealth, which is "filth."

I know people, however, who handle their business with as much sacredness as a minister handles the Bible in the pulpit. And they are both sacred callings. This passage is to the point: "And now the LORD God has sent me with his spirit" (Isa 48:16). When I am sent, the Spirit is sent and adds a plus to all I do, say, and am. Any dedicated Christian can say the same, "The Lord God has sent me with his Spirit into business to turn the sordid into the sacred by dedication." We need nothing more than we need businesspeople who feel that God is sending them and the Holy Spirit into commercial life to lift it to a higher level and to make money for God.

A Roman Catholic businessman wrote to a Protestant businessman and said: "When I think of you, I think of integrity. You have made integrity and your business dealings the same." The Lord God had sent him and his Spirit into that situation to lift it to the Christian level. A boy was grumbling over cleaning shoes. He saw a carpenter singing at his work and asked him why; the carpenter said, "Nothing exciting in this? Nothing to sing about? But I do it for Jesus; therefore I sing." Everything is done for Jesus; therefore everything has meaning, the highest meaning.

O Christ, you touch my body and make it a temple of the Spirit; you touch my mind and I think your thoughts after you. Everything is different now for there is a different motive. Amen.

AFFIRMATION FOR THE DAY: My life is a Spirit-touched life; therefore everything has a plus added to it.

HE LEFT IT ALL

Luke 12:13-21

We are seeing the principle of stewardship at work when all the powers of a person's life are in control of God's Spirit. Then the principle controlling the early disciples will control us, "And the disciples determined, every one according to his ability, to send relief to the brethren who lived in Judea; and they did so" (Acts 11:29-30 RSV). Note two things: "according to his ability," the principle of giving; according to his need, the principle of receiving. And note further: When they "determined," they did so. They didn't promise themselves and others and then slip out of it; they did it.

Many a person determines to make a will giving money to kingdom causes but doesn't do so. And then? Well, somebody asked an African American about a certain man who had died recently, how much he had left, and got the reply, "He left it all." He left it all for relatives to quarrel over, possibly, and to squander. Only what you give away do you take with you. The story goes of a rich man who died and was shown around the heavenly city before he was shown his own abode. He was surprised to find his gardener had such a lovely house and expected to see a much larger one for himself, but was disappointed to find his own was smaller than the gardener's. When he asked the reason, he was told, "Well, that's all the material you sent up."

The Lushai and Naga people of Assam, India, were head-hunters until Christianized. When I asked some of their leaders if they could give me illustrations of people among them being transformed by Christianity, they laughed and said, "Look around you. We are all examples of the transforming power of Christ; we were all head-hunters." One of the signs of transformation was the fact that every household had a vessel in which they set aside a portion of the grain they were about to cook for themselves, the Lord's portion at every meal. They raised eighty thousand rupees in that way one year. The same year a group of them traveled across India singing the "Hallelujah Chorus" in marvelous harmony. Those two facts are connected: Give and your heart sings.

O Spirit Divine, take my powers and use them. I hold nothing that is not at your disposal: money, time, talents, everything. And as you use them, I too shall sing. Amen.

AFFIRMATION FOR THE DAY: All my determinations shall become doings; my consents shall become conclusions.

GATHERING UP THE LESSONS

Luke 12:27-32

We come now to our last week together, and we shall spend it in gathering up the lessons we have learned and pointing them to our individual and collective lives.

As I have gone along with you, the conviction has deepened that the main thesis of this book is sound, namely, that in the society of the Acts of the Apostles we have the fulfillment of the prediction of Jesus that "some standing here won't die before they see God's kingdom arrive in power" (Mark 9:1). In the structure of the individual and collective life that emerged after the coming of the Holy Spirit, we see the very nature of that kingdom. Take a cross section of that society and you will see the essential nature of the kind of order that constitutes the kingdom. The kingdom did come with power—not fully or perfectly—that will come when Jesus Christ returns to set up his kingdom. But this is preview. The kingdom Jesus will set up will be, not different from, but more than the kingdom as seen in the Acts.

Just as Jesus was the incarnation of God, so this group in the Acts became the incarnation of the kingdom of God. They were the Word of the kingdom become flesh in a group. Two new words had to be coined to express the nature of that New Order and the Spirit that animated it: *koinonia*—the fellowship—and *agape*—amplified, human-divine love. This was a brand new thing and had to have a brand new vocabulary to describe it.

When Jesus said, "Don't be afraid, little flock, because your Father delights in giving you the kingdom" (Luke 12:32), that literally became true. For the ideas and outlook and spirit of this little group became the ruling ideas, outlook, and spirit of advancing civilization to the degree that it did advance and was civilization. The real rulers of humanity have been this "little flock"; they have ruled the development, basically ruled it, for they were the kingdom in miniature.

O Jesus, Master, heaven and earth may pass away, but your word shall never pass away. If we build upon your word, we build; if not, we blast. We are yours forever. Amen.

AFFIRMATION FOR THE DAY: I belong to the "little flock," and therefore the kingdom belongs to me; its powers are behind me.

NO LONGER RELIGIOUS BUSYBODIES

John 15:16, 26-27

We continue to sum up the conclusions and point to the lessons of this book.

The outlines of this New Order, the kingdom, were laid by Jesus in the three years of his ministry; but that Order couldn't come until the divine dynamic came in the Holy Spirit.

Jesus was the kingdom. He used interchangeably "for my sake" and "for the kingdom's sake." But he had to leave them in order to come back to them in the Holy Spirit universalized. He changed his presence for his omnipresence. In the Acts, the Son of Man came in his kingdom.

I said in the beginning that we need two things for human living: light on the mystery of life, and Life for the mastery of life. Those two needs were completely met in Jesus. In three years of his life we get light on the mystery of life. We look at him, and we know he is light—light in everything, everywhere. But we find in him more; he is Life for the mastery of life. He moves into us in the Holy Spirit, and then our inadequate lives move out into adequacy; we move out on top of this thing called life, masters of it.

Greater changes in human living took place in the thirty years after the coming of the Holy Spirit than in any period before or since—basic changes.

And those changes began at the right place, with the Christians themselves. All other proposed reformers start to change the world by starting to change others. They have petered out. These people began with themselves; it was from the inside out and from themselves to others. For ten days they waited to have themselves changed, and for twenty centuries we have felt the impact of that change. They were no longer religious busybodies meddling in other people's problems; they were radiant witnesses to a mighty solution, a solution that had begun within and was now working out to others. They weren't meddling moralists; they were messengers, and their message was a witness. That struck the world as new. The word of the kingdom had become fact.

O Blessed, Blessed Master, you have taught us where to begin, with ourselves. Now with assurance we move out to other persons and problems. Amen.

AFFIRMATION FOR THE DAY: My answers for the world will all come out of me; they shall be operative with me.

THEIR PROBLEMS TURNED TO POSSIBILITIES

John 16:7-11

We have been summing up the masteries that came with the coming of the Holy Spirit. Mastery began with the Christians themselves; they were mastered by the Master. And that was the right place; it all began within them and then moved out in concentric circles to the total life.

Had they tried to bypass the upper room and go straight to their tasks, their movement would have petered out. It would have exhausted itself upon the hard outer circumstances. But changed within, they began to change the without. The very first mastery was Jerusalem.

Jesus had told them not to leave Jerusalem, for in that city they had all caved in; Jerusalem had mastered them. So they walked out of the upper room straight into the heart of their problems. And all their problems turned to possibilities. Jerusalem was no longer something to run away from but something to run into and seize for Christ. Everything was that way. They had Life for the mastery of life.

They mastered all human relationships. They were related to God in a firsthand, saving contact. Secondhandedness was gone; it was all firsthand and face-to-face with nothing between. There were no outstanding issues between them and God; they were one in purpose and spirit. And when they came to right relations with themselves, they began "to express themselves" (Acts 2:4 MNT). They were at home with themselves— all self-hate and self-loathing were gone—they loved themselves because they loved something more than themselves.

Then being rightly related to God and themselves, they naturally fell into right relationships with the other immediate disciples; Peter stood with the other eleven (2:14), not against them as before. And further they were related to all believers; "all who believed were together" (2:44 RSV). All believers who belonged to Christ automatically belonged to one another. Further they righted their relations with their enemies—they overcame evil with good and hate with love—they called them brothers and sisters and, treating them like family, turned them into family. All barriers went down before people who had no barriers within themselves.

O Christ, all this seems so effortless and easy and natural. Help me to live in you with effortless victory, victory not of my trying but of your enabling. Amen.

AFFIRMATION FOR THE DAY: I am not a reservoir; I am a channel, a channel attached to Infinite Resources.

DISTRIBUTION ACCORDING TO NEED

2 Corinthians 8:13-15

We continue to gather up the masteries actual in the disciples and possible to us.

They mastered the material by a very simple but effective attitude: they would keep as much of the material as they needed, "distribution was made to each as any had need" (Acts 4:35 RSV). They went straight to the heart of a problem; need not greed was the controlling principle. Each person was to have as much of the material as would make that one more mentally, physically, and spiritually fit for the purposes of the kingdom of God. The rest belonged to other people's needs. That was solidly wise and operative for today.

Then this mastery of relationships brought about the most beautiful human society that ever existed—the *koinonia*, the fellowship—a new word for a new fact. That *koinonia* was a classless society and a raceless society, animated by *agape*—love—a new word expressing a new fact. *Eros*—human, sex love, was replaced by *agape*—divine love. Out of the *koinonia* as the soul, the church as a body was formed. Where there is *koinonia*, there is the church; but where there is no *koinonia*, there is no church. The *koinonia* was the organism out of which the organization, the church, was formed.

Then there was the mastery of the relationship between the material and the spiritual. The twelve missed their step and said they would give themselves to the spiritual and turn the material over to the seven. They put asunder what God had joined together in the incarnation when the Word became flesh. They drove a wedge between the material and the spiritual and impoverished both. The seven kept them together. They became the center of revival power; the center of spiritual awakening shifted from the twelve to the seven. Through the seven the spiritual contagion went to other peoples; they became the center of the missionary movement. They mastered the material; the twelve dodged it.

O God, our Lord, we thank you that you tipped the weight of your power to those who keep life a unit, all controlled by you. For in you, life is one. Amen.

AFFIRMATION FOR THE DAY: All my material relations shall express the spiritual this day.

361

VARIOUS MASTERIES REVIEWED

John 16:20-24

We continue to gather up the masteries that are disclosed in the early Christian movement.

They mastered fear. A group of people who, before the coming of the Holy Spirit, were behind closed doors in fear (John 20:19) were now calling upon the very people of whom they had been afraid to repent and receive the gospel. And they did. "The council was caught by surprise by the confidence with which Peter and John spoke.... They also recognized that they had been followers of Jesus" (Acts 4:13). His quiet courage had caught on in them. Fears had dropped away with the coming of this amazing adequacy to meet anything that life held. They didn't fight the fears; they took the adequacy, and the fears dropped off.

They mastered ingrown self-preoccupation. They forgot themselves, for they were seeing Christ. They fulfilled this statement of Paul, "We have different gifts that are consistent with God's grace that has been given to us. If your gift is prophecy, you should prophesy in proportion to your faith. If your gift is service, devote yourself to serving. If your gift is teaching, devote yourself to teaching. If your gift is encouragement, devote yourself to encouraging. The one giving should do it with no strings attached. The leader should lead with passion. The one showing mercy should be cheerful" (Rom 12:6-8). All of these—prophecy, service, teaching, encouraging, giving, leading, acts of mercy—were outgoing, not one turning in toward itself. Life had mastered life and had turned its flow outward, hence release from self-preoccupation.

They mastered gloom and sadness. Theirs is the most joyous account of the most joyous people that ever existed. They laughed their way through prisons and sang their way through death. They had an incorrigible joy. And joy is the most health-giving emotion that can run through us. Hence they mastered sicknesses that are rooted in sorrow and heaviness of spirit.

Sickness, both functional and structural, went out before the incoming tides of new, abundant living. Inner conflicts gone, the body registered the harmony of the soul. Body and spirit under the control of Wholeness became whole. A new, healthy race came into being.

O Christ, you are Life; and when I have you, I have no gaps of death in me. You have banished death; I live by Life and feel it coursing within me. Amen.

AFFIRMATION FOR THE DAY: I shall open the channels of my being to health by right thinking and emotion.

A KINGDOM THAT CANNOT BE SHAKEN

Matthew 7:24-29

There isn't space left to sum up the masteries available for us. So I can do no more than point to the mastery that gives validity and basis to all the other masteries, namely, the mastery of the total life by the totalitarianism of the kingdom of God. Seek first the kingdom of God; and all these things—all the other and lesser masteries—will be added unto you. The kingdom of God gathers up all the loose ends of life and weaves them into total meaning. It is the Cosmic Loom upon which all the little things and big are woven into fabric, into meaning.

If that is true, then how can we find the kingdom in which are included all the lesser kingdoms of mastery? I want to drop into your thinking a verse that has been the most steadying verse I have ever had given me. It was given me in my quiet time in a hotel in Moscow in 1934. Russia had hit me hard. I needed reassurance. It came in this verse, which arose out of the Scripture and spoke to my condition: "Let us be grateful for receiving a kingdom that cannot be shaken" (Heb 12:28 RSV).

"A kingdom that cannot be shaken"—that has run through my heart and mind like a steadying refrain for years. I've seen people building up kingdoms that I knew were shakable: the kingdom of money, the kingdom of position and pride, the kingdom of honor and glory, the kingdom of pleasure, the kingdom of learning, the kingdom of physical love. I knew in my heart of hearts they were shakable, for I'd seen them shake and fall before my very eyes. When I was trying, before World War II, to get the Dutch minister to agree to let Japan have New Guinea for her surplus population, with the understanding that America would agree to give compensation, his angry reply was, "No part of the Dutch empire is for sale." Alas, where is it now?

Gone, it was shakable. And where are the lesser empires, personal and collective, people have built up? They were shakable by disease, by death, or by sheer inner unhappiness. It is everything to have one unshakable kingdom!

O God, amid shakable kingdoms I stand with my feet in the one unshakable kingdom. What security, what meaning, what ultimacy—what Life this is! I thank you. Amen.

AFFIRMATION FOR THE DAY: Amid a shakable world I shall walk and live and have my being in an unshakable kingdom.

WE BUILD THE CHURCH;
WE RECEIVE THE KINGDOM

Hebrews 12:25-29

Our last day will be a meditation upon the unshakable kingdom.

The wonder of it is that we don't have to double our fists, knit our brows, and clench our teeth to attain this kingdom. We don't have to attain it at all; we obtain it. "Let us be grateful for receiving a kingdom" (Heb 12:28 RSV)—for receiving! We don't have to be fit, to be worthy, to have enough to earn it; we simply have to receive the kingdom. It is prepared to invade us, to redemptively invade us, provided we take down the barriers! That's all! That is the meaning of surrender; it means the taking down of the central barrier, the unsurrendered self. That is the real crux. Let go there, and everything goes with it. Then the kingdom possesses you.

We have missed the point when we talk of "building the kingdom." Nowhere are we told in the New Testament to build the kingdom. The kingdom is built from the foundation of the world, built into the structure of reality. We build the church, but we receive the kingdom. Then we let its powers work in us and through us. We become agents of forces and powers not our own. We are transmitters of the grace of God. We love with a love not our own, rejoice with a joy not our own, and we have a mastery that is not ours; it is of Grace. And it is all effortless and compelling.

One night in Japan, I was on my way to speak to a large new church packed to the doors, largely by non-Christians. They belonged to a kingdom that had been shaken to the dust; now they wanted an unshakable kingdom. On the way at important intersections men stood in the dark, holding lighted Japanese lanterns with a cross upon each one. These men were waving the people toward the church. In this book I have stood like those sentinels in the dark, waving my candlelit-lantern with a cross on it—waving confused people toward the kingdom—the one unshakable kingdom in a shaken world. The cross is the way to that kingdom.

O Gracious Lord, you have shown us yourself in your Son, and you have shown us the kingdom in this New Society, and we will never, never get over the spell of it. Amen.

**AFFIRMATION FOR THE DAY: Mastered by the Master,
I go out to master all things.**